A Regulatory Framework to Remediate the Planet

Environment and Society

Series Editor
Douglas Vakoch

As scholars examine the environmental challenges facing humanity, they increasingly recognize that solutions require a focus on the human causes and consequences of these threats, and not merely a focus on the scientific and technical issues. To meet this need, the Environment and Society series explores a broad range of topics in environmental studies from the perspectives of the social sciences and humanities. Books in this series help the reader understand contemporary environmental concerns, while offering concrete steps to address these problems.

Books in this series include both monographs and edited volumes that are grounded in the realities of ecological issues identified by the natural sciences. Our authors and contributors come from disciplines including but not limited to anthropology, architecture, area studies, communication studies, economics, ethics, gender studies, geography, history, law, pedagogy, philosophy, political science, psychology, religious studies, sociology, and theology. To foster a constructive dialogue between these researchers and environmental scientists, the Environment and Society series publishes work that is relevant to those engaged in environmental studies, while also being of interest to scholars from the author's primary discipline.

Recent Titles in the Series

A Regulatory Framework to Remediate the Planet: Strategies, Outcomes and Implications, by Robert Smet

Climate Diplomacy at the Crossroads: A Multidisciplinary Perspective, edited by Şuay Nİlhan Açıkalın

Political Ecologies of Futurity: Storytelling Plantation Afterlives, Climate Erasures, and Socioecological Justice, edited by Alex A. Moulton and Dylan M. Harris

Concrete Mirage: Governance, Equity, and Sustainable Cities in the United States Southwest, by Erin Heinz

Building Sustainable Agrifood Systems and Resilient Rural Communities in Japan, edited by Raymond Jussaume, Keiko Tanaka, and Kiyohiko Sakamoto

Strategic Rebuilding and Affordable Housing in the Muslim World, edited by Akel Ismail Kahera, Sultan Barakat and Ghadanfar

Encounters with the Posthuman and the Environment, edited by İnci Bilgin Tekin and Zeynep Talay Turner

Canals in a Changing Britain: Construction, Culture, and Environment, 1760–1968, by Jules P. Gehrke

Urban Narratives About Nature: Socio-Ecological Imaginaries Between Science and Entertainment, edited by Carlos Tabernero

The Age of Capitalism, Consumer Culture, and the Collapse of Nature in the Anthropocene, by Jack Thornburg

Sustainable Energy Development: Technology and Investment, edited by Kimarie Engerman, Elizabeth A. Keenan, Dmitry Kurochkin, Elena V. Shabliy

Making Nature Social: Towards a Relationship with Nature, by Rembrandt Zegers

Earth Polyphony: Law, Ecocriticism, and Eco-Activism in Postcolonial India, by Suhasini Vincent

Staying Together: Natureculture in a Changing World, Edited by Kaushani Mondal

Learning in the Anthropocene: Reimagining Education in the Twenty-First Century, by Carl A. Maida

A Regulatory Framework to Remediate the Planet

Strategies, Outcomes and Implications

By Robert Smet

BLOOMSBURY ACADEMIC
NEW YORK • LONDON • OXFORD • NEW DELHI • SYDNEY

BLOOMSBURY ACADEMIC
Bloomsbury Publishing Inc, 1359 Broadway, 12th Floor, New York, NY 10018, USA
Bloomsbury Publishing Plc, 50 Bedford Square, London, WC1B 3DP, UK
Bloomsbury Publishing Ireland, 29 Earlsfort Terrace, Dublin 2, D02 AY28, Ireland

BLOOMSBURY, BLOOMSBURY ACADEMIC and the Diana logo are trademarks of Bloomsbury Publishing Plc

First published in the United States of America 2026

Library of Congress Control Number: 2025947361

ISBN: HB: 978-1-66694-775-5
ePDF: 979-8-21626-916-8
eBook: 978-1-97876-759-1

Typeset by Deanta Global Publishing Services, Chennai, India

For product safety related questions contact productsafety@bloomsbury.com.

Contents

Preface ix
Acknowledgments xii
Abbreviations xiii

Introduction 1

Part 1 Prepping for Regulatory Surgery

1 The Fundamentals of Regulating Air Pollution 23
2 The Inherent Design Flaws of Regulating Stationary Sources under the CAA 45
3 Past Discussion of Clean Air Act Reform 63

Part 2 The Comprehensive Strategy

4 A New Framework for Regulating Air Pollution from Stationary Sources 87
5 Insights and Commentary on the Comprehensive Strategy 139

Part 3 The Adapted and Generalized Strategies

A Brief Description of the Core Strategy 191

6 Adapting the Comprehensive Strategy to the Generation of Solid Waste Pollution 195
7 Generalizing the Adapted Strategy to the Generation of Multi-Media Environmental Pollution 231
8 Commentary on and Implications of the Adapted and Generalized Strategies 239

Part 4 Pursuing a Grand Unified Theory of Environmental Law and Regulation

9 Expanding the Use of the Strategies 293
10 The Implications for Environmental Law 325
Conclusion: Looking Back and Looking Forward 335

Bibliography 355
Index 365
About the Author 377

Preface

I have always been a strong advocate for the environment for much of my life, but my early passion was mathematics and later, physics and engineering. After obtaining my doctorate in engineering mechanics and a brief unsatisfying stint in the private sector, I made the career decision to channel my work ethic and analytical skills to environmental protection, my other passion. With that as my goal, I became an environmental protection engineer regulating, as luck would have it, air pollution.

I have spent most of the past 30-plus years developing construction permits for new and existing major stationary sources of air pollution for my state's environmental protection agency. Such major sources included natural gas-fired combined cycle power plants, coal gasification plants, industrial boilers, gas-to-energy plants at landfills, wood furniture manufacturing facilities, etc. Permitting at and for major sources requires the full suite of knowledge of applicable federal air pollution rules and regulations as well as a wide array of applicable state rules and standards. As a permit writer, I have also played a role in rule development, enforcement, compliance, stakeholder outreach, dealing with "bureaucratic pollution," and more.

Long story short, I have been a regulatory practitioner in the trenches with an eye on what works and, equally as important, on what does not.

However, as my knowledge, skills, and abilities matured in regulating air pollution, my concerns about regulation expanded toward addressing air pollution and other environmental issues in China. I voraciously consumed all I could on international air, water, solid waste, and soil pollution, most notably as they related to China. The works of Stern, van Rooij, Economy, Lo, etc., are just some I have enjoyed.

I began to focus my sights on seeing what, if anything, I could do to work with US-based and other environmental nongovernmental organizations (NGOs) in Beijing to assist Chinese air pollution regulators, since they were obviously having difficulties addressing their cities' poor air quality. In 2009, I attended a four-day presentation on how American regulators address air pollution for managers of the Beijing Municipal Environmental Protection Bureau Research

Institute. Occasional visits to Beijing and elsewhere in China allowed me to develop what I think was a fairly respectable understanding of the real issues that Chinese air pollution regulators were facing. Figuring that what should comprise the efficient regulation of air pollution from stationary sources should likewise apply worldwide, it was only natural to re-examine the Clean Air Act itself. As a consequence, the comprehensive strategy was developed as a means to reform the Clean Air Act for regulating stationary sources.

I wanted next to tackle the Big Kahuna, namely sustainability, so I was extremely fortunate to have chosen *Cradle to Cradle* among the various books on the subject. While progress has already been made to facilitate material reuse and recoverability, that book opened the door wide to achieving further progress to reform environmental regulation as developed in this book. Having read just two chapters in *Cradle to Cradle*, it became immediately apparent that there was a means to adapt and later generalize the strategy for regulating the generation of air pollution to regulating the generation of all multi-media environmental pollutants and surrogates. Although a good portion of this book appears to focus on the efficient regulation of air pollution, do not be misled—its framework forms the underlying foundation for a strategy that will demonstrate, among its noteworthy outcomes, that a circular economy is a direct result of minimizing the generation of solid waste pollution. Adopting methods from the circular economy strategy further allows for a means to rigorously mitigate global climate change.

As if following a consistent pattern, one idea led to another. By asking why the methodology could not be "reversed," I was able to surmise a framework to achieve a means to restore ecosystems as well, which, by extension, leads to a framework to achieve sustainability with Nature by reaching a state of equilibrium between Nature and the human economy embedded within it. By doing so, we can reach a state where we won't have to populate other planets to survive.

Lastly, among the other significant outcomes, not the least of them will be the ability to circumscribe environmental regulation, which will clearly have significant implications for the application of environmental law. It is not too far-fetched to assert that a Grand Unified Theory of Environmental Law and Regulation is possible.

And to think this whole adventure all started with the desire to simply find a better way to regulate air pollution.

Disclaimers

Please understand that being an author is not my day job, so I must apologize for whatever errors I have made. Unless otherwise noted, the assertions and opinions expressed in this book are strictly mine.

Acknowledgments

The team at Bloomsbury was key to getting this book published. My acquisitions editor Courtney Morales, Breasia Boyd, and Taylor Breeding at Bloomsbury were key to turning the manuscript into this book.

Candace Johnson and Dorothy Erstling are also owed my gratitude for their early editing of my proposal. I wish to extend my sincere thanks to Allan Graubard, who provided his editing of the proposal and manuscript early on. His advice on publishing was extremely invaluable throughout the process. Likewise, John Bond's advice throughout the entire publishing process was useful and critical to getting this book to this publisher. Likewise, Dana Compton's advice on peer review was also very useful.

I want to thank Allie Boman for her input on how to conform to the Chicago Manual of Style and Bridget Brown for developing the figures. Karen Ehrmann deserves my gratitude for her advice on permissions and for taking care of the hassle of acquiring required permissions. I want to thank Gina Guilinger for developing the index on a tight deadline.

Rob Brenner, Bill Pedersen, and Carl Dalhammar deserve my gratitude for performing their economic, legal, and/or technical review of the manuscript. I also want to thank Gary McCutchen, Colin Campbell, Eric Hiser, and Joss Tantram for providing valuable insights, helping to catalyze some of the concepts in this book.

Lastly, I want to thank my PhD advisor from graduate school, Dr. Bob Johnson, for helping me to approach problem-solving with the right mental discipline. Without that, this book would never have been possible.

Abbreviations

AA	attainment area
AEGD	Additional Earths at Global Development
AQM	air quality management
ARP	Acid Rain Program
BACT	Best Available Control Technology
BART	Best Available Retrofit Technology
BECCS	Bioenergy with Carbon Capture and Storage
BTL	Breaking the Logjam
Btu	British thermal unit
CAA	Clean Air Act
CaC	Command-and-Control
CAIR	Clean Air Interstate Rule
CaT	Cap-and-Trade
CDC	Centers for Disease Control
CE	circular economy
CFC	chlorofluorocarbons
CMPED	Construction and Modification Permitting and Emission Determination
CO	carbon monoxide
COP	Conference of Parties
CO_2	carbon dioxide
CSAPR	Cross-State Air Pollution Rule

CSR	Corporate Social Responsibility
DfD	Design for Disassembly
DfE	Design for Environment
DoD	difficulty-of-disassembly
EE	energy efficiency
EJ	Environmental Justice
ELI	Environmental Law Institute
EMS	Environmental Management System
ESG	Environmental, Social, and Governance
ESPS	Existing Source Performance Standard
ETU	Equivalent Trading Unit
ETVP	Environmental Technology Verification Program
EU	European Union
FEMA	Federal Emergency Management Agency
FDA	Food and Drug Administration
FLoER	Fundamental Law of Environmental Regulation
GHG	greenhouse gases
HAP	hazardous air pollutant
HCFC	hydrochlorofluorocarbon
hr	hour
H_2S	hydrogen sulfide
IDPC	inherently detrimental product characteristic
JIE	Journal of Industrial Ecology
LAER	lowest achievable emission rate
LCA	life cycle assessment

lb	pound
MACT	Maximum Achievable Control Technology
mGigaton	metric Gigatons
mmBtu	million British thermal units
MoD	Measure of Detriment
mtons	metric tons
NAA	nonattainment area
NAEM	National Association for Environmental Management
NAPA	National Academy of Public Administrators
NESHAP	National Emission Standards for Hazardous Air Pollutants
NGO	nongovernmental organization
NHI	noncompostability harm intensity
NOx	nitrogen oxides
NRC	National Research Council
NSPS	New Source Performance Standard
NSR	New Source Review
NTSB	National Transportation Safety Board
NUPS	New Unit Performance Standard
OECD	Organization for Economic Co-operation and Development
PCPS	Per Capita Performance Standard
PM	particulate matter
PM_{10}	particulate matter with an aerodynamic diameter of 10 microns or less
$PM_{2.5}$	particulate matter with an aerodynamic diameter of 2.5 microns or less

P2	pollution prevention
pos	product-to-soil
ppm	parts per million
PSD	Prevention of Significant Deterioration
RACT	Reasonably Available Control Technology
RFC	regulatory food chain
RFF	Resources for the Future
RGGI	Regional Greenhouse Gas Initiative
SIP	State Implementation Plan
SoB	statement of basis
SO_2	sulfur dioxide
tpy	tons per year
TtC	time to compostability
TtD	time to degradation
TU	Trading Unit
UNFCCC	United Nations Framework Convention on Climate Change
USEPA	United States Environmental Protection Agency
VMoD	Volumetric Measure of Detriment
VMT	vehicle miles traveled
VOC	volatile organic compound
WBCSD	World Business Council for Sustainable Development
WEFE	Water-Energy-Food-Ecosystem
YDFYON	You Don't Foul Your Own Nest

Introduction

The Vision

The concept of achieving environmental sustainability with Nature seems, to many people, to be as far removed from our daily lives as living in the Yukon does to city-dwellers living in the hustle and bustle of Manhattan. Yet, reaching sustainability with Nature is what we must achieve unless we resign ourselves to the very possibility that the generations that follow can no longer sustain themselves on the unsustainable lifestyles we in the developed world have grown accustomed to. Much like obesity, which is associated with many serious health afflictions, unsustainability with Nature is a force multiplier of several calamities here on Earth. One key measure of unsustainability, among others, is the number of Additional Earths at Global Development (AEGD) that would be required if global citizens were to live as well as those in developed countries.[1] However, were we to continually use and reuse materials to the point where we attain a circular economy (CE), adopt measures that mitigate climate change, restore ecosystems, and achieve other sustainability milestones, we might actually be able to live in harmony with Nature without having to leave the planet. The primary purpose of this book is to develop a foundational framework that will not only flatten and reverse the current trajectory of the AEGD curve but achieve an AEGD of zero and remediate the planet.

Achieving "attainment of sustainability with Nature" occurs when the economic system that is embedded within and obtains sustenance from Nature is at a stable, steady-state equilibrium with Nature.[2,3] This concept is not commonly found in the literature, but Mamlyuk was a rare scholar to have posited a biosphere quality model that promotes an equilibrium state.[4] The strategies developed in this book will go a long way to showing how to reach this equilibrium.

To achieve attainment first requires setting limits on various pollutants and resource use and then reducing them in conjunction with increasing ecosystem measures over a baseline until milestones that together achieve environmental sustainability with Nature, thereby approaching some semblance of equilibrium between Nature and humanity.[5] Within this equilibrium state, the further goal is to maximize per capita development.

What has been missing to this point has been a blueprint to solve our global environmental crises. Till now, we have mostly relied on economists and legal scholars who we thought were addressing key environmental problems, but instead they have been trying to achieve global fixes without a large-scale blueprint. As an analogy, consider how successful the construction of a ten-story building would be if only the laborers were relied on to erect it—no architect, no general contractor, no project manager, just the laborers working among themselves to construct the building by "ad hoc committee." After some trial and error, sure, some type of building would be erected, with some level of success, but it would be far from structurally optimal. The same has happened with addressing today's development of regulation to address our current environmental calamities. The economists and legal scholars have metaphorically been calling the shots without a lead architect, the structural engineers developing the fundamental blueprint, and the project managers who oversee the systematic construction of the underlying regulatory structure.

A rigorous examination of current regulatory practice is required where such rigor has rarely been the norm, because environmental legal scholars and lawyers, economists, other academics, etc., have been hopelessly siloed within their own fields and subfields.[6] Legal scholars in environmental law have particularly focused on addressing isolated micro-issues, such as how to better use market instruments, cost-benefit analysis, or applying the polluter pays principle. Rather than using standard old-school regulation and common law techniques applied to separately siloed environmental media, this book will demonstrate that multiple tools can and must be applied macroscopically and holistically with a focus on hierarchically regulating real-world, global-scale, multi-media environmental problems to facilitate sustainability with Nature.

Strategies are developed that reduce human harms to Nature by, for example, facilitating the transition to a circular economy and mitigating climate change, as well as a means to restore Nature,[7] making major inroads toward a methodology that achieves sustainability with Nature. These and other strategies developed in the book fill in major gaps in environmental regulation whereby such regulation can now be applied holistically rather than as the disjointed package of approaches for the various siloed environmental media as currently conducted. Broadly circumscribing environmental regulation in this way to achieve sustainability will also have profound implications for international environmental law by properly elevating the legal status of Nature relative to that of humanity.

Sustainability as a Legal Area of Study

Only a small fraction of legal scholars have raised the issue of achieving sustainability, but they mostly sound the alarm that "something needs to be done." Bratspies expresses the daunting nature of achieving sustainability and posits the need for a new legal framework to do so but only provides commentary on what must be done.[8] Fischman speaks well for those few environmental legal scholars who promote resilience as the more heightened goal than that of achieving sustainability.[9] This is due to the reality of ecological adaptation, rather than the misplaced notion that ecosystems can simply snap back elastically to a previous equilibrium state.

Bratspies, Fischman, and the few other environmental legal scholars who tackle sustainability and/or resilience deserve credit for truly being on the cutting edge of legal scholarship. With the large universe of environmental legal scholars, one would expect that they would likewise have done a great deal of the dirty work of reforming environmental law, but they have yet to significantly do so *for decades*. Yet, as Fischman himself admitted, he was only proposing "a way of thinking about resilience in environmental law rather than a particular set of reforms."[10] We will see later that legal scholars have tended to *think* more about problems in the environmental legal field than actually *solve* them. In contrast, it took this book's author, an environmental engineer and experienced regulator, to "put chalk to blackboard"[11] by making significant inroads to uncover a framework to achieve sustainability with Nature.

As it relates to planetary boundaries, Louis Kotzé argues that "it is evident that environmental law has failed to meaningfully contribute to regulatory efforts that aim to keep humanity from reaching and breaching these boundaries,"[12] and "that the idea of the Anthropocene and its accompanying imagery has not yet been taken up with overwhelming enthusiasm by general and environmental law scholars."[13] This book and the strategies herein will demonstrate that enthusiasm by meaningfully contributing to those regulatory efforts.

Some Fundamental Ground Rules

So, how can attainment of sustainability with Nature be accomplished? Peculiarly enough, probably the best starting point to demonstrate this is by first showing how air pollution should best be regulated; this is because many aspects of how it is currently regulated can readily be transferred to other media and progressing further from there.

Key ground rules must first be established. If there was ever a first, and most significant, Fundamental Law of Environmental Regulation (the "first FLoER"), it would be that where systematic regulation is not aligned with achieving sustainability and preserving Nature first and foremost, then it is flawed and must be scrapped and replaced. The implicit point here is that if we do not prioritize actions that promote sustainability with Nature and an AEGD of zero, then what exactly is the point of environmental law and regulation anyway?[14] Allowing economic forces to cannibalize the conditions that facilitate the economy's very existence by exploiting Nature unsustainably is calamitous for long-term survival. The Second FLoER is that regulation must be aligned with addressing human health and welfare. The third FLoER would be that where the first two FLoERs are met and attainment of sustainability with Nature is reached and maintained, then where regulation does not threaten both attainment of sustainability with Nature and human health and welfare but is onerous to the economic operating system,[15] then that regulation must be relaxed or replaced.

If we follow these fundamental laws and assuming we have the will to apply the appropriate methods, then we won't have to inhabit other planets to escape the fallout of our catastrophic behaviors here on Earth. If we still hope to achieve sustainability with Nature by only applying our collective sheer will, then adapting to our self-made calamities and/or planning for planetary departure will be our only options. It is simply a choice—do we wish to reach sustainability with Nature if it means possibly sacrificing aspects of our current consumptive lifestyles, or do we maintain our current business-as-usual mindsets and live with the consequences?

Getting Started: Reducing the Generation of Pollution

Developing a regulatory strategy that holistically decreases multi-media-generated environmental pollution and facilitates the transition to a CE—where products are designed for disassembly and/or continuous reuse/recycling/

remanufacturing, etc., of their constituent materials within the economy—are only two of the key results of this book, with the former promoting the latter.

Where physical parameters can be measured and quantified, such as the amount of pollutants emitted or discharged into the environment, then pollution can more effectively be regulated. This is the current case today with regulating the generation of environmental pollution, most notably air pollution. In fact, as will be shown in this book, the deliberate generation of air pollution and, in general, the deliberate generation of environmental pollution from stationary sources (think industrial pollution) can be *optimally* regulated. To gain such optimality for regulating the generation of environmental pollution, which includes facilitating our transition to a CE and mitigating climate change, requires a generalized, integrated strategy that will include a cap-and-trade scheme for regulated pollutants, such as for "inherently detrimental product characteristics" (IDPC) and their surrogates (e.g., difficulty-of-disassembly or complexity), the rationing of both resource inputs and carbon-based fossil fuels/feedstocks, and most critically, taking enforceable credit for the reuse of post-consumption materials. Even where regulation of pollution cannot be rigorously specified by using quantifiable means, for example, through the use of work practices, a certain set of guidelines or "operating laws for the application of regulation" can dictate what works and what does not in reducing pollution. Unfortunately, as we know all too well, the misapplication of regulation and excess bureaucracy ("bureaucratic pollution") leads to suboptimal outcomes. And just to be clear, minimizing pollution, of course, is just one prerequisite for achieving sustainability with Nature.

Framing the Development of This Book

The Foundation: A Comprehensive Strategy for Regulating the Generation of Air Pollution

Back in 2001, Richard Stewart asserted the following:

> For all its past successes, the U.S. environmental regulatory system has a fundamental flaw. It consists of a patchwork of detailed and rigid laws that are largely unrelated to each other and are lacking in any unified vision of environmental problems or EPA's mission.[16]

To reiterate again, the strategies developed in this book and the implications drawn therefrom will do nothing less than holistically tie together regulation for the generation of multi-media environmental pollution and the restoration of Nature. In order to best present the generalized strategy, air pollution and the optimal application of regulations required to reduce its generation will be examined first. The reason is clear: many of the same principles that apply to regulating air pollution will form the foundation for regulating IDPCs and their surrogates, resource inputs, and more.

After many years of regulatory reform dormancy, the comprehensive air pollution regulatory strategy will bring reform back to life by developing a comprehensive blueprint for the most optimal regulatory scheme for air pollution generated from stationary sources, that is, industrial, commercial, and institutional polluting facilities. This strategy is not restricted by locality; rather, it is designed for regulators and policymakers worldwide, that is, it is just as relevant to federal and state regulators and policymakers in the United States and elsewhere, where they have the capacity to apply it.

As such, the strategy resurrects and resolves the decades-long problem of how to reform key aspects of the US Clean Air Act (CAA). No doubt, there have been reform proposals that have languished on the shelves of national regulators that, due to opposition by the powers that be, never saw the light of day. Outside of those walls, while much has been written in the academic literature on how to reform the CAA, mostly by environmental legal scholars, very little substantial headway has been made. Clearly, there are scholars and members of the concerned public who wish to see significant progress, but it is difficult for this author to shake off the perception that the more recent discussion of reform appears to be characterized by both misguided environmental legal scholars who espouse generic tweaks (e.g., emissions trading, emissions taxes, cost-benefit analysis) as panaceas for the various ills of the quagmire and skeptical environmental organizations that perceive *any* change as backsliding. In between these two poles is an optimal comprehensive strategy that can be used to great effect.

Lest the reader concludes that the author is a laissez-faire pro-business type, do not despair. Certainly some practices that the corporate community favors (e.g., simplified regulations, emissions trading) are advocated but only *where properly utilized to reduce environmental and ecological harms and minimize bureaucratic pollution.* The reader can rest assured that the author is a true environmentalist, albeit an anti-bureaucratic pollution, optimal-outcomes environmentalist. To arrive at the optimal regulation of production-based environmental pollution requires taking a half-step back but four steps forward. It will be seen that setting absolute limits with tightening caps over time (good for the environment) is the yin of a command-and-control-based regulatory program while emissions trading (flexibility for participants) is the yang. Thus, the goal of setting and tightening rigorous limits will come to be seen as an indispensable component of environmental regulation to reduce harms[17] while emissions trading, an economic instrument distrusted by environmentalists, is simply a practical tool to achieve those reductions.

Engineers are quite familiar with correcting design flaws and identifying optimal solutions. As such, the strategy solves the more comprehensive problem of what common sense, optimal regulation of air quality management (AQM) for stationary sources must be. The reason why a solution has eluded us until now involves two issues, among others: (1) nonpractitioners who may propose solutions commonly view the subject from too far above, as if at 10,000 feet, rather than at ground level, where actual practitioners reside, and (2) given that the regulatory process of the CAA operates under resigned, unquestioned obedience[18] and Stockholm Syndrome-like autopilot in an era of Congressional gridlock, there has been no appetite for reform or for determining just what is "optimal." Simply speaking, any creative solution to the policy and bureaucratic logjam in regulatory innovation is not going to be found "inside the box" as that box (or cage, to be more precise) exists today.

If implemented, a rigorous comprehensive air pollution regulatory strategy will go a long way toward reducing harms inflicted on Nature and preserving for us, and for generations to come, a healthier environment, enhancing the quality of, and in some cases saving, millions of lives. Consider, if only for a moment, what this will mean for those living in the hundreds of cities around the globe with one million or more residents enduring current levels of harmful pollution.

The Broader Problem: A Generalized Strategy for Regulating the Generation of Multi-Media Pollution

It obviously stands to reason that the comprehensive strategy to regulate the generation of air pollution can also be utilized, with appropriate tweaks, to regulate the generation of pollution for other environmental media, namely, water and on-site waste-generated pollution. Moreover, one major outcome developed in this book is the adaptation of the comprehensive strategy to regulate the generation of solid waste pollution, and much more. Altogether, a generalized strategy can be developed to regulate the generation of all multi-media pollution.

Based on principles espoused in the book *Cradle to Cradle*,[19] a leading publication in the sustainability field, the authors state that we don't have a pollution problem, but rather a design problem. Obviously we do have a pollution problem, but their point is quite clear—the basis of the pollution problem is that our "take, make, consume, dispose" economy is one of poor design. With that as a backdrop, because a manufacturing facility consists of many inputs and outputs, *including the product itself*, the comprehensive strategy, upon adaptation and generalization, allows regulators to address the following: resource inputs (e.g., clean water), environmentally harmful inputs (e.g., fossil fuels/feedstocks used in the production of plastics or solvents), environmentally harmful outputs (e.g., air, water, and hazardous waste pollution, product toxicity), and IDPC surrogates (e.g., complexity). In this way, a generalized strategy can thus be developed to integrate the regulation of *all* aspects of the generation of multi-media environmental pollution. Rather than through its current ad hoc, piecemeal development and complicated approach per siloed environmental media, the generalized strategy will facilitate the use of the same approach to regulate these media holistically. In addition, it provides an objective methodology that will achieve true milestone-based reductions of environmental pollution while manufacturers are provided with the flexibility to achieve required reductions.

Along with limiting or rationing resource inputs in conjunction with allowing credit for use of post-consumption waste materials, the generalized strategy includes all relevant multi-media environmental pollutants and pollutant surrogates within a separate trading scheme for each, as applicable. In very simplistic terms, applying a trading program for the generation of IDPCs and IDPC surrogates and the use of "market-based incentives" to reuse post-consumption materials in combination with the "choking off" of virgin resource inputs will, by regulatory design, provide the critical means to reduce multi-media pollution, including the means to facilitate the transition to a CE based on *Cradle to Cradle* principles.[20] The practical uses and policy implications of adopting such a generalized strategy applied to *all* relevant environmental multi-media pollutants cannot be overstated.

The upshot is that IDPCs and IDPC pollutant surrogates for manufactured products that later create environmental distress after discard can now be properly regulated *at the point of production*. This regulatory scheme will in turn facilitate, through process redesign, the reduction and potential elimination of those detrimental characteristics "inherently embedded within" products at the sources that generate/manufacture them so that these characteristics are optimally reduced or eliminated *before* the products become unregulated externalities at, for example, a landfill, ocean, or the side of a country road.

By extension, the strategy's use is expanded so that it can also include imports and supply chains. Although applying environmental regulation to them would likely be controversial in the short term, requiring imported products not to exceed worst-case, numerical "characteristic standards" and applying the generalized strategy to supply chains is feasible and unquestionably necessary.

While remediation technology already exists to remediate surface or groundwater to meet drinking water standards, in theory, the generalized strategy developed in this book would not only allow legacy solid waste pollution to be recirculated, but it also provides a means to remediate CO_2 through a mitigation strategy (described in the next section). The Holy Grail of an ideal generalized strategy would be one that would remediate all legacy pollution, a topic that will be discussed in Chapter 10.

Developing appropriate measures of both IDPC and IDPC surrogate pollution and then finding a means to properly regulate them breaks significant new ground within the environmental sustainability field. Moreover, the generalized strategy bridges the gap between environmental law and industrial ecology, two disciplines that have heretofore existed in relative isolation from one another.

The consequences of adopting the generalized approach to holistically regulate the generation of environmental pollution in an integrated fashion are elegant, timely, and far-reaching. This is particularly significant, given that we, as a global society, are anxiously waiting for answers on how we must solve our mounting environmental problems, particularly in the face of population and economic growth.

Developing Strategies to Solve Other Calamitous Problems

Not to be left out are techniques that use quantifiable measures within the regulatory strategy that allows for the expanded use of the generalized strategy to address other key areas of the sustainability problem. For example, a mitigation strategy will be developed to rigorously address the global climate crisis, incorporating even more than the existing aspects of the Paris Agreement, including a means to take credit for sequestration (e.g., reforestation). Unfortunately, there is as yet no adequate technology to remediate legacy carbon dioxide, that is, that which has already been generated and lingers in the atmosphere.

It is one thing to reduce harms to Nature, but it is another thing to restore it back to health; a basic strategic framework to restore ecosystems via reverse cap-and-trade is developed. Having reduced harms and restoring ecosystems, the concept of achieving an AEGD of zero by finding an "Equilibrium Point" between Nature and humanity, including the economy embedded within it, is the obvious next step.

The Underlying Assumptions Made in This Book

Before discussing and developing the strategies developed in this book, one has to start with basic assumptions.

1. In order to achieve an Additional Earths at Global Development of zero, it shouldn't have to be stated as an assumption when it is an indisputable fact, but just to remind the reader, Nature's resources, biodiversity, waste reservoirs, etc., are not infinite. Nevertheless, there are significant numbers of very learned people, including economics scholars, who prioritize economic orthodoxy over ecological realities, e.g., by basing their theories and conducting their livelihoods as if Nature and all it provides is free, infinitely abundant, and resources are replaceable.
2. It is assumed that the reader knows enough about AQM and how air pollution is regulated without reiterating that in great detail here. For example, the reader will hopefully be familiar already with the following terms: State Implementation Plan (SIP), New Source Review (NSR), National Ambient Air Quality standards, performance and emission standards, and cap-and-trade (CaT). Nevertheless, Part 1 will provide some background for those readers who do not possess this background.
3. The environmental protection regulatory program's capacity is assumed to be sufficiently mature; that is, it is already well along (e.g., with the requisite human resources to conduct inspections, write permits, and enforce regulations). The strategies provided in this book may not be entirely useful to those countries whose capacity to operate an AQM and other environmental media programs is far below what is necessary to optimally or even adequately conduct the program. Likewise, where there exists substantial inertia for a country to change its method of regulation (e.g., when regulatory capture by industry exists), the strategies

developed in this book will not perform miracles; they will not overcome poor governance. So while these strategies are based on participants having to achieve quantifiable milestones, making it much more difficult for them to circumvent regulation, policymakers must still possess the will to use these strategies and commit to their success.

4. While AQM generally encompasses all sources of air pollution, in this book the focus will be on technologically-induced air pollution generated from stationary sources, typically from industrial, commercial and institutional sources. The same assumption would apply to the generation of water, on-site, and solid waste pollution.
5. As this book's strategies address the "intended" technologically-induced generation of pollution during operation and production, it will not address how to prevent unplanned pollution releases, such as those resulting from accidental discharges into water bodies, or those from natural occurrences, such as forest fires or volcanic eruptions. Unless otherwise noted, mobile or biogenic sources are also not included in the discussion.
6. Optimality in this book is assumed to mean the most effective and efficient means to, foremost, reduce pollution to the environment *to reach environmental sustainability with Nature*[21] via bureaucratic efficiency (i.e., by achieving "bureaucratic sustainability"), particularly as it applies to *regulators, and hence to citizens and taxpayers*. It does so by providing sources flexibility beneath declining caps on quantities of generated pollution to best meet their individual trading allotments. Achieving these milestones per source while declining area-wide caps via market-based means is as much an aspect of optimality as achieving attainment of environmental sustainability because optimality entails rewarding the innovative actors and punishing the recalcitrant ones; a suboptimal program would simply treat all sources equally.
7. As a direct consequence of our current "nonattainment of sustainability with Nature," these strategies do not immediately factor in at "first order" any "second-order" effects, such as economic costs or, in some cases, social inequity issues affecting other stakeholders, which instead should be considered only *after* solving the first-order pollution-reduction optimality problem first. One could liken ignoring second-order effects to assuming frictionless springs or ideal gases that are typically made in introductory physics courses.[22] An analogy is in order. Recall the public

safety announcement provided on airlines—if oxygen masks drop, take care of yourself first and your child second—there's no sense in providing care to your child if you pass out first. The logic is the same here. Make sure that the "parent," that is, Nature (which includes human welfare), gets preserved and the environment gets clean and restored first, and only then worry about the "dependents," that is, economic costs, etc., later. Using another analogy, asking the strategies developed in this book to immediately incorporate economic costs and, in some cases, social justice concerns would be like demanding that the Wright Brothers' first airplane immediately be one that includes first-class seating and lavatories; clearly, the idea is to first get the plane off the ground. This assumption is particularly critical as it pertains to achieving a circular economy.

8. Whether or not the implementation of the strategies developed in this book is immediately unrealistic or politically infeasible, it is not relevant at this stage. Thus, regardless of their chances for immediate application, the point is to first get the strategies *right*. It's better to think outside the boundaries of the current box and wait for consensus to come around than it is to think inside the currently constrained box and continue to live with substandard, but politically tenable strategies. The economic and legal squabbling within our existing suboptimal environmental regulatory regime,[23] while unsustainability with Nature continues exponentially, is an indication that we are obviously moving in the wrong direction overall.
9. The strategies developed in Parts 2 through 4 in this book will apply universally, such that there will not be an "EU strategy" or a "North American strategy"; there is just a *best* strategy. Thus, there is no need to discuss how to modify this strategy to any country's particular legal structure; each country, in fact, would need to adapt its legal structure to fit the strategy so as to reach sustainability.[24] To arrive at the best strategy, however, the discussion, primarily in Part 1, will exhibit an American bias, but that bias will hopefully not be too burdensome to non-US readers.[25] However, some reference to the American system is unavoidable since developing a best strategy must be motivated by what already exists today. Nevertheless, to avoid having readers who are regulators in the European Union (EU) and elsewhere feeling left out, detailed aspects of the US system will be kept to a minimum (although it may not appear that way to some). Practitioners outside the United States

should be able to relate to similar aspects of regulation as they apply to their countries and/or regions. In any event, readers outside the United States may skip Chapter 3 that addresses past attempts at regulatory reform in the United States.

10. As researched by Kirchherr,[26] the term "circular economy" has many definitions in the literature. Breaking free from those typical definitions of a CE that typically speak to such requirements as reduce, recycle, reuse, etc., the "definition" of a CE in this book would simply be the outcome that is achieved by minimizing the generation of solid waste and potentially other pollution, relative to the amount of materials already in use and where waste materials are properly incentivized for continual use. To add another element of precision, it would also include the requirement that resources be sufficiently constrained. While such a definition facilitates reuse, recycling, and other "Rs" and more, note that a CE is based on reducing the generation of environmental, but mostly solid waste, pollution. Circularity facilitated by environmental regulation will *not* include the use of renewable energy or social equity, as is sometimes found in the literature. This is because the strategies developed in this book are first and foremost strategies to regulate the generation of pollution and restoring ecosystems.

The significance of specifically focusing on reducing the generation of environmental pollution in Item 7 above cannot be overstated and will be expounded on further. The narrative and task of regulating has often been hobbled, if not hijacked, whether purposefully or otherwise, by a number of distractions. This overburden on regulation includes the relentless obsession with costs,[27] determining which market instruments are best applied, and the slavish attention paid to ensuring that all legal guidance and procedural steps are stringently followed. Any discussion of pollution limits and actual harm reduction is oftentimes relegated to second-class status, particularly as the discussion relates to costs and their association to climate change.

The notion that economic costs must be treated as or more important than preserving or harming Nature, which includes the welfare of humanity, *is a fundamentally flawed premise* because making value judgments regarding Nature and the environment should not be the role of economics or any other social science; economic costs must not be primary in the discussion when sustainability with Nature is in nonattainment (i.e., an AEGD above zero).

Moreover, it is important to remember that the economic system is subordinate to and embedded within Nature, not the other way around. So, where preserving Nature is subordinated to economics within an existing state of "nonattainment of ecological and environmental sustainability," it will clearly be impossible to do so. If it is any consolation, optimality nevertheless does provide the next best thing—flexibility for sources to reduce harms and achieve compliance.

While it is absolutely critical to address social inequities, such as hotspots in environmental justice areas, it is important to reiterate that this issue is subordinate to solving the multi-media pollution-based harms that adversely affect Nature itself. Much like the emergency room doctor having to stabilize the trauma patient first and only later prescribing antibiotics to prevent infection during recovery, solving the social inequity problem is a second-order, locally embedded problem that is still open to a localized solution later (think antibiotics) within the larger global and regional solution (think stabilizing the trauma patient).

The goal here then is to use regulation first and foremost to specifically laser-focus on rigorously restoring ecosystems and reducing the generation of multi-media environmental pollution so that global and regional environmental issues are appropriately addressed. As long as negative environmental externalities are being internalized, inequities can be addressed.

The Layout of This Book

Part 1 provides background on key regulatory aspects under the CAA. So that the reader is on the same page of the comprehensive strategy as it develops in the book, Chapter 1 provides the success story of the CAA and how regulation of stationary sources of air pollution is typically practiced here in the United States. Chapter 2 highlights the major design flaws of the current AQM system for stationary sources. Chapter 3 briefly documents past discussions of CAA reform in the United States, which date back decades, even before regulation became much more complex than it was just twenty years ago.

Readers who are already familiar with, do not understand or otherwise do not need any of the background information regarding regulation of air pollution in Part 1 may skip directly to Part 2 without losing too much context.

Part 2 provides the development and commentary of the comprehensive strategy. Chapter 4 presents the core elements of the proposed transformation/reformation of key aspects of the CAA and develops the optimal, comprehensive strategy for regulating the generation of air pollution from stationary sources. While the strategy is inspired by experience with the CAA, it maintains some of the elements of the current system while restructuring others and utilizes noticeably more streamlined approaches that will achieve what is optimal, or near-optimal, regulation. Chapter 5 provides detailed insights and commentary if the comprehensive strategy is adopted.

Part 3 provides the development and commentary for adapting and later generalizing the comprehensive strategy when applied to the generation of solid waste pollution and multi-media environmental pollution, including how to facilitate the transition to a CE. In Chapter 6, the comprehensive strategy is adapted to "pre-solid waste," that is, product-based pollution, such as a product's difficulty-of-disassembly and toxicity characteristics. The adapted strategy is then generalized further in Chapter 7 by integrating the regulation of all relevant environmental regulatory pollutants to holistically apply to multi-media environmental pollution, including the usual suspects of water pollution and on-site generated waste. This broader strategy, including but not limited to the application of characteristic standards to products, the rationing of resource inputs, and incentivizing the reuse of post-consumption materials, will facilitate the broader transition to a CE. How legacy pollution fits into the picture is also explored. The implications and consequences of applying the generalized strategy to reach a more likely variant of a CE are found in Chapter 8. Here, several topics are commented upon, including regulatory insights, the rebound effect, the flaws of current thought in the CE field, changing mindsets, ecological and economic considerations, imports as transboundary pollution, market economics as a prerequisite to a CE, etc.

Part 4 consists of Chapters 9 and 10, which look at the "deeper" strategic layers and the overall implications of applying the core aspects of the strategies developed in the book. Chapter 9 extends the use of the generalized strategy to even greater problems of our day, namely, mitigating global climate change, postulating a possible regulatory strategy to address resource use in the production of agricultural food products and the restoration of ecosystems. Achieving a "sustainable equilibrium" between a restored Nature and humanity is next postulated. Lastly, the chapter includes a discussion on the role of both the rate of material complexity and entropy increase as they apply to other environmental harms. Chapter 10 posits a Grand Unified Theory of Environmental Law and Regulation and an overarching global blueprint of environmental law. We will also see that the interplay of holistic regulation applied to pollutant harms, resource use, and restoring Nature arises out of the methods developed in this book. Lastly, Chapter 10 posits a Global Constitution for Nature that subordinates human-based constitutions to ensure sustainability with Nature.

The Conclusion looks backward and forward by asking how we got here and how we should proceed into the future. Looking back, candid commentary is provided on the conspicuous absence of economists, environmental legal scholars, NGOs, and others with regard to tackling the calamitous problems we are currently facing. Looking forward, homework is assigned to scholars and others to facilitate the implementation of the strategies developed in the book.

The book ends with a Bibliography that includes websites cited in the text.

To highlight salient points of significance, textboxes are scattered throughout the book.

While the use of regulatory jargon has hopefully been kept to a minimum, there is no way to avoid its use entirely.

A final word—the goal first and foremost is to get things right, so this author welcomes pushing the envelope in the right direction, so hopefully some assertions, where wrong, will be minor in nature. In any event, this book will be considered a success if it properly reorients regulation to achieve sustainability with Nature and motivates the further development of better solutions to our mounting environmental crises.

Notes

1 A related measure provided by the Global Footprint Network is Earth Overshoot Day, which "marks the date when humanity has exhausted nature's budget for the year." https://www.footprintnetwork.org/our-work/earth-overshoot-day/.

2 It should be noted at the outset that the notion of an equilibrium state of Nature is disputed by ecologists because Nature is characterized as a complex adaptive system that continues to change over time. The goal of a resilient and transient steady-state-like equilibrium will be assumed to be that between Nature and humanity (itself a part of Nature) rather than treating Nature and humanity as discrete, stand-alone entities in opposition to the other. If ecologists object to this approach, this author would assert that for now this is still a far better goal than that of our continual unsustainable trajectory. Discussing what an idealized resilient

Nature should be before we even take action must not supersede the immediately pragmatic necessity of initiating the process of achieving sustainability with Nature today. Once we are on the path of achieving sustainability with Nature, ecologists can sort out a better, more defined goal later since they are the experts best equipped to do so.

3 While the reader may find it annoying that the term "with Nature" is used after the term "sustainability," it is being done intentionally to specifically define what type of sustainability is to be achieved and to avoid using the term "sustainable development," which has a human/economic bias, or letting the term "sustainability" be otherwise open to vague interpretation.

4 Boris N. Mamlyuk, "Analyzing the Polluter Pays Principle Through Law and Economics," *Southeastern Environmental Law Journal* 18, no. 1 (2010); downloaded at https://ssrn.com/abstract=1679245. Mamlyuk deserves credit for taking an ecologically holistic approach within environment law.

5 With all the serious academic journal literature out there on the subject of sustainability and achieving a circular economy, it is simply astounding just how few of those seriously mention the fundamental need to limit pollution and resources or even restoring ecosystems. The current paradigm is still one where attaining sustainability or a circular economy is doable only where we all just collectively apply brute force and muster our goodwill at ground level. It is as if academic scholars are too squeamish to venture outside the social norm, indicating just how linear our current mindset remains. That mindset will be fundamentally challenged in this book.

6 It is not uncommon for many of these professionals, particularly environmental legal scholars, to be mired within their own subdisciplines (e.g., experts in air pollution know little about the specifics of regulating hazardous waste), so much so that they are ill-equipped to think innovatively outside their respective boxes. It's unrealistic then to expect that environmental experts would cross disciplines into the areas of the circular economy, industrial ecology, and sustainability, particularly in the United States. The existing lack of such a track record with regard to using regulation to facilitate a circular economy speaks for itself.

7 While how to regulate the amount of cattle on the pasture gets all of the attention in the discussion of the Tragedy of the Commons, what gets lost in the same discussion is the role of the natural pastureland.

8 Rebecca Bratspies, "Sustainability: Can Law Meet the Challenge?," *Suffolk Transnational Law Review* 34, no. 2 (2011).

9 Robert L. Fischman, "Letting Go of Stability: Resilience and Environmental Law," *Indiana Law Journal* 94, no. 2 (2019).

10 Fischman, "Letting Go of Stability," 693.

11 In order to enter the PhD program in graduate school, the author was required to solve problems posed by four professors in subject areas within the field of engineering mechanics. Simply pondering how to solve them without actually solving them by putting chalk to blackboard was grounds for rejection to the program.

12 Louis J. Kotzé, "Reflections on the Future of Environmental Law Scholarship and Methodology in the Anthropocene," in *Perspectives on Environmental Law Scholarship*, ed. Ole W. Pedersen (Cambridge University Press, 2018), 142.

13 Kotzé, "Reflections," 148.

14 This point cannot be overstated. It is this author's contention that if, within the first hour of a first course in environmental law, the professor does not mention the achievement of sustainability with Nature as the underlying, fundamental purpose of environmental law and regulation, then that professor is committing malfeasance. Teaching anything less is simply teaching mechanistic, anthropocentric law as it applies to the environment.

15 The European Union's "do no significant harm" policy is somewhat analogous to the FLoERs proposed here. https://knowledge4policy.ec.europa.eu/glossary-item/do-no-significant-harm_en.

16 Richard Stewart, "A New Generation of Environmental Regulation," *Capital University Law Review* 29, no. 1 (2001): 153.

17 In contrast, restoring ecosystems requires a *reverse* "cap-and-trade" system whereby economic tools are used to facilitate the use of ecological instruments to restore Nature. More will be said about this in Chapter 9.

18 To drive home the point of the current unquestioned obedience to the CAA, the following quote from George Bernard Shaw's Caesar and Cleopatra is salient here: "[he] . . . thinks that the customs of his tribe are the laws of nature." So ingrained is the culture and practice of the CAA that there is so little fresh, innovative thinking to properly reform it.

19 William McDonough and Michael Braungart, *Cradle to Cradle: Remaking the Way We Make Things* (North Point Press, 2002).

20 It is worth noting that the US military has stated that depending on unstable countries to obtain rare metals is a threat to national security. Hence, it behooves nations to adopt a CE.

21 The point cannot be asserted strongly enough that optimality is impossible to achieve where environmental sustainability with Nature is not the primary goal. Arguments that attempt to justify and maintain the status quo of the economic system that are fundamentally predicated on the *unsustainable*, ecosystem-destroying use of resources and the generation of pollution, a situation that is

inherently contradictory to sustainably maintaining the economic system itself, are untenable.

22 One reason why economic costs are not immediately considered is that in a world of improperly priced externalities in a linear economy, it has proven difficult to know exactly how to properly quantify those costs.

23 Even if the Supreme Court were to rule in favor of the environment in every case as much as constitutionally possible, the inherent limitations of existing environmental laws are still not sufficient to ameliorate all the ongoing harms inflicted onto Nature.

24 To those who might object with this assertion, note that achieving sustainability with Nature does not respect political boundaries.

25 Two papers that compare the US and EU systems of air quality management and policy are the following: Karolina Kuklinska, Lidia Wolska, and Jacek Namiesnik, "Air Quality Policy in the U.S. and the EU—A Review," *Atmospheric Pollution Research* 6 (2015); and Assessment of the Effectiveness of European Air Quality Policies and Measures. Case Study 2: Comparison of the EU & US AQ Standards & Planning Requirements. https://ec.europa.eu/environment/archives/cafe/activities/pdf/case_study2.pdf.

26 Julian Kirchherr, Denise Reike, and Marko Hekkert, "Conceptualizing the Circular Economy: An Analysis of 114 Definitions," *Resources, Conservation and Recycling* 127 (2017). https://doi.org/10.1016/j.resconrec.2017.09.005.

27 The discussion of cost inequities as it relates to cost per ton of air pollution removed is not uncommon in the literature. It is important to realize that in the world of manufacturing, cost inequities abound, irrespective of the use of pollution controls. The cost to produce a widget at Company A is different than the cost to produce the very same widget at Company B, so focusing on the cost inequities to control emissions is overstated and distorts the control cost inequity narrative.

Part 1

Prepping for Regulatory Surgery

1

The Fundamentals of Regulating Air Pollution

It All Starts with Optimally Regulating Air Pollution

The regulatory foundation for the development of a circular economy (CE) and restoring ecosystems is best established by first developing a regulatory scheme for media that is well suited for regulation, namely, regulating the generation of air pollution. Many of the same underlying principles and essential building blocks that will be developed for regulating the generation of air pollution are generally applicable to the regulation of other media-generated pollution. In particular, the scheme can be adapted to the generation of solid waste, and more critically its surrogates or precursors to facilitate the transition to a CE.

Prescriptive regulation under the US Clean Air Act (CAA) of 1970 (and its subsequent amendments) was a reasonable response to the air pollution crisis of that time, and air quality has unquestionably improved as a result. Nevertheless, after decades of regulating air pollution in the United States, policymakers and regulators alike have seen that the concentration of certain pollutants in many major cities and other areas is "nonattainment" with, that is, have yet to attain, the National Ambient Air Quality Standards (NAAQS), not to mention the inability to address the problem of climate change. At the same time, the practice of air quality management (AQM) over these many years has turned into a quagmire as a result of the gradual increase in the layering and complexity of regulation, resulting in a cumbersome AQM regulatory system. The reader doesn't have to take this author's word for it. As will be discussed in Chapters 2 and 3, besides legislative gridlock, there is plenty of evidence of inefficiency in the practice of air pollution regulation and a corresponding dearth of reform ideas. Regulation continues on autopilot, and this is especially true as it applies to regulating air pollution generated from stationary sources.

Given the sluggish progress addressing air quality in the United States, and other countries as well, a strategy to optimally address air pollution from stationary sources becomes necessary. That strategy is developed in Chapter 4.

The Past Success of the Clean Air Act

Any discussion of developing an optimal strategy to regulate air pollution, and by extension, reforming the CAA must first begin with highlighting its successes. An informative overview for this can be found in the USEPA's document titled, "Progress Cleaning the Air and Improving People's Health."[1] Among its highlights are the following:

- From 1970 to 2020, the combined emissions of the six common pollutants ($PM_{2.5}$ and PM_{10}, SO_2, NOx, VOCs, CO, and lead) dropped by 78 percent
- Emissions reductions have led to dramatic improvements in the quality of the air we breathe. Between 1990 and 2020, national concentrations of air pollutants improved 86 percent for lead (from 2010), 73 percent for carbon monoxide, 91 percent for sulfur dioxide, 61 percent for nitrogen dioxide (annual), and 25 percent for ozone. Annual fine particulate concentrations improved 41 percent (from 2000), and 24-hour coarse particle concentrations improved 26 percent
- These air quality improvements have enabled many areas of the country to meet national air quality standards set to protect public health and the environment
- Environmental damage from air pollution, such as to the health of ecosystems, is reduced
- The value of CAA health benefits far exceeds the costs of reducing pollution
- New cars, trucks, and nonroad engines use state-of-the-art emissions control technologies
- New power plants and factories use modern pollution control technology
- Power plants have cut emissions that cause acid rain and harm public health
- Interstate air pollution has been reduced
- Actions to protect the ozone layer are saving millions of people from fatal skin cancers and eye cataracts and
- Scenic vistas in our national parks are clearer due to reductions in pollution-caused haze.

As far as not tampering with the CAA is concerned, it would be too naïve and simplistic to assert that "if it ain't broke, don't fix it." In similar fashion to a reliable decades-old coal-fired utility boiler that belches out large quantities of pollution, the CAA has itself been reliable but, over time, its capacity for regulating air pollution has now become inefficient and suboptimal.[2] There are still over 100 million Americans who live in areas of poor air quality sometime during the year. Clearly, certain aspects of the CAA that have been successful must be kept while others, such as the labor-intensive and inefficient State Implementation Plan (SIP) process and the New Source Review (NSR) program for new major source construction or modifications at existing major sources, must be overhauled due to their process-oriented rather than results-oriented nature, not to mention the "bureaucratic pollution" they generate. Nonpractitioners who enjoy the benefits of the CAA without experiencing or observing its downsides do not realize that air pollution regulation is failing to perform optimally.

Schoenbrod et al. make the point that significant reductions occurred when the federal government, not states, was directly responsible for overseeing mandated reductions.[3] These reductions resulted from the following four provisions of the CAA: trading programs were implemented to address the Acid Rain Program,[4] the phasing out of chlorofluorcarbons (CFC), the requirement that automakers cut emissions by 90 percent from new cars, and the mandated use by motorists of lead-free gas in new cars.

While setting caps and establishing an associated trading system was successful, another problem with the current system is clear: although it is complicated by complex rules, numerous guidance documents and procedures that must be followed, it is effective in facilitating emissions reductions, except that it is difficult to specifically quantify how, or pin down just where and why it was effective.

The "comprehensive strategy" to regulate air pollution to be developed in Chapter 4 addresses these and other issues in several ways. It removes nonessential excess bureaucracy to best promote the regulation of air pollution while achieving results that should be similar to if not better than current efforts. The strategy is simpler, but to be truthful, "less complicated" may be more accurate.

Quantifiable emissions targets are to be set in areas that do not attain the NAAQS for a given pollutant while an emissions trading program is used as the tool to facilitate the achievement of those targets. One can think of this as putting sources within a region on a pollution budget. It's a more rational systematic strategy than the one that exists today.

Essential Concepts of AQM

The task of addressing air pollution for stationary sources (think factories) through an AQM program in the United States has typically been administered through an evolving, ad hoc and piecemeal process. Over a span of decades, the American AQM program has progressed from being relatively straightforward to implement[5] to being quite complicated and unnecessarily bureaucratic. This is the result of several moving parts within the program. Such moving parts include:

- Constantly evolving regulations for the same types of source categories, emission units and pollutants, and regulatory interpretations and procedures;
- Overlapping rules that apply to the same pollutant and the same type of emission unit; for example, for NOx emissions from the same coal-fired boiler, the following requirements may apply: the Cross-State Air Pollution Rule (CSAPR), the Acid Rain Program, Reasonably Available Control Technology (RACT), and a NOx trading program within the state;
- Developing detailed permits for major sources, including the CAA's Title V operating permits and major source permits, including the determination of Best Available Control Technology (BACT) and/or Lowest Achievable Emission Rate (LAER), and the mandatory development by regulators of the rationale for their permitting decisions (in the United States these documents may be called Statements of Bases or Project Summaries), that can each be lengthy documents (both time-consuming and labor-intensive to develop), making the issuance of such a permit very difficult to achieve (this also includes multiple procedures in the process);
- Being required to revise and re-revise Title V (major source) operating permits too frequently (particularly for the larger and more complex facilities, such as refineries) by incorporating all recently issued construction permits due to the need to add new units or change operations;
- Difficulties in determining what does and does not constitute a modification (e.g., physical changes to existing equipment, changes in the method of operation);
- Addressing modifications in conjunction with construction of new equipment and often the complexities and nuances associated with them;

- Addressing multiple regulatory requirements at major sources, for example, RACT, NSPS, compliance assurance monitoring (CAM), hazardous air pollutant standards (for major and area sources), emissions trading;
- Seeking guidance from higher regulatory authorities;
- Changes in attainment or nonattainment area status for a pollutant, and the required changes to applicable rules, rule development (including emissions standards) that then requires among things, revisions to permits to reflect these changes; and
- Following and tracking multiple guidance documents and critical legal interpretations.

With many years of experience in AQM to draw from, regulators can now provide fundamentally better suggestions and strategies based on what has worked well and what has not. This book hopefully provides not only a significant upgrade (reform) of the CAA but also an optimal, better organized strategy for regulators elsewhere whose programs are still in their developmental phases. There is no one rigid method of regulating air pollution, of course, but there are those methods that are certainly far superior to others. Some of these methods can be classified into the narrow category of those methods that "work" to reduce pollution over time. Equally as useful, if not more, is what *does not work*, for example, an AQM program designed with a strong permitting program but whose enforcement capacity is structurally weak; such a program will not function well at all.

One good indication that fixing what ails the regulation of air pollution is correct is that the core strategy developed in Chapter 4 also forms the basis for developing a strategy to regulate the generation of solid waste pollution that facilitates the transition to a CE. Given that no one has yet to develop a regulatory strategy to achieve a CE, this provides confidence that the comprehensive strategy is itself correct.

The Command-and-Control v. Market Instruments Debate

There is a good deal of literature, mostly written by economists and legal scholars, debating, on the one hand, the virtues of Command-and-Control (CaC) and the use of market instruments (e.g., emissions trading, taxation) to regulate air pollution. Whether in China, India, or elsewhere, where the need for an organized AQM program is crucial, it is premature to engage in a needless academic debate as to whether CaC or trading is the best method to utilize to regulate air pollution. Elliott has this to say about the matter:

> The debate that still rages in some quarters about whether environmental markets are better than command-and-control regulation strikes me as about as nonsensical as a debate about whether airplanes or trucks are a better method of transportation. Obviously, each has its inherent strengths and weaknesses. Therefore, each has its role, or "ecological niche," and a composite system composed of both is likely to be more adaptable than a "pure" system composed of either one alone.[6]

Besides Elliott being proven prescient, we will see later in Chapter 4 with regard to the use of a composite system that the largely simplistic academic debate of CaC v. market instruments shows that economists and lawyers live in a bubble but know little about the practical nature of regulating air pollution "in the trenches."

First, there is far more to regulating emissions than framing the environmental mission around the narrow lens of CaC versus market instruments. It is arguable that the *bulk* of the core mission of addressing the problem of air pollution involves monitoring concentrations and measuring emissions; for example, determining the actual emissions from an emission unit and, by extension, the total emissions at a source from all the units at that source and the total emissions within the region where those sources are located is critical. Determining pollutant concentrations via ambient monitors and crunching air quality models to identify how to attain the NAAQS for a pollutant forms the foundation of any AQM program for stationary sources. Management scholar Peter Drucker's famous axiom that "you can't manage what you don't measure" fits well here. There is a very good reason why the bulk of employees that conduct the AQM program within a state's environmental protection bureau are engineers (i.e., permit writers, field inspectors, air quality planners, air quality modelers, ambient monitoring personnel, etc.)—you have to measure and count before you can regulate.

Second, the CaC versus market instruments academic debate is inane because of its binary either-or nature among academics. The strategies developed in this book attempt to achieve the regulatory "sweet spot" between the blended use of both CaC and the use of market instruments. Briefly, this is accomplished at the macrolevel by the use of CaC: by setting caps and, where necessary, forcing their decline and allowing flexibility to attain those reductions by the use of market instruments (primarily CaT); and also at the source level, by requiring equipment to meet specific performance standards while providing sources the flexibility as to how to achieve those standards. Market instruments such as trading and taxation, while playing a key role, are nothing more than tools employed to facilitate emissions reductions. The details of the use of these tools within the comprehensive strategy will be discussed in Chapter 4.

Grasping AQM's Small and Big Picture

The following statement is undeniable:

> *The "Fundamental God Particle" of any AQM program is the determination of actual emissions for a specific emission unit or operation.*

Stationary source AQM all begins with determining actual emissions for an emission unit or operation. From there, once all the emissions for a given pollutant at a source are quantified for all the units and processes, only then can sourcewide emissions be determined.[7,8] The collection of all sourcewide emissions for that pollutant within a region provides the total emissions for those stationary sources in that region.

Complicating the problem of conducting a successful AQM program for stationary sources is the fact that the vast majority of emission units within an airshed cannot have their emissions measured using a continuous emissions monitoring system (CEMS). Except where mass balance can be used to determine emissions (e.g., CO_2 emissions based on the amount of carbon in the fuel), the most common means of determining actual emissions at a source is by stack testing. Stack tests, if properly conducted, will determine the emission factors (e.g., lb of pollutant emitted per ton of product) for specific units and processes at a source.[9,10]

Measure, Count, then Regulate: The Role of CaC Regulation

Aside from determining emissions from all sources within an airshed, a great deal of engineering-specific, prescriptive regulation dictates that the ambient pollutant concentrations in the airshed be monitored. In addition to using the monitored ambient air data as a backdrop to regulation, a large amount of air quality modeling must be conducted using sourcewide emissions data to determine to what degree emissions must be reduced.

Basically, there are three supportive legs of the current AQM program stool that achieve its desired goals, namely: (1) determining emissions from the individual units at stationary sources and by extension the sources themselves within a region, (2) monitoring ambient air concentrations, and (3) conducting computer modeling to determine what routes must be taken to achieve attainment of the NAAQS. These data are used to determine how much regulation is ultimately required to ensure that the air pollution generated is sufficiently reduced.

Whether using CaC or economic incentives (e.g., emissions trading) to address sourcewide emissions in order to implement and achieve AQM program goals, it should be becoming clearer that emissions measurement accuracy and accounting are the heart and soul of regulating stationary sources. One major reason why many countries have a very difficult time regulating air pollution is because, except for some of the large major sources (e.g., coal-fired power plants), regulators cannot quantify the amount of emissions that are being generated by individual emission units at a vast multitude of sources.

After the determination of emissions is complete, the next task is actually the "easy" part: specifying how to achieve these reductions through CaC and/or economic instruments. Some might think that this is finally the point where the real philosophical and academic debate on pollution control regulation begins. Economists and others have studied in great depth whether CaC or trading, or some combination of both, should be used to improve air quality at the least cost. Unfortunately, the study of trading programs has focused mainly on the US Acid Rain Program,[11] where the determination of emissions by use of CEMS renders the process more straightforward than determining emissions by less accurate means in the majority of situations.

Unfortunately, the nature of air pollution and the location of its generating sources complicate the academic debate regarding "CaC vs. market instruments," pushing the debate further to the margin. Which tool is more suitable should realistically depend on such factors as whether the source generates intra- or inter-state air pollution, whether the geographical area is in attainment or nonattainment to the NAAQS for a given pollutant, and the number of major sources in that area. Thus, depending on these and other essential characteristics, the debate hinges on the appropriate combination of CaC and market instrument rather than in considering the binary either-or merits.

The Basics of Source-Specific and Regional Regulation in the United States

To motivate how we will proceed in later chapters, we need to know what the common practice of regulating looks like in the United States today. We start with the specific topic of what constitutes a stationary source of emissions, based on the quantity of individual air pollutants a source emits. Although there is no "typical" source, the current method of regulating both major and minor sources of air pollution will be briefly described to flesh out critical concepts, providing the reader with a real perspective on what situations regulators might typically confront.

In the discussion that follows, it should be noted that only some of the more critical aspects of regulation are described here; regulatory purists may object that there are gaps or corners cut, but the point here is to provide the layman with enough of the key essentials for the later chapters of the book.

Major and Minor Sources

Currently, a major source in the United States is one where the potential emissions[12] for any one pollutant are above that pollutant's legally specified major source threshold. The threshold that identifies a major source under the Title V operating permit program of the CAA is 100 tons per year (tpy) for a pollutant (except for hazardous air pollutants or greenhouse gases).[13] Thus, a source where the potential emissions of NOx are 110 tpy and all other pollutant emissions are each below 100 tpy is a major source under Title V due to its NOx emissions being over the 100 tpy threshold. In actual practice, however, a slightly different situation prevails. For a source to be truly considered major for Title V purposes, *actual* emissions of a regulated air pollutant, rather than its *potential* emissions, must be emitted over its major source threshold.

There are typically three types of minor sources. The first is where actual emissions for each regulated air pollutant are below their respective major source thresholds while the potential emissions of at least one pollutant are above the major source threshold for that pollutant. When such a source takes federally enforceable limitations to limit their plantwide pollutant emissions to below their respective major source thresholds, the source becomes a "synthetic minor" source and can elect to operate under a Federally Enforceable State Operating Permit (FESOP).[14] Such sources will still have to meet applicable federal and/or state emission standards for individual emission units while maintaining emissions from individual operations below prescribed limits (in tons per year). Setting enforceable operating and emission limits in the permit by themselves is not enough—sufficient recordkeeping and reporting requirements, among other requirements, must be imposed. Stack testing may even be required to ensure that capture and destruction efficiencies of control devices, in percent reduction, are met.

The second type of minor source is one where the source's actual and potential emissions are both below the major source threshold for each pollutant, but where the equipment itself and/or emissions levels still require a permit. Such sources are truly minor sources. Some states may require such a source to have a permit throughout its duration; that is, without expiration, until a physical change is made at the source that necessitates a revision. Such sources would have to pay an annual fee and still have to obtain a permit if there are changes (e.g., new construction and/or modifications[15]) at the source. As usual, recordkeeping and reporting and other requirements are imposed.

The third and last type of minor source is one where the source's emissions are so low that registration rather than a permit is all that is necessary. Registration may nevertheless require an annual fee.

There are three fundamental, discrete bases of generated emissions from stationary sources: (1) the individual emission unit where the generated emissions are typically governed by an emissions standard for that specific type of emission unit[16] which must not be exceeded but where there may be flexibility to achieve that standard; (2) the source comprised of its emissions units and other generating activities (e.g., fugitive emissions); and (3) the entire regional airshed itself where those sources are located.

With these as building blocks, we are now ready to follow how regional air quality is regulated in the United States. This will be followed by a discussion of construction of major and minor sources. To serve as a guide for later discussion, other relevant aspects of the regulatory program will be briefly described. Lastly the discussion of regulation in the United States would not be complete without mentioning the role of "bureaucratic pollution."

The Role of Limits and the State Implementation Plan (SIP) Process

Where emissions are quantifiable, it would only be natural to assume that the CaC-based regulatory practice to set regional limits is quite common in AQM.

While establishing limits is quite common for an individual source's plantwide emissions and particular emissions units and operations at a source, readers might likewise assume that regional caps are set and reduced quite routinely in those areas that do not attain the National Ambient Air Quality Standard (i.e., the concentration above which there are harmful impacts to health) for a given pollutant, but that assumption would be incorrect.[17] Instead, under the CAA, a very convoluted, circuitous method is employed to (supposedly) achieve pollution reductions in areas that are not in attainment of the NAAQS for subject pollutants.[18]

State regulators in the United States are mandated under the CAA to use an established process, called the State Implementation Plan, or SIP, to, among its many requirements, reduce emissions of subject pollutants in nonattainment areas to below the NAAQS. Once regulators have all the actual emission data from the sources and knowledge of the emission units that generate those emissions, they must then determine how far those emissions must be reduced to achieve attainment based on the pollutant concentration data measured by ambient monitors. Where the area is still nonattainment or is redesignated to an even worse condition of nonattainment, state regulators must revise their state's SIP (to be approved by the USEPA) by developing a very detailed and sophisticated plan to reduce emissions further. They do this, in part, by developing more stringent RACT rules that apply in those nonattainment areas (NAA) for various types of emission units that are able to make further reductions.[19] For example, bakeries may have to install afterburners in order to reduce volatile organic compounds (VOC) emissions (i.e., ethanol) to address the new capture and control requirements in a newly designated ozone nonattainment area. After regulators tighten the rules, they monitor ambient concentrations to determine how to proceed with rule changes in the future (if necessary) until attainment is achieved (or maintained). By its nature, the process is clearly very deliberative and hence not a de facto means to urgently address health and welfare impacts.

We see that rather than applying limits regionally, a convoluted process is used to reduce emissions in areas that are harmful to public health. Unfortunately, this has been the accepted method of reducing regional emissions for decades.

Construction at Major Sources

New Source Review (NSR) is the regulatory program under the CAA that addresses the construction of new major stationary sources or major modifications at existing major stationary sources. NSR was designed as a program to slow the growth of emissions in both nonattainment and attainment areas. There are two prongs of NSR: (1) the Prevention of Significant Deterioration (PSD), that is, the rules that apply in those areas where the NAAQS is met (not exceeded) for a subject pollutant; and (2) nonattainment NSR, which applies to those pollutants whose concentrations exceed the NAAQS. A brief description of the NSR program follows, but it would take far more than a few paragraphs to convey the true nature of the full program.

For purposes of major source regulation under NSR, the location of the source, its source category, and the quantity of emissions of each regulated NSR pollutant[20] generated by that source will dictate whether the source is a major source or not. In attainment areas (AA), that is, where the ambient concentration of a given pollutant is below its specified NAAQS concentration, if the source category is a "named source" under the PSD program (i.e., among the "dirty 26" named source categories) the major source threshold is 100 tpy, whereas if the source category is not named, the threshold is 250 tpy.[21] Companies seeking to construct a new major stationary source or undertake a major modification at an existing major stationary source in an attainment area ("triggering PSD") will be required to conduct air quality modeling and apply Best Available Control Technology (BACT) to those units and processes that emit pollutants where the source's emissions of that pollutant are (1) major and (2) where major emissions of other attainment area pollutants are above pre-established significance thresholds. Thus, a source emitting a pollutant above either 100 tpy (for a named source) or 250 tpy will trigger PSD for that pollutant but will also trigger PSD for pollutants that emit over their much lesser significance thresholds. In addition, modifications at existing major sources can also trigger PSD for pollutants that exceed their respective significance thresholds (e.g., 10 tpy for hydrogen sulfide).

Under the CAA, the definition of Best Available Control Technology, contrary to its name, is actually an emissions limit, which is determined by examining possible technologies that are able to cost-effectively achieve that low emissions limit. The determination of BACT requires the following detailed top-down process to be conducted for each emission unit that emits the attainment area pollutant for which PSD is triggered: (1) identify control options; (2) demonstrate the technical feasibility of those technologies by examining their availability and applicability; (3) rank the remaining control options; (4) consider economic, energy, and environmental impacts (note: unlike LAER in NAAs, sources subject to PSD for a given pollutant can reject technologies if they can justify that they are cost-prohibitive); and (5) select BACT and set the limit (including the technology that achieves that limit). Note that the detailed Top-Down BACT process applies even to emission units that are projected to emit negligible emissions. Needless to say, for a proposed new major source with multiple emissions units emitting many pollutants that are subject to PSD review, the determination of BACT and the accompanying documents to justify those determinations is a very labor-intensive process.[22] In conjunction with the determination of BACT, significant air quality modeling must be conducted to ensure that the project will not, among other requirements, violate the NAAQS for the subject pollutant, deteriorate air quality by consuming an established amount of increment for that subject pollutant concentration in the area, or result in significant impacts to soils, vegetation, and wildlife.

In nonattainment areas, where the NAAQS concentration for a given pollutant in that area is exceeded,[23] the severity of nonattainment dictates the major source threshold—in extreme ozone NAAs, the threshold is low, 10 tpy, whereas in marginal ozone NAAs, the major source threshold is 100 tpy. Clearly, constructing sources in extreme NAAs is much more difficult than in marginal areas since it will require more stringent, expensive controls. Constructing such major sources requires use of LAER, the acquisition of offsets,[24] an analysis of alternatives to the project, and a demonstration that other sources owned by the applicant in the state are in compliance. Unlike installing BACT, where cost can be considered, LAER does not consider costs since the air quality in the NAA already adversely impacts human health.[25] While still an involved process, the determination of LAER is not as arduous as that for BACT since it basically requires the highest achieving control technology to minimize emissions. Due to being located in more densely populated areas, projects in NAAs tend to be more controversial than those in AAs.

The requirements above for AAs and NAAs highlight just a few of the key aspects of NSR, but the discussion does not do justice to its full scope. Nevertheless, it provides a flavor of the foundation for what is typically required for major source construction and major modifications. The reader may already be confused by the description so far, but do not despair, this confusion is a natural symptom of just how convoluted air pollution regulation can be in the United States.

The permitting consequences for all kinds of major sources, for example, those located in AAs and NAAs or those source categories that are named or unnamed, are multi-varied. One of the major complaints about NSR regulation under the CAA involves its complexities and design flaws, a few of which will be highlighted in the next chapter. For the time being, it is important for the reader to understand that the regulatory process and fulfillment of that process to issue an NSR permit is not simple and straightforward. Determining BACT and/or LAER for each subject pollutant emitted from each emission unit is tedious and supposedly rigorous but subject to second guessing, making it an even more arduous, labor-intensive, and time-consuming process. This does not include sorting out the requirements involved in imposing applicable performance standards, other federal standards and requirements, state emission standards, testing, monitoring, recordkeeping, reporting, notifications, etc., which can significantly bog down the various processing tasks involved. For regulators to impose the requirements above within complicated permits and their accompanying documents, developing these detailed documents from scratch and doing so multiple times is not trivial.

Some Complications of New Source Review

It is worth reiterating that NSR was not developed to reduce emissions, but to make increases in regional emissions more difficult. Note that this does not imply that emissions cannot increase in nonattainment areas. A quirk of nonattainment NSR is that a source can theoretically increase, for example, NOx emissions by 24.9 tpy in a serious ozone NAA today and increase emissions again by 24.9 tpy six years from now, and so on. It is the SIP process, rather than nonattainment area NSR, that attempts to force reductions in the NAA (via tightening of RACT) through the convoluted process described earlier.

Among other bureaucratic aspects of the NSR rules is netting. A rather simple concept in theory but sometimes complicated in practice, netting refers to the determination of a current project's significant emissions such that past actual increases and decreases in emissions during a "contemporaneous period" prior to the new project are used to determine whether the net emissions increase is significant. Thus, when the proposed project by itself is a major modification at an existing major source, rather than undergoing NSR and its stringent requirements, the source can choose to "net out" by conducting the netting procedure when the sum of the net emissions' increases and decreases is not significant over a contemporaneous time period, the determination of which is not always straightforward at major sources. This process is particularly complicated when physical modifications at a source occur in conjunction with new construction at the source and the source attempts to use past emissions increases and decreases to net out of NSR if the source can show that the net increase is below the "significance threshold" for the subject pollutant.

As a quick example, a major stationary source in a NAA seeks to install a new unit that will potentially emit 44 tons per year of NOx. Because the new unit's emissions increase is over the NOx significance threshold of 40 tpy (which would normally require full review), the source chooses to net out of NSR because of recent past decreases. To do so, they calculate that the removal of a unit from two years earlier actually emitted an average of 38 tpy of NOx over its previous two years of operation prior to removal, so that the overall project, including contemporaneous decreases, will see a net emissions increase of 6 tpy, which is now below the 40 tpy significance threshold. Yet, this project will have to undergo significant permitting requirements—development of a draft permit, a draft project summary that explains the project in detail and a thirty-day public notice and comment period (with a possible extension if a hearing is requested), all for a permitted net increase of 6 tpy of NOx emissions. In the world of air pollution regulation, an increase of 6 tpy at a source is not very much.

Debottlenecking occurs when a change at one or more emission units has implications for emission increases at upstream and/or downstream emission units that are not being physically modified. Increased utilization can occur when a new unit to be constructed will increase the utilization of an existing unit elsewhere, thereby increasing emissions from that existing unit. Debottlenecking and increased utilization at a source can each complicate the processing of permitting due to the extensive back-and-forth communication between applicant and regulator to clarify just where and by how much emissions will change and whether NSR will apply.

There is far more to NSR than what was just described above. Nevertheless, the reader should hopefully have formed a basic understanding of just how varied the regulation of major sources can be and the difficulties involved in navigating the regulatory gauntlet while not losing sight of the goal: minimizing emissions growth.

Note for future purposes that much of what we have seen above reflects the current "process-based" nature of regulation of stationary sources, when the goal instead should be a far more "results-based" emission reduction program.

Construction at Minor and Synthetic Minor Sources

Constructing minor sources of pollution or modifying units at a minor source is nowhere near as complicated as constructing major sources. The smaller the maximum permitted emissions at a source, the lesser the requirements imposed. Minor sources are typically only required to ensure that individual emission units meet given federal performance and/or state emissions standards. Certainly, sufficient growth of emissions at a minor source would trigger NSR if the emissions increase is sufficiently high to warrant it.

Other Relevant (but Brief) Aspects of the Regulatory Program

Other aspects of conducting AQM should not be neglected. While regulatory purists may again object, some of these aspects will be mentioned only briefly here since this book is not a primer on the general practice of environmental regulation but a means to more proactively reform it.

Stack testing is performed by inserting a probe into the stack gases to ultimately determine the mass rate in lb/hr of emissions coming out of the stack. It is used when it is not clear exactly what the emissions from a process are. Such tests only represent a snapshot in time, which is fine to determine instantaneous compliance but not always useful to ensure ongoing compliance and the actual emissions over the long term. Where possible, to ensure long-term compliance and to determine the actual emissions being generated, continuous emissions monitoring systems (CEMS) are often used.

Ambient monitors are used throughout regions of a state to measure the ambient concentrations of various pollutants. Such monitors are not cheap, so they need to be placed where the data they measure will provide the best information to regulators.

Rules are written by engineers in combination with regulatory attorneys to ensure that the regulations do what they are intended to do. Air pollution permits are written by engineers to ensure that the rules that apply to pollution sources are spelled out clearly to those sources. Inspections of sources are often conducted by regulatory agency inspectors to determine whether source units and operations conform to what is specified in the permit. If violations are uncovered, violation notices are later developed by compliance personnel and may lead to enforcement by enforcement attorneys.

The Bureaucratic Tasks to Regulate Air Pollution in the United States

We've seen above just some of the requirements set by law that are imposed on regulators to achieve the mission of regulating air pollution from stationary sources. The basic description of how regulatory practice is conducted would not be complete without examining the unnecessary generation of "bureaucratic pollution." From high-level regulators on down to lower-level managers, multiple procedures are imposed, all arguably applied to address the requirements of established law, although many are arbitrarily imposed for the supposed sake of preventing possible problems later. Air pollution regulation has a plethora of required procedures, some of which will be discussed further in Chapter 2.

The Role of the Public

The public rarely comes into the regulatory process until, usually, public notice and comment are required when either new rules are being developed or permits have been drafted where the public's input is solicited. Rule development rarely brings out the general public, although environmental organizations may weigh in. The general public is more likely to attend a public hearing and provide comments on draft permits for controversial projects that are to be constructed in their local area.

Final Remarks

In this chapter, we've seen that current air pollution regulation in the United States follows a procedure-oriented path. We've seen examples of the process-oriented SIP procedure and NSR regulation and how that can get complicated very quickly without the guarantee of significant emissions reductions. And we've also seen that the actual tasks of accomplishing the goals of regulation are no simple matter either.

The Clean Air Act was expected to be updated ten years after the 1990 Amendments were enacted, but that never happened. As a result, the process of regulating air pollution under it has not evolved well, and talk of reform has been a common theme in the literature for a while but appears to have tapered off.

The next chapter focuses on the US AQM program's design flaws, some of which have already been discussed and continue to play a significant role in contributing to what some legal scholars call the policy or political logjam.[26] Although there is superficial discussion in the literature on the complicated rules and regulations in play, there appears to be even less discussion on, or acknowledgment of, the existence of the inherent design flaws that contribute to the bureaucratic logjam, such as those resulting from the rulemaking process and the day-to-day bureaucracy itself.

So while reforming the CAA for the regulation of stationary sources is the immediate focus, as we'll see throughout this book, when the goal is to truly limit and reduce pollutants in an adverse area, there is *absolutely no substitute* for setting a hard, limited cap on the pollutant and then tightening that cap over time.

In this regard, we have not taken our eyes off the larger goal of developing a general strategy for regulating the generation of solid waste pollution (Chapter 6) and later, multi-media environmental pollution as well (Chapter 7).

Notes

1 https://www.epa.gov/clean-air-act-overview/progress-cleaning-air-and-improving-peoples-health.

2 One stark example that immediately comes to mind is the treatment of greenhouse gases (GHG). While one could say that our global climate is in a state of "nonattainment for climate stability," whereby concentrations of carbon dioxide and other GHG are significantly affecting the climate, it is treated as an "attainment" area pollutant under the CAA.

3 David Schoenbrod, Richard B. Stewart, and Katrina M. Wyman, *Breaking the Logjam: Environmental Protection That Will Work* (Yale University Press: New Haven & London, 2010), 83.

4 According to the USEPA website, the program "requires major emission reductions of sulfur dioxide (SO_2) and nitrogen oxides (NOx), the primary precursors of acid rain, from the power sector. The SO_2 program sets a permanent cap on the total amount of SO_2 that may be emitted by electric generating units (EGUs) in the contiguous United States." Likewise, "NOx reductions under the ARP are achieved through a program that applies to a subset of coal-fired EGUs and is closer to a

traditional, rate-based regulatory system." https://www.epa.gov/acidrain/acid-rain-program. Key aspects of the Acid Rain Program will play a major role with regard to the strategies developed in this book.

5 It is interesting to note that even in the 1990s, when the rules and regulations were far simpler than they are now, there was discussion even then in the reform literature about reinventing regulation.

6 Elliott, E. Donald, "Environmental Markets and Beyond: Three Modest Proposals for the Future of Environmental Law," *Capital University Law Review* 29, no. 1 (2001): 246. https://openyls.law.yale.edu/bitstream/handle/20.500.13051/1512/Enviro_markets.pdf?sequence=2&isAllowed=y.

7 Determining emissions at a source is still easier said than done. In the absence of using a continuous emissions monitoring system (CEMS), stack testing and material balance are two other means of determining emissions. Nevertheless, to determine compliance, parametric emissions monitoring is sometimes used, but this method only ensures proper performance, a surrogate for compliance, so is not really a means of determining emissions.

8 As a sample calculation, suppose a source has six spray booths whereby five are controlled by an afterburner (100 percent capture, 95 percent control for volatile organic compounds) and the other a touch-up spray booth that is uncontrolled. If the uncontrolled emissions from the five controlled spray booths are 100,000 lbs/year and the uncontrolled emissions from the one uncontrolled booth (using compliant coatings) are 10,000 lb/yr, then the annual VOC emissions E from the source are:

E = 100000 x (1–0.95) + 10000
= 5000 + 10000 lb/yr
= 15000 lb/yr, or 7.5 ton/year.

9 Only where stack test results for the same type of emission unit are numerically precise and presumably accurate can sector-wide emission factors be used with some confidence without resorting to further stack testing. Where wide variability in emission rates exists from an emission unit at one source relative to the same type of unit at another source within the same source category, stack testing must still be relied on.

10 It is important to note that it may take a significant amount of time, effort, and expense to determine the actual emissions of several pollutants from a given emission unit via a stack test, for example, NOx, CO, SO_2, PM_{10}, pursuant to appropriate test methods.

11 Now is as good a time as any to state that the underlying premise of the article by the Environmental Defense Fund called "How Economics Solved Acid Rain" (https://www.edf.org/approach/markets/acid-rain) is clearly flawed. *First, the task*

of abating pollution is a team effort whereby the engineering, legal, and economic disciplines, as well as regulators, all play a part. No one discipline "solves" the overall problem. But just as significant, it was the setting of limits and their required decline that "solved" the acid rain problem. Trading, a market instrument of economics, was just the most practical tool that best facilitated those required reductions. The credit for the success of the Acid Rain Program was clearly misplaced.

12 Loosely speaking, actual emissions of a pollutant may reflect those pollutants actually emitted, such as during the day and evening shifts, while potential emissions reflect operation as if all shifts were operating throughout the full year (8,760 hours) at maximum capacity.

13 A source can also be major under Title V for its emissions of hazardous air pollutants (HAP) whenever one HAP has potential emissions of 10 tpy or greater, or potential aggregated emissions of all HAP are 25 tpy or greater. In the United States, to be a major source of greenhouse gases when its emissions are over 75,000 tons per year, the source must first be major for another regulated air pollutant.

14 It is possible that a source will still seek a Title V permit where its actual emissions for a pollutant are below the major source threshold while its potential emissions are above it. This is atypical; most sources, when given the choice of opting out of being a Title V source, usually choose to become a synthetic minor source. This is because the regulatory obligations on the source are more detailed and demanding under the Title V program of the CAA.

15 The regulatory definition of the term "modification" is a tricky one as it is used in the US AQM program. For example, in some cases, a physical change to an emission unit is not necessarily a regulatory modification if hourly emissions do not increase.

16 The usual emission standards encountered in practice are the federal New Source Performance Standards (NSPS), found at 40 CFR Part 60.

17 It is a bit different in the European Union, where national emission levels are set but where "the EU system is geared much more to peer pressure and persuasion" to reduce emissions. See Kuklinska, Wolska, and Namiesnik, "Air Quality Policy in the U.S. and the EU—A Review," 135.

18 Only nonattainment areas will be addressed here. How attainment areas are addressed is not instructive for our purposes.

19 SIPs also include strategies to reduce emissions from new major sources, mobile sources, nonroad engines, consumer products, etc., but the focus here is on stationary sources.

20 Without specifically adhering to the purist's desire to use the actual legal definition, the term "regulated NSR pollutant" basically means any pollutant regulated under

the CAA. Greenhouse gases meet this definition but are regulated only when another pollutant triggers NSR first. CAA purists may cringe, but since this book is not a legal document, the term "pollutant" will be used hereafter instead of "regulated NSR pollutant" without loss of too much generality.

21 Among the CAA's many quirks, under NSR, source size is determined differently than under Title V of the CAA, where the major source threshold is 100 tpy. Thus, a major source under NSR will always require a Title V operating permit, but not all Title V sources are major sources under NSR.

22 For example, a proposed new major source with ten emission units that each emits six PSD-triggering AA pollutants would require sixty detailed determinations of BACT.

23 It should be noted that under NSR, a source can be located in a NAA for one pollutant but be in an AA for another.

24 For those NAA pollutants emitted in major quantities, emission offsets are also required for that pollutant's total sourcewide emissions in a greater than one to one ratio, depending on the air quality severity of the area. Offsets ensure that there are decreases in regional emissions overall.

25 According to NSR guidance, however, there is support for the argument that the cost of controls cannot be high enough to cancel the project.

26 While legal scholars speak of the logjam as a policy deficiency occurring at the national level, it should be noted that in this book, the term logjam should also include the bureaucratic burdens that currently exist that stifle progress at the lower reaches of the regulatory food chain as well.

2

The Inherent Design Flaws of Regulating Stationary Sources under the CAA

Knowing What Doesn't Work Is Essential to Knowing What Will

Robert Nordhaus was a rare author that wrote in some detail of the macro design flaws of regulating under the CAA, including the SIP process, grandfathering, GHG regulation, and overlapping, uncoordinated regulatory requirements.[1] While this author concurs with his assertions, more can be added, both at the macro and micro levels. Aside from GHG regulation, the flaws that Nordhaus dealt with can be considered as resolvable through, among other means, external and internal trading, as will be developed in Chapter 4.

Over the last several years, there has been little doubt that regulatory practitioners, if prompted, would cite as a leading design flaw the complexity of the current system, which has been growing exponentially, while the necessary human resources for the air quality management (AQM) system to function have only seen linear growth, where it has grown at all. One need only examine the complexity of New Source Review (NSR) for attainment areas, found at 40 CFR 52.21 for the rules governing the Prevention of Significant Deterioration (PSD), and the accompanying guidance documents that have been developed to supplement implementation of PSD.[2]

Whether it's making Best Available Control Technology (BACT) determinations, addressing the bureaucratic aspects related to physical and nonphysical modifications, or performing cost-effectiveness calculations for various technologies, the process of analyzing projects is fraught with complicated obstacles. Permit engineers, company personnel, and environmental attorneys (for both the regulators and the regulated community) struggle with these issues on a daily basis. Some attempts at so-called reform of the CAA's NSR program have tended to only "reform" it for the benefit of the regulated entities and not for that of regulators, consultants, environmental lawyers, the public, and most importantly, the environment and Nature itself. Reform in this case was certainly not synonymous with simplification for regulators; rather, it was geared toward helping regulated entities by granting them more latitude.

Although air quality has certainly improved over the decades, there is no clear indication as to whether or not the environment has significantly improved in justifiable proportion to the growth in regulatory complexity.[3] Regarding the improvement in air quality during the earlier decades, Coglianese, citing a US EPA study of significant air pollution regulations from the previous century, the results of which showed the benefits far exceeded its costs, made a very insightful observation:

> But by itself this summary result does not help decision makers who want to seek to improve air quality, as it does not reveal anything about which specific regulations worked better than others. *As it happened, many of the benefits estimated in the EPA study reportedly came from just a small number of regulations, suggesting that the other regulations in the study could possibly either be withdrawn or improved dramatically.*[4] [Emphasis added]

This indicates that, in the early years, when there were far fewer stringent air pollution rules, only a *fraction* of the regulations to address air quality were responsible for *most of the resulting benefit*. Given this insight, what is the rationale for the growth in rule complexity since those early days?

At the heart of the issue of the growing complexity of rules and their implementation are a number of program design flaws that require our immediate attention. While there are arguably plenty more, five will be discussed here.

Design Flaw #1: The Sluggish Emission Reduction Process

Design Flaw #1 involves the ongoing circuitous, *ad infinitum-like* process of conducting SIPs, the failure to address grandfathered sources and administering the complex requirements of NSR. As such, these will be treated as a single package here.

It doesn't take observing our ongoing infliction of harms onto Nature and human health to show that we are not sufficiently resolving our sustainability crisis through the appropriate application of environmental regulation. To attain sustainability with Nature on a large scale requires that caps be set on pollution and mandating their decline. Other than a small number of targeted programs, such as that to address acid rain, the United States has generally not taken the setting and reduction of regional or statewide emission caps very seriously. The layman might think that these caps or limits are the bread and butter of regulating air pollution—that assumption would be wrong. Instead, limits are focused more at the individual source and emission unit levels than at the regional level.

As noted in the previous chapter, the process of reducing regional emissions in NAAs is facilitated by monitoring air quality concentrations to determine what changes must be made to the SIP. Specifically where the National Ambient Air Quality Standards (NAAQS) is exceeded for a pollutant, a series of regulatory requirements is imposed within a state's SIP to "ensure" emissions of that pollutant are reduced (e.g., requiring that specific standards be met for most equipment that emits the pollutant). For example, state regulators impose, in the vernacular, Reasonably Available Control Technology (RACT) on subject emission unit categories, such as for the volatile organic compounds (VOC) content of a coating, limited to 0.40 kg of VOC per liter of solids in the coating, as applied.

After RACT is established for various types of equipment, regulators measure regional concentrations of the pollutant (e.g., ozone), and if the area's air quality has gotten worse, then regulators must tighten RACT for the various emission units that emit that pollutant in the area. The success of these measures is to be reviewed again in five years until attainment of the NAAQS is achieved. Peculiarly enough, this long, circuitous, drawn-out process can nevertheless allow emissions in the region to increase. In fact, in NAAs, where a subject pollutant's concentration exceeds its specific NAAQS, that is, where the air quality is unhealthy, growth in a NAA pollutant's emissions at a source in a serious ozone NAA can increase by 24.9 tpy now and again in six years, as explained in Chapter 1. This flaw is a key reason why the current program for regulating air quality under the CAA is suboptimal. Yet this existing methodology is simply an artifact of an antiquated approach legislated by Congress decades ago and is still adhered to, to this day.

If the reader believes this is a cockeyed method of reducing emissions rather than simply setting a regional cap and targeting its reduction head-on until the NAAQS is met, then—spoiler alert—the reader's instincts are 100% correct.

Nordhaus provides what is arguably the best synopsis of the problems associated with regulating under the CAA, most notably the macro design flaws of the CAA and grandfathering in particular. The following says it well:

> Left unmentioned in 2010's congratulatory reviews, and the subsequent Capitol Hill political din, were a number of fundamental design flaws and structural limitations in the original statutory scheme, its subsequent amendments and its administration, which have limited the CAA's effectiveness, unnecessarily drove up compliance costs, spawned political controversy and seemingly endless litigation, and arguably retarded rather than advanced deployment of efficient, low emission technologies. These design issues include the "grandfathering" policies which were embedded in the 1970 Act and subsequent amendments, extensive reliance on state implementation plans to carry out much of the regulatory system, the Act's interstate transport provisions, and the "layering" of multiple (and sometimes redundant) regulatory requirements on the same source. The end result is a regulatory regime that achieves less than what the public needs and costs more than what it wants to pay.[5]

His further point on grandfathering is likewise on target with this cogent observation:

> Much of the complexity and redundancy of the CAA regulatory structure can be laid to attempts to remedy gaps in the original scheme: the acid rain program, NSR BART [Best Available Retrofit Technology], and the current transport rules (CAIR [Clean Air Interstate Rule] and CSAPR [Cross-State Air Pollution Rule]) are all attempts to remedy the CAA's original grandfathering policy, to deal with the limitations on authority to regulate interstate transport, or to prevent significant deterioration of air quality in clean (attainment) areas.[6]

There is little to disagree with here.

As we saw in Chapter 1, NSR is a complicated process to address emissions of regulated air pollutants from new major stationary sources or modifications at existing major stationary sources that experience significant increases in emissions. The goal of NSR is to generally ensure that the more a major source generates emissions of a pollutant, the more accountable the source must be held to control and minimize those emissions.

The following are just some of the peculiar aspects of applying NSR:

1. If a major source in an attainment area undertakes two projects, each with an increase of 39 tpy for SO_2, it would normally be subject to PSD because together, the two projects would exceed the 40 tpy significance threshold for that pollutant. Yet, if it can be demonstrated that there is not a substantial technical or economic dependence between the two projects, then they can be considered as separate projects. In either case,

the environment will experience the same harm of an additional 78 tpy of SO_2, yet the lack of a relationship between the two projects allows a legal carve-out to supersede protecting the harm the projects would inflict by avoiding the application of more stringent controls.

2. NSR allows for a source in a NAA that is major for pollutant A to not be subject to PSD for Pollutant B, while if that same source were to be constructed in an AA, pollutants A and B could both be subject to PSD. The problem here is that a quirk in the rules allows pollutant B to escape NSR review entirely in an NAA while it would be subject to BACT for subject pollutants in an AA.
3. From a regulatory standpoint, the increase in emissions of a pollutant from new emission units at a major PSD source are treated differently than the same increase in emissions of that same pollutant from modified emission units at the same source. While emissions are emissions no matter how they are generated, PSD first requires regulators to determine whether the unit generating those emissions is new or modified.
4. When only regulating sourcewide emission limits is what should matter regionally, NSR still requires records to ensure that individual units meet specific monthly and annual emission limits.

To understand why the foibles of NAA NSR have been tolerated for all these many decades, it is important to note that it has been common for elected officials in communities to prefer NAA NSR rather than cap-and-trade to repair the harm inflicted upon the area. They wanted prospective new major stationary sources to contribute to economic growth without being completely shut out of nonattainment areas due to the area's failure to meet the NAAQS.[7,8] In other words, despite the trading option being at their disposal, elected officials' concern was that imposing a cap would likely have inhibited economic growth.[9] The peculiarities of NSR then, such as the quirks cited above, have been intentionally built into the program.[10]

Clearly, many aspects of NSR are not just needless but needlessly bureaucratic. Much of what we have seen to this point reflects the current "process-based" nature of regulation of stationary sources, when the goal should be a far more "results-based" program of directly addressing harms instead.

If the underlying issue of Design Flaw #1 is the sluggish emission reduction process, then what is the strategy that should replace it? The answer to that question will be briefly conceptualized here by focusing upon the underlying regulatory philosophy, but the actual mechanics will be provided in Chapter 4.

As federal bureaucracies go, the National Transportation Safety Board (NTSB) has proven its value. Although most readers probably haven't given the NTSB much thought, consider what it does: tasked, as it is, with solving post-catastrophic problems (i.e., determining the cause of transportation-related accidents). Does the NTSB wait until the Monday morning after a Saturday night plane crash before they begin investigating? No, they're at the scene as soon as possible. When they're on their game, they are catastrophe problem solvers.

Much the same can be said of the Federal Emergency Management Agency (FEMA). In their case, they may even have enough time before a catastrophe to prepare for it, such as a looming Category 5 hurricane. When they're on their game, they too, are crisis problem solvers.

There are also the Centers for Disease Control (CDC). When an epidemic outbreak is discovered and must be contained as quickly as possible, the CDC mobilizes and becomes emergency epidemic problem solvers.

In stark contrast, and certainly no less critical in its importance, is the Food and Drug Administration (FDA), which, among its many federally required tasks, must approve or disapprove medications prior to their release for use by healthcare consumers. The FDA must jump through any number of necessary hoops to ensure that no drug is approved that could significantly harm the consuming public.

So where do the federal USEPA and the state EPAs generally fall within this regulatory spectrum? Are they more CDC-like or FDA-like in their current approach? In particular, in areas that are not in attainment with the NAAQS for one or more pollutants—recall that these are areas where people's health is *already* (not theoretically) in danger—do regulators treat this situation in an NTSB/FEMA/CDC-like or an FDA-like fashion?

Anyone who has worked directly in AQM, for example, within the SIP process, participated in a nonattainment NSR program, or just anyone paying attention to AQM at all even at a distance, would have to say that the federal and state EPAs have been addressing environmental protection in more of an FDA-like fashion, regardless of the health impacts within the many areas where air quality remains impaired.

While acknowledging that nonattainment NSR was meant more to deter emissions increases in a regional nonattainment area (NAA) than to outright prevent them, requiring that RACT and Lowest Achievable Emission Rate (LAER) plus offsets apply in NAAs within the SIP process is, simply, too little too late to reduce emissions to mitigate adverse health impacts. The process treats with kid gloves what should be addressed more as a CDC-like health crisis. Addressing regional health impacts by focusing on emissions one source project at a time under NSR to deter regional emissions increases, while periodically reviewing and revising State Implementation Plans to achieve attainment of the NAAQS, is a very slow, laborious means to achieve the goals of the CAA. Any violation of a NAAQS, particularly for those areas where environmental justice (EJ) areas are located within nonattainment areas, should instead be treated as an emergency, perhaps not as a catastrophic or epidemic-like emergency, but an emergency nevertheless.

While the current process has certainly been successful to some degree,[11] it has been and continues to be suboptimal. The "CDC-like solution" to this flaw will be addressed further in Chapter 4.

Design Flaw #2: Flaws in Complicated Rules and Processing Requirements

For an AQM program to succeed, it is essential that the rules and regulations be developed so that they provide proper coverage to all of the essential components of the process (e.g., definitions, nonattainment area rules) all the way down to the rules governing emission units and operations. These rules must also be able to be interpreted clearly by everyone, and not just by the people who wrote them.

Statutes written by lawmakers are later transformed for implementation into regulations by administrative agencies to achieve the goals of those statutes. Environmental regulations are typically developed by engineers within an "air quality planning section" while working with a small team of regulatory attorneys (separate from the attorneys who enforce the regulations). Not all rules are written well enough to be interpreted clearly. One such example is the following from 40 CFR 96.42(b)(2) of the now-defunct Clean Air Interstate Rule's Budget Trading Program:

> If the initial total number of NOx allowances allocated to all NOx Budget units under §96.4(a)(1) in the State for a control period under paragraph (b)(1) of this section does not equal 95 percent in 2003, 2004, and 2005, or 98 percent thereafter, of the number of tons of NOx emissions in the State trading program budget apportioned to electric generating units, the permitting authority will adjust the total number of NOx allowances allocated to all such NOx Budget units for the control period under paragraph (b)(1) of this section so that the total number of NOx allowances allocated equals 95 percent in 2003, 2004, and

> 2005, or 98 percent thereafter, of the number of tons of NOx emissions in the State trading program budget apportioned to electric generating units. This adjustment will be made by: multiplying each unit's allocation by 95 percent in 2003, 2004, and 2005, or 98 percent thereafter, of the number of tons of NOx emissions in the State trading program budget apportioned to electric generating units divided by the total number of NOx allowances allocated under paragraph (b)(1) of this section, and rounding to the nearest whole NOx allowance as appropriate.

Needless to say, this requirement is difficult for even most regulators themselves to navigate and understand. Arguably, the only people who understand it are the rule writers themselves. A rule such as this has to be understandable to as many people as possible, not just highly paid lawyers and engineers. That is not meant to be a smear. The success of any AQM program demands that rules and regulations be as simple to understand as possible.

Going further, there are the horribly complicated National Emission Standards for Hazardous Air Pollutants (NESHAP), found at 40 CFR Parts 61 and 63, and the New Source Performance Standards (NSPS), found at 40 CFR Part 60. It is not hyperbole to say that they are horribly complicated. While the earlier developed NESHAPs and NSPSs were relatively straightforward, since the 1990s, the NESHAP and NSPS rules have become only more detailed and complicated. To drive home the point, the reader is urged to take some time before reading on to fully read *and* understand, as examples, the Miscellaneous Organic NESHAP (40 CFR 63 Subpart FFFF), the NSPS for Stationary Compression Ignition Internal Combustion Engines (40 CFR 60 Subpart IIII),[12] and the NSPS for Commercial-Industrial Solid Waste Incinerators (40 CFR 60 Subpart CCCC).[13] These regulations are not usually incorporated by reference into permits, meaning that applicable language from these regulations is required to be spelled out in sufficient detail within permits, that is, language to be read later by inspectors and plant personnel, among others.

Complexity is just part of the problem. Cynthia Giles and her colleagues at the USEPA proposed Next Gen principles that would attempt to build compliance into the rules rather than developing poorly written regulations and leaving the task of determining compliance to an understaffed enforcement team whenever they are fortunate to uncover noncompliance.[14] More will be said about Giles's Next Gen principles in the next three chapters.

Aside from the current problems already cited, a quiet parasite of our current FDA-like AQM program is the large amount of informational and procedural hoops that must be jumped through to justify that the regulatory decision process was properly followed. In many states, the Statement of Basis (SoB) is the term used for the support document developed for Title V permits, whereas the Project Summary is the term used in some states for support of NSR permits. The level of detail contained in these documents (which mandate the detailed documentation for the determinations made in the permitting process) has ballooned over the years. It is not unusual, for example, for the USEPA to require that SoBs sufficiently justify all conditions of the Title V permit, including justifying why an emission unit's negligible emissions for a pollutant in the permit are, in fact, negligible. Likewise, under PSD, the USEPA requires that a detailed Top-Down BACT demonstration be made even for negligible emitting emission units where adding expensive controls is laughably cost-prohibitive.

Elliott noted this several years ago when he cited the need to build documentation to support EPA decisions:

> Our system of legality and administrative law requires building a huge "record" that will withstand judicial review as a precondition to government regulation. These high transaction costs for *government* caused by the current style of regulation by bureaucratic standard setting in the United States result in a system of environmental regulation that is "an inch wide and a mile deep" – a system that regulates both too little and too much at the same time. Thus, we should condemn the overuse of inefficient command-and-control systems in the United States not just because they waste industry's money, but also because their inefficiency and high demand for information processing by government as a precondition for environmental improvements results in *under regulation* by leaving large segments outside the regulatory umbrella.[15]

Stewart said it well himself with regard to the required justification for regulatory decisions:

> In reviewing agency decisions, courts have gone beyond ensuring that agencies obey relevant statutes. In order to curb agency bias and promote decisions that are responsive to the full range of affected interests and values, they have also reviewed administrative discretion, requiring a detailed agency explanation, supported by the administrative record, of why an agency chose a given alternative and why it rejected others advocated by those challenging its decision. In doing so, courts have attempted to ensure that agencies take a "hard look" at the relevant evidence, analysis, and considerations of policy, as well as the legal arguments advanced by the contending interests, and justify the policy choices that they make.[16]

Clearly, where discretion must be a part of the process (e.g., prioritizing enforcement on the larger emitters), oversight is justified, but exercising discretion when making technical determinations is a gaping flaw within the current NSR regulatory process and significantly contributes to the generation of bureaucratic pollution. As proposed later in Part 2, reform in part should be based on minimizing this type of discretion as much as possible, thereby minimizing bureaucratic logjam-creating oversight.

The Congressional Research Service (CRS) authored a paper on the implementation and complexity issues associated with Title V permitting. Among the notable issues highlighted there is the following:

> At the same time, there also has been widespread dissatisfaction with the program as it exists, due to program complexity; confusion and uncertainty about some of its requirements; and criticism of costs to regulated entities, permit agencies, and even the general public.[17]

And later:

> Consolidating existing requirements (some dating from the 1970s) into a single, comprehensive document, while undoubtedly beneficial, also has resulted in permits that are lengthy and detailed, making it difficult to read them without precise knowledge of the individual source's operations, according to some stakeholders.[18]

Likewise, the National Research Council (NRC) stated separately that the "complexity of the effort required to issue these permits was underestimated at the time the 1990 CAA Amendments were passed."[19]

Needless to say, regulation that requires the above level of justification, documentation, and processing is contrary to the mission of CDC-like or NTSB-like emergency situations characterized by the unhealthy air quality in nonattainment areas.

Design Flaw #3: Flaws in Multiple Bureaucratic Procedures

Let's begin with a metaphor about pack mules as a prelude to directly stating the problem of multiple bureaucratic procedures within Design Flaw #3.

A pack mule can usually carry up to one-third its weight, which makes using one a practical means to carry small cargo through rugged terrain over long distances. If the carrying capacity of the pack mule is not considered, people will (not may) have a tendency to pile on more cargo that they *think* is critically essential, as the desire to carry more intensifies. Of course, if the weight of the multiple items carried remains well below one-third of the weight of the mule, then there is little issue here; the mule can carry the weight on its back. But let's say, over time, that the weight limit is not only exceeded, but also the number of people piling items onto the pack mule, and the number of items to be carried on its back, also increases. In this situation, things have clearly gotten significantly dicier for the pack mule.

So let's say that the USEPA piles on one-quarter of the mule's weight with 100 items (think rules, guidance, and procedures of all kinds) and the pack mule ventures a few yards. Then the state EPA managers pile on another eighth of the mule's original weight with another fifty items (again, think rules, guidance and procedures of all kinds). At this point, the pack mule is now being tasked with carrying greater than one-third of its weight and carrying 150 items, some of which could easily fall off during travel over the rugged terrain. Needless to say, such a beast of burden will very likely move slowly and drop a few items along the way.[20]

As noted, the pack mule here represents the "downstream" implementers and/or interpreters of the regulations (primarily permit writers and inspectors, but can also include enforcement attorneys, company environmental staff and/or their consultants, environmental organizations, etc.), and the cargo being carried is both the output requirements of those rules (e.g., permits,[21] voluminous statements of bases, project summaries, detailed checklists for inspectors, citations for the compliance and legal teams, responsiveness summaries to comments, voluminous applications, etc.) and the workplace procedures (detailed calculation sheets, multi-step permit logout procedures, providing information onto the RACT/BACT/LAER Clearinghouse forms, etc.). It is the multitude of procedures that regulators must perform that is often hidden from the view of the public.

Let's look at one example of bureaucratic pollution. While permit issuance procedures vary from state to state, some or most of the following steps are likely.

Example: Permit Issuance Procedures

Once a permit is to be issued, there are several tasks required to finalize the process. Aside from having the final permit properly formatted by typists, the engineer must (1) print out all the emails associated with the development of the draft permit;[22] (2) obtain approval from the Environmental Justice Unit that community outreach was completed without any concerns having been raised; (3) input onto the permit database several permitting milestone dates, of which two are the "tech review complete" date and later the "tech review final" date; (4) fill out a page within the permit file on what the total allowable emissions for each pollutant in the new permit will be, as well as many of the database milestone dates; (5) prepare a copy of the calculation/analysis sheet documenting the permitting action; (6) if necessary, obtain approval from the Legal Department and/or Field Section that the permit is ready for issuance;[23] (7) ask the word processing office associate to print out the final permit; (8) if the permit had gone out for public comment, notify the Community Relations Office that the permit is being issued; and (9) develop one or more "cover sheets" for the permitting materials, which are to be used by the clerical employees in the Records Unit to scan the paper materials onto an electronic database.

Bureaucracy can be a force multiplier. As requirements, procedures, and documentation exponentiate, the more regulators must impose requirements, procedures, and documentation to ensure that the early round of requirements, procedures, and documentation are met. One can say that the bureaucratic pollution of the regulatory process itself has achieved a state of "nonattainment."

Although the regulations are designed to both (1) support the science and (2) provide protection from lawsuits, there is actually a third leg to the regulatory rule-writing stool. This is the necessary reliance on the people who must actually carry out the mission of applying those rules and regulations. To this point, lawmakers, the USEPA, and others below them in the hierarchical AQM regulatory food chain (RFC) have considered the first two as equally essential legs of the stool, while they have yet to consider the third in the same manner. The RFC's tendency is to assume that the downstream pack mules and their concerns regarding the bureaucratic pollution that rolls downhill upon them are irrelevant. Cynthia Giles in her book laments much the same thing regarding how rules are written.[24]

The immediate question isn't whether implementing procedures are important or not. Most of the goals they support are important. The real question involves priorities and how they are determined. Managers believe that they can always add one more task onto the back of the pack mule under the assumption that it isn't going to make a difference. Conveniently appropriating the regulatory term "insignificant activity" from Clean Air Act terminology, there are too many managers who believe that the sum of a large number of insignificant activities and procedures is itself insignificant. That is rarely so. One doesn't have to take this author's word for it. Ask any experienced permit engineer. They will tell you the same thing.

AQM is difficult enough as it is without treating the pack mule as a lowly beast of burden. The worst thing the higher-ups in the RFC can do is lose buy-in from the people they must absolutely depend on to get the heavy lifting of AQM done.[25] Yet buy-in cannot be taken for granted these days. High turnover rates for permit writers at state agencies, and the varying quality and quantity of issued Title V permits issued, best characterize the situation.[26]

There is another aspect to the complexity of the process as it exists that requires consideration: loss of institutional knowledge. If only a small fraction of regulators understand the complex rules and numerous difficult-to-interpret guidance documents,[27] then that should be a red flag to policymakers and managers. What happens when those who possess the institutional knowledge of the historical nuances of NSR, Title V, the NSPSs, NESHAPs, Acid Rain Program, etc., retire? Do policymakers at the national level assume that the next generation of regulatory employers and employees will be able to easily navigate the current system of complex rules as if they possessed the experience and skills of their predecessors? Don't count on it.

Anyone attempting to address the reform of AQM, if they truly care about the mission, must confront the following nonrhetorical question:

> *What is the absolute minimum amount of necessary regulations, requirements and procedures that must be imposed within the regulatory process to achieve its necessary outcomes?*

While there's no simple answer to determining the path to the lowest generation of bureaucratic pollution, this issue will be addressed further in Chapter 4 as the comprehensive strategy is developed. In the meantime, the reader is implored to always think about this most critical of questions as they proceed through this book.

Design Flaw #4: Misapplication of Labor

Design Flaw #4 is the under-reliance of attorneys and the overreliance on engineers in AQM. It was noted earlier that to avoid rule interpretation and compliance hazards, rules could be better developed by attorneys, in particular by following Next Gen principles by building in compliance as the default option into the rules. In addition, rules are currently written as if compliance is assumed and the onus to detect noncompliance is oftentimes put on the shoulders of inspectors; an enforcement attorney's role is to wait passively for such detection. A key takeaway that Giles makes throughout her book is that this process misses a large amount of noncompliance by sources. Next Gen principles instead dictate that compliance be built into the rules "upstream" to minimize the need for uncovering noncompliance "downstream."[28]

Likewise, AQM is also overreliant on permit engineers to develop permits and other supporting documentation when attorneys should play a more active role in their development, since permits are supposedly legal documents; yet not many attorneys assist in drafting them, the task (and sometimes, blame) being imposed onto the permit-writing engineers.[29] As it is now, it is not unusual for permit writers, after all these many years, to still write many portions of a permit with specific legal language tailored uniquely to a source, based on a case-by-case review of each individual permit application. One would think that, after all these years with a track record of what permit language works and what does not with regard to enforcement, the USEPA enforcement attorneys would have developed a permit language manual by now.

Design Flaw #5: Minimal Inclusion of the Public in the Process

Design Flaw #5 is the neglect of proactively including the general public within the AQM process. When implementing any environmental protection program, public involvement is essential. Unfortunately, for all the attention paid to involving the public in the process, a different situation prevails. Due to the complicated nature of implementing an improved AQM program, the general public (and that does not mean the environmental NGOs) has been effectively excluded. Discussions about the program commonly take place without, or with minimal, public input. As a result, on one end of the spectrum, we have rules that even environmental professionals can find difficult to understand and interpret while, on the other end of the spectrum, a public that has little idea, and misperceptions of, what these same environmental professionals actually do and the role they play.

If the reader does not believe this, it cannot be suggested strongly enough that they attend a heated public hearing for a draft air pollution permit and observe the character of the discussion, the gap between what the public demands, what regulators can actually deliver, and the effect of the public's input after a permit is issued. In hearings during public comment periods, where the general public can voice their concerns in person, the vast majority of comments have very little to do with the actual conditions within the permit. This is in part due to the unreadability of many of these complicated permits. More to the point, though, is the world of difference between what the public believes the regulatory agency's role is and its actual role.

As an indication of the lack of public participation in the permitting process, when the permitting agency does receive comments regarding a permit from someone other than the USEPA, it is usually from an environmental group and less likely from the general public.

Although there may be other design flaws that require discussion, the five discussed above are just some of the key ones this author considers to be significant.

A Quick Thought on the Design Flaws

Let's face facts. From lawmakers all the way down to regulatory agency managers, these design flaws create problems largely of their own making. It seems particularly disingenuous of environmental legal scholars in academia to decry a logjam in environmental policy when it is their own legal culture that creates a bureaucratic logjam, such as requiring complex documentation to justify decisions, thereby slowing the process down to a crawl in some cases.[30] As Esty has pointed out:

> Notably, the "legalism," or perhaps more pejoratively the legalistic nature of American environmental law, has become a major drag on the process of evolution toward more efficient and effective regulatory structures.[31]

Based on the author's personal experience, the more legalistic the process has become, the more attention is devoted to navigating through the myriad regulations, their complexity, pettifoggery, and procedural hoops and less to the underlying engineering basis for the generation of air pollution itself.

In Chapter 3, key aspects of the past discussion of reform of the CAA will be spelled out. Certain authors will propose reform ideas to address the environmental policy logjam, but as we'll see later their strategies to address that logjam fall far short of curing the CAA of its existing ills. We will also see that while there has been a good deal of very general discussion on what reform should look like (e.g., use more trading), preciously little has actually been proposed as usable strategy. Not only that but the design flaws as highlighted in this chapter, where the human element is being factored in, have been woefully neglected in the literature as well.

So what would a transformed or reformed CAA for stationary sources look like exactly that includes properly addressing the above design flaws? In Chapter 4, a new paradigm that facilitates the achievement of results-oriented milestones while minimizing process-oriented practices is proposed and developed. As far as this author is aware, the comprehensive strategy proposed for the proper regulation of air pollution generated from stationary sources breaks new ground. In addition, this "reorientation" of regulation will later set the stage for generalizing the strategy's essential components to regulating the generation of multi-media environmental pollutants, and more.

It should be noted that readers, such as those from the European Union or Asia who are not interested in past reform attempts in the United States, may go directly to Part 2 with little loss of context to the strategies developed there.

Notes

1 Robert Nordhaus, "Modernizing The Clean Air Act: Is There Life After 40?" *Energy Law Journal* 33, no. 2 (2012).

2 One can think of guidance documents as the legal equivalent of making imprecise measurements in engineering, that is, if the rules were written precisely as to their intent, there would be no need for detailed interpretations.

3 Bureaucratic growth over the last twenty years is at least an order of magnitude worse than in the 1990s when scholars and policymakers began speaking of reform.

4 Cary Coglianese, "Evaluating Regulatory Performance," *University of Pennsylvania Journal of Law & Public Affairs* 8, no. 1 (2023): 125. https://scholarship.law.upenn.edu/jlpa/vol8/iss1/8.

5 Nordhaus, "Modernizing The Clean Air Act," 368.

6 Nordhaus, "Modernizing The Clean Air Act," 387.

7 The author would like to thank Rob Brenner for this insight.

8 Often lost in the discussion of cap-and-trade is that the process is *corrective*. We will find that cap-and-trade can generally be applied to the generation of pollution for all environmental media.

9 Note that this policy decision violates the First and Second FLoERs.

10 Brian Potts, "Trading Grandfathered Air—A New, Simpler Approach," *Harvard Environmental Law Review* (2006). https://harvardelr.com/wp-content/uploads/sites/12/2019/07/31.1-Potts.pdf; and National Academy of Public Administrators, "A Breath of Fresh Air: Reviving the New Source Review Program," *Report by a Panel of the National Academy of Public Administration* (NAPA 2003). https://napawash.org/academy-studies/a-breath-of-fresh-air-reviving-the-new-source-review-program. Both articles provide an excellent discussion of the process of conducting NSR.

11 Regulators should not take credit for improved air quality where otherwise environmentally responsible companies are forced to relocate elsewhere.

12 The Engine rules (both NSPS and NESHAP) are an object lesson in bureaucracy in how it specifies applicable requirements. Most engines that the rule typically regulates—emergency engines—emit very little pollution in relative comparison to nonemergency engines, yet the level of detail of the rules are mind-numbing.

13 For extra credit, the reader should try to differentiate the applicability of Subparts AAAA through FFFF of the NSPS from each other—for example, which rule does nonprogram tire pyrolysis fall under? What about pathological waste generated at a university veterinary hospital?

14 Cynthia Giles, *Next Generation Compliance: Environmental Regulation for the Modern Era* (Oxford University Press, 2022).

15 Elliott, "Environmental Markets and Beyond," 253.

16 Stewart, "A New Generation of Environmental Regulation," 36. The "hard look" doctrine was reaffirmed by the Supreme Court in *Citizens to Preserve Overton Park v. Volpe*, decided in 1971.

17 Claudia Copeland, "Clean Air Permitting: Implementation and Issues," *Congressional Research Service* (2016): 7. https://fas.org/sgp/crs/misc/RL33632.pdf.

18 Copeland, "Clean Air Permitting: Implementation and Issues," 7.

19 National Research Council, *Air Quality Management in the United States* (National Academies Press, 2004), 191.

20 To add insult to injury, some managers and supervisors within the regulatory food chain infrastructure blame the poor quality of pack mules under these conditions.

21 Drafting a permit is no simple task, due to the hashing out of technical issues, permit language, etc., that can take several iterations.

22 The email history is printed out to memorialize the decisions made in the permitting process within the electronic database (in the event that the permit is challenged or there is some need to review the record in the future). The vast majority of the time, accessing the record is rarely necessary.

23 Getting the a-okay from others outside the permit section (e.g., the Legal Department and/or the Field Section) relegates the permit engineer to both a go-fer *and* a pack mule. The author remembers one time that an attorney did not respond to three separate emails when the green light to issue a permit was being sought. The inclination was to just issue the permit anyway without the attorney's concurrence (since he failed to respond to the emails), but the author was instructed by his manager to personally visit the attorney to get that concurrence.

24 Giles, *Next Generation Compliance*, 87.

25 For confirmation, one need only refer to: Terry Davies, Robert Hersh, Aracely Alicea, et al., *Reforming Permitting* (Resources for the Future [RFF], 2001); and Copeland (cited previously). Both noted the burdens of conducting an air quality permitting program. Note that the RFF report was written in 2001, long before the current logjam was noted.

26 Amid this discussion on Title V, it is worth pointing out that, according to Rob Brenner, who was in the USEPA's Office of Policy, Title V was not well thought out at the Congressional level at the time the CAA Amendments were adopted.

27 Speaking of guidance documents, the reader is strongly encouraged to look up how many guidance documents there are that just address NSR and Title V. With these various guidance documents, it's not hard to get confused keeping track of interpretations. Likewise, there are the various applicability determinations that have been developed for NSPSs and NESHAPs over the years.

28 The reader should observe a common theme of upstream redesign being made throughout this book, whether it is to reduce pollution or facilitate rule compliance.

29 Interestingly enough, lawsuits have been filed by practicing attorneys when estate wills are drafted by non-attorneys. Is it not peculiar then that permits, which again are supposedly legal documents, do not engender that same level of concern by the legal profession?

30 This need for justification seems logical in the abstract, but when one considers that the bulk of these legal belts and suspenders carry little actual load, then it simply becomes a sink of wasted time and effort.

31 Daniel Esty, "Next Generation Environmental Law: A Response to Richard Stewart," *Capital University Law Review* 29 (2001–2002): 187. Here, Esty cites a quote within a footnote from Richard B. Stewart, "Environmental Regulation and International Competitiveness," *Yale Law Journal* 102, no. 8 (1993): 2050.

3

Past Discussion of Clean Air Act Reform

Reform Ideas: A Brief Discussion

Before the proper strategy regulating the generation of air pollution can be developed, it is first necessary to examine previously suggested reforms of the US Clean Air Act (CAA) for regulating stationary sources. Sadly, within the constraints of the existing CAA, a literature review identified the redundant discussion that generally revolved around the more expansive use of market instruments like emissions trading as a means to reform the US program but did so without the necessary rigor or detail to support this general tack. In 2008, though, the Breaking the Logjam Symposium held at New York University School of Law provided some degree of clarity with regard to reforms, whereby its presenters actually did put some "chalk to blackboard." Later, in 2012, Robert Nordhaus, at the time a law firm partner and Professorial Lecturer in Law at George Washington University Law School, also provided some provocative ideas on reforming the CAA as well.

These attempts at explicating beneficial reforms tended to focus only on macrolevel national issues (such as interstate transport and the SIP process) rather than addressing the equally critical micro-level state and local issues (such as intrastate contributions to NAAs, rule complexity, and the required reliance on excess bureaucratic pollution).

General Discussion of Reform

There has been discussion of reform of the CAA for decades, even dating back to a time when the practice of regulating air pollution was much less of a hassle (*for regulators*!) than it is today. Clearly, there will always be those, such as Oren,[1] who believe that the CAA has been successful in reducing emissions and needs little improvement. In his case, he acknowledges that addressing ozone remains a problem, but also asserts that, because the CAA has done well in reducing mobile source emissions and sulfur dioxide emissions under the Acid Rain Program, if the Act isn't broke, then there is no need to fix it.[2]

Be that as it may, and given that the CAA was supposed to be updated ten years after enacting the 1990 CAA amendments, there have justifiably been authors who have argued in the academic literature that the CAA is in serious need of reform. Their rationale is addressed next.

The "Old" Reform Ideas

The reform discussion in this chapter is arbitrarily chosen to begin with the thoughts of Richard Stewart, who made a serious attempt to present the best argument for reform. While he didn't serve up a substantive blueprint of just what a reformed CAA would look like, his insights were nevertheless prescient.

Like many authors, Stewart asserts the following regarding command-and-control regulation in general: "The defense of the current command regulatory system is also well known. It 'works.'"[3] While that may be true, he further asks with regard to the current regulatory system:

> How suited is it for addressing what some have termed "second generation" environmental problems, including those generated by small sources of pollution and waste sources and the burgeoning service economy? How capable is the command system of promoting an integrated, ecosystem-based approach to environmental and natural resource management? How can it address entirely new environmental problems, such as climate change? Can and should the command system be modified to better deal with these challenges? Can other regulatory instruments and approaches better address them? How can needed changes in our environmental regulatory system be accomplished, given the current political gridlock on environmental legislation? What initiatives or new developments might favor more fundamental change?[4]

This book will make significant progress toward addressing these very questions.

In some academic papers a common subject arises, namely, how the current air quality management (AQM) program is in a state of logjam or stalled at a crossroads. Unfortunately, the solutions proposed tend to be vague: for example, there is the oft-cited "next-generation" agenda to reform regulation, without detailed discussion of just what that might mean or how it would function. Typically, there is also the usual mention of the success of the Acid Rain Program as proof that trading is a promising regulatory tool, with the usual obligatory mention that use of a trading program should be expanded (in some vague and unspecified way) to carve out another niche of CAA regulation. The authors then tend to extrapolate their discussion of trading to other possible areas, without ever putting chalk to blackboard to work out the details. Two examples may suffice here: the Environmental Law Institute (ELI) backed the idea of trading, but they only briefly addressed it;[5] Fiorino[6] does the same as just one of several components of his *New Environmental Regulation* proposal. The absence of detail is telling. Neither ELI nor Fiorino, nor, as far as this author is aware, has anyone else before Nordhaus and the Breaking the Logjam Symposium, bothered to spell out how exactly to demonstrate the details regarding what a reformed regulatory regime would look like.

Examples of such unaddressed questions pertaining to trading are which sources located where, should participate, and using what criteria? What pollutants should be traded and what should not? For example, should particulate matter dust be tradable? Lead? Hydrogen sulfide? How should trading be conducted? Where should it apply? Should it mimic the Acid Rain Program? And if so, how? What would the permitting program even look like? What about the role of continuous emission monitoring systems (CEMS) and stack tests, particularly when a source wants to take credit for reductions via improvements to energy efficiency? How different would inspections become, if at all? What about enforcement actions? How can trading be expanded outside the usual well-trodden topics of air pollution and acid rain, say, for example, solid waste? In short, it's trivial to suggest "more trading," but when the critical specifics are lacking it's mostly all form and no substance.

As it turns out, and as we will see in more detail in Chapter 4, trading should be expanded, only because it is the best tool *when and where properly applied.*[7]

David Case

In 2014 David Case published a paper that nicely surveyed the general "state-of-the-literature" on the subject of policy gridlock and logjam in air pollution regulation and air quality improvement since the 1990s.[8,9] It is no secret that there has been a great deal of criticism of the current environmental regulatory system, its inefficient and ineffective approach, and its associated costs. Case later goes on to mention the "Breaking the Logjam" symposium (to be discussed later), and the usual "Next Generation" environmental reform proposals, including, but not limited to, the following: market-based regulatory instruments, environmental management systems (EMS), voluntary (self-regulatory) environmental programs (e.g., National Environmental Performance Track and Project XL), and public information disclosure. Case lays blame for surrendering the responsibility to set environmental policy at the feet of Congress by asserting that "Prospects for robust and meaningful results from experimentation with regulatory reform programs have been squandered by many years of congressional inaction."[10,11]

A few comments are in order. While Case's points are legitimate, it seems arguably better to first achieve solid and final consensus from top practitioners on what is optimal and then, and only then, petition Congress to act on such consensus. In Congress's defense, what solid ideas, in fact, have they had to work with over the years? Most scholars on the subject haven't actually practiced AQM or regulated pollution, so they in turn haven't proposed anything of practical substance other than citing the *need* for reform and the vaguely defined expanded use of trading. Do we really want Congress to prematurely develop a politically determined next generation of the CAA without first hearing what top practitioners have to say? The time to admonish Congress is after consensus based on solid principles and practical experience has already been developed but where they have intentionally ignored it for the sake of political expediency. As it stands now, Congress can argue that they don't have much guidance to work with. What papers that support reform far outnumber the even fewer papers that put chalk to blackboard that actually attempt to provide that reform.

On paper, regulatory reinvention programs such as public disclosure, EMS, and market-based incentive programs are great, and some have successfully reduced pollution. Several years ago, Fiorino likewise advocated for greater use of programs such as Project XL and Performance Track, extolling their virtues. Be that as it may, one reason why some past attempts at reform failed for voluntary programs (e.g., Project XL) is clear: they were simply unsuitable for environmental *regulatory agencies* to adopt on a wide scale.[12] For one thing, nowhere in the literature is there even an attempt to detail how these alternative regulatory models would realistically be put into widespread practice. However beneficial these programs may seem, imagine the amount of state agency resources that would have been required to attend to *thousands* of such labor-intensive requests. The idea of expanding such voluntary programs for several companies within a state would bring meaningful pollution regulation for most sources to a virtual standstill.

Likewise, no one can argue against the usefulness and significance of pollution prevention (P2). In fact, in the 1990s, there was a strong push to promote P2, and progress was made to implement it, but industry generally fought it tooth and nail, while regulatory agencies themselves were too focused on pollution control instead.[13] There was arguably some progress to be made if requiring P2 was given a regulatory spine through legal authority,[14] but the fact that P2 and pollution control have, to this point, been in "regulatory opposition" with each other does not imply that they are fundamentally incompatible. In fact, this opposition indicates that the current regulatory paradigm is flawed, which will be corrected in this book, most notably in Part 3, by developing a regulatory framework that sets limits on pollution whereby implementing P2 and controlling pollution are by design properly aligned.

Gray and Shimshack

With regard to the current need to promote proper regulatory construction, Gray and Shimshack made this very salient point:

> Recent survey evidence suggests that a traditional regulatory structure with rigorous monitoring and enforcement remains the number one motivator for many facilities' environmental compliance decisions.[15]

While it has been generally asserted that little progress had been made on suggesting viable routes to reform the CAA, several authors have offered more practical suggestions, particularly when NSR was undergoing reform in the early years of this century. These include the NSR reform ideas offered by Potts[16] and the National Academy of Public Administrators (NAPA).[17] Some of the flaws of NSR were noted in the last chapter, but the Potts paper and NAPA document each provide a dated but nice background on NSR's shortcomings and both proposed reforms. However, because NSR requires a far more radical overhaul when their proposed reforms rely on working within this flawed program, their input will not be discussed further here.

Freeman and Farber

Freeman and Farber[18] provided their own opinion on prescriptive regulation versus the use of economic instruments. Freeman and Farber rationally felt that trading would not necessarily be a panacea for the ills of AQM. They acknowledge that both Command-and-Control (CaC) and economic instruments can realistically coexist:

> And so the debate goes. Framing the debate between prescriptive *versus* market-based regulation in either-or terms echoes the dichotomous nature of the federalism debate. In reality, both environmental law and natural resource management rely on a mix of mechanisms. Moreover, neither kind of instrument is as "pure" as the two poles of the debate would suggest: virtually every market mechanism of environmental regulation depends on some prescribed government limit, such as setting a cap, in the emissions trading context, beneath which trades occur. And in all of these regimes, the government—either Congress through legislation or agencies through regulation—plays a crucial role in monitoring and adjusting the rules to respond to new events or information.[19]
>
> The point is this: twenty years of experience suggests that it is impossible to declare a clear winner in this debate. Whether an instrument works optimally depends on a variety of factors, some of which are easier to predict and control than others. These include: the sophistication of the market participants; the size and diversity of the market; the vulnerability of the environmental "good" or "service" to accurate valuation; the vulnerability of the regime to political rigging in the allocation process; and the potential for gaming, shirking, and cheating by the regulated entities, among other things. The challenge now is to mix and match instruments in a way that is sensitive to the contexts—political, economic, geographical—in which they are deployed, and to remember that no matter how well-designed regulatory or management tools might be in theory, for their success they each require effective implementation and monitoring.[20]

This last paragraph is without question correct, supporting Elliott's contention in Chapter 1 regarding the academic nature of the binary debate between command-and-control and the use of market instruments. The one major caveat to proposing a comprehensive strategy including a trading scheme is that, for it to work, *the success of the trading program relies on its design.*

Schmalensee and Stavins

If one studies the track record of emissions trading, as well as noting Freeman and Farber above, it is difficult not to conclude that a trading program's success simply comes down to how well it is designed, one of two key lessons made by Schmalensee and Stavins based on 30 years of experience with cap-and-trade systems.[21] The other lesson they provide is that:

> First, cap-and-trade has proven itself to be environmentally effective and economically cost effective relative to traditional command-and-control approaches. Moreover, less flexible systems would not have led to the technological change that appears to have been induced by market-based instruments or the induced process innovations that have resulted.[22]

The reader is urged to be constantly aware of these lessons as pollutant trading is discussed throughout the rest of this book.

The National Research Council–Air Quality Management in the United States

The National Research Council (NRC) of the National Academy of Sciences set out in their book "(1) to evaluate from a scientific and technical perspective the effectiveness of the major air quality provisions of the Clean Air Act and their implementation by federal, state, tribal, and local government agencies; and (2) to develop scientific and technical recommendations for strengthening the nation's air quality management system with respect to the way it identifies and incorporates important sources of exposure to humans and ecosystems and integrates new understandings of human and ecosystem risks."[23] The authors of this book (hereinafter referred to as the NRC) discussed the ways in which the CAA has been successful but likewise addressed its deficiencies. They did not propose reform of the CAA per se; instead, their suggestions for changing direction were based on working within the constraints of the CAA.

Before highlighting their recommendations and proposed actions, it is worth noting some of their observations of the current AQM program for stationary sources under the CAA. Like the previous authors cited above, the NRC is also in favor of an expanded role of cap-and-trade. They cite the obvious success of the Acid Rain Program but also that of the phaseout programs for lead and chlorofluorocarbons. Just for the record, they do go on to say that "Even in the case of the acid rain SO_2 emissions-trading program, which has been the most successful application, there are issues to be addressed and improvements that could be made."[24]

The NRC provided a few limitations of the stationary source control program under the CAA, but the following are noteworthy:

> The NSR and PSD programs do not affect a large fraction of the existing facilities that have not undergone major modifications but have remained in operation.[25]
>
> Achieving the full potential of cap-and-trade will require applying the technique to a broader range of pollutants, implementing a less cumbersome process for revising caps and targets, developing enhanced and more cost-effective CEM [continuous emissions monitoring] and other monitoring technologies, and guarding against deleterious geographical and temporal distribution of emission reductions.[26]

The NRC also asserts that the success of a cap-and-trade program among sources, or even possibly applying caps among source categories, does not presume the imposition of emission unit performance standards.[27] While the imposition of performance standards is not a prerequisite to the success of a trading program, there should be no question that the goal of facilitating the reduction of emissions is enhanced by imposing such standards. More will be said about this in Chapters 4 and 5.

The NRC acknowledges that "The importance of CEM systems raises a challenge for extending the cap-and-trade approach to other pollutants for which cost-effective CEM technology is not available."[28] They add that "With the exception of CEM, there is limited ability to quantify stationary source emissions."[29] While this is generally true, this problem can and must be minimized and overcome in order to expand the use of emission trading and minimize the use of prescriptive regulation on a source-by-source basis.

The NRC also saw how the current program is too process-oriented:

> An overemphasis on procedures can produce an AQM system that is overly complex and rigid and insufficiently focused on measuring performance. Indeed, participants in the existing AQM system at all levels (the public; stakeholders; and local, state, and federal officials) have expressed concern that the current system is sometimes overly driven by rules and procedures, focusing too much time on paperwork and not enough time on tracking efficacy of the statutes, rules, and methods that were enforced. Insufficient tracking makes it difficult to identify weaknesses and flaws in the technologies and strategies used to control air pollution, and it makes it difficult to help in the development of technologies and strategies that are more cost-effective and thus capable of attracting broader community support.[30]

In their thorough review of the current program the NRC saw the big picture:

> The AQM system must be flexible and vigilant in the coming decades to ensure that pollution mitigation strategies remain effective and sufficient as our climate changes.[31]

They provide five recommendations and actions, of which two are relevant for purposes of our discussion (the other NRC recommendations are outside the scope here). Their two recommendations are:[32]

> Recommendation 2: Expand National and Multistate Control Strategies
>
> Actions—Expand federal emission controls, emphasize technology-neutral standards, use market-based approaches, reduce existing-sources emissions, and address multistate regional transport.
>
> Recommendation 3: Transform the SIP Process[33]
>
> Actions—Replace state implementation plan with integrated multi-pollutant air quality management plan and reform process to focus on tracking results using periodic reviews, encouraging innovative strategies, and retaining conformity and federal oversight.

The NRC promotes the use of practical technology-neutral standards within Recommendation 2: "that is, standards that set clear performance goals without specifying a technological solution—and provide flexibility for sources to achieve those goals in the most cost-effective way possible and provide incentives for developing new technologies."[34] They state that this can be done in at least two ways: (1) by setting an emissions cap on a source without setting emission standards on generating units, and (2) setting rate-based standards for diffuse sources (e.g., mobile, consumer, and area sources).

It is unclear whether the NRC promotes the combined use of both performance standards for units at a source and trading among sources, but it only seems logical that they would have. Nevertheless, employing an emission unit that meets a performance standard allows sources to generate a lesser quantity of emissions at the source, so that the source can emit more under its equivalent source allotment within a trading program. In this respect, it behooves the source to install units that meet, if not are more compliant than these standards. What's not to like about that?[35] And last of all, one can see that a performance standard has a certain yin and yang quality to it—the standard itself is a prescriptive limit (the yin) while how a source chooses to meet that standard for a particular emission unit provides a vendor-supplied, market-based option (the yang).

Regarding their Recommendation 3 and its associated actions, the NRC notes the following regarding some of their findings on the SIP process:

> The SIP process has mandated extended amounts of local, state, and federal agency time and resources in an iterative, often frustrating, proposal and review process that focuses primarily on compliance with intermediate process steps and not on the more germane long-term indicators of performance.[36]

This is a common complaint shared by many authors, and as the reader is aware by now, this author as well.

The "Breaking the Logjam" Book and Symposium

With regard to the AQM flaws of the CAA, one of the very few contributions addressing the CAA's current issues came in *Breaking the Logjam* (*BTL*), a book by Schoenbrod, Stewart, and Wyman, and the related article by Schoenbrod, Schwartz, and Sandler (hereinafter referred to as "Schoenbrod").[37] *BTL*, published in 2010, and the 2008–09 paper that preceded it,[38] arose from a symposium to address various aspects of what they and others characterized as a (policy) logjam.[39,40]

After years where the reform literature spoke generally to the subject of reform without much detail or rigor, Schoenbrod's article focused on only a portion of regulating interstate, and to a lesser extent, intrastate air pollution. To address interstate pollution, they present a few interesting ideas, namely, to have Congress:

1. Extend the Acid Rain Program from power plants to all categories of sources whose members are the biggest contributors to interstate pollution;
2. Integrate all pollutant limits into a common framework, rather than regulate them piecemeal;
3. Regulate through cap-and-trade (rather than command-and-control) all source categories for which it is possible to measure emissions, with the same emission limits for existing and new sources;
4. Decide how to set emission caps and allocate emission credits; and
5. Choose which sources to subject to direct federal regulation so as to address most *inter*state pollution while minimizing the total number of federally regulated stationary sources.[41]

With regard to regulating the remaining interstate pollution sources, Schoenbrod would let Congress leave that choice to the states. We first summarize Schoenbrod's approach to regulating interstate air pollution.

In effect, what Schoenbrod/BTL proposed was to shift who and how the major sources of interstate air pollution are regulated under the Acid Rain Program, by first expanding its use to more sources than just power plants.[42] Next, they appear to advocate establishing limits per individual source category, rather than having limits set for each pollutant across all industries combined.[43] They would apply CaT to rope in new and existing (think grandfathered) sources that are within federally regulated source categories using the best emissions monitoring technologies,[44] it being unclear however as to what those federally regulated source categories are.[45] Lastly, Congress would decide which sources fall under the federal interstate regulatory umbrella and those under state oversight, as well as be tasked with the setting of caps and allocating credits.[46]

Although regulating interstate pollution-generating sources in the fashion that Schoenbrod proposes is a key step, in the big picture, it will still take regulators only so far. While we need regulatory reform, there is much more to addressing the logjam than simply sorting out who does what and moving from a slow-walking SIP process to emissions trading, as the reader will see in Part 2.

The idea of segregating major sources into source categories, as Schoenbrod proposes, is imprecise because it micromanages the AQM program where it is unnecessary. In fairness, the NRC appears to suggest that the same approach be taken. However, emissions are emissions no matter where they are generated, so if certain source categories find it more difficult to reduce emissions than others, then they have the option of either purchasing trading units and/or redesigning their processes to reduce emissions, a common theme espoused in this book. Congress can certainly set interstate emission caps and deadlines for achieving National Ambient Air Quality Standards (NAAQS), but doing so per source category, as noted above, is suboptimal. Besides, a trading program for individual pollutants will quite adequately solve this problem where the percentage reductions required at participating sources are proportional to their achievable reductions if the program is well-designed, rendering moot any proposed scheme that relies on a per source category reduction.

Let's not forget that, irrespective of the source categories from which emissions are generated, improving the overall air quality for the primary benefit of addressing adverse environmental impacts to Nature and human health is the ultimate goal. Singling out source categories for targeted control of air pollution seems as inefficient to apply regulation differently as doing so under NSR based on whether the emission units are new or existing. Thus, focusing on the aggregated improvement in air quality per source category is an inefficient step backward in the effort to break the logjam.

At the state level, Schoenbrod unfortunately advocates that "Congress should eliminate the NAAQS-SIP process and its manifestations dealing with 'non-attainment' and 'Prevention of Significant Deterioration' as well as the Title V permit program."[47] They suggest that states should have the option to be stricter, if they so choose.[48] They recommend that "states should provide each source with a comprehensive list of emission limits to which it is subject, rather than dribbling them out pollutant by pollutant and program by program"[49] and the use of "cap and trade for those source categories for which it is possible to measure emissions accurately and with appropriate safeguards against hot spots."[50] Rather than doing what is best to reduce impacts on Nature and human health, this would only allow business-friendly states to do the bare minimum (or worse) to address those impacts.

While Schoenbrod would streamline the CAA by excising a good portion of the NSR rules, without providing specifics, they would use cap-and-trade to address the shortfall.[51] The *BTL* authors would retain the requirement to "vet" major new or modified sources,[52] which can only be assumed to mean conducting air quality modeling including the determination of how much increment[53] is consumed in attainment areas—but they were vague about what "vet" meant exactly. This is particularly concerning given that this does not mesh with the use of cap-and-trade in existing AAs as they propose; with the details missing, it leaves the method very unclear and confusing.[54]

Since they would eliminate Prevention of Significant Deterioration (PSD) and nonattainment area (NAA) New Source Review (NSR),[55] the *BTL* authors would also eliminate Best Available Control Technology (BACT) and Lowest Achievable Emission Rate (LAER) determinations, relying instead on the use of (what else?) a trading program that applies in both attainment and nonattainment areas, where their distinction is eliminated. We will see that eliminating LAER and BACT with no adequate plan to replace them is just a bridge too far.

The *BTL* authors also propose to eliminate new source performance standards (NSPS) that apply to individual emission units,[56] instead relying on states, which could resort to trading if they choose to do so, to sort out the emissions reduction details. It will help to understand the general significance of performance standards. One can think of the "performance standard for a region" for a given pollutant being the emissions cap for that pollutant when attainment of the applicable ambient air quality standard is achieved in a region. Likewise, the "emission standard for a source" for a pollutant is its sourcewide emissions limit for that pollutant when, ideally, no localized health impacts result from only that source alone (i.e., singling out other regional and local contributors). Lastly, the allowable emission rate of that pollutant from an emission unit set by rule is the unit's performance standard. In effect, there is a hierarchy of three performance standards for a given pollutant: one for an individual region, one for each individual source, and one for an individual emission unit. An optimal AQM program for stationary sources should ensure that all three standards are imposed and met until at least regional attainment of the NAAQS is achieved.

While Schoenbrod's/*BTL*'s focus is on expanding the Acid Rain Program, and with the elimination of distinctions at the state level between NAAs and AAs, their proposal would allow emissions to increase in existing NAAs while emissions could decrease in an existing AA. This would be a major step backward in the mission.

Nevertheless, while the NRC provided reasonable reform recommendations, Schoenbrod deserves credit for breaking away from the timid crowd and taking a stab at a different approach. As the reader will later see, some of Schoenbrod's ideas, or variants of them, fit within the comprehensive strategy for the regulation of interstate air pollution as developed in Chapter 4, while their other ideas related to regulating many aspects of intrastate air pollution veer far off the path of meaningful reform. Chapter 5 will provide a critique of their suggestions in the context of the comprehensive strategy.

Robert Nordhaus

Robert Nordhaus addressed reform by providing two options, A and B.[57] In simple terms, in option A, Congress would simply upgrade existing regulatory programs by "making them more workable and better coordinated."[58] The areas he cites as possible examples for improvement include: grandfathering and New Source Review, National Ambient Air Quality Standards, the SIP process, interstate transport, and hazardous air pollutants.

Option B, on the other hand, is more aggressive. Here Nordhaus proposes to restructure the CAA in the following manner:[59]

- Phase out grandfathering (and NSR) for existing sources, establish ESPS (existing source performance standards), and streamline regulation of existing stationary sources

- Expand EPA authority to use market-based regulation while protecting local air quality
- Give the EPA effective tools to control regional transport
- Retain the current NAAQS process with less frequent revisions
- Reform the SIP process
- Accommodate GHG regulation
- Transition without backsliding.

Regarding the first bullet point on grandfathering, Nordhaus proposes an "existing source performance standard" (ESPS) program, similar to the current NSPS, that would replace NSPS, BACT, and LAER for modified sources and replace the interstate program, BART and National Emission Standards for Hazardous Air Pollutants (NESHAPs) for existing sources.[60] Nordhaus explains in detail how the bullet points in Option B would function, including the ESPS and an associated two-tier operating permits program. The ESPS for a pollutant from an emission unit would merge BACT, LAER, and NSPS together at modified existing sources and would represent the ESPS-tier. The source-specific tier standard would factor in air quality aspects relevant to the source's location, such as being in an extreme NAA. In the context of a trading program, emissions at the source would only be allowed where the source-specific standard is not exceeded, but a tighter ESPS can be exceeded for an emission unit at the source if allowances are purchased to make up the difference. Nordhaus provides praiseworthy but somewhat confusing ideas in his other bullet points, but he was clearly constrained by the existing CAA, limiting his capacity to think outside its box.

Next Gen Principles

While not espousing broad reform of the CAA itself, Cynthia Giles, in her book, *Next Generation Compliance: Environmental Regulation for the Modern Era*, focuses more narrowly on improving how the actual rules should be better written. Her tenure within the Obama EPA's Office of Enforcement and Compliance Assurance promoted the use of Next Gen regulation whereby environmental rules themselves are designed so that compliance is built into them, that is, where compliance is the default option.[61] Some quotes provide a nice flavor of Giles's proposal to redesign regulations:

> It is taken as given that compliance is the job of enforcement, so if there are violations, then enforcers need to up their game. This perspective—held by most environmental policy practitioners, including government regulators, regulated companies, legislators, academics, and advocates—assumes compliance is about what happens after environmental rules are written.[62]
>
> Poorly designed rules that create opportunities to evade, obfuscate, or ignore will have dismal performance records that no amount of enforcement will ever fix. Compliance isn't consistently achieved by force-fitting it on the back end; it results from careful design up front.[63]
>
> I discovered that comprehensive evidence supports what I have anecdotally observed over decades of experience: significant violations are far more prevalent than everyone thinks.[64]
>
> Rules that work use command-and-control creatively, to smooth the path to compliance and block the violation exits.[65]
>
> Each poorly designed rule can collapse in a different way. But the lack of structural integrity eventually reveals itself in large numbers of violations.[66]
>
> The Acid Rain Program . . . worked well not because it was a market program, but because it created a regulatory box so tight that compliance was the only way out. NSR is the opposite of a tight box.[67]

The discussion of simplicity in rule writing is nicely addressed in the excellent paper by Giles's colleagues at the USEPA, David Hindin and Jon Silberman:

> Environmental agencies will often tailor regulations to recognize differences among the members of a regulated universe, maximize the regulated entities' compliance options or flexibility, or otherwise meet sector or facility-specific technical needs or problems. Consequently, rules may have complex applicability criteria, exemptions, exclusions and conditions. Such complex, tailored rules, while protective and cost-effective on paper, are not always beneficial in practice. Poor compliance can undermine complex rules. When circumstances suggest equivalent compliance under either simple or complex rules, the latter may be preferable because they provide tailored flexibility or for other reasons. Simplicity, however, should not be undervalued. Simple rules are easier for regulated entities to understand and for regulators to apply. Ultimately, relying on a simple rule may result in better overall compliance. Regulators should thus consider whether a simple rule, despite appearing less protective, might actually achieve higher compliance and greater environmental benefits.[68]

They later assert:

> Whether a rule or permit is viewed as complex or simple will often depend on the intended end user. For example, a permit for a manufacturing facility with environmental engineers and consultants can be more complex than a permit controlling stormwater at a retail shopping center. Rules and permits should be intelligible to, and meet the needs of, facility managers and staff, and government inspectors.[69]

Clearly, it is far better to be a master of simplicity than a slave to complexity.

Lastly, in his PowerPoint presentation, Hindin asserts the factors that contribute to compliance:

- Vigorous Government Inspection & Enforcement
- Clear, Simple Applicability
- Structural Factors
- Effective Monitoring (Periodic or Continuous)
- Independent Third Party Verification
- Real Time Information
- Electronic-Reporting to Government
- Public Accountability Transparency
- Market Forces
- Community Engagement
- Training/Technical Assistance Programs.[70]

Based on more than just the quotes above, the contributions of Giles, Hindin, and Silberman, and Gray and Shimshack contain a significant amount of wisdom based on a generation of practical experience useful to *all regulators*.

More will be said in Chapter 4 about the issue of designing rules, but for now, it can be said that Next Gen adoption is an unquestionably necessary, but not necessarily sufficient, condition for the reform of the underlying regulatory system.

A Response to the Above Authors

While the literature does present some beneficial ideas for reform, many veer off course and remain incomplete. Other than the NRC and Giles, typically missing in the literature to date is the regulator's perspective; and that does not mean the perspective from the high-level managerial and policy personnel at USEPA who have rarely experienced the regulatory grunt work. Quite simply, input from r*ea*l ground-level regulators who perform actual day-to-day tasks is lacking. It is fair to say however that the authors discussed above have at least raised their voices while practitioners of day-to-day regulation of air pollution, other than Giles and her colleagues, have been conspicuously silent; perhaps this is because speaking out would be fruitless, if not also frowned upon by upper-level management and political appointees.

In any event, past reformers have been held back by two shortfalls. First, is their lack of direct experience with the actual practice of regulating air pollution. The majority of 'reformers' are academics who study regulation abstractly and from a distance, without appreciating the finer points of what works and what does not. Second is the blind spot created by their incapacity (or unwillingness) to break away from CAA orthodoxy. Whether reformers are environmental legal scholars, environmental activists, economists, or even USEPA or state regulators, they rarely think outside the CAA regulatory box/cage.

As a regulator concerned with what works best by dovetailing theoretical principles with real-world, practical regulatory experience, this author does not consider the limitations or constraints posed by thinking within the CAA as applicable to devising an optimal solution. Seeking cures from within an already flawed system is itself a flawed concept. Let us not forget that the larger goal here is to assist regulators not just in the United States but also those worldwide (e.g., China and India) by providing them with a blueprint of the most optimal strategy to regulate air pollution. This is being done by throwing off all encumbrances of current CAA biases and limitations and proposing what the most optimal regulatory program should be instead. In Chapter 4, this optimal, comprehensive blueprint will be spelled out with follow-up commentary in Chapter 5.

It is again important to remind the reader that much of what will be presented in the following chapters on optimal strategy development for regulating air pollution from stationary sources will form the underlying basis for generally regulating multi-media environmental pollution. This includes those pollutants and surrogates associated with inherently detrimental product characteristics that will play a key role in facilitating the transition to a circular economy. In this respect, while Parts 1 and 2 focus on air pollution, and limiting the generation of multi-media environmental pollution is the focus of Part 3, finding a means to achieve other key milestones, such as mitigating climate change, restoring ecosystems, and attaining sustainability with Nature, is the higher, overarching goal.

Notes

1 Craig N. Oren, "Is the Clean Air Act at a Crossroads?" *Environmental Law Review* 40, no. 4 (Fall 2010).

2 As just one counterargument, if more people were aware of the consequences of conducting intensive inspections of emission sources from a contemporaneous Government Accountability Office (GAO) report (to be discussed later), people would not be as sanguine with regulating stationary sources under the CAA.

3 Stewart, "A New Generation of Environmental Regulation," 21.

4 Stewart, "A New Generation of Environmental Regulation," 26.

5 Environmental Law Institute, "Barriers to Environmental Technology Innovation and Use," *Environmental Law Institute Research Report* (January 1998): 32–3.

6 Daniel Fiorino, *The New Environmental Regulation* (The MIT Press, 2006).

7 More generally, we'll see in Part 3 that trading *must* play a *very significant* role in regulating the generation of multi-media pollution.

8 David Case, "The Lost Generation: Environmental Regulatory Reform in the Era of Congressional Abdication," *Duke Environmental Law & Policy Forum* 25, no. 1 (Fall 2014).

9 Other authors before Case mentioned many of these alternatives. Typical is this worthy article by Wyeth: George Wyeth, "'Standard' and 'Alternative' Environmental Protection: The Changing Role of Environmental Agencies," *William & Mary Environmental Law and Policy Review* 31, no. 1 (2006).

10 Case, "The Lost Generation," 92.

11 It could clearly be argued that these programs have been quietly subverted by lobbyists representing many regulated entities.

12 For the record, EMS is an exception and is essential and should be required for all sources.

13 Joel S. Hirschhorn, "Why the Pollution Prevention Revolution Failed-And Why It Ultimately Will Succeed," *Pollution Prevention Review* (Winter 2000).

14 That said, asking a regulatory agency whose primary focus is on regulating pollution to play the additional role of environmental consultant is outside the scope and reach of pollution control agencies, much like asking police departments to also teach literacy.

15 Wayne Gray and Jay Shimshack, "The Effectiveness of Environmental Monitoring and Enforcement: A Review of the Empirical Evidence," *Review of Environmental Economics and Policy, Association of Environmental and Resource Economists* 5, no. 1 (Winter 2011): 3. https://www.journals.uchicago.edu/doi/full/10.1093/reep/req017.

16 Brian Potts, "Trading Grandfathered Air—A New, Simpler Approach."

17 National Academy of Public Administrators, "A Breath of Fresh Air: Reviving the New Source Review Program."

18 Jody Freeman and Daniel A. Farber, "Modular Environmental Regulation," in "Thirty-Fourth Annual Administrative Law Issue: Incrementalism and the Administrative State," special issue, *Duke Law Journal* 54, no. 4 (February 2005). https://scholarship.law.duke.edu/dlj/vol54/iss4/1/.

19 Freeman and Farber, "Modular Environmental Regulation," 819.

20 Freeman and Farber, "Modular Environmental Regulation," 820. Here they cite: James Salzman and J. B. Ruhl, "'No Net Loss': Instrument Choice in Wetlands Protection," in *Moving to Markets in Environmental Regulation, Lessons from Twenty Years of Experience*, ed. Jody Freeman and Charles D. Kolstad (Oxford University Press, 2006).

21 Richard Schmalensee and Robert N. Stavins, "Lessons Learned from Three Decades of Experience with Cap and Trade," *Review of Environmental Economics and Policy* 11, no. 1 (Winter 2017): 74.

22 Schmalensee and Stavins, "Lessons Learned from Three Decades of Experience with Cap and Trade," 73–4. Here, the authors cite three papers: Nathaniel O. Keohane, "What did the Market Buy? Cost Savings under the U.S. Tradable Permits Program for Sulfur Dioxide," Working paper YCELP-01-11-2003, Yale Center for Environmental Law and Policy, New Haven, CT (2003); Robert N. Stavins and Richard Schmalensee, "The SO_2 Allowance Trading System: The Ironic History of a Grand Policy Experiment," *Journal of Economic Perspectives* 27, no. 1 (2012); and Joseph A. Doucet and Todd Strauss, "On the Bundling of Coal and Sulfur Dioxide Emissions Allowances," *Energy Policy* 22, no. 9 (1994).

23 National Research Council, *Air Quality Management in the United States, xi.*

24 NRC, *Air Quality Management in the United States*, 205.

25 NRC, *Air Quality Management in the United States*, 215.

26 NRC, *Air Quality Management in the United States*, 215.

27 NRC, *Air Quality Management in the United States*, 177.

28 NRC, *Air Quality Management in the United States*, 210.

29 NRC, *Air Quality Management in the United States*, 266.

30 NRC, *Air Quality Management in the United States*, 282.

31 NRC, *Air Quality Management in the United States*, 278.

32 NRC, *Air Quality Management in the United States*, 269, Figure 7–1.

33 The NRC summarizes the CAA requirements for SIPs (NRC, *Air Quality Management in the United States*, 94–5, Box 3-3) and later provides examples of bureaucratic overload that go into nice detail with regard to the shortcomings of the process (NRC, *Air Quality Management in the United States*, 129, Box 3-7).

34 NRC, *Air Quality Management in the United States*, 293.

35 In fact, the use of standards and trading is absolutely essential to the larger strategy of regulating multi-media pollution, including the means to achieve a circular economy.

36 NRC, *Air Quality Management in the United States*, 296.

37 David Schoenbrod, Joel Schwartz, and Ross Sandler, "Air Pollution: Building on the Successes Breaking the Logjam: Environmental Reform for the New Congress and Administration: Panel III–Climate Change, US Domestic Regulation, and the Future of the Car," *New York University Environmental Law Journal* 17, no. 1 (2008–2009).

38 Note that the *BTL* book (first cited in Chapter 1) and the Schoenbrod article address many of the same issues, but the article provides more details.

39 The four principles around which the BTL Project was organized were "Cross-cutting regulatory approaches that address underlying causes, openness about trade-offs, scaling regulatory authority to the problem, and expanding the use of market incentives and information." Lawrence Huntington, Philip Sharp, E. Donald Elliott, et al., "How Did We Get Into The Logjam, And How Do We Get Out of It?" Summary of Panel I Discussion at the *Breaking the Logjam* Conference Held at the NYU School of Law, New York, March 28–29, 2008, 20. https://nyuelj.org/wp-content/uploads/2013/03/HOW-DID-WE-GET-INTO-THE-LOGJAM.pdf.

40 While this was interpreted as the BTL symposium's general thinking on the policy logjam as generally being a legislative one, the interpretation of logjam taken in this book includes the bureaucratic aspects as well.

41 Schoenbrod, Schwartz and Sandler, "Air Pollution: Building on the Successes Breaking the Logjam," 289–90.

42 Between Schoenbrod and the *BTL* authors, these would include power plants, electric and other services combined, petroleum refiners, paper mills, hydraulic cement mills, pulp mills, organic chemical plants, primary aluminum plants, carbon black plants, blast furnaces, lead smelters, and raw sugar mills.

43 It should be noted that it is not entirely clear whether their use of the term "limit" means the usual tons per year or something else. Thus, specifying an aggregated ton per year limit for each pollutant for the cement manufacturing industry (as one example) seems to be micromanaging. In any event, a well-designed trading scheme would render this matter moot.

44 Schoenbrod, Schwartz and Sandler, "Air Pollution: Building on the Successes Breaking the Logjam," 296.

45 If these are those sources subject to NSPSs and/or NSR, this would be in conflict with Schoenbrod's/*BTL*'s proposal later to eliminate those programs.

46 Schoenbrod, Schwartz and Sandler, "Air Pollution: Building on the Successes Breaking the Logjam," 299–300.

47 Schoenbrod, Schwartz and Sandler, "Air Pollution: Building on the Successes Breaking the Logjam," 320.

48 Schoenbrod, Schwartz and Sandler, "Air Pollution: Building on the Successes Breaking the Logjam," 320–1.

49 Schoenbrod, Schwartz and Sandler, "Air Pollution: Building on the Successes Breaking the Logjam," 322.

50 Schoenbrod, Schwartz and Sandler, "Air Pollution: Building on the Successes Breaking the Logjam," 322.

51 As noted earlier, NSR is used to analyze the implications of emissions increases due to construction of new major sources or modifications made at existing major sources. Other than such sources in NAAs having to obtain trading units to account for their emissions increases, it is difficult to see how a Schoenbrod-proposed trading program addresses NSR.

52 Schoenbrod, Stewart and Wyman, *BTL*, 96.

53 According to the USEPA (https://www.epa.gov/nsr/prevention-significant-deterioration-basic-information), "PSD increment is the amount of pollution an area is allowed to increase. PSD increments prevent the air quality in clean areas from deteriorating to the level set by the NAAQS. The NAAQS is a maximum allowable concentration 'ceiling.' A PSD increment, on the other hand, is the maximum allowable increase in concentration that is allowed to occur above a baseline concentration for a pollutant. The baseline concentration is defined for each pollutant and, in general, is the ambient concentration that existed at the time that the first complete PSD permit application affecting the area is submitted. Significant deterioration is said to occur when the amount of new pollution would exceed the applicable PSD increment. It is important to note, however, that the air quality cannot deteriorate beyond the concentration allowed by the applicable NAAQS, even if not all of the PSD increment is consumed."

54 As will be seen in Chapter 4, the comprehensive strategy will maintain a scaled-down NSR program that retains its essential regulatory strengths by keeping its effective "crew," while purging its ineffective "cargo."

55 *BTL*, 96.

56 Schoenbrod, Stewart and Wyman, *BTL*, 96.

57 Nordhaus, "Modernizing the Clean Air Act," 388–401. Robert Nordhaus, who passed away in 2016, was the brother of economics Nobel Laureate William Nordhaus.

58 Nordhaus, "Modernizing the Clean Air Act," 388.

59 Nordhaus, "Modernizing the Clean Air Act," 391–401.

60 Nordhaus, "Modernizing the Clean Air Act," 392.

61 A good example of a manufacturer's production of compliance-ready emission units are engines, whereby sources that purchase them will not have to test them for compliance once the manufacturer can certify to their compliance after production.

62 Giles, *Next Generation Compliance*, 1.

63 Giles, *Next Generation Compliance*, 1–2.

64 Giles, *Next Generation Compliance*, 2.

65 Giles, *Next Generation Compliance*, 172.

66 Giles, *Next Generation Compliance*, 42.

67 Giles, *Next Generation Compliance*, 42.

68 David A. Hindin and Jon D. Silberman, "Designing More Effective Rules and Permits," *George Washington Journal of Energy & Environmental Law* (Spring 2016): 107. Here, at the end of their quote, Hindin and Silberman cite: Martha G. Roberts, "Integrating Compliance and Regulatory Design in EPA Rulemaking," *New York University Environmental Law Journal* 20, no. 3 (2014): 556–61, where compliance can influence rule design via cost-benefit analysis.

69 Hindin and Silberman, "Designing More Effective Rules and Permits," 108.

70 David Hindin, "Next Generation Compliance: Research Questions," Slideshow presented at Session 4: Enhancing Compliance by Leveraging Forces Beyond Inspections and Enforcement of the Research on Effective Government: Inspection and Compliance Workshop, June 1, 2015, Slide 6. https://mcep.umd.edu/sites/mcep.umd.edu/files/David%20Hindin%20Next%20Gen%20Research%20Questions%202015.pdf.

Part 2

The Comprehensive Strategy

4

A New Framework for Regulating Air Pollution from Stationary Sources

The Need for a New Approach

Although the decades-old US Clean Air Act has a number of positives going for it, the Act most definitely has its downsides. Among these are two key areas in the regulation of stationary sources that scream for reform: streamlining the regulatory process and curing its design flaws. One can certainly appreciate that a few of the authors cited in Chapter 3 also identified these same needs. Nonetheless, some authors, with the notable exceptions of Schoenbrod and Nordhaus, simply proposed the expanded use of trading as "solutions" without ever putting "chalk to blackboard"; that is, doing the required work to sort out the troublesome details. Even in the case of Schoenbrod, less rigor than was necessary was provided to support their proposal.

The current antiquated air quality management (AQM) program to regulate stationary sources under the CAA reflects "overbureaucracy," which unfortunately accepts as normal the current regulatory sluggishness and the much broader logjam, which one can characterize as bureaucratic pollution. The fact that there is so much legal overburden and USEPA guidance within the current system is an indication that the program is flawed, for which a multitude of fixes applied over a period of years has not resolved. It is this author's contention that, among the CAA's flaws, too much discretion in making technical determinations has also led to too much bureaucracy and conflict.

What then is the optimal "regulatory infrastructure" that achieves the best air quality improvement outcomes? We know already that the God Particle of an AQM program is the determination of actual emissions, so what is the God Particle of regulatory effectiveness? Given that optimality and correcting design flaws are tasks that engineers feast upon, in this chapter an optimal strategy for regulating air pollution and a comprehensive framework for adoption will be proposed; the framework would allow the United States to escape from its current bureaucratic rut, if it chooses to. As a key component of that strategy, the earmarks of an emissions cap-and-trade scheme are spelled out that can also be applied to mitigate global climate change, as laid out in Chapter 9. As counterintuitive as it may seem, many aspects of the framework will play a very significant role in regulating the generation of multi-media pollution, including a means to achieve a circular economy.

In Support of the Yin of Setting and Declining Limits

Before we develop the framework of the comprehensive strategy, let's begin with this question: If a plant's overall emission limit for a given pollutant is not exceeded and does not impact "Nature's welfare" or public health, would exceeding a set limit for that pollutant generated from just one of the source's several emission units be as impactful? The answer is that it is not; but acting on violations of internal limits at a source when source-wide limits are not violated is yet another flawed aspect of current air pollution regulation in the United States. This problem is compounded by the peculiar fact that the limit on total regional emissions of a given pollutant in a nonattainment area (NAA) is not even set and systematically reduced through regulation, indicating that regulation can be pennywise and pound foolish.

What policymakers and regulators should really be concerned about and fixated upon is not micromanaging how a source's individual unit's emissions increases meet individually applicable limits but instead focusing on how much a source's emissions will impact ambient concentrations. The current regulatory program is unfortunately focused on micromanaged, process-oriented regulation at the source when more milestone-based, results-oriented regulation should be the focus instead.

Common sense dictates that limits on pollution from a source and likewise within a region are far more critical than limits set for individual emission units. If measuring emissions is the fundamental God Particle of AQM at the micro level, then a regional limit is the God Particle at the macrolevel. For any areas where there are adverse health and welfare effects, reductions in those limits are mandatory.

> One can think of the process of regionally capping a pollutant with its subsequent decline within NAAs as the ecosystem "getting its harm reduction cut up front," that is, committing to no further harm, while the economic system,

which is embedded within the larger ecosystem, "reimburses" the environment for the damage it has incurred. In other words, while setting the initial limit and not allowing increases represents the down payment on repayment, subsequent declines in the cap are installment payments while the tool of trading simply sorts out who gets what and at what cost.

In Support of the Yang of Trading[1]

To ensure that the total emissions limit for a pollutant from stationary sources within a region is reduced, "external trading" (i.e., trading between sources or intersource trading within the region) should be expanded beyond its current use. This has reduced acid rain and is being used to address climate change in some regions, but it can and must also be expanded as a tool to address natural welfare and regional health impacts for those nonattainment area pollutants emitted by sources that emit that pollutant in major amounts. The characteristic of fungibility of plentiful pollutant emissions and the units that emit them can be exploited by trading those pollutant emissions externally under a regionally capped and declining limit where possible. Furthermore, setting but not reducing a maximum allowable limit for a pollutant and using "internal trading" within a source (i.e., *intra*source redistribution of pollutant emissions from units within the source) can and should be used for pollutants emitted in either major or minor amounts in attainment areas, and for nonattainment area pollutants emitted in minor amounts.

As seen earlier in Chapter 3, some skeptics of external trading include members of the environmental community. Unfortunately, the narrative has been hijacked by some within the trading opposition camp when the narrative should instead be focused on the setting and reducing of *limits*. Expanded use of trading is advocated because it is the right tool to use *when applied appropriately*; establishing, as it does, an efficient means to reduce emissions under a regional quantified cap that tightens over time. At the same time, external trading is a tool that can actually simplify the practice of regulation. Elliott says it well:

> ...in some circumstances, markets can be far more efficient for *government* regulators than old-fashioned case-by-case command-and-control regulation.[2]
>
> One statistic illustrates how important and pronounced this advantage [economizing on the resources] can be: there are about 15,000 government

> employees working on air pollution control in the United States, of whom only about fifty (0.3% of the total) work in the acid rain program at EPA, yet this single market-based program has produced a substantial portion of the reductions in air pollution over the last decade.[3]

Those opposed to trading because it gives polluters a "right to pollute" should instead be focusing on the sin of pollution rather than the polluter-as-sinner. Using a trading program to facilitate pollutant reductions underneath the cap goads[4] sources to redesign their process(es) and/or take measures to substitute fuels and/or resources. In this respect, it is an *ideal* tool for nonattainment areas or other adverse environmental areas[5] where emissions must be practically and effectively reduced; with sources allowed only to trade with other sources that emit the subject pollutant in major amounts within the same nonattainment area.[6] The more objective the means to verify emissions and quantify violations, the more the program can be trusted to do what it is designed to do. Besides being reminded by the National Research Council (NRC) of the benefits that trading has already provided to improve the environment,[7] anti-trading diehards should withhold judgment until after reading Part 3, where trading is used to facilitate the transition to a circular economy (CE); and Part 4 where reverse cap-and-trade can be used to restore ecosystems. In fact, regulating the generation of inherently detrimental pollutant characteristics to facilitate the transition to a CE or restoring ecosystems seems all but impossible without applying an external trading scheme.

Where some countries in the European Union (EU) have been using an emissions tax for a number of years now, it has done far more to increase revenues than to meet its goal of reducing emissions.[8] This is because taxation, a dissuasive market instrument, does not bake in absolute, milestone-seeking reductions the way that cap-and-trade (CaT), a corrective market instrument, does. Trading is more effective because it operates beneath a Command-and-Control (CaC)-based, numerical cap that systematically declines until the goal of remediation is reached. Where a discrete regional emissions and concentration goal is to be achieved, CaT is the optimal method since it is based on that goal being met by the collective actions of all major contributors within the region irrespective of who does or does not reduce emissions. On the other hand, taxation only acts on sources individually, without any source having met, or having to meet, an established discrete numerical goal for meeting regional emission limits. Clearly then, emissions-wise, corrective CaT is far more deterministic while purely dissuasive taxation is not. A successful trading program is like putting all the major sources for a given pollutant within a region on an enforceable, hard-capped pollution budget. What's not to like about that?

One major goal of this chapter, then, is developing the optimal regulatory "sweet spot," which includes the sweet spot between the use of CaC and the use of market instruments, and among market instruments, the role of trading and taxation.

Critical Terms of Usage

- External and internal trading: External trading refers to the trading of source trading units (TU)[9] between individual sources, while internal trading refers to the redistribution of pollutant emissions between units within a source itself under a plantwide cap. Here, no official trading actually occurs but emissions are "exchanged" without required reductions under a Plantwide Applicability Limitation (PAL), which is an emissions bubble usually used for an attainment area pollutant at the source; the source is simply allowed to operate in compliance as long as its emissions for subject pollutants do not exceed its PAL for that pollutant. Stringent recordkeeping is required to document and track emissions.
- Adverse Area: An area suffering from adverse air quality impacts directly due to air pollutants, such as ozone NAAs, acid rain-affected regions, areas of impaired visibility, and environmental justice (EJ) areas located within one or more of these areas.[10] The climate stability NAA, that is, the entire planet, is indirectly affected by greenhouse gas pollution and is better addressed by the mitigation strategy in Chapter 9.
- Sources that emit pollutants in major and minor amounts: Where possible in the discussion of the comprehensive strategy that follows, the current definitions of major and minor sources under the CAA will be replaced with two simple phrases: "a source that emits a pollutant in major amounts" and "a source that emits a pollutant in minor amounts."
- Demand-based emissions growth: This is emissions growth resulting from an emissions increase from emission units currently operating at the source that results from an increase in production demand.
- Capacity-based emissions growth: This is emissions growth that is projected to occur due to an increase at a source resulting from adding new emission

units and/or making physical modifications to existing units that increase the production capacity and increase the potential emissions of at least one pollutant at the source.[11]

Note: A truly like-for-like replacement of a unit at a source would fall under the category of demand-based growth, since it will not increase the capacity and potential emissions of the source. On the other hand, replacement of a unit at a source with a larger capacity unit would fall under the category of capacity-based growth, since it will increase the capacity and potential emissions of the source.

- Potential to Emit (PTE): Pursuant to 40 CFR 52.21(b)(4), the USEPA's definition of PTE under the PSD rules is the maximum capacity of a stationary source to emit a pollutant under its physical and operational design. Any physical or operational limitation on the capacity of the source to emit a pollutant, including air pollution control equipment and restrictions on hours of operation or on the type of material combusted, stored, or processed, shall be treated as part of its design only if the limitation or the effect it would have on emissions is federally enforceable.

The Framework of an Optimal Comprehensive Strategy

As the term is used in this book, optimality is loosely defined as the most effective and efficient means of reducing the generation of emissions/pollution to the environment at the lowest effort/cost *to regulators*, and with any luck, others as well (most notably taxpayers). Whether regulators use command-and-control, taxation, or emissions trading, there will always be a cost, so the best approach is that combination of their use that reduces pollution optimally, including bureaucratic pollution, with the least effort. As a case in point, the administrative time to process complex permits is often cited as a cost to regulated entities, but from a regulatory practitioner's point of view, the excess bureaucracy associated with developing and administering complex permits is first and foremost an unnecessary cost to regulators, and therefore to taxpayers and the environment itself.

The approach taken to developing a new strategy reflects the well-known aphorism from computer scientists Brian W. Kernighan and P.J. Plauger: "Don't patch bad code—rewrite it."[12] Simply patching the flawed regulation of stationary sources under the current CAA is not sufficient. It is far better to determine what an optimal program looks like and progress forward diligently and with speed.

Here, the overarching goal fixes its focus on objective (quantifiable) results-oriented milestones while minimizing the amount of subjective (qualitative) process-oriented practices. The strategy is developed first by addressing climate-altering greenhouse gas (GHG) pollutants[13] and other types of pollution on both a global and regional basis by setting comprehensive limits on inputs and outputs in a rational hierarchical order: from the global and regional levels, and so on to the source and emission unit levels. More will be said about the hierarchy for regulating air pollution in Chapter 5.

Globally limiting, by rationing, fossil fuels and applying CO_2 (and/or GHG) trading will be required to reduce concentrations of CO_2 (and/or GHG) and other collaterally generated pollutants; adopting a CE which facilitates material efficiency and thus energy efficiency will not be sufficient by itself to mitigate climate change, but it is nevertheless necessary.[14] Next in the hierarchy is limiting regional emissions (e.g., nitrogen oxides) through the appropriate use of external and internal trading applied respectively to sources that emit those pollutants in major and minor amounts. Regulation proceeds further down the hierarchy to simple minor sources, etc. Figure 4.1 provides the hierarchy of regulation.

Next, the proper division of labor (to appropriately distribute and minimize workload) is also a focus of the comprehensive strategy. This includes the different, sometimes supporting other times leading, roles played by the feds and states. Academia and environmental research centers will also have a key role to play. At the staff level, a brief discussion of who does what between engineers and lawyers must be clarified. The design flaws in the current system, as discussed in Chapter 2, are addressed next. Other key issues are discussed, such as what the external trading scheme might look like, what pollutants should be traded, the roles of permitting and other essential functions, and the necessity of stack tests.

Developing the Underlying Foundation for Optimal Regulation

To set the stage for the development of the comprehensive strategy, the optimal means of regulating air pollution from the highest to the lowest levels will be addressed.

The macro or global level will address limiting both fossil fuel usage[15] and CO_2 emissions, as well as addressing interstate transport. The focus of this section will first be on the regulatory approach to addressing global climate stability

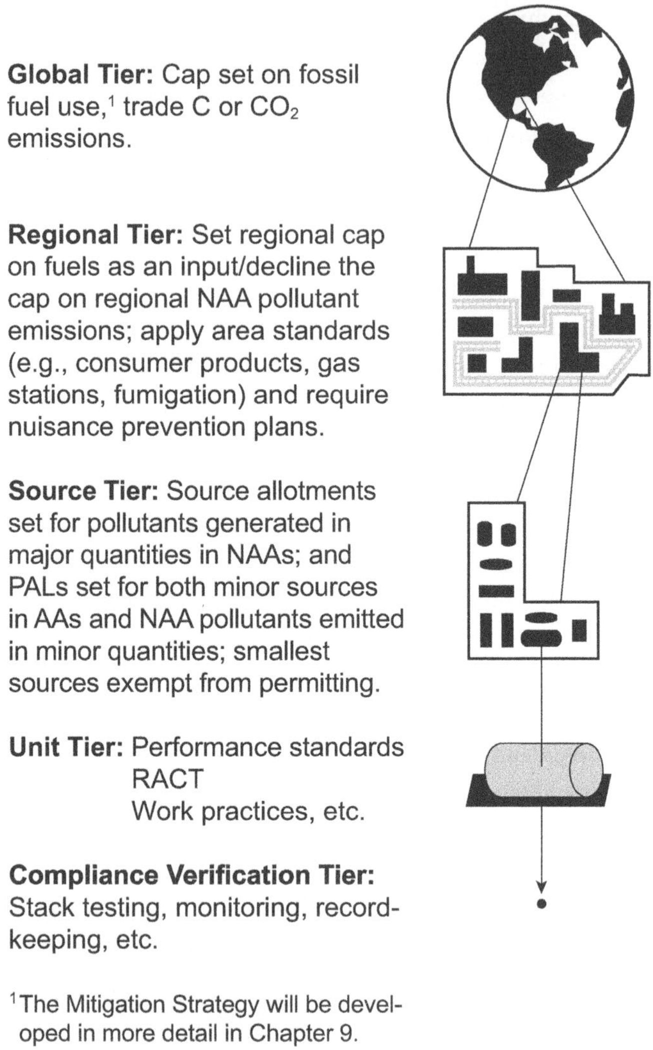

Figure 4.1 Hierarchy of regulation.

nonattainment. In this respect, the national narrative has usually been either taxing carbon dioxide emissions or utilizing emissions trading, most typically the external trading of carbon dioxide emissions from power plants. This narrative will be seen to be woefully deficient. The full approach to addressing climate change will be further developed in Chapter 9.

Next is regional regulation, for example, by limiting emissions of a pollutant in adverse areas and using external trading to protect both Nature's welfare and human health by meeting the National Ambient Air Quality Standards (NAAQS).[16] At the regional level, reductions will also occur in ozone nonattainment areas in major metropolitan areas. Given the multitude of sources that generate precursors to ozone pollution in major metropolitan areas,[17] the best, although certainly unpopular, means to regulate stationary and nonstationary combustion sources (e.g., mobile sources and nonroad engines) is to limit the amount of regional fuel usage. It makes no sense to focus on limiting emissions only from large stationary sources if ubiquitous mobile emitters (think "vehicle miles traveled") and nonroad emitters are left unregulated other than by setting engine performance standards, as current practice dictates. Doing so only invites nonattainment in perpetuity.

While regional air quality degradation caused by existing stationary sources that emit pollutants in major amounts in NAAs comes next in the hierarchy where external trading is to be used to reduce emissions, "internal trading" can be used to limit emissions of both AA and NAA pollutants emitted in minor amounts at sources through the use of Plantwide Applicability Limitations (PALs).

This discussion is followed by how to address construction of new sources (i.e., major, minor, or negligible emitters) as well as modifications at existing sources. While the major focus of this book is how to remediate the planet due to the existing harms from pollution that impact Nature and human health, the discussion on construction or modification is focused on preventing pollution from becoming future harms. Thus, how to prevent significant deterioration of air quality, while secondary to the primary discussion with regard to reducing harms, is still important in its own right. The discussion here is just one approach among other possible approaches.

The hierarchy then focuses regulation at the unit level (e.g., the use of performance standards). Lastly, regulation requires compliance verification, such as the use of stack testing.

The Top of the Regulatory Hierarchy: Rationing the Use of Fossil Fuels

Starting at the top of the air quality hierarchy is our global climate where the Earth itself is the critical "nonattainment area" for climate stability. Clearly, the CO_2 concentration curve must be flattened and then lowered. Without mincing words, the quantity of all fossil fuel-based carbon must be limited by all users of these fuels;[18] there is just no other alternative. *This requirement simply reflects Air Pollution Regulation 101*, that is, to limit outputs, inputs must be limited. That said, where a global usage limit on fossil fuel-based carbon is set that still allows countries some flexibility to use them, then such a strategy will be more palatable. The mitigation strategy developed in Chapter 9 would do this by first setting a fossil fuel-based carbon usage limit. Limiting and then declining global CO_2 emissions (from both fossil fuels and biomass) via an international, treaty-based CaT system is utilized. Enforceably limiting and declining the quantity of carbon-based fossil fuels combusted is not only a prerequisite to mitigating climate change but is far more preferable than simply externally trading or taxing post-combustion CO_2 emissions solely at the back end because this *guarantees* specifically planned reductions of CO_2 emissions, rather than remediating the harms of CO_2 via CaT or dissuading their generation via pure taxation. In effect, limiting by rationing is just a special case of capping whereby trading is performed in real time with real currency and by all consumers, designed to allow the environment to get a guaranteed reduction up front.

The Role of External Trading to Address Regional Emissions

Adverse welfare impacts such as those caused by acid rain and health-impacted areas such as nonattainment areas are addressed next. As tempting as it is to address first those areas directly impacting health, who says both types of impacted areas shouldn't be considered within one program?

Where rationing of fossil fuels is at the top of the global hierarchy of pollution regulation, at the top of the regional hierarchy is the setting of limits for subject pollutants and the use of a trading program beneath the umbrella of declining caps in adversely impacted areas. While further CaC-based regulation could be utilized to facilitate necessary reductions, trading is an efficient, practical tool tailored nicely to reduce emissions to address the immediate problem of adverse impacts, namely nonattainment of the NAAQS, as well as reducing acid rain. One can do this by combining together an adapted, more comprehensive Cross-State Air Pollution Rule (CSAPR), that is, one that applies nationwide to major, interstate pollution-generating sources. This approach would address pollutants that contribute significantly[19] to NAAs (including the EJ areas within them) and the Acid Rain Program, while incorporating Schoenbrod's suggestion of including *all* major interstate polluters (e.g., steel mills, refineries) for NOx, SO_2, $PM_{2.5}$, and

CO_2 (i.e., those pollutants emitted in major quantities that participate in interstate transport).[20] This includes the required participation of grandfathered emission units that also contribute to interstate pollution and the alteration of climate stability. Major sources that externally trade a pollutant because those sources' emissions of that pollutant contribute significantly to, say, both acid rain and nonattainment of some kind (e.g., ozone) would continue to trade until one area is no longer an adversely affected area, so thereafter it trades within the other existing adverse area. Since capped limits decline for each adverse area air pollutant emitted in major quantities, who reduces and how is irrelevant. In addition, interstate-polluting sources that contribute significantly to NAAs (and the EJ areas within them) will continue to be regulated via state-determined Reasonably Available Control Technology (RACT) by the states, and where reductions in emissions through use of RACT are not sufficient for the area to reach attainment area status, then RACT must be tightened even further while the trading program continues. And as long as there are grandfathered sources that emit one or more pollutants in major quantities that contribute significantly to downwind adverse air quality, then those sources *must* participate in trading for those subject pollutants.[21]

Where appropriate, external trading will play a key and expanded role in the comprehensive strategy, but certainly not comprise the strategy itself. It is important to note that there are grandfathered sources in attainment areas that do not affect any downwind adverse areas. These attainment area sources should not be included in any external trading program with nonattainment area sources because doing so allows their emissions to be a source of "clean" emissions to the worst polluters in NAAs, thereby defeating the purpose of the AQM mission. Simply requiring grandfathered sources to trade just because they are grandfathered is not always appropriate. Instead, such grandfathered sources can simply take a PAL, subject only to state RACT and federal performance standards, as applicable.

The Acid Rain Program was successful in part due to its exceptional nature, namely, it applied to boilers that utilize continuous emission monitoring system (CEMS) where fuel switching and/or installation of add-on controls was possible and where aspects of Next Gen compliance were built into the rule. While Elliot noted that about fifty USEPA employees administered the Acid Rain Program to address SO_2 and, to a lesser extent, NOx, expanding the corrective external trading program to more stationary source categories, as Schoenbrod recommends, is quite possible. However, expanding it to more pollutants could potentially be problematic, particularly if it possibly leads to regulatory capture whereby states are left out of the enforcement loop. A cooperative arrangement between the feds and states in this regard may be more appropriate. While this shifting of responsibility from the states to the feds improves the practice of regulation overall, it is only a modest step. More will be said about the role of the feds and states later in this chapter.

It is important to realize that interstate pollution is a contributor to downwind NAAs, but it is too simplistic to assume that it is the only contributor affecting Nature's welfare and/or the public's health. Some might scoff at focusing on anything but interstate pollution because they perceive regional issues like interstate transport, where pollutants are emitted on a far wider scale, as more critical to the deterioration of the environment than the contributions from *intra*state polluting sources. There is some truth to that, but let's not forget that we have several states whose sources generate intrastate pollution that significantly contributes to NAAs within their own and neighboring major cities more than interstate contributors.

External trading within adverse areas will facilitate reductions from many of the sources that emit the pollutant in major quantities while reducing regional emissions from stationary sources overall. In this way, the regional cap for a pollutant is "tuned" to decline sufficiently over time to meet that pollutant's National Ambient Air Quality Standard. With the lowering of pollutant concentrations, the area of adversity should also reduce in size geographically, but only to the extent that external trading is no longer effective due to all potential emissions reductions having been tapped out. In the case where the adverse area remains adverse but at a lower ambient concentration for the pollutant in question, and where there are no further options to reduce emissions, regulators must then require stationary sources that emit that pollutant in this stubborn NAA[22] to take an all-hands-on-deck approach to addressing the ongoing problem. Sources must take appropriate measures by (1) being required to meet stricter RACT and (2) submitting for approval a Lowest Achievable Emission Rate (LAER) Retrofit Contingency Plan. This plan would outline preparations for the possible future scenario where the source contributes to a localized hotspot during the trading program. Should that occur, the source will have in place a plan for the installation of LAER on all appropriate emission units. However, if the LAER Retrofit Contingency Plans are ineffective in a nonattainment area that exists in part due to the use of a dirty fuel, then use of a cleaner fuel must be mandated. Lastly, as a last resort to comply with the First and Second FloERs, not to mention achieving compliance with the regional performance standard, relocation of the remaining problem sources or portions thereof must be mandated.

Trading should continue until attainment is achieved. While one can think of attainment of the NAAQS as a performance standard for the region (where nonattainment represents a "violation" of the regional air quality performance standard), regulators may elect to require additional trading until ambient concentrations are a PSD increment below the NAAQS for the subject pollutant.

To better measure emissions and provide integrity to the program within the CDC-like corrective trading approach, regulators must require sources to use a CEMS wherever possible, and where sources cannot, frequent use of stack tests to determine and verify emissions used in its place. Use of "certified sustainability accountants" must also be required to verify and sign off on the pollutant quantification used in the trading program. These accountants are not environmental consultants who simply crunch the emissions numbers for their clients; due to the necessity to achieve sustainability with Nature, they are more like, and higher in stature than, certified public accountants.

By addressing nonattainment area pollutants separately, external trading under the comprehensive strategy takes care of the fragmented and staggered SIP process as currently constituted. Given the various pollutant concentration levels throughout the country, Congress and/or federal and state regulators can more easily and directly tune the external trading programs to address compliance to the NAAQS in various regions.[23]

The Role of Internal Trading, or Plantwide Applicability Limitations (PALs) to Address Source Emissions

One question, among many that the reader might ask at this point, is this: if external trading is appropriate for addressing areas of poor air quality (i.e., adverse areas), what happens where the air quality is not adverse, for example, where pollutant concentrations are well below the NAAQS, thereby being in attainment for the given pollutant? How should air quality be regulated to ensure that it does not become an NAA? There is also a related question: how should a source that emits pollutants in minor quantities in the NAA be regulated?

In attainment areas, sources that emit pollutants in either minor quantities or major quantities that do not contribute significantly to an NAA should take a Plantwide Applicability Limitation (PAL),[24] whereby the source can emit that pollutant from various emission units at the source as long as the source does not emit over their PAL. It is important to note that "internal trading" is not technically conducted; a source is allowed to generate emissions of AA pollutants as long as the source does not exceed its total plantwide limit for the pollutant and meets all applicable performance and emission standards.

Likewise, a source in a NAA that emits an NAA pollutant in minor quantities would take a PAL for that pollutant rather than be required to externally trade.[25] This includes those sources that were previously in an NAA for a pollutant that are now in an AA due to the successful operation of the trading program that resulted in attainment. No longer should regulators in these cases be hassled by having to limit emissions from individual emission units or groups of emission units at a source when all that should really matter, as far as regional air quality is concerned, is what total emissions of a pollutant are being generated by the entire source itself.

Thus, internal trading of emissions among individual emission units at a source within an attainment area is elegantly symmetric to that of external trading among sources within nonattainment areas, with this exception: external trading for sources that emit a NAA pollutant in major quantities is always required to reduce emissions. It is important to note that a source that emits a NAA pollutant in major amounts cannot isolate itself from NAA-required external trading by obtaining a PAL for that pollutant. They absolutely must trade in order to address the health and harmful impacts to Nature that their emissions are contributing to.

The Role of Source Location and Source Categories

Where do source location and source type fit in, and how should these aspects be addressed? Much like the current regulatory regime under the CAA, how an existing source is regulated will depend on what pollutants are emitted in major or minor amounts and what the existing air quality status is (i.e., attainment or nonattainment) with regard to where the source is located for those particular pollutants. To be more specific, it is worth keeping NSR's demarcation of major source thresholds (for purposes of both construction and operating permits) in nonattainment areas and establishing new major source thresholds for sources in attainment areas, as shown in Table 4.1.

Under the current rules for the Prevention of Significant Deterioration (PSD) of Air Quality, that is, in attainment areas for subject AA pollutants, as noted

Table 4.1 Source Thresholds for Pollutants Emitted in Major Amounts

Area Status	**Air Quality Severity**	**Source Threshold tons/year**
Nonattainment Areas	Extreme	10
	Severe	25
	Serious	50
	Moderate	100
	Marginal	100
Attainment Areas	Dirty 26	100
	All Other	200

previously in Chapter 1, there are special types of sources classified under a list of twenty-six named source categories.[26] These sources oftentimes belong to generally higher-emitting, multi-pollutant source categories (e.g., steel mills, chemical process plants), having a major source threshold of only 100 tpy for any one pollutant. All other source categories (e.g., an auto manufacturing plant) are allowed up to 250 tpy before being deemed as major. In the comprehensive strategy, the major source threshold for pollutants emitted from sources within the named categories (plus other source categories regulators might choose to include) should retain the threshold of 100 tpy, regardless of the air quality of the area. Otherwise, the threshold for all the other source categories is 200 tpy for sources located in pristine-like areas. These source thresholds are important because they will determine how much sources will be able to increase emissions of an AA pollutant under their PAL threshold before they must address a proposed increase in emissions over that threshold, whether due to the growth in emissions from existing units, the addition of new units, or expansion due to both.

Thus, for purposes of mandatory external trading, a source located in a serious nonattainment area for SO_2 that emits 80 tpy of SO_2 must participate in the external trading program, since it is a source that emits SO_2 in major quantities (i.e., $80 > 50$). On the other hand, a source that emits 20 tpy of SO_2 in that same NAA would take a PAL for its emissions of SO_2 (since $20 < 50$).

A quick word about the density of sources: Where regulators observe that a few adjacent sources each emit a pollutant in minor quantities but when considered as a whole, collectively emit that pollutant in major quantities, regulators should seriously consider treating these sources as a major contributor within an NAA. Some judgment will be necessary here, such as exempting sources that truly emit a pollutant below a de minimis quantity. Addressing the density of sources in an NAA may also help to clarify the issue of "single source determinations," which in the current NSR and Title V permitting program is fraught with a great deal of confusing legal guidance and interpretation, particularly when two "separate" sources have an economic relationship with each other.

Replacement of BACT and LAER with the Tightening of NSPSs

Under the current CAA, triggering PSD for a major project (i.e., either a new major source or a major modification at an existing major source) requires that Best Available Control Technology (BACT) be imposed on those emission units that emit that pollutant (even in de minimis quantities), and where necessary, air quality modeling must be conducted to determine the effects on air quality resulting from that project's worst-case generation of that pollutant. Likewise, triggering NSR in NAAs requires that LAER be imposed on those emission units that emit that NAA pollutant, as well as the requirement to obtain emissions offsets, plus other requirements.

In the comprehensive strategy, in almost all cases, BACT and LAER should be replaced by BACT-like New Source Performance Standards (NSPS)[27] that are tightened every five years, an idea suggested by Colin Campbell and an idea that will play a very key role in the strategies developed in this book.[28,29] As will be discussed later in this chapter, it is more appropriate for expert environmental engineers at federal research centers and/or academia to make these NSPS determinations, using a disciplined Food and Drug Administration (FDA)-like approach.

As stated above, new and modified units should be required to meet an NSPS,[30] rather than LAER or BACT, which are currently determined uniquely for each subject unit through a very labor-intensive, time-consuming process (see Part 1). Some might argue that this relaxes current requirements under nonattainment area NSR, but in the end the pluses will outweigh the minuses. First, NSPSs will be revised for *all* new subject emission units and control technologies every five years by environmental research centers and/or academia. Under this new scheme, the tightened NSPSs will apply not only to units constructed or modified at major sources but also to *all* newly constructed units or modifications made to existing equipment (where an increase in hourly emissions occurs). All sources, *major and minor*, that wish to install a new boiler, for instance, must install the latest, modern boiler type that meets the most recently imposed standard.

Secondly, in those rare instances where the tightened NSPSs may not generally be as stringent as what LAER would be, the source in the NAA must nevertheless "pay" for this supposed "relaxation" in standards by having to purchase more trading units during periods of a declining cap.[31] Thus, it behooves the source to think and plan ahead for minimizing emissions.

One can think of emission unit performance standards as addressing more localized effects on human health and the welfare of Nature, so where global and regional strategies are not viable, say for regulating hydrogen sulfide, emission unit performance standards are the next best means to address localized impacts.

Thirdly, and this may come as a shock to readers, LAER and BACT, as tight emission rates, are actually over-rated. First, in the very early days of NSR the process and control technologies were not as well-developed as they are today, but over the years, the LAER and BACT rates determined by regulators have generally been leveling off. As a second point, the reader is urged to count the number of sources at the RACT/BACT/LAER Clearinghouse[32] that were required to obtain LAER and/or BACT in any given year; relative to the number of major sources in the United States, the number of determinations is minor.

As a result of revising and tightening NSPSs every five years, the need to expend precious regulatory resources around the country to determine LAER and/or BACT at subject sources will be virtually eliminated. This also reduces regulatory discretion and many redundant justifications for decisions made at the various state regulatory agencies. This innovation alone will save a significant amount of effort in developing project summaries and statements of bases (for Title V permits), which are just two of the many process-oriented contributors to the current bureaucratic logjam.

The Environmental Law Institute raised a point regarding the use of performance standards that is salient here.[33] They found that performance standards set too tight may only be met by one technology at the exclusion of other possible control technologies and where process designs stifle innovation. In brief, a company would be forced to use the default technology to meet what is in effect a specific technology standard rather than a performance standard. What nonpractitioners fail to appreciate is that each innovative technology carries with it unique regulatory scrutiny for purposes of operation, such as, testing, recordkeeping, and monitoring. From a practical standpoint, the drain on resources to develop these tailored requirements for each individual innovative technology would be significant. As a consequence, the feds should set a stringent enough standard that nevertheless supports innovation by allowing sources the flexibility to use a small number of distinctive technologies that meet the performance standard.

To briefly recap, we have seen how the strategy addresses fossil fuel-based carbon nationwide and how it should function for existing sources in NAAs and AAs; namely, rationing of fuels and external trading for NAA/adverse area pollutants emitted in major amounts and internal trading (PALs) otherwise. We have established pollutant thresholds for certain source categories in NAAs and AAs. We have also seen that, when properly addressed, more stringent NSPSs must replace BACT and LAER determinations. But how should an increase in emissions at major sources resulting from the construction of new units or the modification of existing units be addressed?

Construction of New Major Sources or Modifications at Existing Major Sources within Adverse Areas and AAs

Addressing demand-based and/or capacity-based growth in adverse areas (e.g., NAAs or acid rain-affected regions) is relatively straightforward under the comprehensive strategy. Whether that growth in the area is the result of demand-based or capacity-based emissions increases of one or more pollutants at existing major sources, or even due to new major sources proposing to construct in the adverse area, including an upwind location that significantly and adversely contributes to that area's health or welfare impacts, such sources must acquire the requisite number of trading units beforehand from sellers or from a pool of trading units that were set aside from reductions for just this purpose. If there are not enough trading units for the source to construct in the area, then that proposed source simply cannot locate there. Moreover, how construction of a new source that emits a given pollutant in major amounts, or a modification at a similar existing source, will or will not affect participation in a trading program should only depend on the existing ambient air quality for that pollutant and the increase in that pollutant's emissions. Lastly, construction in adverse areas requires that the proposed source utilize whatever current NSPSs apply for new emission units.

Alternatively, where TUs are not available for purchase, policymakers could certainly impose the requirement that, in adverse areas, proposed new sources must be redefined (i.e., a proposed coal-fired power plant to be sited in an adverse area can be redefined as a power plant of another type, such as wind, solar, etc.). It bears reiterating that because adverse areas identify as areas where detrimental health or welfare impacts occur, regulatorily, they should be treated as such with CDC-like urgency.

In any case, for proposed new combustion emission units at new major sources, existing major sources in nonattainment areas, or from those upwind sources located in AAs that contribute significantly to NAAs, the rules must require the use of the cleanest fuel regardless of cost.

As for attainment areas, can any proposed new source simply construct and consume as much clean air quality as it so desires? This question will be addressed as the comprehensive strategy is further developed, but to do so, a current component of NAA NSR and PSD must first be excised.

Along with seeking the reduction of the 250 tpy threshold to 200 tpy for many major sources in AAs, the complete elimination of significance thresholds[34] under NSR is proposed, be they for NAAs or AAs. For those who fear that this borders on environmental protection apostasy, note that significance thresholds have been a "fool's gold" requirement under NSR; that is, while seeming to be protective of air quality, in reality, the usefulness of significance thresholds to protecting the environment has been negligible and only contributes to bureaucratic pollution. Whenever air quality modeling is conducted for the pollutant where it is shown to exceed its significance threshold (but is below the major source threshold), in very rare cases does that modeling indicate that the pollutant's emissions will cause or contribute to adverse welfare and/or health impacts. In other words, in almost all cases there is a negligible modeled impact on the air quality resulting from the project for the subject "minor" pollutant. Thus, undertaking air quality modeling for the pollutant is nothing more than a formal but ineffectual hurdle that must be jumped only for legally mandated, procedural purposes.

When constructing a source that will emit one or more pollutants in major amounts in an AA, all that should really matter is what the existing concentrations for the subject pollutants at the source location are, what the source's projected emissions will be, and the source category that the source falls under.[35] *That is all that should really matter.*[36] While experience has shown that significance thresholds have little to no value in aiding regulators to protect the environment, appropriate backstops can still be built in.

Increment consumption[37] is one aspect that cannot and should not be eliminated from NSR for attainment areas. It is absolutely appropriate that applicants that propose to construct sources that may emit pollutants in major amounts, that is, over the applicable source threshold in an attainment area (i.e., either 100 or 200 tpy), be required to investigate the effect of the source's annual emissions on air quality. This is truly the backbone of the Prevention of Significant Deterioration of air quality and must be retained.

In an attainment area, regardless of its source threshold, an existing minor source will operate such that pollutant emissions are emitted in quantities that are under their respective PALs. These pollutant limits will be the minimum of either the pollutant's potential to emit (PTE) or its applicable source threshold (i.e., 100 tpy or 200 tpy). Likewise, for a source in a nonattainment area that emits the NAA pollutant in minor amounts, the source's PAL is also equal to the minimum of either the pollutant's PTE or its applicable source threshold (e.g., 25 tpy in a severe NAA).

If the source now wants to increase its emissions by demand-based growth (e.g., by adding a night shift using existing equipment), then it can increase its PAL, and if its PTE is greater than the source threshold, then it can take the limit of the source threshold. If the source seeks to increase emissions over its applicable source threshold by demand-based growth, the source must conduct air quality modeling to ensure that the PSD increment,[38] including the contribution of pollutant precursors (as applicable), is not consumed in the region. To avoid a source from gaming the system, it is allowed a one-time increase of its plantwide limit over the threshold for this pollutant over a ten-year period. This ten-year moratorium on expanding a source's PAL gives the source incentives to continually reduce emissions to remain under the PAL. Likewise, to avoid the situation where the source proposes absurd operating and production rates that allow for extreme open-ended operational flexibility, the emission rates corresponding to these same operating and production rates must be modeled against the allowed increment consumption for the applicable attainment area pollutants.

Likewise, for increases due to capacity-based growth (e.g., by adding new units or modifying existing units where there is an increase in overall emissions), if the source in an attainment area wishes to increase its PAL where that PAL already exceeds its assigned source threshold for that pollutant, then it must also conduct air quality modeling to ensure that the allowable increment for the area is not consumed.

Of course, if the minor source is in a nonattainment area for a subject NAA pollutant and it seeks to increase its PAL above the major source threshold (e.g., 50 tpy in a serious NAA), it will have to participate in the external trading program for that pollutant by purchasing TUs for the whole amount of its emissions, not just the amount over the threshold. And if there are no TUs available for purchase, the increase over the threshold is not allowed.

In general, then, if the source's PTE for a pollutant is below that pollutant's threshold, it can only take its PAL equal to the pollutant's PTE. If the source will emit one or more pollutants—for which actual emissions are emitted in major quantities—it will be required to conduct air quality modeling, including the amount of PSD increment consumed, if the source cannot accept the source threshold as its PAL. Naturally, new large-emitting sources constructing in attainment areas would be allowed to take a PAL limit if they truly have the potential to emit at or above the applicable source threshold, but they would still have to conduct modeling to determine how much increment is consumed, much like the case today.

Lastly, for very small sources, state regulators will determine (through state-based regulations) the de minimis threshold under which small sources would require permitting. For example, regulators could propose that very little or no pre-construction approval would be required for a project where (i) the NAAQS is far from being threatened for subject pollutants, (ii) no HAPs are to be emitted, and (iii) the proposed source's PTE for each pollutant is less than or equal to 20 tpy.

Clearly, very minor sources should be at the low end of the sources-to-be-regulated hierarchy via permitting and inspections, while the lowest of the low should only be required to register.

Sample Scenarios

Several instructive cases follow that will clarify for the reader how the regulatory strategy developed so far would apply to sources. In each scenario, a source's regulatory status is determined simply by (1) the NAA or AA status where the source is located and (2) the pollutants that it emits in major and/or minor quantities. For the sake of simplicity, GHG emissions are ignored, but they could easily be incorporated into the discussion.

I. For New Sources:

   a. A new source is proposed to be constructed in an ozone nonattainment area, where the NAA threshold is 100 tpy. The proposed source will only emit NOx in major quantities, with all other pollutants emitting at the following PTEs: 41 tpy for CO,[39] 11 tpy for VOC, 3 tpy for SO_2, and 8 tpy for $PM_{10}/PM_{2.5}$. Note that NOx is a precursor to the creation of ozone in the lower atmosphere.

Assuming the proposed source meets all other compliance requirements and conditions for issuance of a permit (e.g., meeting New "Unit" Performance Standards and state rules), the source must later participate in the regional external trading program for NOx emissions. As such, it must, as one prerequisite to permit issuance, acquire NOx trading units from existing sources in the NAA prior to construction and in perpetuity, cognizant of the future tightening of the regional cap, until attainment is reached. The source will accept PALs for its other pollutants equal to their respective PTEs (i.e., 41 tpy for CO, 11 tpy for VOC, 3 tpy for SO_2, and 8 tpy for $PM_{10}/PM_{2.5}$).

b. A new natural gas-fired combined cycle turbine power plant is proposed to be constructed in an ozone nonattainment area. The proposed source will only emit NOx and CO in major quantities and all other pollutants in quantities each less than 90 tpy.

This situation is very similar to (a) above (having to secure NOx TUs from existing sources in the NAA before construction of the source) except that the source must also conduct air quality modeling for CO because it would be a major source named as one of the twenty-six "dirty" categories where the threshold in an AA is 100 tpy. The source will accept PALs equal to the PTEs for the other pollutants.

c. A new source is proposed to be constructed in an SO_2 nonattainment area, where all the pollutant emissions will be emitted in minor quantities.

The source will simply take PALs equal to the PTEs for each pollutant since the PTEs for these pollutants are each below their respective applicable source thresholds.

II. For existing sources:

a. Six years later, the now existing source in (I)(b) wants to add a new emission unit that will emit modestly more NOx, CO, and other pollutants at the source. The current actual emissions from the source are such that it should be able to absorb the NOx emissions into its current allotment (e.g., by having initially purchased NOx trading units from a shutdown facility already), but the proposed higher level of CO emissions is projected to exceed the source's existing PAL limitations.

The source must maintain its current PTE for CO emissions since it must wait ten years to raise its PTE in the attainment area for CO. For pollutants such as VOC, $PM_{10}/PM_{2.5}$, and SO_2, the source will simply bump up their PAL limits to their new PTE levels if they each remain below 100 tpy.

b. An old, existing source that emits all pollutants below 100 tpy has seen its NOx emissions rising to that threshold. Seeing that its auxiliary boiler is over 50 years old, it proposes to replace it with another auxiliary boiler of the same size but will be subject to the New Unit Performance Standards for industrial boilers.

Being a more efficient boiler with a tighter NOx standard, it will allow the source to operate comfortably with the lower PTE.

Hopefully, these examples provide the reader with a feel for how the strategy would address new projects. A summary of the regulatory strategy is provided in Table 4.2.

We have seen that the comprehensive strategy, in effect, establishes more straightforward criteria to directly address air quality impacts, including those

Table 4.2 Summary of Regulatory Elements of the Comprehensive Strategy

		Required Action or Limitation	
Pollutant Emission Amounts	**Regional Pollutant Status**	**During Operation**	**Upon Constructing a New Source or Making Modifications at an Existing Source**
Major	NAA[a]	Must trade NAA pollutant in the region	Must purchase trading units
	AA	Must take PAL	If Sourcewide Pollutant PTE < ST[b], then PAL = PTE; Otherwise, accept either PAL = ST or PAL = PTE > ST, but this requires modeling & increment consumption[c]
Minor	NAA[a]	Must take PAL in NAA pollutant; no trading	
	AA	Must take a PAL for each AA pollutant	

a. Here NAA is generally meant to be any adverse region.
b. ST is the applicable source threshold for a pollutant emitted in major amounts.
c. Increasing the PAL when over the ST is allowed only once every ten years.

resulting from new constructions and modifications. This is in contrast to utilizing the convoluted, process-based components of the existing SIP and NSR programs. While there will be essential aspects of NSR that will and should be kept and other aspects that will be eliminated, what replaces it should be as good if not better with regard to environmental protection. This is true if only because what does replace it is more tailored to its underlying goal of mitigating the air quality health and welfare impacts in adverse areas and preventing significant deterioration of air quality in AAs.

This section provided the blueprint of the strategy where air quality is most effectively and efficiently regulated. However, an optimal program also includes identifying the most appropriate division of labor, namely who should do what.

Division of Labor

We now turn to the associated roles of the critical participants: this includes the tasks of the feds and states, academia and environmental research centers, and in terms of human resources, the roles of the regulatory engineers and legal staff.

The Role of the Feds and the States

The feds should only regulate the interstate sources that they are capable of regulating and only those pollutants that cause downwind impacts. If SO_2 and NOx are the only pollutants causing such downwind impacts, then the feds should only regulate those pollutants—while the states regulate the other pollutants at those same sources.[40]

Clearly, the workload of the USEPA will increase significantly. An obvious prerequisite for success here is that there be sufficient fees collected and resources allocated to accomplish the tasks. Otherwise, asking the USEPA to do the heavy lifting of regulating the major interstate polluters may be biting off way more than they can chew. Also, to ensure that possible but improbable regulatory capture does not occur at the federal level, states should still maintain adequate backup oversight of the program. Sources that do not contribute significantly to local NAAs but to acid rain only should still participate pursuant to the above strategy. The caveat to this scheme is that the feds should have the capability to undertake this added responsibility and that the loss of funds to the states does not hamper their ability to regulate the other sources within their jurisdiction. If robbing Peter (i.e., the states) to pay Paul (the feds) causes a problem for Peter, then a more equitable program must be developed.

Nevertheless, having the feds and the states oversee large interstate-polluting sources is appealing. The long, drawn-out SIP process that states conduct can in part be replaced by external trading at the level of the USEPA for these sources. Team effort, however, is essential if for no other reason than the likely resource constraints at the state level make it so.

The Role of Academia and Environmental Research Centers

Although the feds will have less of a role in the SIP process under the comprehensive strategy, they can play a more pivotal role elsewhere within the new strategy by focusing on the more technical aspects of AQM for stationary sources. For example, federal academic and environmental research centers should determine and tighten NSPS/NUPS every five years[41,42] as a replacement for LAER and BACT, since these determinations should be left to technical specialists.

These tasks must be conducted to minimize discretionary technical decisions made by regulators throughout the country. The process of determining BACT or LAER is, for the most part, rigorous, but the process nevertheless requires justification and substantiation. States making these "rigorous discretionary decisions" require bureaucratic pollution to support oftentimes controversial technical decisions. Leaving these determinations to academia and/or environmental research centers, in what should properly be conducted in a disciplined FDA-like process, provides the necessary rigor citizens expect.[43]

Currently, when a permit application that triggers NSR is submitted where the demonstration of Best Available Control Technology (BACT) and/or Lowest Achievable Emission Rate (LAER) is required, state regulators must spend a great deal of time and effort to make determinations of BACT and/or LAER for each subject pollutant emitted from each emission unit subject to NSR.[44] For major projects (e.g., chemical manufacturing, refineries, integrated steel manufacturing), this review sometimes requires making determinations for many pollutants emitted from several emission units for the proposed major new source or modification at an existing major source. On top of that, an air quality impact analysis must be performed for the project's AA pollutants, not to mention other numerous necessary collateral tasks associated with the review.

There should be no reason why state, county, or municipal environmental protection agencies should be conducting essentially the same LAER/BACT determinations when many of them are redundant. An excellent argument for why the responsibility should be shifted from state and municipal regulators to academia and/or applied environmental research centers is the bureaucratic hurdles associated with determining Best Available Control Technology for Carbon Capture and Storage (CCS)[45]—as a potential control "device" for the capture and control (actually sent far underground) of carbon dioxide from exhaust gases. A number of applicants throughout the country have applied for a PSD permit where they have to demonstrate (yet again and again for each new application where GHG emissions are major) that CCS is not feasible and, where it is, showing that CCS is not cost-effective for a proposed plant's emissions of CO_2 (e.g., from a natural gas-fired combined cycle power plant). The current PSD rules dictate that this demonstration be conducted. Inevitably it is shown, yet again, after a great deal of time, effort, and expense (*as much for the regulators* to review as for the applicant to conduct), that CCS is not technically feasible and, where feasible, cost-effective. The various state regulatory agencies scattered across the United States would be better off if these redundant detailed determinations were made by experts in academically affiliated environmental research centers. Must the current requirements of the detailed, legalistic, procedure-oriented process be strictly followed when the obvious engineering facts on the ground (i.e., that CCS is infeasible) are already known beforehand?

More problematically, where there is otherwise no reason to do so, a determination of BACT in one region can be more lenient than the determination of BACT in another region for the same type of unit. This arbitrariness is a definite inequity of the process. Having academia and research centers revise these standards every five years to be more stringent based on state-of-the-art technology is why BACT and LAER can be scrapped. Since BACT and LAER are only determined at a relatively small fraction of major sources nationwide per year anyway, why eat up so much time making these determinations when a tightening of NUPSs can be utilized instead (and which applies to *all* sources that use such a technology). And where there would be regional operational differences for the same type of equipment that would create varying emission rates, e.g., the sulfur content of natural gas varying around the country, states could seek exceptions from what would be the fed's base-case determination of NUPS.

Thus, it would be best to let state and local engineers at regulatory agencies focus on determination methods for a source's emissions within their permits and conducting inspections at those sources. Centralizing technical determinations to the feds and avoiding redundancies, inequities, discretion, and controversy at the state level is imperative.

Environmental research centers, including those affiliated with academia, would directly target their applied research to solving immediate problems rather than being theoreticians competitively applying for research grants. They would perform multiple functions:

- Determining Maximum Achievable Control Technology (MACT) standards
- Conducting technology verification studies[46]
- Overseeing emission testing and emission factor development
- Approving innovative technologies[47]
- Determining the optimal combination of ambient monitoring and air quality modeling to use to achieve air quality goals
- Overseeing the role and development of air pollution models
- Developing new or alternative emission test methods
- Determining what qualifies as routine maintenance, repair, or replacement for various industrial source categories
- Etc.[48]

Leaving the heavy lifting of technology determination to the feds/research centers while leaving the administrative tasks to the states, thereby eliminating redundancies, should significantly simplify the practice of regulating pollution generated from stationary sources and would do so for the better.

The Role of the Regulatory Engineering and Legal Staff

Sorting out how the roles of engineers and lawyers fit into the strategy is briefly discussed here. While engineers will continue to play key roles in permitting, inspecting, monitoring, etc., there should be much more focus of engineering expertise on intensive inspections. The Government Accountability Office (GAO) report cited in the last chapter speaks to this issue by stating that intensive rather than routine inspections uncover substantive violations.

For their part, lawyers should focus much more of their efforts on developing permits. More will be said about this when Design Flaw #4 is addressed in more detail in the next section.

Correcting the Inherent Design Flaws

It is worth recalling the question posed in Chapter 2: *What is the absolute minimum amount of necessary regulations, requirements, and procedures that must be imposed within the regulatory process to achieve its necessary outcomes?* Addressing the design flaws below will make answering this question much easier. While the deeply rooted design flaws discussed in Chapter 2 will not be trivial to excise from the practice of the US AQM program, they must still be aggressively addressed.

Addressing Design Flaw #1: The Sluggish Emission Reduction Process

Since the strategy developed to this point effectively addresses Design Flaw #1, its key aspects will be briefly reiterated and summarized here: utilize a streamlined, results-oriented scheme that includes an external (*inter*source) trading program between sources within adverse areas (e.g., NAA and acid rain-impacting) for pollutants emitted in major quantities (including grandfathered sources), which sets hard quantitative milestone goals, rather than using risk-averse, baby-step regulation within a long, drawn-out, labor-intensive SIP process. For everything else, internal (*intra*source) trading under a sourcewide PAL by sources is utilized. In this way, NAAQS violating/health- and/or welfare-impacted nonattainment areas must be addressed more in a CDC-like fashion. Also included is a streamlined but effective pre-construction NSR program.

Also, stringent NSPS-as-BACT/LAER determinations would be made by technology experts at the federal level at research centers and academia, following in the mold of the FDA whereby medicines are approved at the federal level. To optimally redistribute expertise, the feds and states will have their defined roles while engineers and attorneys will have theirs.

Addressing Design Flaw #2: Complicated Rules and Requirements

The second major design flaw involves the complexity of rules imposed by the regulatory food chain (RFC) itself and the responsibility put onto the thousands of downstream "consumers" (e.g., permit writers, field engineers, environmental attorneys, regulated sources, and the public itself). Economists would identify this situation as an externality: decision makers and rule writers privatize the benefit of dictating the rules while socializing the costs to those downstream consumers by saddling them with an extremely complex regulatory system.

First, as a preliminary matter, it is worthwhile to refer again to Coglianese, cited in Chapter 2, who made the observation that based on an EPA study, only a fraction of regulations were actually beneficial. With that in mind, if a 96 percent reduction in SO_2 emissions is achieved by six pages of streamlined, easy-to-understand regulations, whereas thirty pages of very complicated regulations are projected to achieve a 97 percent reduction, which is more preferable? This is more than a hypothetical question.[49] The reader is urged to mull this over, particularly if required SO_2 external trading with a declining cap can pick up where this regulatory "relaxation" leaves off.

Complicating the complexity issue further are confusing rules that require interpretations by layers of bureaucratic review. One can think of these interpretations as the legal equivalent of imprecise engineering measurements. Obviously, such rule interpretations must be kept to a minimum.

Engineers and lawyers helped to design the current crop of complex regulations, so it only seems reasonable for more insightful engineers and lawyers to redesign them.[50] Taking this a step further, the comprehensive strategy optimally redesigns the broad regulatory umbrella of the AQM program for stationary sources, and we saw earlier in Part 1 that Giles postulated the redesign of environmental rules themselves so that compliance is built into them and making compliance the default option.[51] Wherever and however possible, her proposals must be incorporated. Speaking from her years of experience, Giles exhorts that "The belief that most companies comply, and that noncompliance should be left to enforcers, has been stubbornly persistent, despite the reality that serious violations are common, and the design of the environmental rules themselves is the main driver of good, or bad, performance."[52] If we simply assume that rules will automatically elicit compliance, then, according to Giles, "we will continue to suffer from pervasive violations."[53]

There are solutions, however. The place to start is by "internalizing the externalities." Here, a convenient analogy that the environmental community is quite familiar with will be instructive. Years ago, in the old days of beverage can manufacture, the can's pull-off top was tossed aside, creating not just a simple litter problem but also a public hazard for people walking on their bare feet (i.e., getting cut by the sharp edge of the tab lying on the ground). In fact, it was the *ingestion* of pull-off tabs that led an engineer at Reynolds Metals to develop a patent for stay-on tabs—whereby the externality of the fugitive pull-off tab would be internalized onto the can itself.[54]

Much like the externalized hazards of the pull-off tabs, the externalized hazard of rule complexity (and by extension, regulatory process complexity) is felt by the people forced to interpret, impose and implement those rules. Naturally then, the solution to the second design flaw is for the people who write the rules to internalize the externality. It probably borders on heresy to say it, but rule writers should be the first ones on the firing line to test/implement *other rule writers'* rules (i.e., not their own). This would significantly reduce the burden imposed on the people who interpret, impose and implement those rules down the chain.

For these rule writers to determine how user-friendly their rules are, it is not enough to develop a permit, provide rule interpretations for company personnel, or explain it to the public *just once*. Anybody can write a Title V permit with two or three applicable, complex NSPSs and/or National Emission Standards for Hazardous Air Pollutants (NESHAPs) and a long detailed Statement of Basis, but the real acid test is doing this *several times over*, finalized within established timeframes amid other required duties, all done without flinching to criticism, burning out, or applying for a job transfer.

> A fact of life in the regulatory trenches is that it is difficult to develop complicated permits and their supporting documentation from scratch but extremely easy to criticize how they were written.

For the RFC to fully grasp the scale of the problem, several such permits, rule interpretation discussions, etc., must be conducted and completed.

The point here is this: by internalizing the externalities, not only will the rule writers feel the confusion and frustration inflicted on others downstream in the process, but more significantly, they will no doubt *reinvent/redesign the process*,[55] hopefully by downsizing the requirements within the rule, the supporting documents, procedures, etc. Would any of these proposed changes ever happen if the lowly permit and rule-writing staff engineers and attorneys at the state level made the request up the chain of command? The answer is an obvious no. That is why the design flaw has to be corrected *at the point of origination*. Do that and this contribution to the bureaucratic logjam will significantly ease.

The downstream rule interpreters should likewise be included in the process, a point Giles reinforces in her book as it relates to rule writers within the USEPA who should listen to their fellow enforcement attorneys' suggestions regarding Next Gen. Is it logical under a "Design, Build, Operate" paradigm for the builder of a refinery to take on the design and build responsibilities while handing the metaphorical keys over to the refinery personnel to take on the refinery's operational responsibility? Obviously no, because those who operate a refinery should also be included in the design and build aspects in order to identify problems and resolve them before full-scale transfer and operation.

It should be noted that no less than the Congressional Research Service report (Copeland, cited in Chapter 2) addressed the complexity and implementation issues associated with Title V permitting, but it did not appear that the USEPA has yet to take advantage of the opportunity to correct those flaws. If they had done so, it is certainly not at all obvious. Reducing the complexities of the Quad-Letter NSPSs, limiting the requirement for excess and needless information in Statement of Bases (SoBs),[56] and more, should be priority goals. Clearly, policymakers have wasted a major opportunity to simplify bureaucratic logjam-creating rules, regulations, and procedures for the sake of improving effectiveness.

Some further commentary follows on the need for simplifying the process as it relates to excess complexity:

1. Given that rule writers form a kind of monopsony, what if there was competition for rule writers to develop rules, *as if their livelihoods depended on it*, and which achieved the same environmental results but did so with much less rule complexity? It should not be forgotten that because simpler rules are easier to implement and thus provide a greater likelihood to achieve intended outcomes, regulatory simplification is as much a benefit for the environment as it is for the public/taxpayers, regulators, and the regulated. Most importantly, regulations should be written so that the public can understand them. Compliance effectiveness of, and simplicity in, the writing of rules to achieve intended outcomes should be the only presiding value that matters.
2. Due to the historical development of inflexible and obsolescent rules that atrophy over the years, mandatory evaluation of some or all environmental laws and regulations is an idea worth exploring. Evaluation would occur every ten years by asking what works and what doesn't, what have been the loopholes, what parts and sections create constant headaches, and where are they confusing and least effective, etc. One principal problem holding back reform of AQM in the United States is this: because backsliding is to be avoided at all costs, major and minor rules and regulations are virtually locked into place in perpetuity

irrespective of effectiveness, preventing their potential reform based on ongoing practice and experience. With proper checks and balances, evaluating rules every ten years, for instance, would facilitate replacing poorly designed laws and regulations with better ones. For example, it goes without saying that MACT standards should be simplified by collapsing them into NSPSs wherever possible to minimize the current hassle of separate NSPS and NESHAP rules applying for the same type of emission unit within a given source category.

3. What simplification giveth away, external trading in adverse areas and stack testing can taketh back. A well-designed trading scheme supplements the process of source-specific regulation in adverse areas. Thus, where rule simplification may possibly threaten deterioration of air quality in adverse areas, an external trading system in NAAs can be used to offset this by tightening the regional cap; whereas in attainment areas, simplification and growth in emissions are slowed and offset by requiring modeling to ensure that significant deterioration of air quality is minimized.
4. If necessary, the "translation" of rules and regulations into plain language should be outsourced to neutral experts/observers, so that everybody can interpret them, not just the people who wrote them.
5. To simplify the understanding of the regulations, corresponding flowcharts should be required. Pictures speak louder than words.

As we've seen, a chunk of the bureaucratic logjam is due to an underlying hierarchical culture in rulemaking and implementation wherein a small group high up the regulatory food chain dictates what items to carry, leaving the downstream pack mules to carry the heavy load. If, in the hierarchical process of writing rules, creating numerous complicated legal guidance and regulatory interpretation documents, etc., the people at the top strongly resist internalizing the externalities that they pass on to those down the chain, then the underlying cultural flaw is clear. Regulating the generation of environmental pollution should not be subordinated to the preservation of a hierarchical culture.

Addressing Design Flaw #3: Multiple Bureaucratic Procedures

The third design flaw was the proliferation of procedural or bureaucratic pollution, namely the multiple bureaucratic procedures created and imposed by the regulatory food chain onto the downstream pack mules.

Bureaucracies bureaucratize such that procedures grow exponentially while the workforce grows linearly, if it grows at all. In fact, during recessionary times, budget cutbacks, or post-covid, the workforce decreased in numbers while the complexities of the system either remained or continued to grow.

To resolve the proliferation of bureaucratic pollution, regulatory agencies should be required to undergo Kaizen review of operations every few years, just to ensure that growth in regulatory and bureaucratic pollution does not run amok, that is, creep back to nonattainment. Instead, or in addition, managers should be required to obtain Kaizen or Six Sigma certification to prevent that same kind of growth.

In addition, in terms of bureaucracy, and its tendency for unchecked growth, "bureaucracy monitors" should be installed at the state and national levels; their function—to put a check on such growth. As ludicrous as this may sound to some, particularly those high up the RFC, this is a serious suggestion. At the national level, this independent authority can be called the Inspector General of Bureaucracy. His or her task would be to monitor the functioning of the bureaucracy, help resolve complaints from the downstream regulatory practitioner community, anonymously if necessary. Most importantly, this authority must keep its eye on the overall goal at all times and not be distracted or corrupted. The Inspector General must act as the natural prey to the invasive species of excess bureaucracy. Currently, managers who supposedly monitor workload and procedures too often fail to observe the parasitic effects on results due to bureaucratic creep.[57]

Addressing Design Flaw #4: Misapplication of Labor

The fourth design flaw was the overreliance on engineers for much of the pack mule labor and the underapplied talent of staff attorneys.

Rather than staff attorneys passively waiting for permit engineers and inspectors to feed them enforcement cases, the regulatory legal staff can become proactive problem solvers by utilizing more of their muscle within the new strategy. Rather than Next Gen being just an abstract concept, regulatory attorneys, environmental lawyers, and legal scholars, with the assistance of the USEPA, should develop an extensive compendium of real-world Next Gen regulations and concepts that can be used "in the field." The goal is for Next Gen principles to build compliance into the "upstream" rules rather than relying on "downstream" enforcement.

AQM is also overreliant on permit engineers to develop permits when lawyers should be playing a more active role in their development. Permits today, particularly Title V permits, contain technical information and regulatory requirements that are nevertheless *legal* documents written by engineers, whereby developing many of the more complicated and controversial ones is characterized by an oftentimes tortuous process up to the point of issuance or denial. The fact that engineers develop legal documents should be a red flag that something is fundamentally flawed. Why? As legal documents, permits should be treated and written as such, preferably without the incomprehensible legalese. A newer revised AQM program should engage attorneys more in the crafting of permits and consequently participate in the accountable process of issuing them. Attorneys have crafted sophisticated conditions in Consent Decrees, so why not permits as well? Asking non-attorneys to craft legal documents in their entirety, as they do now, naturally subjecting these non-attorneys to second guessing later, is clearly suboptimal and thus not what works best to achieve sustainability with Nature.

In the many years of taking multiple enforcement actions at the national level and writing Title V permits for tribal lands, the USEPA has not yet developed for permit writers a "Permit Language Condition Manual": a proven compendium of "canned" permit language that is battle-tested, appeal-proof, and lawsuit-resistant. Attorneys, particularly those federal and state-level enforcement attorneys with significant institutional knowledge, should be tasked with developing such a manual with national application based on their enforcement experience.[58] But this invitation is also left open for all environmental lawyers, academic and otherwise, who are truly committed to protecting and remediating the environment. The goal is for lawyers to play a more proactive role in the permitting process by preemptively crafting enforceably airtight permit language (in Plain English, of course). Thus, if seven out of every ten critical permit conditions are boilerplate, and the other three are written to support the technical requirements on a source-specific basis by engineers around legally approved language, then permit-writing becomes far more efficient and the permits themselves stronger to enforce, thereby allowing engineers more time to focus their efforts on what they do best.

Since regulated sources appreciate certainty, here is a worthy proposal from Schakenbach, Vollaro, and Forte:

> Automatic penalties built into a statute or regulation can reduce the burden on any implementing agency by decreasing the amount of discretion allowed in calculating penalties and by reducing the amount of time adjudicating them.[59]

Thus, attorneys should develop "certainty guidelines" for regulated entities, such as categories of violations and penalties based on deviations, excursions, minor violations, etc. In the spirit of Schakenbach et al., enforcement attorneys should specify the relationship between violations and penalties: to wit, *if a source commits this particular violation, then this will be the specific penalty.* Doing so would help to facilitate compliance as the default option for sources, as noted by Giles with regard to the success of the Acid Rain Program. Transparency is just good policy. Regulators providing certainty only *after* a violation has occurred, that is, regulating by enforcement, only facilitates resentment when cooperation is necessary.

Addressing Design Flaw #5: Minimal Inclusion of the Public

The fifth design flaw was neglecting the more proactive inclusion of the general public within the AQM process. Information is the God Particle of environmental pollution protection, so providing all critically relevant information to the public is critical to that end. Applying transparency on polluters is a regulator-imposed "work practice" that can only help to reduce pollution at those sources; even though a source may be in compliance, disclosure of information may encourage sources to further reduce emissions and discharges. Overwhelming the public with arcane techno- and regulatory-babble does not do that. Better would be to post online all the relevant information that the public really should and wants to know. Included on such a digital information agency dashboard, among a multitude of possibilities, should be information regarding source emissions data (e.g., annual emissions, stack testing results) as well as what the regulatory agency's responsibilities and limitations are and are not.[60] Since it is their air being polluted, after all, a well-structured survey of the public would help to elicit what information should be provided on the dashboard.

With regard to correcting the above design flaws, a word of advice is in order—if there is ever the possibility that a blue ribbon panel were to look further into fixing these and other design flaws and problems, take notice as to how many of the panel members are selected from management and how many are actual ground-level practitioners. Managers, particularly those who have written few, if any complex permits and Statement of Bases/Project Summaries or inspected complex sources, should be excluded from this panel. Bureaucracies bureaucratize, so managers are likely to never surrender their power and admit failure by being asked to correct the design flaws that they played a key role in creating or perpetuating. With nonpractitioners on the panel, cosmetic changes (e.g., "reorganizations") are more likely.

Truly environmentally conscious reformers in the United States have to be vigilant to see that the process is corrected to the final endpoint. Reformers should not let people who are incapable of putting chalk to blackboard to solve complex problems. Before reinventing regulation, then, policymakers must reinvent the regulatory process itself. To allow them to simply reconstitute existing or incorporate other design flaws in the future will only handicap the process further. At the risk of redundancy, that's why it is a good idea to first seek consensus on what comprises an optimal strategy before anyone acts on reform.

Key Issues

The Trading Scheme

Based on their research on cap-and-trade, Schmalensee and Stavins concluded that "cap-and-trade systems, if well designed and appropriately implemented, can achieve their core objective of meeting targeted emissions reductions cost-effectively."[61] While the basics and actual mechanics of the external emissions trading scheme will not be discussed in detail here—leaving those fine-tuned details to designers later—the reader is encouraged to review the informative USEPA and Resources for the Future reports, both cited in Chapter 2.

Instead, the big picture focus of the external trading program here will be on stationary sources that emit pollutants in major amounts in adverse areas, namely those that have not attained the National Ambient Air Quality Standards for that pollutant. Let's say that a source is located in a moderate ozone nonattainment area and has actual emissions of 400 tpy each for nitrogen oxides (NOx), volatile organic compounds (VOC), carbon monoxide (CO), and sulfur dioxide (SO_2), and negligible emissions of particulate $matter_{10}$ (PM_{10}). The source would be subject to the trading program for NOx and VOC (as ozone precursors), while CO, SO_2, and PM_{10} would be subject to a Plantwide Applicability Limitation (PAL) because they are attainment area pollutants that presumably do not contribute significantly to downwind NAAs.[62] If the source chooses to expand, it must purchase TUs for NOx and VOC while increasing the PALs for the AA pollutants but also requiring that CO and SO_2 undergo modeling to determine whether the NAAQS will be violated for each, and further determining whether PSD increment for SO_2 will be consumed.

When it's time to develop baselines for the trading scheme, sources must use actual compliant emissions typically from the previous two years prior to initiation of the program. Upon program initiation, sources must thereafter utilize the same methodology to determine their generated emissions as they had for their baseline. Thus, one key ground rule of the program must be that sources will only have one "bite at the apple" to determine their baseline. This is because if regulators blindly accept source data, sources may later undercount emissions, whereby they would not have to purchase as many allowances as necessary during reconciliation. Worse yet, sources could be sellers in the market when in fact they may need to be buyers. In addition, as the program progresses, it is not unusual for sources to mysteriously "find" hidden emissions they did not know they had for some of their emission units. Under the Santiago trading program for PM_{10},[63] the reality was that some companies learned they had to revise previous years' annual emission reports because they found they had missing or undercounted emissions (which may have then subjected them to an enforcement action) within their baseline determination. Thus, sources that later renege on that one bite must suffer the consequences, so getting the baseline right the first and only time is important not only for source participants but for the integrity of the trading program.

To ensure further integrity of the program, certified sustainability accountants must put their imprimatur on emissions determination and verification. When it comes to undercounting within an ironclad trading program, there's nothing quite like the embarrassment of a company (including its shareholders) having to buy Trading Units until attainment is achieved that they could have claimed as theirs when calculating its baseline or, where there are no TUs to acquire, having to pay significant Trading Unit (TU) deficiency penalties. To add injury to insult, sources that are discovered later to have undercounted their emissions must be penalized not just for noncompliance to the rules but possibly for certification-of-compliance fraud.

Next, for each nonattainment area pollutant emitted in major quantities, sources would obtain an allotment based on their actual emission rates over a previous timeframe. In determining baseline allotments, actual emissions must be adjusted for any noncompliance (including accidental releases) and for any revisions due to rule applicability, either of which occurred since the beginning of the lookback period. If regulators choose not to penalize the generation of noncompliant emissions after startup of the trading program, they could instead require that both compliant and noncompliant emissions be included in the total generated emissions as the trading program proceeds, which would require obtaining the acquisition of TUs to reconcile emissions generated at the source. In effect, the cost of reconciling noncompliance through the prices of TUs would substitute for the penalties they would otherwise have to pay.

So that those companies that had already made pre-program voluntary reductions are not penalized, two possible options for them are to (1) allow them to reduce emissions at a much slower rate (say by 1 percent per trading period rather than 3 percent for other participants) or (2) delay their entry into the program until other sources catch up with their reductions.

One can loosely think of the trading allotments that a source is required to hold as a de facto sourcewide emission limit for the source. This limit consolidates many regulatory requirements into one hard and fast number. As such, sources would have to be aware that, as a consolidated limit, it should likewise engender a great deal of consolidated "enforcement significance."

If companies do not make any changes to their emission units once the external trading program is up and running, then all they have to do is determine what their emissions were during the past time period and see whether they are above or below their current allotment. That's straightforward enough.

It should be noted that where emissions occur outside "normal" operation, such as during startup, shutdown, and malfunction (SSM) where they are not addressed separately, they could be addressed within a trading program by one of two options. Where a CEMS is not used, companies could simply use brute force to measure and/or stack test the emissions for units during these scenarios or, as an alternative, accept a Next Gen-like reasonably underestimated rate that counts as part of their initial allotment, while reporting a higher estimated amount thereafter, thereby building in a conservative emissions determination. Regulators also have the option of treating SSM emissions separately within a Work Practices Unit to be discussed later.

Lastly, a way to incorporate technological innovation into the process, long advocated by many authors in the literature, is to first incorporate a regional limit and external trading along with a first-time, sharp decline in that initial regional emissions cap. This is to be followed by a gradually decreasing cap thereafter to allow companies to prepare years ahead of time to seek innovative technologies that later meet tightened NUPSs should they need to replace emission units to meet their future allotment.[64]

Which Pollutants Should Be Externally Traded, When Possible?

To this point, the trading program has been discussed without identifying which pollutants should be subject to trading. One of trading's key advantages is that it exploits the unique fungibility of plentiful emissions for various types of air pollutants.

As stated earlier, an optimal strategy should treat greenhouse gases as a global "climate stability" nonattainment area pollutant, which can best be addressed via the global mitigation strategy in Chapter 9. Limiting the use of fossil fuels will also have the collateral benefit of reducing emissions of pollutants other than GHG. So where these other emissions are still problematic, at the back end, the correct approach will be to regionally trade those pollutants that cause adverse effects. Generally speaking, NOx, SO_2, VOC, and $PM_{10}/PM_{2.5}$ are stronger candidates as tradable pollutants, while pollutants such as PM, CO, H_2S, and individual hazardous air pollutants (HAP)[65] may better be addressed by the next best alternative—performance standards.[66]

Regulating both filterable PM and total $PM_{10}/PM_{2.5}$ (i.e., both filterables and condensables) is currently cumbersome and prone to confusion and error. In general, large filterable PM (think dust) shouldn't be traded since it is too prevalent (e.g., dust coming off raw mills and feed dryers), more diffusely generated, and difficult to quantify. Since the regulation of filterable PM from process operations would be mixed in with combustion-generated PM, it would be more appropriate for combustion-generated PM to be limited by fuel rationing at the front end as well as by equipment performance standards, while process-generated PM is best addressed by performance standards. Virtually unquantifiable PM such as fugitive dust from haul roads, etc., is best addressed by stringent fugitive dust plans.

While $PM_{10}/PM_{2.5}$ emissions are typically condensable particulate matter resulting from combustion, trading combustion-generated $PM_{10}/PM_{2.5}$ is certainly possible. While PM_{10} trading has been tried in Chile, few readers may not be aware that particulate trading is being tried in India.[67]

CO should not be traded because the bulk of these emissions are generated by mobile sources, the pollution from which is best addressed first by limiting fossil fuels and requiring engine performance standards be met. Nevertheless, where practical, nothing stops regulators from trading CO in a CO NAA if they so wish.

How Would Permitting and Essential Functions Change under the New Scheme?

Obviously, there will be more to the external and internal trading programs than what has been discussed here thus far, such as the market dynamics associated with external trading. Of course, to make the program functional, a different type of permitting regime will have to be developed and implemented.

While under the strategy, the legal staff must collaborate far more with permit engineers (e.g., providing appeal-proof language), permit engineers will continue to issue construction permits for new emission units and physical modifications, applying appropriate emission standards, recordkeeping, reporting, and other necessary requirements into the permit. Included in the permit will be PAL limits where applicable, but for pollutants subject to external trading, potential quantities of material usage, operating and production rates,[68] and the methodology of calculating emissions, so as to reconcile emissions to the source-specific allotment based on "measure, count, regulate."

Unlike the Title V program under the current Clean Air Act, within the comprehensive strategy it is not necessarily critical that an overriding, always up-to-date operating permit be required for major sources. Up to a certain point, one large comprehensive permit becomes extremely unwieldy, particularly for an integrated source like a refinery that undergoes many changes in one year alone. One essential aspect of permitting for the large major sources is to avoid constant revisions of the permit. This is done so as not to hinder the critical mission, namely, that of overseeing the numerical determination of emissions for the various emission units and operations at the source, particularly where reductions are required to achieve both attainment and sustainability with Nature.

For larger sources, all of the following should be segregated from the rest of the permit itself: the separate document for the latest "determination of emissions" for the various units,[69] the source allotment (for adverse area pollutants), and PAL pollutant limits.

The role of the permit engineer, whether for the states or the feds (as applicable),[70] should morph into developing and updating permits for new and existing emission units that document the performance standards that apply to them. The engineers would also specify within the source's permit the unit-specific performance standard for each unit at the source, impose stack tests where necessary, specify the recordkeeping and reporting requirements for the source to maintain, etc.[71] These tasks should be left to the engineers at the Environmental Protection Bureau Air Pollution Control Department using boilerplate language approved by regulatory and enforcement attorneys. The unit could be called the Construction and Modification Permitting and Emission Determination Unit (CMPED Unit). One can envision the Permit Section being primarily comprised of a CMPED Unit, which would oversee a Major Source Unit and a Synthetic Minor/Minor Source/Registration Unit. Besides the normal recordkeeping and reporting requirements, a typical permit would require the same records and determination methods for emissions from the various units as those that were used to determine the baseline emissions where a trading program applies.

The CMPED Unit's critical functions would be to (1) determine, in the early stages of the trading program, the baselines and allotments for the major sources within the nonattainment and other adverse areas, (2) set source's Plantwide Applicability Limitations for those attainment area pollutants, regardless of whether the pollutant is emitted in major quantities, (3) track the emission determination factors for the units at the source, so that once process information is provided, emissions can be determined straightforwardly, and (4) issue new construction and revise permits for modifications.

Within the Permit Section, a Work Practices Unit should also be created to address nonquantifiable PM and VOC emissions from sources that require the implementation of work practice requirements, including the provision of plans to minimize fugitive dust[72] and leaks, odors, and perhaps even startup/shutdown emissions. To fill out the Section would be a unit of one or two specialists who handle open burning permits.

Aside from these units within the Permit Section, and the enhanced inspections conducted by the field operations staff, an External Trading Reconciliation Unit within the Compliance Section will be tasked with conducting the administrative functions of the external trading program. They will also work in conjunction with enforcement attorneys to ensure that violations are addressed.

An Essential Adaptation of Adopting the Strategy: Stack Testing

Where a continuous emission monitoring system (CEMS), mass balance, or another means of measurement cannot be used to determine emissions from a unit, stack testing may be required to determine site-specific emission rates and emission factors. In its simplest form a stack test is conducted by inserting a probe into the flue gas stream over a set period of time to collect a pollutant so that a lb/hr and/or pollutant concentration can be determined. Typically, three one-hour tests are conducted and the rates averaged to determine these values.

So let's say that a source makes a physical modification to an emission unit or changes its operation to increase that unit's emissions. If there's no simple way to determine what the emission increase would be (e.g., via a CEMS or mass balance), then a stack test requirement would be imposed to determine the emissions rate. That is simple and straightforward and no different than what is currently required.

But what if a source wants to make a change that *reduces* emissions instead and wishes to take credit for that reduction? In a well-functioning internal or external trading scheme, taking credit for reductions requires measurement, and that measurement may require expensive stack testing (or at the very least use of conservative emission determination factors). Such a test can cost tens of thousands of dollars.[73,74] The other option is to simply make the reduction without a test and not taking any credit for it, that is, by simply using the emission determination factor that applied prior to the reduction.[75]

Let's not forget that those emissions determined at a source aren't just needed to simply reconcile the appropriate amount of trading units, but this same data is also used in air quality modeling and tracking. This emphasizes the point that if regulators do not track the measurements of something as critical as actual emissions, how exactly would regulators be able to manage them? While one would hope that ambient monitors to measure atmospheric pollution would be sufficient to guide the reduction program, the measurement and use of accurate stack tested emissions data from multiple emission points would still serve as a nice backstop.

Summarizing the Key Changes that Result from Adopting the Strategy

The great news about setting hard limits and utilizing an external trading program in adverse areas to reduce them is that, for all intents and purposes, many needless aspects of NSR vanish. For example, the micromanagement of emissions from discrete units at a source will no longer be necessary. Likewise, emissions of nonattainment area pollutants emitted in major quantities from new sources in NAAs will require the source to purchase TUs from the market as a prerequisite to construct and operate, besides also having to demonstrate compliance to other applicable federal and state rules. The required purchase of TUs will replace the need to acquire offsets as currently required under NAA NSR.

To optimally reduce emissions in the NAA, federal and/or state emission unit performance standards must be imposed at the source in conjunction with the use of a trading scheme. These performance standards, for example, can be in the form of lb/mmBtu or lb/MWh for some combustion devices or, say, lb/ton of product (e.g., clinker for a kiln at a cement manufacturing plant). The trading unit allotments assigned to the source dictate the total equivalent of allowed emissions for the source separate from the individual emission units themselves. The emission unit performance standards not only function as an incorruptible backstop to meeting the unit's compliance obligations, but it also contributes to satisfying the required reduction of the emissions trading program.

Be that as it may, and as discussed earlier in Chapter 2 regarding the Design Flaws, many of the current rules that address performance standards are horrifically written and could stand major re-writes. Let it be said here that for any well-designed trading program to get off the ground, thinning down the complexity of the standards without losing emission reduction *performance* would go a long way to making any trading scheme gain traction. The moral here is to simplify without losing effectiveness.

Remarks on the Strategy

The comprehensive strategy is elegant in its relative simplicity and holistic construct. Regional and sourcewide limits can be seen as the "Yin" while the subsequent market activity to effectuate meeting and reducing these limits can be seen as the "Yang" of the regulatory scheme. The strategy thus developed in this chapter shows that while Stewart did not identify the details of how trading should play a better role, his instincts were nevertheless correct. Stewart's instincts will be shown to have been even more prescient in Parts 3 and 4, when trading is extended to both embedded characteristics of products to facilitate the transition to a circular economy (basically, applying a trading program to the generation of solid waste pollution), as well as a means to restore ecosystems.

When dealing with America's current AQM strategy, it is expected that people will argue for more "reasonable" or "practical" solutions than what has been proposed here. But settling for suboptimality under those conditions is not the primary goal. Rather, the path of least resistance that optimally regulates air pollution and promotes sustainability with Nature must be followed. In truth, it is possible that what has been proposed may only end up as a silver standard. In the end, after further refining the strategy and reaching consensus, it will hopefully evolve to become the gold standard. Whatever regulatory system is best for optimally reducing emissions to the environment to achieve sustainability with Nature is ultimately all that really matters.

Final Thoughts

At its very core, the day-to-day activities of air pollution regulators must be to maintain a constant focus on the larger goal of reducing emissions. The comprehensive strategy includes, but is certainly not limited to, correcting the inherent design flaws of the current system and sorting out the proper division of labor (academia and research centers, feds and states, engineers, and attorneys).[76] Just like regulating air pollution, these same elements of the strategy will be critical to regulating the generation of inherently detrimental product characteristics and their surrogates, which will be explained in more detail in Chapters 6 and 7 when the adapted and generalized strategies, respectively, are laid out. Furthermore, other thorny sustainability problems will be explored in Chapter 9 using aspects of the generalized strategy, including a means to mitigate climate change.

Notes

1 Informing the current discussion of emissions trading are the following useful resources: Office of Air and Radiation, *Tools of the Trade: A Guide to Designing and Operating a Cap and Trade Program for Pollution Control* (EPA-430-B-03-002, USEPA, 2003). https://www.epa.gov/sites/default/files/2016-03/documents/tools.pdf; Office of Air and Radiation, *Clearing the Air: The Facts About Capping and Trading Emissions* (EPA-430F-02-009, USEPA, 2002). https://www.epa.gov/sites/default/files/2016-03/documents/clearingtheair.pdf; and Joseph Kruger, *Companies and Regulators in Emissions Trading Programs* (RFF DP 05-02, 2005).

2 Elliott, "Environmental Markets and Beyond," 248.

3 Elliott, "Environmental Markets and Beyond," 247. Here he cites: U.S. Environmental Protection Agency, *Progress Report on the EPA Acid Rain Program* (USEPA, 1999), 6. https://www.epa.gov/sites/default/files/2015-08/documents/1999report.pdf.

4 Other appropriate synonyms that could be used are prods, urges, inspires, nudges, forces, and encourages.

5 Theoretically, adverse areas can include areas of impaired visibility.

6 Setting regional limits is prescriptive, CaC-based regulation, which should unquestionably be the best friend of anti-trading adherents, and a fact that should not be understated. Unfortunately, there is apparent hypocrisy to their opposition to cap-and-trade—they support caps but nevertheless oppose the trading component more, even though it is the mandatory decline of the cap that truly reflects *regulation*. In all the years of opposition to trading, anti-trading adherents have postulated little, if any form of a truly command-and-control-based regulatory method operating under a total capped limit as an alternative to CaT. For example, how exactly would regulators ensure that the regional limit be met and reduced, particularly when new sources propose to construct within the nonattainment area? Would regulators use some form of central planning that dictates reductions and limits for each new and existing source, subject to immediate change to all those sources as newer sources enter the NAA? Such an approach would be as inefficient and logjam-provoking as anything utilized today. It's trivial to criticize others' ideas, but proposing workable solutions is far more challenging.

7 NRC, *Air Quality Management in the United States*, 197, Box 5-5.

8 Sirini Withana, Patrick ten Brink, Andrea Illes, et al., *Environmental Tax Reform in Europe: Opportunities for the Future: Final Report.* A Report by the Institute for European Environmental Policy (The Netherlands Ministry of Infrastructure and the Environment, 2014); and European Environment Agency, *Environmental Taxation and EU Environmental Policies*, EEA Report No. 17/2016 (Publications Office of the European Union, 2016).

9 The term "trading unit" is used here where other authors use the term "allowance" or "permit." An allotment for a source is comprised of its allotted trading units, where, for example, each generated ton of emissions of a pollutant may equate to ten trading units. The use of the term "permit" is avoided since a permit is reserved for the actual written "contract" between a source and the regulatory agency.

10 It might be more appropriate to call EJ areas "economic and environmental injustice" areas instead.

11 To be clear, the emissions increase is not from the actual activities of construction or modification, but from the subsequent operation of the unit after construction or

modification is complete. Note that it is possible for a plant to increase production capacity while reducing emissions (e.g., replacing solvent-based coatings with powder coatings), but this is not typical.

12 Brian W. Kernighan and P. J. Plauger, *The Elements of Programming Style*, 2nd ed. (McGraw-Hill, 1978), 71.

13 Technically speaking, greenhouse gases are not air "pollutants" in the strictest sense of the term since they do not *directly* cause physical harm to human health and natural welfare. Nevertheless, for the sake of simplicity, GHGs will be treated as an air pollutant in this book.

14 Much of the strategy to mitigate climate change discussed in Chapter 9 follows key aspects of the comprehensive strategy.

15 To be more technical, rather than limiting the usage of fossil fuels of varying heat content, the discussion should more properly be based on limiting the total mmBtus of fuels. However, since the bulk of Btus are fossil fuel-based, this book will address the limiting or rationing of fossil fuels with the understanding that Btus are what is to be limited.

16 Under the comprehensive strategy, NAAQS concentrations under the CAA will remain the same here since these are critical to drawing the line on health impacts.

17 A rough breakdown of source types where volatile organic compounds (VOC) are generated is from area (48 percent), on-road (20 percent), nonroad (20 percent), and point (12 percent), while 20 percent of NOx is from point sources.

18 David M. Driesen and Amy Sinden, "The Missing Instrument: Dirty Input Limits," *Harvard Environmental Law Review* 33 (2009). https://harvardelr.com/wp-content/uploads/sites/12/2019/07/33.1-Driesen-and-Sinden.pdf. As the obvious yet not-so-novel approach of limiting inputs appears to be, Driesen and Sinden are two of only a few scholars who seem to have even postulated doing so for fuels at the front end so as to ensure that emissions of CO_2 are limited at the back end. As noted earlier in Part 1, far more is written in the literature regarding the academic debate between applying command-and-control vs. market instruments to reduce emissions than simply limiting inputs. This focus is astounding. It shows where the priorities lie within the economic and environmental legal communities in addressing environmental calamities. The obsessive, abstracted focus on one-dimensional concepts and tools rather than actually applying these tools to solve calamitous problems at the global level is a major indication that many scholars have not been putting their talents to optimal use.

19 "Significantly" is a value well over de minimis, as defined by regulators.

20 The reader is referred to Chapter 3 for Schoenbrod's discussion on regulating interstate polluters for sources other than power plants.

21 For grandfathered units where a performance standard was not imposed, the baseline and associated allotment should be based not on the actual emissions from that unit but on the most stringent performance standard that would apply to that unit. This would "incentivize" such sources to replace that underperforming unit.

22 This approach doesn't have to apply just to NAAs. It can just as easily apply to other adverse areas (e.g., acid rain-affected or visibility-impaired areas).

23 Clearly, reductions in NOx and VOC in ozone NAAs should be compatible with the Haagen-Smit curves (i.e., by specifically considering NOx-limited or VOC-limited areas).

24 The PAL proposed in the comprehensive strategy would definitely *not* be the lenient one allowed under 40 CFR 52.21(aa). The PAL here would be characterized by a tighter limit that requires air quality modeling if emissions increase above source thresholds.

25 Where a source removed emission units, thereby lowering the PTE for one or more pollutants, the PALs for these pollutants may need to be reduced, where necessary.

26 Depending on when the list was published, this number is either twenty-six or twenty-eight. Three certain types of sources listed separately are sometimes listed together as one category.

27 To be more precise, the term should be New Unit Performance Standard since a source represents the entire plant or facility, while the emission unit is a specific piece of equipment or operation.

28 Campbell's idea arose in response to the author's question regarding what could be done to improve air pollution regulation based on 20/20 hindsight.

29 One of the manuscript's technical reviewers, Rob Brenner, asserted that based on his experience in the USEPA's Office of Policy dealing with the Administrative Procedures Act, NSPSs would take much longer than five years from initial development to its rule effectiveness date. In the spirit of simplification and streamlining, it is this author's opinion that the goal of being able to finalize tightened NSPSs every five years should still be the desired goal. If five years is unrealistic, obviously the timeframe for tightening those NSPSs should be minimized to whatever timeframe is possible.

30 As long as an emission unit is not modified to increase emissions of an NSPS-regulated pollutant, a unit subject to a past NSPS does not have to comply with a newly determined NSPS. The new NSPS will only apply to new emission units and those units that are modified that also increase hourly emissions.

31 The author wishes to thank Gary McCutchen and Colin Campbell, both nationally recognized NSR experts, for the following insightful and counterintuitive observation. Under NAA NSR, for major projects that require LAER and offsets, applying a stringent LAER will actually result in *less* of an emissions reduction in

the NAA than if LAER was less stringent (but no lower than an applicable NSPS). Note the following example: if a new major source in an ozone NAA is subject to an NSPS-level LAER with a PTE of 800 tpy of NOx, then if the offset ratio is 1.3 to 1, it is required to obtain 1.3 x 800 or 1040 tpy of NOx from one or more sources within the NAA. In this scenario, the environment will thus notice an overall reduction of at least 1040–800 or 240 tpy of NOx. On the other hand, if that same source is subject to a more stringent LAER with a PTE of 700 tpy, it only needs 1.3 x 700 or 910 tpy of NOx offsets. While the environment will only notice a reduction of at least 910–700 or 210 tpy, the former case with NSPS-level LAER and offsets will, counterintuitively, represent a more environmentally beneficial reduction of 30 tpy (i.e., 240–210) relative to the stringent LAER and offsets case.

32 The Clearinghouse is a compilation of such determinations maintained by the USEPA and supplied by regulators for the beneficial use of other regulators.

33 Environmental Law Institute, "Barriers to Environmental Technology Innovation and Use," 13.

34 Under current New Source Review, simply constructing a source that is major for pollutant X can have collateral ramifications for the review of other pollutants that are emitted in lesser, but "significant" amounts. For example, an applicant that proposes to construct a 180 tpy VOC source (from within the Dirty 26 list where the major source threshold is 100 tpy) in an AA that will also emit 50 tpy of SO_2 will trigger PSD review for both VOC and SO_2 (thus requiring use of BACT for units that emit those pollutants, conducting air quality modeling, etc.). It is by virtue of the fact that because the source is major for VOC that PSD will also apply to SO_2 because the 50 tpy of SO_2 exceeds its 40 tpy significance threshold.

35 The first two factors, the source location concentration and the source's projected effect on ambient concentration, are very important since they are fundamental to the impact on air quality, while the third factor, the category the source falls under, is critically important for prioritizing which sources should get the most regulatory scrutiny.

36 To understand the nature of the excess bureaucratic scrutiny under NSR, imagine if one were required to answer the following questions on whether to take an umbrella out or not: If it is raining, how large are the droplets? How torrential is the rainfall? Is it a light rain? How loud is the rainfall? Is there thunder? Is there lightning? If there's thunder and lightning but no rain, why is that? If it's about to rain, are the clouds gray? Just how gray? Can the sun be seen through the clouds? Are others outside carrying umbrellas? Is the umbrella functioning properly? Is the umbrella big enough to handle the job? If not, why not? On the other hand, the only two questions that should truly matter are: Is it raining now, and does the forecast say that it is going to rain later? Aren't those the only questions worth asking?

37 See Chapter 3 for a description of PSD increment.

38 It should not be assumed that the use of the less stringent Class II increments is implied here. To preserve Nature and/or protect EJ areas, regulators may wish to apply the tighter Class I increments that apply to regions such as national parks and wilderness areas.

39 CO increases are cited in some of these examples, but later in the chapter, it is argued that regulators could choose to regulate CO by the use of performance standards only.

40 To bolster regulators' ability to regulate these interstate pollution sources (including grandfathered emission units that contribute to downwind pollution), the largest of the major sources (e.g., refineries, integrated steel production) require extra special attention. Permitting, inspection, etc., should be addressed by environmental engineers with advanced degrees whose priority career focus has been on these specific types of sources. Critical details such as these have not been addressed by earlier authors.

41 This is not to say that these academic and environmental research centers cannot factor in regional and/or project-specific considerations into the determination of performance standards. On the other hand, specific sources hoping to catch a break by seeking relaxed standards will not get much sympathy from other sources subject to stricter standards.

42 For any unit without an existing performance standard, either a standard that is the tightest in the country for that operation or what the most stringent national rule requires could be used.

43 State-by-state FDAs would be a laughably unthinkable means to approach drug approvals for individual states, so why not ask that the determination of NUPSs be performed at the national level? Seen from another angle, why are NSPSs currently being determined at the national level while BACT and LAER are generally determined at the state level in most cases?

44 As one example, the author has participated in discussions about what should comprise BACT for startup emissions for combustion turbines. If a Brand A turbine has lower lb/hr NOx and CO emissions during startup than comparably sized Brand B and Brand C turbines but much higher VOC emissions than these same turbines, just how should regulators determine what the proper criteria are to challenge applicants as to what BACT is for these three pollutants during startup? And what is BACT in this case, and how would that determination be justified? While startup emissions are usually a small portion of a combustion turbine's annual emissions, jumping through these detailed regulatory hoops is required under the current Top-Down BACT process.

45 CCS can also be an abbreviation for carbon capture and sequestration.

46 The USEPA's Environmental Technology Verification (ETV) Program exemplified the public-private partnership proposed here.

47 These would be for those sources that would see their allotments dropping in the future and would rather have an alternative technology developed in preparation for that.

48 As will be discussed further in Chapter 6, research on various aspects of the circular economy based on *Cradle to Cradle* principles should also be conducted by such centers.

49 The reader is urged to reread the Giles/Next Gen Compliance section in Chapter 3 regarding simplicity. The Hindin and Silberman quotes are particularly insightful as they pertain to the discussion.

50 If regulators themselves encourage industry to reduce solid waste pollution by redesigning products, say for disassembly ("design for disassembly"), rather than landfilling them after use, it should not be asking too much to have regulators redesign and simplify their own rules and regulations to avoid bureaucratic pollution.

51 Thinking outside the environmental regulatory box, one can likewise imagine building compliance to applicable requirements within corporate charters as well.

52 Giles, *Next Generation Compliance*, 2–3.

53 Giles, *Next Generation Compliance*, 2.

54 We also see much the same internalized externality concept when companies take back their large appliances, so that when the customer is ready to toss it out, instead of sending it to a landfill, the item goes back to the manufacturer for disassembly.

55 The reader should keep the notion of redesigning processes in mind throughout the book, with particular emphasis on Part 3.

56 Mandating the documentation of every gory detail within SoBs is overkill. Why not simply require regulatory documentation for only those pollutants emitted in major quantities and use the time savings to address other major pollution issues?

57 If sabermetrics could ever be applied to the regulatory mission, one could observe that for every unit of production, excessive bureaucracy and poor workplace morale would translate into a loss of production (e.g., 0.4 units), a metric that would prove useful to the RFC.

58 Another upside for state agency attorneys to participate in the development of permits is in ensuring that confidential business information is not disclosed in the permit.

59 John Schakenbach, Robert Vollaro, and Reynaldo Forte, "Fundamentals of Successful Monitoring, Reporting, and Verification under a Cap-and-Trade Program," *Journal of the Air & Waste Management Association* 56 (November 2006): 1578.

60 As an example of information the public may be unaware of but should, is the fact that some environmental agencies may have no choice but to issue a permit for a proposed source, no matter how vehemently the public wants the agency to deny it. This is because, depending on the state, the environmental agency is required *by law* to issue a permit if it meets the legal conditions for issuance. This information is necessary for the public to know so that they can focus their attention on legislators to change the law rather than blame the environmental agency for something they have no authority to change.

61 Schmalensee and Stavins, "Lessons Learned," 71. For readers interested in the "what works" lessons of cap-and-trade programs in the article, they are referred to the article's sections on "Lessons" as learned from the US Acid Rain Program on page 63 and "Key Features for System Design and Implementation" on page 72.

62 While it is later advocated that CO be only subject to performance standards from individual emission units, regulators could treat this pollutant as a tradable pollutant.

63 Jeremy Schreifels, "Emissions Trading in Santiago, Chile: A Review of the Emission Offset Program of Supreme Decree No. 4," 2012. https://papers.ssrn.com/sol3/papers.cfm?abstract_id=1910156.

64 Companies would not be seeking these innovative technologies in a vacuum since they would no doubt be collaborating with academic and federal environmental research centers on what technologies are on the cutting edge.

65 While large quantities of hydrogen sulfide and some HAP such as benzene are emitted by a relatively small number of sources in major amounts, in a region populated by refineries that emit sufficient quantities of H_2S and benzene, it is certainly conceivable that regional H_2S and benzene caps could be set and required to be aggressively declined. External trading could then facilitate those reductions in the same way that lead was addressed at those same sources in the past. Critics who might object that allowing benzene trading could create hotspots should note that current regulation allows such increases now.

66 In any case, HAPs such as benzene and lead should have very stringent performance standards relative to other pollutants. In fact, if there was ever an exception where strict technology standards should apply, it is for HAPs.

67 B. V. Kavitha, Chirag Bhimani, and A. Sudhakar, "Issues and Challenges for Emission Trading Scheme for Particulate Matter in India," *Journal of Environmental Research and Development* 9, no. 03 (January–March 2015).

68 For NAA pollutants subject to trading, no tons/year limits are set in the permit for annual emissions, so upon entering the source premises, inspectors must be provided with the current actual emissions based on these potential operating and production rates to conduct intensive inspections with sufficient scrutiny.

Inspectors will also know the source's current trading allotment so that they will be able to determine whether the source is operating above, at, or below what is "allowed" under their current allotment. It should be noted that inspectors should not be expected to crunch the raw data; rather such information must be provided by professionally certified sustainability accountants.

69 Determination of emissions here connotes site-specific emission factors (e.g., as determined by stack testing) or formulae.

70 Under the comprehensive strategy, the feds would conduct the trading program for pollutants from interstate pollution sources that contribute to downwind adverse areas, but the permitting responsibilities will still likely be handled by the states. As such, the discussion will focus on the role of the states.

71 Based on the adage that one can catch more flies with honey than with vinegar, to encourage positive, compliant behavior, it might be wise for regulators to have permits written to include incentive clauses, just like those found in the contracts of professional athletes. This avoids the typically stern tone taken with sources ("The Permittee shall . . .").

72 The notion that roadways should be treated as emission units must be eliminated and handled by fugitive dust plans instead.

73 Of course, for some companies, tens of thousands of dollars may just be a drop in the bucket relative to the cost of complying with or taking credit for future emission reductions.

74 In the literature of the 1990s and early 2000s, the authors who highlighted the virtues of Project XL, and other voluntary programs, spoke of companies wanting to take credit for making voluntary reductions. That same literature did not mention the expense of stack testing to quantify those reductions.

75 It should also be possible that testing only be targeted for emissions generated in major quantities, such as those by sources participating in trading programs. Small emission generators may not need to have stack tests imposed if the consequences are minor.

76 Regulators should also be thoroughly aware of the article from Gray and Shimshack (see Chapter 3) and the GAO Report regarding inspections. These documents will guide regulators to the larger mission of the AQM program. Put another way, ignoring the advice from these papers will render the practice of AQM less optimal than it should be.

5

Insights and Commentary on the Comprehensive Strategy

Filling in Some Gaps within the Comprehensive Strategy

The optimal means of addressing the regulation of stationary sources, what has been termed the comprehensive strategy, offers regulators worldwide a viable means to reduce air pollution while the adapted version applied to the generation of solid waste will support the means to achieve a circular economy, as will be developed later in Chapter 6. This chapter provides further commentary and additional insights on the comprehensive strategy, along with critiques of the leading perspectives offered by Schoenbrod et al. and Nordhaus, with some promotion of Next Gen principles thrown in. This chapter concludes by considering how best to put the comprehensive strategy to the test.

So as to expand on the nature and consequences of the comprehensive strategy developed in the previous chapter, we will address the following topics:

- Redesigning Regulation—The Underlying Basis of the Comprehensive Strategy
- Critical Aspects of the Comprehensive Strategy
- Streamlining Existing New Source Review to be as or more Effective
- Measuring is Fundamental
- Permitting as an Essential Element of the Comprehensive Strategy
- The Legal Aspects
- Repositioning Economics
- The Most Critical Aspect

The reader is urged to pay close attention to the discussion of the comprehensive strategy since it will provide valuable insights that carry over to the adapted and generalized strategies in Part 3 and what comes later.

Redesigning Regulation: The Underlying Basis of the Comprehensive Strategy

1. *Fundamental Redesign.* As noted in previous chapters, among its many problems, the current air quality management (AQM) system allows for increases in emissions of pollutants in NAAs, the reliance on an incredibly excessive bureaucratic process that comes with regulating pollution, and glaringly inadequate regulation of the higher-polluting grandfathered stationary sources that are virtually excluded from significant regulation, while newer and cleaner emission units are regulated more strictly. Continuing use of such a scheme makes no sense. Oddly enough, there are thousands of professionals who have invested *their entire careers* administering this suboptimal program and know no other way to regulate air pollution; it has simply become normal, accepted practice.

   To use regulatory complexity to create the appearance that regional emissions are being strictly limited without *actually* limiting them is at best disingenuous. If reductions are being made at sources within a region, will citizens necessarily see attainment of the National Ambient Air Quality Standards (NAAQS) and a reduction of pollution's impacts on Nature's welfare and human health? Maybe, but there is no guarantee.

   Simply trying to reduce the *rate* of emissions from each emission unit at sources through the periodic tightening of Reasonably Available Control Technology (RACT) is laughably insufficient since total regional emissions can still increase overall due to an increase in the population of emission units therein.[1] Given the continued use of the SIP process decades into the implementation of the CAA, the fact that there are still many nonattainment areas in the United States is the proverbial definition of insanity—doing the same thing over and over but expecting different results. On the other hand, we have seen that there is no substitute for setting absolute regional limits and then tightening those limits to reduce emissions.

   Enforceably setting hard and tightening limits also applies to the use of fossil fuels as a *guarantee* to limit post-combustion emissions. Setting regional limits on total Btus from fossil fuel use affects all sources in a region that combust those fuels: mobile sources, stationary sources, nonroad engines, residential heating, etc. In this regard, limiting and declining the use of fossil fuels to reduce emissions is simply a means to internalize externalities; that is, by better passing on the increased costs of emitting CO_2 to the users and consumers of fossil fuels.

Among stationary sources in adverse areas (e.g., NAAs), the best market incentivizing tool to wield to facilitate the practical and efficient reduction of capped emissions within a region is clear: external trading of emissions. The market will set the price for sources to reduce emissions by using control devices and/or redesigning the process to reduce emissions. Those sources that cannot or will not reduce emissions will have to purchase trading units with appropriate dissuasive taxes applied to those purchases to encourage them to meet emission reduction requirements.

In short, the comprehensive strategy shifts our current outdated ad hoc, regulate-as-we-go strategy to one that is much more rigorous and systematic.

Critical Aspects of the Comprehensive Strategy

2. *Prerequisites*. There are several critical prerequisites for the successful implementation of the comprehensive strategy, including, but not limited to: the tightening of Best Available Control Technology (BACT)-like NSPSs every five years,[2] appropriate recordkeeping for both external and internal trading (i.e., PALs), intensive inspections, and the requisite need for sufficient resources and capacity to conduct the program.

The comprehensive strategy shows that it is far more preferable to have a tightening regional cap in tandem with tightening performance standards (where possible[3]) in contrast to applying BACT/LAER (Lowest Achievable Emission Rate) only to emission units at relatively few sources that undertake major projects and the eventual tightening of RACT[4] at all subject sources under the glacial SIP process. Certainly, under a well-designed trading program, grandfathered emission units that significantly contribute to an adverse area would be squeezed most to reduce emissions.

Regarding the need to keep and maintain adequate records to ensure compliance under either external or internal trading, there is little to add other than that it is no more burdensome than any hardship currently imposed on sources. In fact, it will likely be less.

To better understand the significance of intensive inspections, the reader is referred to the Government Accountability Office (GAO) report, followed by the article by Gray and Shimshack.[5] In the latter article, the authors researched the evidence to support the role of monitoring and enforcement toward the goal of compliance and not only found that it supported general deterrence at a targeted source, but it also influenced reductions of violations at *other* sources. In so doing, emissions are reduced. As the Gray and Shimshack abstract notes:

> The consistent findings from this literature review are as follows: (1) environmental monitoring and enforcement activities generate substantial specific deterrence, reducing future violations at the targeted firm; (2) environmental monitoring and enforcement activities generate substantial general deterrence, reducing future violations at facilities other than the targeted one; and (3) environmental monitoring and enforcement activities generate not only reductions in violations but also significant reductions in emissions.[6]

In a related article, the Norwegian Environmental Protection Agency conducted a natural field experiment on the effects of self-reporting, inspection frequency, and specific deterrence.[7] The results included evidence of under-reporting of violations in firms' self-audits (whereas more violations were detected in onsite inspections than in self-audits). Announcing an increased inspection frequency had no effect on firm compliance, but having had a past inspection raised subsequent compliance substantially.

On the basis of these informative articles and basic common sense, it should be clear that engineers must spend much more time in the field conducting inspections. If there are still those who assert that the existing routine inspection program is sufficient, they have not read the GAO Report. Based on that and other documents, any prerequisite for establishing a cap-and-trade system must ensure that intensive, not routine, inspections are conducted prior to implementation of the program. While regulators must up their game if and when the comprehensive strategy is implemented, sources must up their compliance game as well. Thus, one critical prerequisite for regulators to put the strategy into operation is this: one or two years prior to implementation, regulators must ensure that intensive inspections force sources to scrutinize their operations and emissions determination methods.

Of course, much of what has been asserted here is based on regulatory bodies having adequate resources. If management hopes they will get the same amount of regulatory outcomes while skimping on qualified human and other resources and/or funding, then all bets are off and failure is likely.

3. *The Focus Is on Achieving Results*. Another key aspect of the comprehensive strategy is that it seeks to achieve results-oriented milestones while minimizing the amount of process-oriented procedures. External trading of pollutants emitted in major amounts in adverse areas is Win-Win-Win because (a) it is specifically targeted at reducing welfare- and health-impacting pollution, (b) it is an efficient tool, and (c) when enforcement is necessary, it identifies a clear target (e.g., by focusing on emission exceedances, recordkeeping, etc.), rather than wasting time and effort on inconsequential "paper violations." This does not imply that the regulation of air pollution will be rendered easy, but the program will be much more systematic in the concise way that it needs to be.

   Instead of taking slow-walking steps to address pollution, using the strategy's objective and quantitative focus on determining and quantifying emissions,[8] and weaponizing it to reduce emissions in adversely impacted areas renders it more appropriate. Rules should likewise be Next Gen designed, preferably like composite materials—light yet very strong and effective.

   To reiterate a problem with the current system: it is complicated at the regulatory front end but can be effective at reducing emissions at the back end, without any discernible, clear-cut way to pin down causation. For example, did the application of multiple rules result in reductions, and if so, which rules were responsible? Or did reductions occur only because most companies sought compliance to avoid the harsh consequences, regardless of the quality of the rules and their permits? Or was it some unknown combination of the two?

   The comprehensive strategy, on the other hand, is simpler to use when seeking compliance from sources. By setting quantifiable emission limits/targets at the back end, it puts sources on a practical pollution emission budget that they must meet. As Schoenbrod pointed out, "the greatest and most rapid reductions in air pollution were accomplished when the federal government, by direct congressional act, set actual emission targets."[9]

With external trading, a regional limit is set first. Then the cost for the collection of sources to comply with the limit is simply assessed by the market. If a source fails to reconcile its emissions with its current allotment, the failure to acquire the appropriate quantity of trading units will result in a penalty, leaving much less room for contested litigation.[10] In contrast, simply applying a tax on emissions only serves to act more like the cost of doing business than a penalty, so that even where the tax is mandatory, the presumed future modification of behavior is not.

Thus, external trading applies muscle to the appropriate pressure points. It also provides a direct carrot-and-stick approach, whereas the current SIP program does so only indirectly, being long on process and short on immediately demonstrable results.

A temporary downside to the external trading system involves the initial surge of required activity to determine baselines and allotments for the sources emitting pollutants in major amounts. Why? Because determining baselines is painstaking work and must be conducted while the current AQM program—still active—is phased out. Presumably, once the new program is up and running, the rest is downhill (i.e., straightforward, but not necessarily easy).

The trading program will eliminate much of the sizably bureaucratic stationary source portion of the current SIP process. Of course, whatever SIP planning eventually morphs into, it should include fuel rationing and will still have to address mobile sources, etc.

4. *Hierarchy of Regulation*. Based on the discussion to this point, one can observe a clear hierarchy of air pollution regulation (see Figure 4.1). The top geographical tier involves limiting the quantity of fuels (or Btus) the combustion of which generates CO_2 and other emissions on a global and regional basis, when these fuels are combusted by a multitude of combustion units (e.g., boilers, turbines, mobile sources, leaf blowers, etc.). The next tier involves limiting emissions within a region (e.g., NOx generated from combustion sources) downward to area and nuisance emitters (such as consumer products or fumigation operations).

   Next is the regulation for the top tier of operation, namely individual emission units, such as cement kilns, coating operations, and landfill flare operations. Following that are work practices (such as keeping lids on mixing tanks or implementing leak detection and repair programs at chemical plants). The last tier of regulation involves essential command-

and-control requirements at the micro-scale, such as stack testing, recordkeeping, monitoring, etc.

Unfortunately, current regulation in the United States has addressed the tiers above in an ad hoc, piecemeal fashion, often with an overly pathological focus on more localized issues and minutiae rather than systematically tackling all tiers of the regulatory hierarchy, that is, nationally, regionally, and downward, through a systematic, top-down approach. While compliance at industrial facilities is justifiably the necessary focus at the local level, the need to develop a viable systematic emissions reduction strategy for global and larger regionally generated air pollution seems to get lost in the discussion, the glacial, suboptimal SIP process notwithstanding.

5. *Structural Stability*. With the comprehensive strategy, many aspects within the reformed AQM program are kept as immovable as possible. Ideally, the only significant aspects that should be subject to change over time are the regional cap on emissions and performance standards that are revised every five years.[11] Otherwise, other aspects of the AQM program, such as applicable rules, should be as static as possible.
6. *Continuous Focus on Improvement*. The declining global and regional caps, in conjunction with the tightening of performance standards, require participants to continually strive for process/product redesign and improvement as allotments decrease. Clearly then, performance standards for emission units must absolutely have a place in AQM.[12] Having only a regional cap under an external trading program without performance standards is asking for trouble.

   Removing performance standards would most certainly be a gift for sources (major and minor) but not for the environment. If external trading applies only to sources for pollutants emitted in major amounts where performance standards do not apply, but where standards only apply to emission units at smaller emitting sources, this just defeats the purpose of AQM. Pushing the technological envelope is as important as pushing the regional pollution-reduction envelope. Attempting to aggressively abate the welfare-impacting and unhealthy effects of air pollution by carving out exceptions for the larger polluters in NAAs and other adverse areas is counterproductive.
7. *Optimizing the Use of Human Resources*. The underlying culture in the US regulatory system is currently a legally structured "process-centric" one.

While still a regulatory–based system, the focus instead should be more results-oriented, characterized by engineers becoming industrial and/or environmental engineers with an eye on emissions quantification and away from being "clerical engineers" with only a pinch of environmental engineering thrown in.

Under the strategy, environmental and process engineers in academia who review technologies for NSPSs, etc., would focus their attention on more technical matters that have a direct influence on the broader environment. For their part, governmental regulatory agencies can thus better exploit the comparative advantages of having engineers on the ground as inspectors and within academia, environmental research institutes, and within a variant of the ETV Program. Thus, the more deterministic AQM becomes (i.e., quantifying emissions, setting and then declining those limits, tightening NSPSs, etc.), the less process-oriented the regulatory process becomes, rendering it more streamlined with regard to having addressed the design flaws.

8. *Transparency.* Transparency is critically important, as much for the permit review process as for inspections, enforcement, and other actions conducted throughout the entire AQM program, which tends to be opaque to the general public. Likewise, regulators must make their work more transparent by posting online clear, readable results of their permit review, inspection reports, enforcement actions, and the like. The public can then make more informed decisions with regard to which sources are major concerns and which are not. Information can be seen as the God Particle of environmental protection itself.
9. *Process Oversight.* If and whenever the program gets bogged down, perhaps when excess legal procedures begin to smother the process, it is critical that the Inspector General of Bureaucracy and the state program monitors step in to de-bureaucratize the process.
10. *Improving Air Quality for Nature's Sake and Ours Is Job 1.* One key takeaway here is to first and foremost, get air quality management issues right, and then and only then incorporate the concerns of other stakeholders. Recall the point made in the Introduction regarding the public safety announcement provided on airplanes—if oxygen masks drop, take care of yourself first and your child second. Thus, make sure that the harmful air quality gets clean first, then worry about economic costs later.

Streamlining Existing New Source Review to Be as or More Effective

11. *Streamlining NSR.* The comprehensive strategy, when enacted, will significantly reduce the bureaucracy associated with a reoriented version of New Source Review. Many of the bureaucratic aspects of physical and nonphysical modifications will vanish since emissions increases by projects will be subsumed within external or internal trading (i.e., PALs). The current, complicated piecemeal micromanagement of an individual unit's emission limit or the specific emission limits for a collective group of units under the source roof will end. All that should and will matter under the comprehensive strategy are plantwide emissions. Likewise, all that should and will matter is how total increases at sources affect air quality in a region.

To appreciate the significance of streamlining, note a quirky NSR loophole whereby a source in a nonattainment area (NAA) can skirt NSR by taking a 99 tpy limit for a given group of emission units followed later by constructing more emission units that took another 99 tpy limit. This allows the entire source to become a major source while avoiding the stringent requirements of NAA NSR. With an external trading scheme, this "99+99" NSR flaw would no longer be a problem under the comprehensive strategy where the source emits the pollutant in major amounts in the NAA. Becoming a major source forces that source to account for the increase in emissions through the external trading scheme by having to purchase trading units (with dissuasive taxation) and utilizing a stringent BACT-like NSPS on subject units.

Another good reason to implement a trading scheme in nonattainment areas is that under the current AQM program, thresholds can change in NAA due to varying changes in nonattainment status. For example, if the major source threshold for NOx is 100 tpy in the year 2000, and then changes to 25 tpy in 2007 and back up to 100 tpy in 2015, keeping track of applicable requirements on equipment that was constructed during these respective periods is very complicated and cumbersome for regulators to remember. For example, a unit constructed in 2010 that took a limit of 24 tpy (to avoid major New Source Review) must thereafter maintain that limit to avoid NSR in the future, even after the threshold in the NAA is increased (i.e., relaxed) in 2015. External trading solves this problem without any difficulty simply by facilitating reductions in the NAA until attainment is achieved, which is the whole point anyway.

The gradual growth in emissions allowed under current NSR (i.e., by increasing emissions over a several-year timespan) is offset by the periodic need by regulators to tighten regulation for certain units at *all* sources in an area, including those sources that may not ever increase emissions in the NAA or AA. Emissions growth within NAAs will no longer be allowed under the comprehensive strategy without suffering regulatory consequences because addressing welfare and health impacts must be the top priority.[13,14] For the sake of the environment, it would be improper to ever remove the hard cap to allow for any relaxation when that is the job of policymakers.

The simplification via external trading, and the streamlining of NSR, more than offsets the potential difficulties in transitioning from the current system to the new strategy. No longer will regulators be tasked with tracking individual operating and emission limits at a source and constantly referring to countless arcane USEPA guidance documents (both major red flags for the need for rule redesign). Critics of trading might argue that external trading relies on the inexact measurement of emissions; but inexact measurement exists in prescriptive regulation already and can be worked around with a properly designed trading program.

Lastly, another aspect that should hopefully go away under the strategy is the NSR statute of limitations enforcement time bar whereby construction of a major source or making modifications to an existing major source without undergoing NSR before it is discovered can escape punishment. Under the strategy, it can be argued that the trading program is an ongoing requirement such that sources cannot be shielded from enforcement via a statute of limitations due to their failure to, among other violations, account for their past emissions.

12. *Proper Use of PALs.* Inspired by the current Prevention of Significant Deterioration (PSD) program for AAs, an altered, less generous PAL will be utilized. With a PAL, sources typically in attainment areas only need to ensure that emissions of a pollutant emitted in minor amounts are limited under a sourcewide "bubble limit." Thus, pollutant emissions from individual

or grouped emission units at the source are no longer limited to specified levels. Limitations apply exclusively to sourcewide emissions, with worst-case limits on production that correspond to what was previously modeled.

13. *Addressing New Constructions and Modifications.* In the comprehensive strategy, permit review requirements for construction of new sources, new units, and physical modifications at existing sources would still continue, including the requirement for stack testing. However, where some new sources seek to set a PAL or where a source undertakes a modification to increase its existing PAL, air quality modeling and determining whether increment is consumed will still be necessary to ensure that air quality does not deteriorate significantly. Furthermore, setting a constraint on the number of years that a source is limited to its PAL is another useful requirement to ensure that further deterioration of air quality within a region is avoided.
14. *Even Where Flawed, the Strategy Is Still the Best Option.* Trading is an ideal tool to reduce emissions under declining caps in adverse areas; if measurements are flawed, adopting any program that does not force the reduction in regional limits would be no better. What gets lost in the discussion is the fact that whatever program is used when measurements are flawed, be it trading or prescriptive regulation, will always be less than 100% adequate. Nevertheless, CaT will still be best because there is less interpretation to complicated rules in CaT, and any flaws in measurements can be adequately addressed (e.g., setting aside an escrow account of TUs, requiring continuous emissions monitoring systems (CEMS) on as many emission units as possible in NAAs).

Measuring Is Fundamental

15. *Measure.* The author's doctoral adviser would always say that when one gets in over their head tackling a complex problem, go back to fundamentals. The same fundamentals should apply with regulating air pollution: measure, count, regulate. After program is functioning and the performance standards set, the core operating processes of the program will include the following: (1) stack testing after physical modifications are made and/or measuring emissions with CEMS or mass balance, etc., (2) determining plantwide emissions using process data and emission determination factors, (3) trading either internally and/or externally

depending on whether the pollutant is emitted in major or minor quantities in AAs and/or NAAs, and (4) imposing performance standards on both the operation and/or emissions from various units.[15]

16. *Count.* Under the comprehensive strategy, summing the *uncontrolled* emissions at a source determines its pre-control sourcewide emissions total (e.g., in tons/month). This is no different than current practice, except for one key improvement: under the comprehensive strategy, the integrity of the determination of emissions should improve as regulators will have more time to devote to this task.
17. *Measuring Being Independent from Regulation.* Measuring emissions will always be the most critical part of AQM, but it cannot be stressed enough that it is no less rigorous when using an external or internal trading program than when using a prescriptive one.[16] Measured emissions are measured emissions no matter how they are later regulated. One may attempt to argue that a prescriptive program that regulates on a source-by-source basis relegates bad measuring at one source to only that source, but the SIP program that addresses all the sources in the region has no means of correcting the sum of the accumulated errors in measurements at all sources any more rigorously than an external or internal trading program would.

Permitting as an Essential Element of the Comprehensive Strategy

18. *Role of Permitting.* Under the new strategy, the behemoth Title V permits, which will no longer require constant revision, can be managed more efficiently as well. First, with the crucial methodology for determining emissions to be integrated into Title V permitting, incorporating new units into Title V permits would include incorporating the use of that methodology as well. More specifically, permits would include the necessary emission determination factors (EDF) used for determining and quantifying the emissions from the emission units addressed by the permit. For transparency purposes, the EDF portions of the permit can be published online for public review. Of course, the public would not have access to process data since this may be confidential business information and/or trade secret.[17]

Also, aside from the specific emission standards that apply to subject emission units, the Title V permits will not need to specify emission limits for NAA pollutants for the entire source either, only the initial allotment and the schedule of reduced allotments thereafter. On the other hand, the Title V permit would incorporate the PAL emission limits for each of the AA pollutants and the NAA pollutants emitted in minor amounts.

As originally established, the Title V operating permit program was only meant to function as an administrative program; it was not intended to reduce emissions and was also not meant to improve welfare and health benefits. Under the comprehensive strategy, the Title V permit will play a much more focused and effective role. There may still need to be a degree of gap filling and periodic monitoring to ensure that emissions are correctly determined and compliance is determinable, but these requirements can be focused only on pollutants emitted in major quantities. For pollutants emitted in minor amounts, regulators have the option to apply lesser requirements for testing and documentation. In fact, if determination methods are less exact for minor emitting units for AA pollutants, the AQM program can live with that inexactness far more than for unhealthy NAA pollutants emitted in major amounts.

The more the Title V permit can be segregated into portions that better reflect relevant emission unit operating requirements and separate emission determination methods, particularly for pollutants emitted in major amounts, the less cumbersome these permits will be.

Legal Aspects

19. *Adopting Next Gen-like Principles.* Giles's Next Gen principles for redesigning regulations to build compliance into the rules, where compliance is the default option, are a significant step in the right direction. In this respect, any reformed CAA should have precisely written statutes to strongly discourage regulatory capture. For example, if the emissions trading scheme is compromised,[18] the reformed CAA should default to a harsh form of prescriptive regulation on sources, such as requiring sources to onerously reduce emissions in adverse areas.

Likewise, if research centers renege on their responsibility to tighten NSPSs (where the technologies exist to do so), then the statute should be written to ensure that the NSPS is automatically reduced by 10 percent. In general, triggering a fallback that is even more draconian and punitive to sources during regulatory capture will coax compliance by default.

If, after implementation, the "enforcement community" continues to distrust the new strategy, that same community is certainly encouraged to propose the development of the penalties within the regulations themselves. Recall that the Acid Rain Program set a given dollar penalty per ton of excess emissions within the regulation.[19] When applied, this underutilized tactic proved a success, so why not expand on that? This can and should certainly be used more, given that the business community often says that uncertainty is one of their biggest concerns; setting a penalty within a rule may help to resolve that. Or "bad actors" could also be required to meet individual limits and to maintain a higher level of regulatory detail and oversight until they become good actors. A more extreme possibility would be penalizing violators by requiring them to fund projects for their most compliant competitor rather than funding lame Supplemental Environmental Projects decided on by enforcement lawyers.

20. *Addressing Fraud*. If fraud is discovered, companies must be punished severely. Among other penalties, losing Confidential Business Information and/or Trade Secret protection is just one possible means of punishment for failing to take the preservation of Nature's welfare and human health seriously. This, of course, should be written into the statute.
21. *CaC v. Market Instruments*. The use of Command-and-Control (CaC) legal instruments versus economic incentives correlates to rigid determinism versus flexibility, respectively. From an academic standpoint, measuring (e.g., monitors, stack testing, modeling) is command-and-control-based (i.e., rigid determinism) as are limiting regional emissions. On the other hand, when there are multiple pathways available for sources to not exceed those limits, then the economic incentive to comply has been demonstrated via an external trading scheme (by providing flexibility) at the sourcewide level in an adverse area. At the emission unit level, using NSPSs as a guide, performance standards are just smaller "modules" of CaC—while sources have the option to meet a standard for an emission unit as they choose, they must nevertheless meet both

the given CaC-based limit and the underlying compliance requirements to do so. Thus, if the AQM program functions optimally and citizens breathe cleaner air as a result, then the proper symbiotic balance between CaC and market instruments will have been determined.

Repositioning Economics

22. *The Misuse of Dissuasive Taxation.* It has already been noted that the nature of cap-and-trade is corrective while that of taxation is dissuasive. On top of that is the observation that economics, as a social science, uses its tools to address what it perceives to be a social problem. When it comes to addressing pollution, there is both a blessing and a curse for the use of economic instruments. The blessing is that the generation of environmental pollution, in many cases, unlike many social problems, can be quantified, which means it can be properly regulated. The curse is that by the time the pollution problem has caused significant harm to Nature and the planet at large, it is too late to use the simple dissuasive economic instrument of taxation to solve the problem. It is much like trying to cure an alcoholic's liver cirrhosis—the dissuasive act of simply taxing alcohol is far too little and far too late to address the problem. Cirrhosis is best addressed by a doctor, not an economist. When an area is nonattainment for anything, the corrective nature of cap-and-trade is called for, rather than the dissuasive use of taxation, the use of which is better suited to punish individual polluters who choose to buy trading units.
23. *So Where Are the Economists?* Much that is lacking in the discourse on regulation is the critical input from economists, mainstream and otherwise, who are purportedly as concerned about the environment as economic growth. How, in fact, would economists *optimally* address the regulation of air pollution, particularly with the market instrument tools at their disposal (e.g., emissions trading and taxation)? Why have they been so reluctant to *optimally* address solving environmental problems where they seriously impact health and welfare? While this is only a rhetorical question, the reader is referred to the Conclusion for a harsher discourse on their relative silence in the discussion. In short, economists

appear to be conspicuously absent when it comes to participating in any discussion of addressing harms to Nature.

Probably the Most Critical Aspect . . .

24. *Making Regulating Rewarding.* At the end of the day, to keep everyone engaged in the program (particularly the downstream pack mules of various stripes), how do regulators make the whole AQM process rewarding? Transitioning from the sometimes soul-crushing bureaucracy that regulators must currently endure to a more equitable load brings its own issues. After adopting the new strategy, employees from top to bottom must continually be motivated and committed to the mission. Improving the environment while the downstream pack mules depart for greener pastures due to burnout and boredom is suboptimal over the long-term.

    Believe it or not, continually motivating employees to commit their efforts to attaining and maintaining clean air is probably the most critical issue of all. Finding extremely conscientious and motivated employees is not enough due to the drudgery of the current suboptimal program. Simply making the work less drudgerous, even under the comprehensive strategy, may not be sufficient. Many engineers and attorneys like challenges; typing up reports that few people will ever read and performing procedures dulls morale. Thus, regulators must try to make it professionally fulfilling and enjoyable. To attract talented and motivated people, employees should be encouraged to continually strive to pursue the goals of the AQM program and their own goals by allowing them the ability to obtain advanced degrees, professional licensure, career growth, etc. The National Research Council (NRC)'s recommendations for attracting talent for the USEPA, which can be adapted to the general needs of the state and local regulatory agencies is praiseworthy.[20]

    The dirtiest and most complicated major sources should be handled by those engineers with more extensive educational backgrounds than usual (e.g., PhD in Chemical Engineering for refineries and chemical plants). Thus, the absolute top talent for permitting, inspections, and enforcement should be reserved for the major sources. Furthermore, the employees must enjoy solving puzzles, meaning that prospective employees who just want routine employment are probably best suited for addressing less complicated sources. Being a regulator requires a special type of temperament. It is not suited for just anyone with the required degrees. It requires curiosity, dedication, and attention to detail.

Various facets of implementing the strategy have been laid out above. The comprehensive strategy will clearly be more straightforward to implement than the current outmoded program used in the United States today, if for no other reason than all the pieces fit together rationally and cohesively. Aspects of applying a well-designed trading program are explored next.

Comments on Applying a Trading Scheme

25. *Large Scope Regulation.* How will the trading scheme optimally address criteria pollutants over the long term? For the majority of stationary sources, consider the following:
    - CO_2 will ultimately be reduced by globally rationing and phasing down the use of all fossil fuels on the front end and, where necessary, by global (and regional) cap-and-trade programs for CO_2 at the back end, with renewables replacing the electricity-generating combustion units.[21]
    - SO_2 will ultimately be reduced by rationing and phasing down the use of high sulfur fossil fuels at the front end; and at the back end by a regional cap-and-trade program and by the application of desulfurization control technologies.
    - NOx will ultimately be reduced by rationing and phasing down the use of fossil fuels at the front end; and at the back end by a regional cap-and-trade program and by the potential application of denitrification control technologies (e.g., Selective Catalytic Reduction, or SCR).
    - $PM_{2.5}$ will ultimately be reduced by rationing and phasing down the use of all fossil fuels at the front end (since $PM_{2.5}$ is principally the result of combustion); and at the back end by a regional cap-and-trade program and the potential use of add-on controls (e.g., electrostatic precipitators).

- Volatile Organic Compounds (VOC) will be reduced by rationing and phasing down the use of fossil-based carbon feedstocks and all fossil fuels at the front end; and at the back end by a regional cap-and-trade program as well as by the application of add-on controls (e.g., afterburners) and low-VOC solvents, etc.

26. *Voluntary Measures Rendered Moot.* A well-designed external trading program can address complaints by industry about undertaking voluntary reductions rather than simply achieving just enough reductions to attain compliance to applicable rules. Companies that want to "overcomply" to applicable rules can also do so by using the external trading scheme to their economic advantage by selling any of their excess trading units.

    Note: The labor-intensive voluntary programs of the past (e.g., Project XL) can now automatically fall by the wayside under external and internal trading programs. By being required to not exceed their declining allotment in NAAs and staying below their PALs in AAs, pollution prevention is something that companies can profitably adopt under the strategy without being coaxed into doing so. Under a trading program, sources can now take credit for those reductions but by doing so, however, it may require the need for more frequent (and expensive) stack testing. At the larger sources where an operational change is being made to reduce emissions, the cost of stack testing would likely be relatively small to measure those reductions compared to the cost of performing the operational change itself.

    The exploitation of the fungibility of certain ubiquitously emitted pollutants makes regionally regulating these pollutants more efficient for regulators by streamlining bureaucracy. For industry, trading promotes flexibility, a collateral co-benefit when adopting an external cap-and-trade system. So Hooray! for industry being able to exploit the benefit of making reductions that would otherwise be voluntary under the current system.

27. *CaT Facilitates Integrity.* Within the new strategy, the integrity of determining and quantifying emissions should be at peak form with the adoption of a CaT program. In fact, a CaT program should operate better than it does now, given that the scrutiny it applies tends to unearth hidden emissions that were not previously accounted for. At a base level, when real money is involved in the buying and selling of trading units, industry will seek to achieve compliance.

Critics of trading may have concerns with regard to trusting the monitoring and verification of emissions. It is important to note that monitoring and verifying emissions is as much an issue in our current prescriptive regulatory system as it is in cap-and-trade. Sometimes sources undercount emissions, and sometimes they go unreported for years. Sometimes source emissions are approximated, even though they are to be used in Rate-of-Further-Progress demonstrations within the SIP process to determine what the next level of regional regulation should be. Sometimes a source makes what it thinks is not a modification but, in fact is, all without receiving a permit for it. That's the reality we live with *today*.

Cap-and-trade no more incentivizes suspicious activities than a prescriptive program does now. In fact, a cap-and-trade program should make regulating the generation of air pollution more streamlined, allowing more attention to be devoted to targeting inspections, emissions verification, and enforcement. The Acid Rain Program is Exhibit A in that regard.

28. *Addressing Hotspots*. The literature has discussed well the topic of "hotspots," that is, areas of concentrated nonattainment, particularly in EJ areas where an external trading program is adopted. Unfortunately, this discussion indicates that its critics do not appreciate the realities of *current* regulation. While experts discuss hotspots as a possible outcome that must be avoided if a trading program is implemented, current regulation *already* allows for those very same hotspots to occur now. In fact, decades into the implementation of the CAA, the continued existence of NAAs alone is proof that the current program is still not achieving its desired results. Current law, in fact, allows for construction of new major sources or major modifications at existing major sources of pollution in an EJ area within a NAA and requires that offsets be obtained from elsewhere within the same NAA but potentially outside the EJ area.[22] This requirement will possibly and even likely increase emissions within the EJ area itself. Let's also not forget that current NSR for nonattainment areas allows growth of emissions; for example, in a serious NAA, an increase of 24.9 tpy at a major source is allowed now and again six years from now, and so on.[23]

The anti-trading mindset is misplaced because it is not the well-intentioned use of emissions trading that delivers unequal outcomes; instead, it is the underlying system itself. At the heart of the hotspots problem is the combination of the substandard SIP process and outdated National Emission Standards for Hazardous Air Pollutants (NESHAPs) and NSPSs[24] and, unrelated to air pollution regulation, redlining and zoning, which are hidden instigators of present and future hotspots. While redlining narrows down the locations where low-income and/or minority populations can live, through zoning, city planners deliberately load the dice further against low-income and minority populations by narrowing the choice of possible locations of new pollution sources of pollution, away from high-income areas and, adding insult to injury, increasing the likelihood that those new sources will be sited in EJ areas.[25,26] As an indication that trading should not be blamed for the existence of hotspots, note again that EJ areas within NAAs *already* exist in many locations, oftentimes for *decades*, where trading is not even used.

Furthermore, trading is highly unlikely to facilitate the formation of hotspots[27] any more than the current regulatory scheme does, particularly when individual emission units are required to meet performance standards. What seems to get lost in the discussion is the fact that the area will experience "de-hotspotting," that is, air quality improvement, sometimes to the full achievement of attainment of the NAAQS, all *due to the forced decline of the regional emissions cap*. For a hotspot to occur, production at those contributing sources must coincidentally be much higher than usual while their emissions controls are not as effective as the sources outside the hotspot. The former scenario seems statistically unlikely to occur in a given area at the same time that the latter will because all emission units at contributing sources will have to meet some minimally required level of control (e.g., meeting performance standards such as RACT and/or NUPS).

Nevertheless, if upon trading, hotspots do occur, then CaC and economic tools together can be utilized as remediating agents using one or more options; for example, (1) only requiring trading from sources within the EJ area to sources outside it within the same NAA; and/or (2) setting maximum emission limits on sources that cannot be exceeded during trading and/or (3) if trading occurs between sources within the same EJ area, requiring the imposition of a stiff deterrence tax on the purchase of trading units by the source buying those trading units (i.e., an additional "EJ TU tax" on top of the "NAA TU tax"); and/or (4) when sources become too few to trade effectively in a NAA, these same sources will then be required to implement their "LAER Retrofit Contingency Plans" (since it best addresses concentrations at the local level rather than at the regional level); or as a very last resort, (5) the forced relocation of the source (so as to achieve the regional performance standard), particularly where it is located in an EJ area, so as to avoid violating the Second FloER.[28,29] Following the emergency room doctor analogy in the Introduction, some of these prescriptions represent the use of "antibiotics" or other further measures only after the doctor has stabilized the patient (i.e., by using the emissions reduction scheme via the CaT program).

Because NAAs and the EJ area hotspots within them still exist today after all these years, without use of a trading program to address those hotspots, one could justifiably argue that the anti-trading mindset combined with the fear of future development of hotspots has only allowed otherwise reducible pollution to continue being emitted in the meantime. While applying an external trading program to directly reduce emissions may take time, at least it puts attainment on a compliance schedule.

29. *TU Dilution.* Inflating source allotments by allowing credit to sources for overcompliance or excess banking only dilutes the effectiveness of the external trading program. There is no point in using an external trading program if too many sources have more TUs or allowances than they will ever generate in equivalent emissions. If there is a sizable glut of TUs, it is certainly possible to accelerate trading until the glut is erased.
30. *Design of the Program is Critical.* At the risk of overstating the point, what dictates whether or not the trading program functions the way it should is how well the trading program is designed.
31. *Addressing Multi-Media Pollution.* In the literature, there is discussion about incorporating cross-media regulation within an overall regulatory scheme, for example, by mixing water pollution regulation in with the regulation of air pollution. In Part 3, a much better option is offered, whereby the comprehensive strategy is adapted and generalized to regulate all relevant resource/fuel inputs and multi-media environmental pollutant outputs, including inherently detrimental product characteristics (IDPC) surrogate pollution,[30] as inspired by principles espoused in the book *Cradle to Cradle.*[31,32] The generalized strategy, among its attributes, allows for cost balancing, that is, sources can

decide for themselves how much they will expend overall for process redesign, pollution control, and/or trading units for the various types of pollution they generate. This has always been a goal of many reformers of environmental law and economics.

The authors of *Cradle to Cradle* may not have known it, but their goals of reducing IDPCs and their surrogates to zero, as in a fully functioning circular economy (CE), correspond to idealized "attainment" for these pollutants on a regional basis. Idealized attainment in air pollution regulation is demonstrated by not just meeting or being below the NAAQS, but where the concentrations of pollutants are zero. More realistically then, attainment of the IDPC surrogate pollutant standards, which are relevant to regulating the generation of solid waste pollution, represents a state where the regional pollutants associated with these characteristics still exist but where the solid waste is environmentally manageable.

The Support for, and Advantages of, Rationing and Preserving Fossil Fuels

Crossing our collective fingers in the hope that taxing or trading fossil fuel-based CO_2 emissions solely at the back end, and only then from the large sources[33] to sufficiently reduce CO_2 emissions runs the unacceptable risk, among others, of doing too little too late. Doing so begs the obvious question: why bother spending precious time trying to reduce a fraction of CO_2 emissions when globally rationing fossil fuels *guarantees* targeted reductions? The point is that trading should be conducted only after first rationing and gradually reducing fossil fuel-based carbon at the front end. The mitigation strategy developed in Chapter 9 does this and more.

The reader should note also that rationing fossil fuels does not just apply to coal since CO_2 emissions generated from its combustion are just a fraction of the CO_2 being generated. Nor should rationing apply to just the major sources of air pollution that combust fossil fuels. In fact, hierarchically, fossil fuel rationing must apply globally and then nationally because greenhouse gas emissions, as a global issue, must also be dealt with on a national scale. Thus, it is important to note again that rationing at the national level can simply be thought of as another form of CaT—set a limit and let the market sort out who gets what, but where everyone participates in real time using actual national currency.

Whether limiting or rationing carbon at the front end would be politically acceptable is, for now a tangential, second-order concern that should not affect the first-order need to determine how to achieve both attainment of climate stability and sustainability with Nature-correct solutions first, political feasibility later. Nevertheless, the rationale for rationing, relative to other alternatives such as taxation, is explained in greater detail next. This is being done since there will be a good fraction of people who likely experience cognitive dissonance—they support action against climate change, but they are not yet comfortable with the concept of limiting the use of fossil fuels. The following discussion will attempt to overcome that dissonance.

By far the most critical reason for rationing fossil fuels is to *flatten and then lower* the CO_2 concentration curve (with the larger goal of achieving an Additional Earths at Global Development [AEGD] of zero, remember). While this is the primary purpose of rationing fossil fuels, there are other practical reasons to limit the use of fossil fuels as well:

- It provides the collateral benefit of reducing emissions of other combustion-generated pollution, such as nitrogen oxides (NOx), carbon monoxide (CO), etc.
- With the large number and variety of sources emitting CO_2 throughout the economy, a subset of source sectors emitting CO_2 exists that are not easily amenable to tracking and permitting, such as ocean vessels and office buildings. To address these and similar sources (where tracking and permitting will be overly burdensome), it is far more rational to ration/limit carbon at the front end, such as setting production limits from fossil fuel suppliers (think refineries) and phasing this limit downward to a level of maximum achievable reducibility. The market will sort out demand and supply from there.
- Fossil fuels do not recycle, so once used, they are not recoverable like aluminum cans are. Do the arithmetic: multiply the current world population by 50 years and the world per capita Btu usage rate and ask whether we have that much fuel content left by 2075 and whether we can live on a planet with the proportional amount of additional CO_2 in the atmosphere. Clearly, we need to wean ourselves off the use of fossil fuels. Fossil fuels instead should only be used as a backup, reserve supply for when no other alternatives exist. The production of steel and cement, which

currently relies on the generous use of coal, may be such candidates for that need.

- Austerity is often preached by mainstream economists, for example, lenders from the International Monetary Fund imposing austerity measures as a pre condition of providing assistance to financially challenged third-world countries with weak governance. Thus, where developed countries have been voraciously living it up on Nature's credit card, imposing austere measures to preserve *natural*, not just financial resources should not be up for debate.
- Rationing and preserving fossil fuels have their advantages. Realizing the actual, not just perceived, benefits of energy efficiency (EE) and pollution prevention (P2) is far more possible for the following reasons:
    - Implementing EE and/or P2 is far more likely to be implemented when energy input and material usage are constrained. Where corrective CaT or purely dissuasive taxation is only applied to the source to reduce emissions at the back end, then there is a lesser incentive to implement EE and/or P2. Furthermore, conducting EE and P2 so as to provide credits within a trading program will not usually work since emissions that result from such practices are not directly measurable. Lastly, if EE were widely implemented at a national scale, it would result in the shutdown of a number of power plants due to lack in energy demand, but there is no incentive to do so; with rationing and the subsequent incentivized implementation of EE that would result, this outcome would occur automatically. Being on a fuel budget ensures that *every* Btu is utilized much more wisely, so that pollutant reductions are made out of necessity whether the emissions benefits are directly measurable or not. Lest we forget, doing this mitigates climate change and preserves Nature.
    - Consequently, the rebound effect is avoided, at least at the macroscale. The typical example of the rebound effect is demonstrated by improving the fuel efficiency of automobiles, wherein improved fuel economy provides drivers the counterproductive incentive to drive more, thereby increasing emissions. Limiting fuel supplies, however, removes that incentive and encourages efficiency, to the benefit of preserving environmental welfare.
    - In terms of jobs, there will be a trade-off. There will be a gain of new jobs associated with EE and P2, particularly within a circular economy, while

there will be a loss of traditional jobs associated with resource extraction. It is probable as well that the job market associated with "circularity" will likely expand exponentially because necessity will be the mother of invention.

It should be noted that we have limited the harvest of timber and set aside lands as national parks, so rationing fuels or materials should not be seen as draconian or come as a collective shock.

> Critics of rationing at the front end who nevertheless support carbon abatement at the back end by taxation cannot escape one of the most fundamental laws of physics, namely, the conservation of mass. In particular, such critics have to demonstrate through appropriate combustion stoichiometry how X amount of carbon atoms emitted at the back end can be reduced to guarantee that Y amount of carbon atoms is being reduced at the front end to achieve attainment. The point is—anything short of *guaranteeing* reductions by setting limits at the front end is disingenuous. Taxation, will power, and sheer determination to reduce CO_2 emissions are substandard control devices.

If limiting or rationing fossil-based carbon[34] as an *input* is not the wiser approach overall, then it begs the question of just how serious global climate change has to become before we focus on limiting fossil fuel-based inputs.

The Impracticality of Controlling CO_2

We will see in Chapter 9 that the external trading of CO_2 emissions and the taxation for the purchase of TUs play a key role in the mitigation strategy, which is a variant of the comprehensive strategy itself. Upon observing current practice, we note that relying on the application of economic instruments in general to sufficiently reduce CO_2 emissions solely at the back end to a subset of emitters has been fraught with high expectations that have fallen far short of flattening the CO_2 concentration curve.

Consider one likely response to CO_2 trading, namely, switching to the use of cleaner fuels as a pre-"control" option.[35] The reductions made under the Regional Greenhouse Gas Initiative (RGGI)[36] trading program for CO_2 and the Santiago trading program for PM_{10} were primarily due to fuel switching (i.e., to natural gas). Fuel switching is certainly a necessary step in the right direction, but it's far from sufficient to achieve the necessary CO_2 reductions to mitigate the ravages of climate change.

For pollutants other than CO_2, such as VOC and PM, controls are much cheaper to retrofit than replacing the emission units themselves. In this light, the Acid Rain Program was successful because control equipment and/or cleaner fuels could be respectively utilized on and fired in existing utility boilers. Trading under the Acid Rain Program was used to strategically mitigate the costs associated with add-on controls that collect and/or transform emissions, which is currently not cost-effective for CO_2. There are no viable add-on control devices to scrub out CO_2 emissions, and energy efficiency measures by themselves, while necessary, are not sufficient; thus, responding to the need to significantly reduce regional CO_2 emissions using an external trading program on only the large emitters requires entirely replacing the emission unit or entire source with a completely new unit or facility.[37] While complete replacement is an impractical but unfortunately necessary means to achieve CO_2 emissions reductions within any regulatory scheme, limiting fossil fuels at a larger geographical (e.g., global) scale will at least cushion the replacement blow better, particularly where there is a shared commitment to be environmentally responsible and accountable, both nationally and globally. Doing so will eke out every opportunity for *all users* of fossil fuels, both large and small, to become more efficient, and where it becomes too costly to operate inefficient utility boilers (particularly under a global trading program), then market signals will dictate that the dirtiest units be shut down.

If NOx and VOC (both precursors to ozone), $PM_{2.5}$ or for that matter, vehicle miles traveled (VMT), cannot be sufficiently regulated due to the ubiquity of a various multitude of emissions generators, what hope is there for individually regulating CO_2 emissions from the ubiquitous number of generators on a mass scale? For example, how does the CO_2 generated by heating of skyscrapers in major cities and the large number of internal combustion engines (e.g., automobiles, nonroad diesel engines, diesel-fired emergency engines, locomotives, lawnmowers) get roped into CO_2 regulation? While CO_2 emissions are quantifiable from many major and minor sources and thus potentially reducible, there are just too many carbon-based fuel-burning emission units and corresponding CO_2-emitting sources that are not conducive to individualized regulation and tracking on a mass scale.

The Rationale for Not Using Economic Instruments to Reduce Carbon Dioxide Emissions Solely at the Back End

Notwithstanding all other significant issues, regulating CO_2 emissions via purely dissuasive taxation is also too little too late. When the scientific consensus presses us to act now to remove legacy CO_2 from the atmosphere,[38] the simplistic notion of only *discouraging* fossil fuel usage by taxing CO_2 emissions is flawed for two reasons. First, it relies on blind faith that economic tinkering at combustion's back end will automatically reduce the use of fossil fuels at the front end. In addition, it smacks of "economic correctness," a cousin of political correctness, since it steers clear of the economic incorrectness of limiting fossil fuel usage outright via CaC-based regulation. Taxing carbon emissions may have been sensible at a time when the concerns of climate change were more uncertain and "manageable," that is, during attainment of climate stability, but this is no longer the case. Taxation might alleviate climate change a bit by facilitating less unsustainable behavior, but settling for this alone—with less CO_2 being emitted—is a copout given the worsening crisis. If sin taxes, such as those on alcohol, haven't eliminated alcohol use, or more precisely, cirrhosis of the liver, then where the combustion of fossil fuels creates a global crisis, purely dissuasive taxation's value as a climate change-solving tool is clearly a nonstarter.[39]

In addition, for many sources, taxation would simply be treated as both a fee and the cost of doing business, where that cost would be passed on to consumers without a proportional environmental benefit. Thus, ultimately delegating the onus of a global climate crisis onto the backs of consumers via dissuasive taxation, as if the underlying climate problem is a simple behavioral one at the individual level, is clearly the wrong tool at the wrong time. More importantly, collecting taxes and spending the revenues for society's benefit may be all well and good, but it still does not ensure a solution to the calamity we face with the rapidly increasing pace of climate change.

As a sign of the compartmentalization of our environmental crises, addressing carbon as only a post-combustion problem is an ill-posed one. Whether solely using CaT or a carbon tax—an idea for which William Nordhaus was awarded a Nobel Prize in Economics[40]—should be used to reduce greenhouse gas emissions is a question that, on its merits, begs a deeper, more fundamental level of examination. Are we truly solving the right problem in the first place?[41] Waste plastics and CO_2 emissions are very much two sides of the same carbon coin, in effect fraternal twins separated at birth, so to speak, at the refinery. Regulating them separately post-consumption seems foolish, while regulating them as a rationed/limited input seems far more reasonable.[42]

Typical is the report, "Pathways to Deep Decarbonization in the United States,"[43] which presented a study on how to significantly decarbonize the economy in order to reach 2°C by 2050. Nowhere in that paper was there any mention of the ubiquitous waste plastics problem, as if the problem is meant to be addressed separately, or worse, ignored. Without minimizing the crisis of climate change, what's the point of addressing that crisis if microplastics significantly deteriorate our environment, as we now know they do? The point is to first address fossil-based carbon as an input (i.e., whether as a fuel or as a feedstock) before it is released to the environment; addressing carbon outputs as emissions and solid waste is too late.

Further Thoughts on Taxation as a Component of Regulating Fossil-Based Carbon as an Input

Would simply taxing the use of fossil fuels be a reliable means to guarantee reductions in greenhouse gas emissions to reach the goal of climate stability? To answer that question, let's ask this: would it have been appropriate to tax DDT, or was it proper for government policymakers to ban it outright? How about taxing thalidomide, or was it also appropriate to ban that outright? While banning fossil fuels immediately is unrealistic, reducing and phasing out fossil-based carbon inputs by rationing, utilizing a global CaT program to limit and then reduce CO_2 emissions, and recycling waste plastics to achieve *guaranteed* results is clearly the better plan.

> Contrary to common popular opinion within policy circles, climate change is NOT a problem to be solved by economics. Climate change is obviously and fundamentally an environmental problem that must be solved by regulatory methods, but the narrative in the United States and elsewhere has been hijacked. If it were possible, we would simply use control devices to reduce GHG emissions in the same way we use them to reduce emissions of NOx and particulates. While there are no control devices to reduce GHG emissions, this doesn't mean that we have to surrender reduction of these emissions to "market solutions," such as taxation; it just means we have to "control" emissions directly at the source, that is, by capping carbon inputs. This reflects the Fundamentals of Air Pollution Regulation 101, the common method air pollution regulators already

use to limit emissions of other pollutants. For example, to limit emissions of VOC from coating operations at a source, it is necessary to put limits on both the amount of coatings used and the VOC content of the coatings applied. To cap global CO_2 emissions at the international level requires capping carbon inputs. There is simply no other substitute.

Global climate change is a pollution problem best addressed by strong limit-and-phaseout regulation at the front end first, *then* followed by the imposition of economic disincentives.

A Comment on Regulating Mobile Source Emissions

While the focus of Part 2 has mostly been on regulating the generation of air pollution from stationary sources, it is worth a moment to discuss emissions from mobile sources. The NRC makes the following comment regarding a limitation of the Mobile Source Emission Control Program:

> Growth in vehicle miles traveled, personal automobile usage, and popularity of fuel-inefficient vehicles (for example, SUVs) has offset a significant portion of the gains obtained from stricter emission standards on individual vehicles. With the exception of the conformity requirements of the 1990 CAA Amendments and subsequent related legislation, air quality managers remain unable to affect these societal and behavioral determinants of mobile-source emissions.[44]

Unlike regulating discrete stationary sources, where it is much simpler to track operations and emissions reductions, the sole tool regulators currently have for regulating mobile sources is setting performance standards per model of vehicle engine and averaged per fleet. Regulating mobile sources to the point where total emissions within a region are assuredly reduced also requires regulating vehicle miles traveled (VMT); that is, collectively regulating drivers' behavior, venturing into legal and political territory that is outside the scope of the discussion here. In a region where mobile source emissions are increasing due to an increase in VMT, regulating mobile sources is a difficult proposition at best.

The point here is that without limiting regional fossil fuel usage, mobile source emissions within the region cannot be regulated in earnest without focusing on limiting VMT. The comprehensive strategy can certainly address the contribution to regional emissions from discrete stationary sources, but other than simply setting performance standards per model of vehicle or average per fleet, how regulators address the portion of regional emissions contributed by mobile sources is far more difficult if fossil fuel usage is not limited.

If regulators are truly serious about flattening the CO_2 concentration curve and reducing emissions from mobile sources in NAAs, rather than just regulating emissions per vehicle horsepower (and per fleet), it is far better tactically to regulate fossil fuel-based emissions. This is best accomplished by limiting and then tightening the total amount of fossil fuels collectively used by all vehicles and nonroad engines globally, nationally, and regionally. That wouldn't be an exact science, of course, but it is better than simply relying on an average performance standard per fleet or per vehicle and hoping for reductions thereafter.

Critiques of the NRC, Schoenbrod/BTL and Nordhaus

Critique of the NRC

Although the NRC report addressed relevant issues with regard to regulating under the CAA, it tended to be grandiose; for example, when they suggest that "The air pollution challenges facing the nation over the coming decades are complex; they are likely to require mitigation strategies that are consistent with the 'principle of one atmosphere,'"[45] that is, the large-scale application of multi-pollutant AQM. Likewise, they later state that "a comprehensive, multisector strategy for the mitigation of both air and water pollution may ultimately prove necessary to comprehensively protect human and ecosystem health."[46]

On this latter point, the NRC is accurate but probably not in a way they foresaw. As will be seen later, the comprehensive strategy is generalized in Chapter 7 to holistically regulate the generation of multi-media environmental pollution, which not only includes air, water, and on-site generated waste pollution as well as resource inputs (e.g., fossil-based fuels and feedstocks), but also inherently detrimental product characteristics. So while mitigating air and water pollution can be accomplished, the NRC's claim is inaccurate if it is to occur within the current constraints of both the Clean Air Act and the Clean Water Act. A fundamental rethinking of both Acts would have to be undertaken first.

While they also mention the complexities of the current program, they do not address how to "de-complexify" the AQM process itself. In effect, if not by intention, the NRC's proposals would do more to add to the current bureaucratic logjam than alleviate it.

Critique of Schoenbrod et al./*BTL*

While the NRC proposed additional impractical and grandiose regulatory tasks to an already flawed and bureaucratically logjammed Clean Air Act as noted in Chapter 3, it was also noted earlier that Schoenbrod's reform proposals included both wise and unwise choices to improve the current regulatory system.

Schoenbrod's suggestion to have other larger sources that emit interstate pollution regulated under the Acid Rain Program is sensible. They recommend that regulation of certain major sources that generate interstate air pollution (e.g., steel mills and cement plants) should be incorporated into the Acid Rain Program and be appropriately regulated by the USEPA rather than the states—given the USEPA's track record of handling the heavy lifting of the Acid Rain Program. Although this is certainly reasonable, determining just which sources contribute significantly to interstate pollution is not as easy and straightforward as Schoenbrod would lead us to believe. Oddly enough, there are some small industrial sources as well as some mobile sources that contribute to interstate pollution above a de minimis level. Nevertheless, whatever obvious interstate sources can be included under the umbrella of both the Acid Rain Program (and an adapted, more comprehensive CSAPR) should be included, while the states should address remaining sources but only if those sources are not significant contributors to other adverse areas outside the state.

The above proposals for improvement notwithstanding, trading with a set target and well-designed, CaC-based compliance-built-in regulation, not simply being under federal control, is likely one key reason why the Acid Rain Program was successful. In fact, in Chapter 6, where the trading scheme for IDPC and IDPC surrogates is developed, we will note that the sources that generate these solid waste characteristic pollutants, which can easily be transported across state boundaries, are not the type of program the feds should undertake. They would be overwhelmed were they to do so. Nevertheless, the sensible strategy for regulating interstate air pollution via an external trading program is one that should be federally run.

Schoenbrod's suggested improvements are more than offset by their flaws, as discussed below. The other takeaways and problems associated with Schoenbrod's proposals can be distilled down to the following:

- Schoenbrod lost sight of the fact that the whole point of addressing AQM issues is to address health and welfare impacts. So after slicing off critical limbs of air pollution regulation (e.g., eliminating the distinction between NAAs and AAs and the removal of performance standards at the state level), Schoenbrod compounded the problem by demonstrating an almost pathological focus on trading between only the largest sources that generate interstate transport, to the exclusion of other localized contributors to NAAs. Their infatuation with trading is out of proportion to its purported benefits.
- While subsuming the regulation of major sources of interstate pollution under the Acid Rain Program and a more comprehensive CSAPR helps to streamline the AQM program, eliminating the distinction between NAAs and AAs under their approach presents a major problem that must still be addressed. This begs the question—by eliminating the distinction between NAAs and AAs, how would regulators address welfare and health impacts in current NAAs when interstate trading would allow sources in AAs to act as "farm teams" for their emissions to sources in NAAs? That is, how can it be justified for sources to provide emissions from areas of good air quality to sources in areas of existing poor air quality? Equally egregious would be where emissions are externally traded from an NAA to a distant or adjoining AA, potentially turning that AA into an NAA. Allowing sources that significantly contribute to adverse welfare and health impacts in NAAs to have pollutants transferred to or from AAs defeats the purpose of using regulation to improve both citizens' health and Nature's welfare. If legally designated NAAs are eliminated under Schoenbrod's scheme, then NAAs could persist indefinitely. Finally, and more fundamentally, by eliminating the distinction of NAAs and AAs, what exactly is the purpose of regulating air pollution at all?

  The whole point of trading is to have the major polluters in NAAs being forced to compete *among themselves* to reduce emissions to improve air quality, including in EJ areas. While it is possible that emissions may increase in some areas within the NAA while decreasing in others as the overall cap declines, the trading program will eventually facilitate reductions everywhere and much quicker than the decades-old AQM program we have in place today.
- Schoenbrod's/*BTL*'s proposed strategy presents another radical flaw: their dismissal of New Source Performance Standards as a regulatory backstop

to reducing pollution. Eliminating them completely at the state level because they believe trading may pick up the slack is a moral hazard that is unacceptable in any AQM program. They provide no discussion on how to appropriately regulate equipment operation to ensure that emissions are minimized or provide any assurance that emissions are correctly quantified. Since the dispensing of performance standards is a critical issue, this topic will be discussed in more detail later in this section.

- Schoenbrod/*BTL* proposes, also quite radically, the elimination of NSR and Title V at the state level. They were vague by failing to mention even briefly how the following significant issues must be addressed: the consequences of physical modifications, the preconstruction *Prevention* of Significant Deterioration of air quality (including how much increment will be consumed), how permitting fits into the program, the necessity for the increased use of stack testing,[47] or the critical role of fees to operate the program.
- The Title V permitting program is complex (and must certainly be simplified), but without it or a similarly designed program, what exactly does Schoenbrod propose regulators use to permit and inspect sources and to ensure that operations and emissions are associated with the sources' trading allocation? What documents would members of the public rely on to scrutinize sources' applicable requirements? How does anyone know what monitoring or recordkeeping requirements apply?
- They fixate on interstate pollution as if the bulk of the problem of pollution is due to it. They miss the point that many regional ozone NAAs, for example, are localized health-impacted areas; they provided no proposal to address them, other than allowing state regulators the option to address them as they see fit with only minimal federal oversight.
- Their almost pathological fixation on trading neglected explicating in any detail the other critical aspects of the regulatory scheme (e.g., assurance of compliance or major and minor source regulation in general).
- Schoenbrod did not address the transition of sources into and out of trading programs. Nor do they establish any criteria to determine when trading ceases.
- They do not detail the flaws due to excess bureaucracy within the current system, or how to address it.
- Lastly, Schoenbrod would have Congress reform the environmental statutes. Do we really want Congress to do what they think is best or, worse yet,

> let special interests write the next version of the CAA? Is it not better for those closest to the regulatory action to develop the best consensus-based approach and put Congress on the hot seat if they don't adopt what the experts claim is best?

One key takeaway from Schoenbrod is that they wanted to use trading as the cure-all for regulating stationary sources and focusing their attention on only a fraction of the problems besetting the current AQM program in the United States while losing focus on addressing health and welfare impacts.

Schoenbrod's argument against eliminating performance standards at the state level must be aggressively countered. They fail to realize that the emissions cap on a source (via its allotment) is the source's "performance standard,"[48] while emission units at the source have their own performance or emissions standards. Without question, regional trading and requiring equipment performance standards are wholly compatible. Performance standards are a virtual guarantee on an emission rate, so why on earth should regulators throw that valuable Ace into the discard pile? New Unit Performance Standards allow sources within an external trading program to lessen their emissions, so that more emissions (likely proportional to production) can be emitted to fit under their allotment. For example, replacing a boiler with a NOx emission rate of 0.12 lb/mmBtu with one that must meet a performance standard of 0.10 lb/mmBtu means that, for the same level of usage, emissions at the source will be lower, so that the source can not only stay below its allotment, but it can also sell excess trading units.

Removing performance standards begs the obvious question that the Schoenbrod team does not address: how will regulators be able to ensure that emission units properly operate? Without that information, it becomes more difficult to determine that unit's emissions, particularly when a CEMS is not used. Furthermore, performance standard requirements are more than just numerical standards or work practices; they also include emissions monitoring or testing requirements to ensure proper operation of equipment, recordkeeping, reporting, etc. The argument was made in Chapter 4 to simplify some of these requirements, but the outright elimination of them would be a huge setback to regulating air pollution.

Furthermore, if performance standards are removed as a tool of regulation, what requirements would be imposed on minor sources that are not subject to trading? For example, if hospitals (unlikely to be major sources) each use a small boiler currently subject to the 40 CFR 60 Subpart Dc NSPS, does this requirement still apply to those boilers if this NSPS is eliminated? If performance standards disappear, what happens to the regulation of H_2S, for example? As there typically aren't enough sources of H_2S within a region to allow trading, would sources be given free rein to emit H_2S with impunity with no underlying performance standards? Regardless of source size, eliminating performance standards would virtually give carte blanche for sources to generate more emissions, which is not conducive to the goal of reducing health and welfare impacts under an AQM program.

Another key reason to require NUPSs for individual emission units is this—would we advise regulators to simply trust sources to rely *solely* on trading to solve their air quality impacts? Performance standards act as a firm, unquestioned regulatory backstop, so a fair question to ask is—if performance standards are eliminated, then what regulatory backstops fill in the gaps that trading cannot?

Moreover, the larger a source's emissions are, particularly where those emissions adversely impact health and welfare, the more performance standards should apply, not less. Getting the most bang for the buck with NUPSs by simplifying them while maintaining their effectiveness (i.e., strong but light, like composite materials) is strongly advised. One key centerpiece of the comprehensive strategy is that BACT-like NUPSs be *tightened* every five years—certainly not eliminated. Again, they recommend the use of a trading program that not only solves the ills of deteriorated air quality but acts as a panacea for all the ills of the current logjam as they perceive it. Instead, in Chapter 4, it was proposed to use trading only as a tool that serves the greater mission of eliminating *existing* deterioration of air quality in adverse areas, not an end in and of itself.

The reader may wonder why this issue is being beaten to death in such detail. This is because the role of performance standards within a trading program will play a very crucial role in the strategies developed later in Parts 3 and 4. In fact, they are fundamentally necessary to regulating the generation of multi-media pollution (including achieving a circular economy), as well as the global emissions of CO_2 as a means to rigorously mitigate climate change, and more. Performance standards are fundamental to regulating the generation of environmental pollution.

The goal of reform here should first and foremost be the reduction of the negative harms to Nature and human health and welfare from air pollution by appropriately and efficiently streamlining the program, not dismembering some of its valuable appendages, such as the elimination of backstop requirements like the NSPSs and the distinction between NAAs and AAs all to promote trading and transfer regulatory flexibility to the states. Unfortunately, Schoenbrod's reform proposals have the facade of environmental reform but have all the earmarks of gifts benefiting industry in business-friendly states. The goal to optimize the regulation of air pollution from stationary sources requires effective strategic streamlining, not the elimination of major programs, which were developed to protect Nature and human health and welfare. Although Schoenbrod saw how complex the current program is, their team impulsively sought a simplistic, quick-fix solution, which is arguably as extreme as the opposite swing of the pendulum.

In contrast to Schoenbrod's reform proposals, the more thorough, well-designed comprehensive strategy represents the pendulum's mid-swing that keeps the baby safe and clean while the dirty bathwater is tossed out. The strategy breaks the impasse erected between the misguided reformers and the risk-averse, anti-trading environmental NGOs.

Critique of Robert Nordhaus

As stated in Chapter 3, Nordhaus, much to his credit, provided what is arguably the best synopsis of the problems associated with regulating under the Clean Air Act, most notably the macro design flaws of the CAA and grandfathering in particular. He focused on what he felt were the obvious "big ticket items," but unfortunately, he did not deal with the big ticket items one sees as a day-to-day practitioner, such as rule complexity and growth in the number of regulatory procedures.

For the level of effort he expended, Nordhaus's ideas are laudatory but they would unfortunately add to complexity. It was a bit difficult to follow the gritty details of his Option B, such as how and when to apply the two-tier operating permits scheme and what and when certain aspects of the CAA should be retained. Moreover, what he claimed would improve results would only do so at the expense of adding more complexity. For example, the merging of several standards into one, where they would still differ depending on whether the emission unit is new or existing, then determining these for multiple source categories, and further determining the specific source-specific tier standards, all just complicate the task of solving the emission reduction problem. He also avoided dealing with the nitty-gritty issues of rule complexity and failed to address the other "micro" design flaws of the CAA as seen from the state regulator's perspective.

In any event, readers are invited to sort it out for themselves, but in the end, though, it won't really matter since the level of complexity of Nordhaus's Option B renders its use moot due to it being too tethered to the CAA and being a bit too convoluted to be incorporated within an optimal, simplified strategy that could be understood by regulators and practitioners. In his defense, and based on his approach, if Nordhaus was not constrained by the existing limitations of the current CAA, he would have had much freer rein to propose a more streamlined approach. What is clear is that Nordhaus was without question on the right track with his breadth of coverage on some of the critical issues that needed to be addressed.

Promoting the Principles of Next Gen Regulation

For optimal regulation of air pollution and later, other environmental pollution, there is absolutely no question that Giles's Next Gen principles for the redesign of regulations must be adopted. This author can muster only minor quibbles with regard to Giles's Next Gen principles. She did not want to give much, if any credit to cap-and-trade for the success of the Acid Rain Program, going so far as to say that "the compliance outcome would have been the same" without it.[49] She asserts that its success came about "because tough, prescriptive rule design gave the regulated utilities no way out. It was a triumph of command and control."[50]

Giles was correct to attribute the success of the Acid Rain Program to rules with built-in compliance that used command-and-control to, quoting Giles from Chapter 2, "block the violation exits," such that compliance was the default option. Without question, trading has received too much hype for the Acid Rain Program's success while CaC has received too little; Giles is correct to revise this history. However, she downplays the means to efficiently reduce emissions via trading. If cap-and-trade was taken away, the question then becomes—how else would those same reductions have been made, with equivalent effectiveness? If CaC would have worked just as well without trading, then why create the Acid Rain Program in the first place? And how would she explain the other successes of trading cited by NRC/Schoenbrod? In short, the success of the Acid Rain Program was a "collective" effort, of which command-and-control played an essential role throughout the program, but where trading played a key role as well.[51]

It can be concluded that the optimal regulation of air pollution from stationary sources functions best with the proper blend of both CaC and market instruments where each serves their specified purpose (i.e., CaC applies well where specific certainty is necessary and a market instrument applies well where options are allowed to meet that specified requirement). As demonstrated in the comprehensive strategy, the symbiotic Yin and Yang aspects of corrective CaC and trading, respectively, show that both CaC-based requirements and market instruments sandwiched between the use of CaC at the upper end (i.e., a regional cap) and lower end (e.g., use of CEMs) were optimal, as was successfully demonstrated in the Acid Rain Program. It is understandable and justifiable for Giles to be a defender of CaC while downplaying the often overly hyped role of markets, but the antagonism is a bit too undeserved. Giles may not appreciate that markets worked well elsewhere to reduce environmental harms, but the flexibility provided under an umbrella of a CaC-based requirement through the use of trading has a role to play, if only passively in the shadow of its more dominant CaC partners. A similar point applies to the use of performance standards, the significance of which Giles also downplays.[52]

In response to a self-posed question about whether a rule is either market-based or one-size-fits-all, she properly asked:

> Who cares? Our goal isn't fighting over label primacy; it is the more exacting practice of building a strong and resilient structure by creatively using all the tools.[53]

It is noteworthy that a couple of actual regulatory practitioners, Giles and this author, are far more aware that the CaC versus market instruments question is not the binary either-or question that those in academia seem to portray it as.

With regard to her very praiseworthy prescriptions for improving regulatory compliance, they unfortunately appear to be more grandiose than practical. Decrying the current state of poorly designed rules and rampant noncompliance, she curses the darkness much more than lights any candles. By not providing copious examples of just how to better redesign rules and regulations, she at best only theorizes about what must be done. Research must be conducted to find the solutions to better-written rules yet, considering the number of years since Next Gen was first theorized and developed, that research has shown few insightful examples. In Giles's defense, however, this is far more an indictment of academic legal scholars who have had every opportunity to lend a hand to assist their overwhelmed practitioner colleagues by tackling this critical real-world problem, yet many such scholars act more like pundits than problem solvers. It is this author's opinion then, that one shouldn't expect legal scholars in academia to tackle the problem due to its applied nature.[54] In contrast, engineers in academia are only too happy to tackle real-world problems.

This author's concerns with Giles are minor. Without a doubt, her principles have a major role to play in the redesign of regulations and compliance. While one of this book's larger goals is to improve environmental quality through a well-designed, generalized strategy to regulate the generation of multi-media environmental pollution as well as to restore ecosystems, it is absolutely essential that Giles's focus on writing well-designed rules plays a significant role toward achieving that goal.

So Will Adopting the Comprehensive Strategy and Curing the Design Flaws Break the Logjam?

Optimistically speaking, adopting the comprehensive strategy, including curing the current design flaws, will certainly go a long way toward relieving the current policy and bureaucratic logjam. There's something for everybody on both sides of the reform debate to like and dislike. The aggressive CDC-like regulatory approach for adverse regions should be much more palatable to environmental NGOs due to the tightening of regional caps, while the use of both external trading in NAAs and PALs in AAs should be acceptable to industry because they provide operational flexibility for emitting pollutants. Likewise, the tightening of New Unit Performance Standards every five years for new and modified units, rather than the use of BACT/LAER, may disappoint environmental groups somewhat, but unlike BACT/LAER, these revised standards will apply to *all* subject units constructed or modified at all sources, not just for projects at major sources.

Nor does much of the comprehensive strategy pose a political threat to the policymaking hierarchy, with the possible exception of correcting current design flaws such as reducing rule complexity. Correcting those flaws will be much tougher, so long as the center of political gravity within the current regulatory food chain avoids clarifying, through discussion with its downstream experts, what works best to reduce bureaucratic pollution. It is obvious that the American AQM system cannot make significant improvements if policymakers and regulators are unwilling and/or unable to address the underlying design flaws and their own blind spots, deliberate or otherwise. When attainment of bureaucratic pollution standards is achieved, regulators can better focus on addressing environmental pollution.

While the comprehensive strategy by itself may be met with stern resistance, it will likely be the generalized strategy developed in Chapter 7 that will gain the necessary traction to adopt the comprehensive strategy. This is because the generalized strategy is holistically applied across *all* environmental media, including regulating the generation of solid waste pollution that facilitates the transition to a CE. That said, it would be logical to assume that the European Union and, to a lesser extent, China, will be further ahead of the United States in adopting a CE because the United States is still naïve to the concept.

Criticism of Past Reformers and Critics

Oddly enough, the policy logjam is in part bemoaned in the literature by scholars who are primarily within the legal profession. However, within the regulatory trenches, a good chunk of the current bureaucratic logjam itself is in part largely the direct result of the risk-averse legal profession itself needing assurances, re-assurances, and re-re-assurances that the rules and regulations, Title V Statement of Bases, NSR project summaries, guidance documents, and many other detailed documents and procedures created by the actions of attorneys, regulators, and managers, are legally impermeable so as to withstand challenge. In other words, isn't the need for these detailed legal defense documents dictated from *within the very culture* of the legal profession that complains of the national policy logjam? One need only recite Stewart, Elliott, or Esty from Chapter 2 again here. So who exactly do reformers expect will lead all of us out of the policy logjam? Are they advocating that the same culture that played a major role in getting us into the current bureaucratic logjam be the ones to get us out of the policy logjam?

There will no doubt be skeptics and critics of reform. Such detractors are urged to go to the blackboard with chalk in hand and rigorously demonstrate why the current system is optimal, for example, justifying why CO_2 should be treated as an attainment area pollutant in the United States or why grandfathered coal-fired boilers should not be regulated further. Being forced to go up to the blackboard to solve such a problem and prove its correctness is a form of "Criticism Repellent," in that it seeks to screen out the armchair critics who only want to criticize without knowing how to find better solutions. It is expected that there will be critiques of the comprehensive strategy, but it is not sufficient to simply be negative—critics must state why a given aspect of the strategy is substandard and then propose how to improve the strategy.

Putting the New Strategy to the Test

Putting the new strategy to the test will determine its efficacy in reducing air pollution and alleviating the welfare and health impacts of it. At the national level, resolving the problems associated with optimality may prompt legislators to finally act. Think about it—wouldn't we really want legislators to have access to an already determined, optimal regulatory scheme *before* the special interests seek to deform it into a shape they dictate? At the same time, it's quite clear that the critically necessary changes we need will only be endorsed from the bottom up and implemented from the top down. Realistically, consensus as to what comprises optimal regulation of air pollution and the pressure that builds to facilitate it may not be sufficient by itself to change the CAA, which might only reach the tipping point by mitigating climate change and regulating multimedia environmental pollutants, particularly those linked to facilitating the transition to a CE. Upon their adoption, it is just natural to collaterally adopt the comprehensive strategy as well.

If there is actual bottom-up interest in enacting an optimal AQM program, particularly after consensus has already been reached, Congress should see that the design flaws are corrected and allow a test run for the strategy in a few attainment and nonattainment areas. Congress could first amend the CAA to allow states to experiment with proposals before adoption at full scale. Policymakers at the national and state levels, in association with clean air organizations, could then work out the kinks during the implementation of the strategy.

Encouraging US Regulators to Adopt the New Approach

After these many decades, it is safe to say that the Clean Air Act is a flawed document. To address its flaws, advice for transforming the CAA was provided in Part 1. Although much has been written about the need for substantial reform of the CAA, precious little has actually been developed as a strategy to this point. For sure, the literature is filled with proclamations to expand the use of emissions trading, but nobody, including Schoenbrod and Nordhaus, has effectively spelled out in significant detail how to do this optimally, nor has there been a comprehensive examination of the full extent of the problems underlying the current policy and bureaucratic quagmire or its resolution. That task has been undertaken in this Part, in part by maximizing the use of results-oriented methods and by striving for rigorous, objective, and achievable quantitative milestones while minimizing the deleterious characteristics of our current practice.

Due to retirements, many of the country's regulators are reaching the end of their careers. With their departure, a significant amount of institutional knowledge is being lost while a complicated, subpar program is sustained. With all its moving parts, the current regulation of air pollution is difficult enough. Rendering it *less* difficult and more effective, if given the opportunity, is the only logical next step.

As an engineer with a scientific method mindset, the author welcomes constructive criticism of the ideas that have been presented so far in this book. Fellow regulators are strongly encouraged to respond so as to refine and improve the strategy based on the lessons they have learned. Of course, this also includes those regulators in the United States who have been raised on the CAA but whose knowledge and experience enable them to "think outside the cage" established by the Act.

Although the United States is, from a practical standpoint, well-equipped to make the necessary changes as laid out here, given the current inertia against reforming policy, it is fair to assume that this will not happen anytime soon. The proverbial act of Congress seems ever distant. This becomes even more apparent when considering the need to adopt a strategy radically different from the current CAA, consensus for a transformed CAA notwithstanding.

Nonetheless, adopting the strategy in the United States is not unrealistic when we are facing the harms that environmental pollution inflicts. It can be strongly asserted that now is actually the best time to address these issues. We know that the best time to buy into the stock market is at a low, not a high, so if consensus is reached during the current "down time" in our country, such consensus will hopefully prompt a future Congress to act appropriately when a more enlightened turn in environmental awareness and political will arrives.

In any event, whether or not Congress even adopts the desired reform is not the most immediate concern. The bottom line is that the CAA is in a state of logjam and quagmire, and reforming its ills from within is a fool's errand. Instead, the approach here was to conduct the analysis outside the box with the goal of clarifying the aspects of the optimum regulatory scheme. This author's "inner mathematician" dictated that the optimality problem be solved first, regardless of how politically realistic it would be implemented by policy makers.

Once known, tested, and activated, the comprehensive strategy then becomes the gold standard that policymakers worldwide can use to help resolve the environmental issues that they face in their individual countries.

Could Regulators Elsewhere Be Open to Adopting the Comprehensive Strategy?

The theory and practice of the comprehensive strategy as presented in Part 2, much like the strategies developed later in Parts 3 and 4, should be deemed universal. There is only a family of optimal or near-optimal methods, with all remaining methods at suboptimal scale. Anything less than what is proposed here, particularly with a weak enforcement program, is likely to be far from adequate. As such, any country's policymakers must not downgrade an optimal system to fit their claim of a specific reality they feel is unique to them.[55] And it is important to note that a uniquely "Western way" of administering AQM for stationary sources is also not being promoted. As a general rule, then, after they have heard from fellow practitioners, policymakers and regulators elsewhere are strongly encouraged to provide counter-approaches, as long as they can demonstrate that their program is obviously better and operates at an optimal scale (if possible).

Thus, the approach taken in this book of presenting a clear blueprint of what optimality looks like for worldwide policymakers and regulators is based on the premise that they must first shore up their own capacity issues. This is as true for adopting the comprehensive strategy as it will be for adopting the later strategies. Taking actions other than what reflects optimality will only return superficial results.

Last Thoughts on Part 2: Giving Credit for Their Contributions

In developing the comprehensive strategy, this author wishes to commend the following environmental professionals for their insights and contributions:

- Stewart and Esty (without articulating the specific details, their prescience in knowing about the notion of regulatory optimality over two decades ago)
- Campbell (suggesting that LAER and BACT be replaced by NSPS/NUPS and tightening them over time)

- Coglianese (most emissions reductions were made with only a minority of regulations)
- Mamyluk (one of the few authors who realized that there is more than one dimension to solving the problem of reducing pollution)
- Gray and Shimshack (the evidence that deterrence results from inspections and monitoring of sources)[56]
- The researchers who put together the GAO Report (whereby intensive rather than routine inspections are critical to finding violations)
- Schmalensee and Stavins (their wisdom with regard to the realities of trading)
- Elliott (insights on regulatory practice)
- Schoenbrod et al. (taking a nice stab at addressing the policy logjam)
- Robert Nordhaus (seeing the macro inherent flaws of the current program and taking a more detailed stab proposing reforms to the CAA) and
- Giles (Next Gen compliance).

The comprehensive strategy, including these reform ideas, will play a role in the chapters that follow.

Notes

1 Most notably, the increase in the population of emissions, emission units, and other sources of air pollution reflects a fundamental flaw overlooked by advocates of dissuasive taxation of pollution, particularly for CO_2 emissions.

2 Performance standards set a CaC-based emission rate that is not to be exceeded, but with an economic option for sources to choose whatever acceptable process and/or control technology is necessary to achieve this rate. This dual, Yin and Yang-like property appears to be the proper balancing point between the use of CaC and compliance flexibility.

3 Unfortunately, not every emission unit has an underlying performance standard. Instead, stack testing to determine emission rates may have to be required for many subject units before a trading program is initiated. This is hardly a major downfall, but if necessary, academically affiliated environmental research centers can be tasked with the development of New Unit Performance Standards where there were none before, based on the results of several stack tests on new vendor-supplied equipment.

4 As a reminder, Reasonably Available Control Technology is a state-based standard that is imposed on emission units. As an example, coating facilities may be required

to use VOC-compliant coatings, whereas a printing facility that wishes to use noncompliant inks will have to use an afterburner to control VOC emissions.

5 Both the GAO Report and the Gray and Shimshack article were cited in Chapter 3.

6 Gray and Shimshack, "The Effectiveness of Environmental Monitoring and Enforcement." The abstract can be found at: https://www.journals.uchicago.edu/doi/abs/10.1093/reep/req017.

7 Kjetil Telle, "Monitoring and Enforcement of Environmental Regulations: Lessons from a Natural Field Experiment in Norway," *Journal of Public Economics* 99 (March 2013).

8 Recall that the core function of AQM—measure, count, then regulate—should *first and foremost* be directed toward the goal of determining emissions, the God Particle of AQM.

9 Schoenbrod, Schwartz, and Sandler, "Air Pollution: Building on the Successes Breaking the Logjam," 287.

10 During trading periods when there are disagreements between sources and regulators, a regulatory escrow account set aside could be utilized to minimize disruptions.

11 To reiterate, a newly constructed or modified unit must meet the new standard while an existing unit is required to meet the standard that applied at the time of its construction.

12 While there are regulations for the treatment of hazardous waste for downstream, off-site processing, targeted regulation of on-site generated hazardous waste at the source level does not yet entail the development upstream of even minimal performance standards for various source categories at the point of generation (i.e., in units of lb/unit of product). In this age of supposed enlightened environmental awareness, this shows just how backward environmental law still is.

13 Just to be clear, growth in emissions in AAs is allowed under the comprehensive strategy, but it should be designed to be progressively (exponentially) more difficult as the air quality worsens.

14 Given that NSR allows growth in NAAs, it is unclear as to how the opposition to trading serves its opponents. Anti-trading diehards would be wise to reserve their opposition until after reading the discussion in Chapter 6, where regulating inherently detrimental product characteristics, as well as rationing resources, facilitates the transition to a CE.

15 Unfortunately, NSR may sometimes follow this process instead: Define the project; what are the projected increases in emissions?; what are the thresholds?; what are the decreases from this and previous projects?; what units are being modified?; are they new or existing units?; what units may experience an increase in emissions without being physically modified?; is this project related to previous projects?;

etc.; develop a draft document for all decisions, and develop the draft permit that follows measure, count, regulate, regulate more, etc.

16 As noted previously, requiring the use of a CEMS (where possible) on emission units in NAAs would make the measurement of emission rates even more accurate.

17 One can think of source transparency as being a "work practice" imposed upon sources by regulators that helps to reduce source emissions. Even though a source may be in compliance to applicable rules and regulations, the mandatory disclosure of information encourages sources to reduce emissions and discharges even further, demonstrating that information is the God Particle of environmental protection.

18 As one example, if ambient monitors may fail to show that emissions were not reduced years after the trading program was implemented, this could indicate that sources have been misrepresenting emissions.

19 Found at 40 CFR 77.6(b).

20 NRC, *Air Quality Management in the United States*, 290.

21 The reader should be reminded that GHG emissions are generated by the "ubiquity of combustion units" everywhere throughout the economy, so reducing GHG emissions without rationing fossil fuels would be a very sluggish uphill battle indeed.

22 This discussion applies to what are called "criteria" pollutants, such as NOx, CO, and SO_2, and does not specifically apply to hazardous air pollutants (HAPs) because under the CAA they are treated separately. Thus, HAP emissions can increase under current regulation to create HAP hotspots.

23 It should be noted that this "loophole" within NSR was agreed to by city mayors when NSR was originally adopted.

24 One such example is the outdated NSPS for Asphalt Plants that should at least have an odor standard.

25 Without question, proper zoning requires that a level playing field be established so that no population is either geographically or disproportionately disadvantaged relative to any other. While this may be accomplished in theory, the uneven distribution of production facilities and hence the uneven generation of pollution still makes this ideal problematic.

26 U.S. General Accountability Office, "Drinking Water: EPA Could Use Available Data to Better Identify Neighborhoods at Risk of Lead Exposure," *Report to Congressional Requesters* GAO-21-78 (General Accounting Office, 2020), 2. https://www.gao.gov/assets/gao-21-78.pdf: "GAO's statistical analysis indicates that areas with older housing and vulnerable populations (e.g., families in poverty) have higher concentrations of lead service lines in the selected cities GAO examined."

27 Meredith Fowlie, Stephen P. Holland, and Erin T. Mansur, "What Do Emissions Markets Deliver and to Whom? Evidence from Southern California's NOx Trading

Program," *American EconomicReview* 102, no. 2 (2012): 991. https://faculty.tuck.dartmouth.edu/images/uploads/faculty/erin-mansur/mansur_emissions_markets.pdf. Researching the role of emissions trading under California's RECLAIM program, the authors found that there was no noticeable effect of trading to increase emissions from one area to the next.

28 The notion of relocation should not be controversial. Multinational companies operating in other countries have relocated factories for any number of reasons.

29 While the approach here is based on regulating pollution, New Jersey's approach to addressing pollution in EJ areas, where much more responsibility is placed on applicants rather than on regulators, is praiseworthy.

30 These act as precursors to the generation of solid waste pollution at the point of product manufacture, prior to the product being shipped, sold, consumed, and later discarded.

31 *Cradle to Cradle* highlights the fact that we don't have a pollution problem as much as we have a design problem. The authors basically propose redesigning production at the upstream end to reduce, and if possible, eliminate pollution at the back end.

32 This step will hopefully represent the "Next-to-Last Generation" of regulating the generation of environmental pollution in general. Without question, the Last Generation of regulation should be one that achieves the Grand Unified Theory of Environmental Law and Regulation that promotes sustainability with Nature. Chapter 10 will lay out the framework of such a theory.

33 Based on per sector Energy Information Administration data for the year 2022, relative to the use of fossil-fuel-based fuels (i.e., coal, natural gas, and petroleum) consumed among the residential, commercial, industrial, transportation, and electric power sectors, the percent of Btu from fossil fuels consumed for electric power generation was only 27.3 percent. https://www.eia.gov/totalenergy/data/monthly/.

34 We will see in Chapter 6 that reducing the generation of plastic solid waste pollution by rationing fossil-based carbon as a resource input, as a parallel regulatory approach to addressing climate change, will play a critical role in both achieving a CE and reducing harms to Nature.

35 Note that the definition of BACT in the CAA treats "clean fuels" as a potential control option.

36 Congressional Research Service, "The Regional Greenhouse Gas Initiative: Background, Impacts, and Selected Issues" (CRS, 2019). https://fas.org/sgp/crs/misc/R41836.pdf.

37 The cost of doing so can easily be hundreds of millions of dollars for large emitters.

38 Fred Krupp and Ernest J. Moniz, "Cutting Climate Pollution Isn't Enough—We also Need Carbon Removal," September 23, 2019. https://thehill.com/opinion/energy

-environment/462609-cutting-climate-pollution-isnt-enough-we-also-need-carbon -removal/.

39 Proponents of taxation as an adequate deterrent should consider that people are not deterred from becoming hedge fund managers, brain surgeons, or even economists just because tax brackets become progressively higher as incomes increase.

40 Coral Davenport, "After Nobel in Economics, William Nordhaus Talks About Who's Getting His Pollution-Tax Ideas Right," *New York Times*, October 13, 2018. https://www.nytimes.com/2018/10/13/climate/nordhaus-carbon-tax-interview.html.

41 Mamlyuk, "Analyzing the Polluter Pays Principle Through Law and Economics." As cited in the Introduction, Mamlyuk laid out his biosphere quality model for reducing limits on pollution harms based on not just the polluter pays principle (which economists tend to focus abstractly on individual sources), but he also proposed incorporating Nature within a regulatory regime. Peculiarly enough, there are articles in the literature that still promote the zombie idea of the per-source examination of the polluter pays principle to reduce emissions.

42 It is worthwhile to take the notion of ill-posed problems a step further. The reader is urged to consider the following nonrhetorical questions—what is the economic cost to elephants of clean water? What is the value of wetlands to biodiversity? The likely response to these questions is that our economic system is not equipped to address them, which is the whole point. Using anthropocentric measures of value to price only what is valuable to *humans* but not to Nature itself is a gaping flaw and a major failing of our economic system. Likewise, a legal system constructed around mediating disputes, maintaining order, and seeking justice, with humans (and their institutions) virtually always front and center, only compounds the problem by being extremely problematic for sustaining Nature in perpetuity. An alternative legal framework to this flawed paradigm will be developed in Chapter 10.

43 J. H. Williams, B. Haley, F. Kahrl, et al., *Pathways to Deep Decarbonization in the United States.* The U.S. report of the Deep Decarbonization Pathways Project of the Sustainable Development Solutions Network and the Institute for Sustainable Development and International Relations, 2014). https://biotech.law.lsu.edu/blog/US-Deep-Decarbonization-Report.pdf.

44 NRC, *Air Quality Management in the United States*, 173.

45 NRC, *Air Quality Management in the United States*, 279.

46 NRC, *Air Quality Management in the United States*, 280.

47 To be fair to Schoenbrod, their proposal relies on sources that use continuous emissions monitoring systems (CEMS) on as many emission units as are feasible, so the review of physical modifications and conducting of stack tests on these emission units may not necessarily be critical. But it is also important to realize that not all of the various pollutant emissions from all major sources are measurable by a CEMS.

48 More precisely, this standard is that which applies when no localized health impacts result from that source alone.

49 Giles, *Next Generation Compliance*, 173.

50 Giles, *Next Generation Compliance*, 173.

51 It is also worth noting, as Giles had, that the accurate measurement of emissions via CEMS also played a key role in the program's success. Its significance can be credited to what might be called the minimization of the degrees of separation between the direct measurement of emissions and its immediate access by regulators and the public to ascertain compliance. This is in sharp contrast with the much higher degree of separation where regulators have to pour over records and data to determine what a source's emissions were and whether those emissions are compliant to applicable rules and regulations.

52 Giles, *Next Generation Compliance*, Chapter 6.

53 Giles, *Next Generation Compliance*, 175.

54 More will be said about this glaring deficiency in the Conclusion.

55 It is difficult to imagine how any unique approach can overcome the need to set absolute limits on pollution and tighten them downward using market incentives since doing so does not have a geographical bias.

56 Previously cited, this document's value cannot be overstated.

Part 3

The Adapted and Generalized Strategies

A Brief Description of the Core Strategy

For those readers who may have skipped to this chapter or who found it too difficult to wade through Chapters 1 through 5 because air pollution regulation was outside their area of expertise, this preliminary discussion to Chapters 6 through 8 provides the core takeaway from Part 2. The key points will play a critical role here in Part 3 to develop the regulatory strategy for not only the generation of solid waste that will facilitate the transition to a circular economy (CE) but also the generalized strategy that will regulate the generation of environmental media in general. In fact, key components of the comprehensive and generalized strategies can be utilized to mitigate climate change (See Chapter 9) and regulate resource inputs in agricultural production.

To guide the reader through the thinking process for the approach taken in Part 3, the core of the comprehensive strategy to regulate the generation of air pollution for stationary sources consists of the steps below, although it should be noted that the following is only a synopsis of the detailed information in Chapter 4 and the follow-up insights and commentary in Chapter 5:

- The rationing and phasing down of fossil-based carbon inputs *guarantees* that the CO_2 concentration curve flattens and drops. Taking any actions less than this are at best "half-hearted, half measures," which are at best ensured to only achieve incremental climate change abatement.
- Within nonattainment areas for a given pollutant, the respective yin and yang of setting limits on total quantities of regional pollutants and trading them is required by those sources that generate those particular pollutants in major quantities. Setting and declining limits represents the environment "getting its cut up front" in the pollution-reduction deal, while trading is nothing more than a simple tool to achieve reductions. By far, the best friend of the environment is setting limits on the generation of pollution and reducing them, thereby ensuring that the strategy Command-and-Control (CaC)-based. There is no "right to pollute" since regional emissions are required to be reduced.
- The required reductions in pollution at sources to meet declining limits send a clear feedback message to those sources to add control devices, switch

fuels, and/or redesign their manufacturing processes in order to minimize emissions to reconcile their allotments or meet plantwide emission limits.

- While regional caps for a pollutant apply to the region and trading for that pollutant applies to all sources that emit that pollutant in major quantities, performance standards apply to actual emission units or operations at all sources, major and minor. These equipment performance standards must be tightened every five years so that new units to be installed or modified units must meet these tighter standards (while existing units continue to meet their previously applicable standards).
- The goal of the strategy is to achieve "attainment" of ambient air quality standards by properly blending the use of CaC-based regulation and market instruments (e.g., trading and dissuasive taxation on the purchase of trading units).
- The division of labor has to be optimal also, in that federal employees and state regulators have their roles, academia and environmental research centers have their roles, and engineers and attorneys have theirs.
- Taxes on the purchase of TUs must act as a deterrent to reduce the generation of pollution.
- Clearly, the rules, regulations, and the trading system itself have to be well-designed (think Next Gen) and not captured by any stakeholder. Also, excess bureaucratic methods and procedures ("bureaucratic pollution") must be minimized so that they do not become a parasitic load on the function of the regulatory program itself.

The ramifications of applying this core strategy and other techniques to the generation of pollution from *all* environmental media cannot be overstated. With the combination of rationing fossil fuels, the tightening of both regional limits and New Unit Performance Standards, there is a constant "regulatory forcing" of emissions reductions. If it can be done for air pollution, it can certainly be done for the generation of pollution from other media as well, even where it would appear there are not yet the quantifiable pollutant characteristics to be regulated. However, we will see that in Part 3, after developing measures of certain hitherto undeveloped pollutant characteristics, this strategy is amenable to not just regulating the generation of water and on-site generated waste but more significantly, *to manufactured products themselves* that later become solid waste. With appropriate constraints, the adoption of a media-wide means to force reductions downward will facilitate the achievement of a circular economy (CE), the restoration of ecosystems, and a prerequisite to reaching sustainability with Nature.

A Quick Note on Terms of Usage

Unfortunately, the terms "circular economy" and "sustainability" get bandied about a lot in the literature, oftentimes without being specifically defined. Some authors play fast and loose with these terms, and the nature of their meaning tends to be vague and implied. Reaching attainment of a CE and making progress toward sustainability with Nature as developed here will not necessarily conform to the terms "circular economy" and "sustainability" as typically used by political leaders, academics, environmental nongovernmental organizations, and others.

While some authors might use the term "sustainability" to only mean environmental sustainability, other authors include a social equity component. Parts 3 and 4 focus on sustainability with Nature, where not just harms to Nature are reduced (to reach "attainment") but also where ecosystems are restored (until attainment of an Additional Earths at Global Development [AEGD] of zero is achieved). Thus, the answer to what a "circular economy" and "sustainability" are is actually deceptively simple—it is whatever attainment outcome that results from appropriate regulation.9

6

Adapting the Comprehensive Strategy to the Generation of Solid Waste Pollution

The Circular Economy: Truly Regulating the Generation of Solid Waste

Limiting the willful generation of air pollution from industrial sources should involve a broader context: limiting the willful generation of the multi-media environmental pollution from such sources. In a world that is nonattainment for sustainability with Nature,[1] this broader context also entails limiting resource use,[2] maximizing the reuse of waste materials, and minimizing the use of fossil-based carbon. Properly regulating these fuel, resource, and pollution components raises the possibility of a "Grand Unified Theory" for regulating not only the generation of environmental pollution from industrial and other sources but also existing legacy pollution, the interplay of resources, and the restoration of ecosystems as well.[3]

Instead of our current practice of treating each environmental media of pollution within separate, fragmented regulatory silos, taking a holistic approach to the generation of environmental pollution can lead to a general means for regulating pollution. In brief, this would be a far more systematic, organized, and eco-centric plan of attack than anything developed to date. Although climate change gets the most attention, the overarching goal of the generalized strategy is to comprehensively minimize the generation of all environmental pollution, whereby its expanded use to mitigate global climate change is just one outcome.

Regulating solid waste in the United States within its current linear economy is primarily being conducted at the point where the consumer good is tossed away into a well-designed landfill. While we dictate the treatment, storage, and disposal of hazardous waste, little is done to actually specify how to *redesign products* further "upstream" so as to minimize solid and hazardous waste pollution in the first place. While the European Union (EU) is requiring manufacturers to take responsibility for the impact on the environment of their products' design, known generally as Extended Producer Responsibility (e.g., of which product takeback is just one possibility), they are still in the very early, primitive stages of implementation.

In this chapter, we will develop a more flexible version of the Extended Producer Responsibility strategy by adapting the use of the comprehensive strategy to regulate the generation of solid waste pollution that will not only facilitate reuse and recoverability of materials but, more specifically, upon applying appropriate constraints, the so-called "adapted strategy" will facilitate the transition to a circular economy (CE). In the next chapter, the adapted strategy is generalized to more generally regulate the generation of all critical multi-media environmental pollutants. The generalized strategy can also be applied to resource/feedstock and fuel inputs, supply chains, imports, and on-site hazwaste generation. Although our goal is to minimize the generation of environmental pollution, the key component—redesigning the processes involved—implicates the broader transformation of our current linear economy to a CE.

Readers unfamiliar with the concept of CE are first referred to this description provided by the Ellen MacArthur Foundation:

> Such an economy is based on few simple principles. First, at its core, a circular economy aims to "design out" waste. Waste does not exist-products are designed and optimized for a cycle of disassembly and reuse. These tight component and product cycles define the circular economy and set it apart from disposal and even recycling where large amounts of embedded energy and labour are lost. Secondly, circularity introduces a strict differentiation between consumable and durable components of a product. Unlike today, consumables in the circular economy are largely made of biological ingredients or "nutrients" that are at least non-toxic and possibly even beneficial, and can be safely returned to the biosphere-directly or in a cascade of consecutive uses. Durables such as engines or computers, on the other hand, are made of technical nutrients unsuitable for the biosphere, like metals and most plastics. These are designed from the start for reuse. Thirdly, the energy required to fuel this cycle should be renewable by nature, again to decrease resource dependence and increase system resilience (e.g., to oil shocks).[4]

The books of Ken Webster[5] and Walter Stahel[6] provide insightful visions of just what the economic, industrial, and societal implications of what a CE should ideally look like.

Just What Does a "Circular Economy" Mean Anyway?

As noted in the Introduction, Kirchherr analyzed various definitions of the term "circular economy" in the literature.[7] The approach taken here in Part 3 is not technically about how to achieve a CE; rather, it is about reforming the regulation for the generation of environmental pollution by utilizing more rigorously such that achieving a CE is not the goal but an outcome. Thus, it is unnecessary to *define* a CE other than to say that it is the outcome that is achieved by minimizing the generation of solid waste and to a lesser extent other pollution. More specifically, it requires that the use of virgin resources be sufficiently constrained while waste materials are properly incentivized for continual use, such that reused materials are incentivized over those of virgin materials.[8] As will be seen in more detail later, many of the resulting benefits that arise within the many definitions of CE in the literature, such as reuse, remanufacturing, etc., will automatically be included by properly regulating the generation of environmental pollution.[9]

Since the economy cannot regulate itself into circularity by leaving it alone, as much as some might like to pretend that it can, the term "circular economy" as used in this book will at its core be regulation-facilitated. So as to avoid the continual use of the term "regulation-facilitated circular economy," CE will simply be used instead.

Outlining the Approach to Achieving a Theoretical/Ideal Circular Economy

Would it be crazy to assert that we can regulate the generation of solid waste pollution by taking a page out of the Acid Rain Program playbook? As we will soon see, this assertion is not at all crazy.

It should be noted early on that the development of the adapted strategy, and what will later be broadened to become the generalized strategy, will primarily focus on manufacturers of consumable and disposable products, such as appliances and plastic forks. However, the adapted and generalized strategies will likewise apply to higher order assembled products such as airplanes and even buildings since these are sources of "complexity" pollution when they are abandoned or demolished. While the bulk of the discussion is on manufactured consumable products, it is important to note that mega-assembled products should not escape our attention toward achieving both a CE and sustainability with Nature. In fact, as we will see in Chapter 9, higher order sustainability issues must also address urban sprawl and ecosystem restoration, but we must start simple and small and work up.

To guide the reader through the thinking process, the development of the adapted strategy for achieving an ideal CE will mostly be comprised of the following components:

- If we want to properly regulate the generation of solid waste, the first step is to change the deeply entrenched mindset of perceiving solid waste as nonhomogeneous junk and trash. As varied as solid waste is within waste streams, these items can be better characterized by just a small number of discrete, unique detrimental properties that are inherent to them, such as volume, complexity, their ability to be disassembled, compostability, and toxicity.[10] Quantifying these appropriate regulatory measures of detriment (MoD) and the pollution associated with solid waste is a prerequisite to developing the details of the adapted regulatory strategy. Complicating matters is the fact that while pollutants such as sulfur dioxide and carbon monoxide are fungible air pollutants, solid waste is "nonhomogeneously unfungible" within the waste stream, rendering it more difficult, but not impossible, to regulate its detrimental characteristics to later facilitate material recirculation.
- The foundation of regulating these measures of detriment (MoD) and the pollutants associated with them is next developed, such as what attainment means as far as the generation of solid waste is concerned and the proper use of command-and-control, limits, and trading/taxation. The total amount of MoD pollution generated as a function of manufactured product per unit time (similar to lb/hr rates for air pollution) must then be calculated.
- The yin and yang of setting limits on the total volumetric quantity of each regional nonattainment pollutant and the use of trading to reduce them are developed, in direct parallel to the comprehensive strategy for regulating the generation of air pollution in adverse areas.
- In order for manufacturers to meet declining allotments through trading, the concept of taking credit for reusing materials through the regulatory use of "Equivalent Trading Units" is developed; this is arguably the centerpiece of the strategy to facilitate circulation of materials, thereby facilitating the transition to a CE.

- Just as in the comprehensive strategy and its use of performance standards (e.g., lb/mmBtu for a boiler), manufactured products must meet, for a given detrimental characteristic, a "characteristic standard," a minimum recovery standard that all products must comply with.
- Rationing of, and taxing the purchase of trading units for, both resources and fossil-based inputs (e.g., organic chemicals) is required to ensure that circularity for existing materials is further incentivized.
- Due to their critical role, addressing how supply chains and imports must be regulated is necessarily included.

As we will see in Chapter 7, the adapted strategy can be expanded even further by applying it to other media, such as the generation of water pollution and on-site generated waste (e.g., for concentrated animal feeding operations). Distilled down to its core feature, probably the most groundbreaking aspect of the generalized strategy is that although unique pollutants are associated with each environmental media, *the same general methodology can be used to regulate the generation of pollution for each media*. In Chapter 9, the core methods employed within the generalized strategy can also be applied to achieve even "higher order" components of environmental sustainability itself.

Metrics: Types and Usage

There has been a great deal of discussion in the literature about a broad range of metrics used to measure some aspect of sustainability. Fiksel cites several examples from the United Nations and the World Bank that are used worldwide.[11] Among these are population density, arable land per capita, annual rainfall, housing costs, and poverty index; among those that are environmentally related are sulfur dioxide emissions and hazardous waste generated. Specific performance metrics that are typically seen include total solid waste generated, gallons of water consumed, and the amount of renewable energy used.

The World Business Council for Sustainable Development also documents several circularity metrics to facilitate the transition to a CE, but they are mostly of a business- and performance-oriented nature (e.g., circular value creation, operational efficiency).[12] In the broader literature specific to environmental concerns, however, performance metrics are typically focused on the usual suspects: water and energy use, the amount of air, water, and on-site waste pollution generated, CO_2 emitted, etc. In fact, if one performs an internet search for "Future Regulation of Sustainability Metrics Examples," the top search results are fairly typical. For example, there is the National Association for Environmental Management's (NAEM) 2014 paper: "The Future of Sustainability Metrics and Reporting."[13] Nonetheless, among the multitude of Environmental, Social and Governance (ESG) metrics currently in use, we are most familiar with those regulated metrics associated with environmental pollution. Unfortunately, companies are mainly measuring and reporting metrics, mostly for the benefit of providing a degree of transparency to their shareholders.

Interestingly, besides sustainability metrics, researchers in the CE community have been developing several different circularity metrics that attempt to tease out the critical elements of measuring, performance tracking, and possibly regulating those parameters, so as to facilitate the transition to a CE. Most notable is the universal Material Circularity Indicator (MCI) developed by the Ellen MacArthur Foundation. This metric includes as inputs the amount of virgin and recycled materials and reused components, usage durability of the product, destination of the product after use, and how efficient the recycling processes are that produce recycled input and after use. This metric produces a value between 0 and 1 where higher values indicate a higher circularity.[14] In the literature, other possible stand-alone environmental circularity metrics of note can also include water efficiency, waste diverted from landfills, and recycled content.[15,16]

Sifting Out the Proper Environmental Pollutants to Regulate

Absent a coherent underlying structure, use of both sustainability and circularity metrics has been ad hoc and piecemeal. Transitioning to a CE will require a more robust systematic methodology that is compatible with regulation.[17]

Those in the CE community tend to look at circularity metrics differently than regulators, namely, from the outside of the manufacturing facility looking in. However, the more appropriate approach should be the reverse—from the inside "regulating" out. In addition to the sustainability, environmental, and circularity "performance metrics" already in use, a few new "product-embedded" *regulatory* metrics will be added. These measures that will not simply be tracked just for performance *must be regulated as pollutants generated upon manufacture*, that is, discharged as pre-solid waste/product and embedded as a precursor of the product's pollution. These pollutants will be called "inherently detrimental product characteristics" (IDPC) and, for some others, "IDPC surrogates." In this sense, while all IDPCs and IDPC surrogates are circularity metrics, not all circularity metrics are necessarily IDPCs or IDPC surrogates.

These new product-embedded characteristics should be the only relevant ones within the environmental sustainability discipline worth focusing on for the purposes of regulation.

The concept of circularity begins with putting the onus of solid waste pollution generation onto its actual generators, not the consumers. So, if a source is held accountable for the air, water, and on-site waste pollution it generates, it must also be held accountable for all the environmentally and ecologically detrimental characteristics that are inherent to the product itself as manufactured at the source.[18] Another way of thinking of a product is as "pre-solid waste," that is, a near-cousin to the pollution that is generated directly to the air, water, and as on-site waste. IDPCs and IDPC surrogates, as specified below, must be measured and treated as actual pollutants to be regulated—because they are essentially those characteristics that adversely affect the environment due to their unfungible nonhomogeneity, unrecoverability, and ubiquity.

IDPCs that are pollutants in their own right are easy to identify; namely, a product's volume, toxicity, and in some cases its noncompostability. There are also inherently detrimental characteristics of products that are more like surrogates of or precursors to solid waste pollution, in that they are not immediately recognized as pollution in and of themselves, but are still instrumental in facilitating the discarding of the product as waste because they inhibit the reuse or recycling of their constituent materials. Inspired, developed, and quantified based on the characteristics described in the book *Cradle to Cradle*, among other sources,[19] these characteristics are: difficulty-of-disassembly (DoD) and complexity, that is, measures of irrecoverability and impurity;[20] for example, an automobile is more difficult to disassemble than a toaster, and a multi-doped copper alloy is more complex than pure copper. Up until now, IDPC/IDPC surrogate generated/'embedded' pollution has been hidden in plain sight because, as consumers, we have tended to consider the product, which, long after removal from the manufacturing facility, is consumed and typically thrown into a waste bin on its way to a landfill, where solid waste regulation is currently focused instead. As will be seen later, regulating these IDPC precursors "upstream" facilitates a means to better reduce them.

Besides regulating the IDPCs themselves, regulation must also be applied to a product's embedded IDPC surrogates prior to exit from the production or "resource transformation,"[21] line. Until very recently, this environmentally detrimental aspect of production has been unaccounted for by regulators. Yet, recent articles indicate that some of what are here called IDPC surrogate pollutants are measurable and, with further development, refinement, and simplification, are ripe for future regulation rather than being used for basic evaluation and tracking.[22] Just as the determination of emissions is the God Particle of air quality management (AQM), quantifying these MoD characteristics per product is the God Particle of regulating the generation of solid waste. Likewise, where stack testing, continuous emissions monitoring systems (CEMS), or the use of mass balance can typically determine actual air pollutant emissions, calculating the total product MoD discharged per hour acts as the solid waste equivalent. An MoD represents the constant, dimensionless "concentration"[23] of an inherently detrimental pollutant characteristic or a surrogate (e.g., complexity) embedded per product, which when multiplied by a volumetric rate of production, in units of ft^3/hour, is analogous to a rate as equivalently determined by an air pollutant stack test, typically measured in pounds per hour. In fact, where an embedded, dimensionless concentration can be accurately determined and then multiplied by a volumetric production rate,[24] determining its generation rate for an IDPC or IDPC surrogate-associated pollutant should be more accurate than measuring the variable air pollutant emission rate by stack testing.

To clarify this point, one can think of a stream of a given pollutant exiting a stack at an average rate of U pounds per hour, where the instantaneous emission rate varies during that hour. In the special case where the rate of air pollution generated during an hour does not vary, one can also think of this hourly emission rate U (the total amount of pollution generated in units of pounds per hour) as P x (U/P), where P is the total weight in pounds of product generated per hour and U/P simply represents the dimensionless ratio of air pollutants generated per unit product manufactured (note that the units of both weight and time cancel).

The equivalent calculation will be made for the generation of solid waste, but volumetrically rather than by weight. One can think of the dimensionless MoDs associated with each IDPC and IDPC surrogate as being directly analogous to U/P. For example, in the same way that a cement kiln generates, say, 6.0 pounds of carbon monoxide per ton of clinker, that is, at a dimensionless ratio of 6/2000 or 0.003, a manufacturing source may likewise generate ("inherently embed," may be more precise), for example, 0.73 units of the complexity IDPC surrogate per unit of product. So, if this product is manufactured at a rate of 100 cubic feet per hour, then the volumetric rate of the complexity IDPC surrogate generated is 73 cubic feet per hour.[25]

We similarly determine the *annual* volumetric equivalent of P x (U/P), namely, the total annual product volume x MoD for each product manufactured for each separate IDPC and IDPC surrogate generated per year and add their values. Let us call the annual volumetric MoD for each product P_i manufactured, $VMoD_i$. These $VMoD_i$ are determined for each product by using the calculation methods in the articles cited earlier or, where these are still crude, via more simplified means, where possible and necessary. The total quantity of the volumetric measure of detriment (VMoD) per year is then found by summing these $VMoD_i$ over all i products P_i manufactured per year for each individual IDPC and IDPC surrogate generated at the source.

So, if a company manufactures 100,000 table lamps of Brand 1 per year, where the volume per lamp and the complexity MoD per lamp are 0.2 ft^3 and 0.55, respectively, then the annual VMoD generation rate of the complexity characteristic for the production of these Brand 1 lamps at the source is 0.55 x (100,000 lamps/year) x (0.2 ft^3/lamp) or 11,000 ft^3/year. This would represent $VMoD_1$ for the Brand 1 lamp. If there were two other brands of lamps manufactured, Brands 2 and 3, then one would likewise calculate $VMoD_2$ and $VMoD_3$, the total sum of which represents the total sourcewide VMoD for the source, namely $VMoD_{Total} = VMoD_1+VMoD_2+VMoD_3$ for the complexity pollutant generated at the source.

It would appear that the only solid waste metrics worth regulating are the IDPC pollutants for volume, toxicity, and noncompostability, and the two IDPC surrogates cited earlier: difficulty-of-disassembly and complexity,[26] although Bakker et al., while not specifically mentioning metrics directly, would argue that reverse logistics and recyclability (or upcyclability) would also be worthy of consideration.[27] The IDPC and IDPC surrogate pollutants now round out the broader, more complete bases for regulating environmental pollutants that can be used to address the usual relevant media (i.e., air, water, on-site generated waste, solid waste).

A Quick Aside Regarding the Rationale of What the Circularity-Regulated Pollutants Should Be

Those who study circularity might argue that what has been termed here as IDPCs and IDPC surrogates are the same as circularity metrics, such as the percent of recycled material or renewable energy used. They are different. The focus on IDPC surrogate pollution is based first and foremost on the generation of a pollution precursor when it is discharged inherently with a product, just like any pollutant, and then finding the pivotal pollutant metric by which to measure it. This will facilitate not just the reduction of the MoD associated with each IDPC and IDPC surrogate but also set the stage for material circularity within the economy. Where IDPC and IDPC surrogate pollution should be treated as just another form of pollution, circularity is approached here from the perspective of what results from directly and appropriately regulating IDPC and IDPC surrogate pollution.

This may seem counterintuitive to some, but just as with sustainability metrics, any environmental study of a CE's circularity metrics should not be "contaminated" with economic metrics.[28] Likewise, it is not appropriate to establish a recycling metric based on the amount of recovered material since market instruments will automatically handle that in response to regulation. It may be noble to track what components of products have been recycled, but it is not a fundamental metric that should be regulated as a pollutant surrogate. Limiting and then minimizing IDPC and IDPC surrogate totals is primary, and market economics is the tool ("engine") to facilitate those reductions.

We now know what new pollutants need to be regulated, but how should they be regulated? We will see that properly regulating these pollutants, with proper constraints applied, facilitates the transition to a circular economy. Maitre-Ekern, a rare legal scholar to do so, attempted to spell out how to use regulation to achieve a circular economy, but her analysis only revolved around the usual regulatory suspects, such as command-and-control (e.g., the European Union's Ecodesign Directive), market-based instruments (e.g., emissions taxes), and information (e.g., energy labeling).[29] It would appear that because she had no awareness of the concept of IDPCs and IDPC surrogates and other key regulatory drivers as discussed here, she was unable to uncover the significant elements of how best to facilitate the transition to a CE.

Developing the Foundation for Regulating IDPCs and IDPC Surrogates

The authors of *Cradle to Cradle* probably didn't realize it at the time, but the goals of a fully tuned circular economy are equivalent to a perfectly idealized "attainment" goal for IDPCs and IDPC surrogates—in much the same way that 0 μg/m^3 for NO_2 represents the ideal attainment goal on an annual basis for the National Ambient

Air Quality Standards under the Clean Air Act for nitrogen dioxide (while 100 μg/m^3 represents attainment). Ideally, products manufactured in a state are consumed in the same general area. If the total quantity of a certain IDPC or IDPC surrogate within that area is ecologically "absorbable" (i.e., at a quantity below which the natural environment can "assimilate" that level of waste without harmful repercussions) with very little solid waste being routed to waste sites, then we can conceivably say that that region has achieved "attainment" for that given IDPC or IDPC surrogate. Clearly, we are "nonattainment" globally for solid waste because the natural environment is unable to absorb, assimilate, accommodate, or otherwise manage the mass quantities of solid waste that have already been generated and exist now as legacy solid waste pollution. Likewise, we would all agree that consumed products currently manufactured cannot all be disassembled; these products, such as cell phones and computers, are simply tossed out after some salvageable metals and components have been removed. Clearly, the environment that stores a large amount of e-waste in this country alone has not yet reached anything close to "attainment."

In the same way that regulators determine a National Ambient Air Quality Standards (NAAQS) threshold concentration below which Nature (not just the landfills within it) can assimilate the "nondisassemble-able" products without incurring harm to the environment, or adverse health or welfare impacts, regulators must determine the equivalent total VMoD thresholds per IDPC and IDPC surrogate in a region. This determination can be guided by what types of materials end up in waterways, landfills, public spaces, etc., and if the natural environment cannot assimilate any quantity, then the attainment threshold will obviously have to be zero.

Thus, to appreciate the larger picture of regulation, let's continue with the calculation procedure from the previous section to determine the total generated quantity of a regional IDPC or IDPC surrogate (measured as total VMoD). We would sum the sourcewide totals of the VMoD for complexity for all the sources within a region. Attainment is reached when the total VMoD for the complexity pollutant in the area of regulation is environmentally manageable; otherwise, it would be deemed to reflect "nonattainment" for that IDPC or IDPC surrogate.

The Role of Product Characteristic Standards

In similar fashion to regulating air pollution through underlying New Unit (Source) Performance Standards for emission units at a source (e.g., operation of a cement kiln having to meet 0.4 lb SO_2/ton of clinker based on a 30-day rolling average), products must also not exceed established characteristic standards. For example, if regulators determine that folding tables can technologically meet a complexity MoD of 0.70, then they may set the characteristic standard at 0.73. Thus, if a company produces such tables with an MoD value of 0.76 for the complexity MoD per table produced, then the company would be in noncompliance with the standard. This standard simply provides a maximum "pre-solid waste" design MoD standard that products must meet within their product category. In a similar fashion with revising New Unit Performance Standards every five years for the next "recruits" of emission units that emit air pollution, product characteristic standards must also be revised every five years for the same type of product so as to continually push the product redesign innovation envelope.

Meeting characteristic standards should not just be a requirement for manufacturers within this country, but this requirement must also apply to imports. Why? Because it makes no sense to import products that are manufactured elsewhere with little to no recovery potential or remanufacturing value that would only later clog domestic landfills or, worse yet, ditches and waterways. The need for characteristic standards is critical. National regulators, through academic and environmental research centers, will determine and set these standards based on the methodologies for calculating the various product characteristics' MoDs, reasonably dictated by what has already been achieved. It would also be wise for regulators to only sign those trade agreements that require minimally acceptable characteristic standards to be met as a condition of import and export.

Furthermore, to ensure both aggressive reductions in the generation of solid waste and energy usage, and the increased reuse of existing stocks of recovered materials, regulators must do everything in their power to ensure that characteristic standards for several products are not simply defaulted to the highest acceptable characteristic value; hence the reason why those standards must be periodically tightened.

How Will the Critical IDPC/IDPC Surrogate Pollutants Be Regulated?

Besides the current regulation of the familiar environmental pollutants (air, water, and on-site generated waste), the discussion of developing an *actual regulatory strategy* to facilitate circularity that will lead to a CE is virtually nonexistent at this time. Besides the work of Eléonore Maitre-Ekern, noted earlier, the only insightful legal discussion of the topic is from Chris Backes and Roger Feldman.

Backes probably comes closest of any author to formulating more appropriate legal requirements to facilitate a CE based on the European Union's (EU) Ecodesign Directive.[30] While the European Union's focus was mostly on conserving energy and reducing waste, Backes notes that they wish to expand their scope of product-specific requirements so as to promote circularity, such as including durability, reparability, upgradeability, design for disassembly, ease of reuse, and greenhouse gas emissions.[31] Unfortunately, as far as creating the necessary framework for facilitating the transition to the CE is concerned, the EU is barely getting out of the starting gate.

Roger Feldman provided a presentation at the Environmental Law Institute and American Bar Association's program: The Circular Economy: Regulatory and Commercial Law Implications.[32] In this respect, Feldman's presentation, "Developing Laws to Facilitate a Circular Economy," was somewhat on point but unfortunately, he focused mostly on property rights, governance, and finance.

The strategy developed here will go a long way toward regulating the generation of environmental pollution. Readers who have already extrapolated from the discussion in Part 2 and earlier indications in this chapter will likely have anticipated that a trading program will play an essential role in regulating IDPC and IDPC surrogate pollution. In preparation for formulating an IDPC trading scheme,[33,34] it is envisioned that regulators will first determine what the attainment level of each IDPC and IDPC surrogate pollutant is within their domain of regulation (e.g., state, country). Given the global ubiquity of detrimental solid waste pollution, it is probably fair to treat all areas as NAAs for IDPCs and IDPC surrogate pollution.

Just like for air pollution, regulating IDPC and IDPC surrogate pollution follows the "measure, count, regulate" scheme. As for measuring and counting, each source generating IDPC and IDPC surrogate pollution must determine the MoD for each product and the total sourcewide VMoD of each regulated pollutant at the point of manufacture by using an accepted calculation method. With the determination of the plant's total VMoD baseline per individual IDPC and IDPC surrogate pollutant, each averaged over a two-year period, then the determination of the corresponding allotments for each pollutant at the source is easily made, adjusted for possible noncompliance to the characteristic standard.[35] As for the "regulate" portion of the scheme, the total of each VMoD[36] representing each IDPC and IDPC surrogate pollutant within a region is limitable and declinable, and hence tradable. This process of required declines of total VMoD for the IDPC and IDPC surrogate pollutants provides a means to facilitate the reduction of the MoD for these pollutants among the region's various manufactured products. This in turn will likewise facilitate the recoverability of materials that would otherwise be generated as solid waste pollution.

Let's say a source that manufactures widgets calculates the complexity IDPC surrogate MoD for Brand X901 to be 0.78, where the characteristic standard is 0.75, thereby subjecting it to penalties for noncompliance. The source produced an average of 70,000 of these widgets per year, based on two years of production prior to the initiation of the trading program. Then the compliant amount of the VMoD from the generation of the complexity IDPC surrogate for the Brand X901 widget, with a volume of 0.2 ft^3 per widget, would be 0.75 x (70,000 widgets/yr) x (0.2 ft^3/widget) or 10,500 ft^3 of complexity per year. Likewise, let's say that when all the other widgets produced by the facility during the two baseline years are averaged and included, the total sourcewide VMoD baseline for the complexity IDPC surrogate is 40,000 ft^3 per year, with a corresponding equivalent allotment of 400,000 trading units, where ten trading units equate to 1 cubic foot per year of the complexity surrogate pollutant. All sources within the regulatory jurisdiction would similarly calculate their total VMoD baselines and allotments in the same manner, not only for the complexity surrogate pollutant but for the other applicable IDPC and IDPC surrogate pollutants.

If state regulators are seeking to reduce the total VMoD of the complexity surrogate pollutant generated within the appropriate geographical jurisdiction[37] by 15 percent over a five-year period, then the widget manufacturer will have an allotment of 400,000 TU x (1–0.15), or 340,000 trading units for the complexity surrogate pollutant by the end of those five years. Thus, if they actually produce/"discharge" a total of 38,000 ft^3/year of the complexity pollutant from the manufacture of their widgets in the fifth year, equivalent to a total of 380,000 TUs within the trading program, then they must buy 380,000 minus 340,000 or 40,000 TUs from other complexity generating sources in the same regulated jurisdiction. As a means to further discourage the deterioration of the environment, the purchase of TUs must be taxed.

Continuing to focus on the complexity IDPC surrogate, assume that trading among sources that "embed this IDPC surrogate in major quantities" proceeds over the years as the cap on the regional total VMoD for the complexity IDPC surrogate declines. This will mean that sources will be prodded by the market to redesign their processes to render their products less complex.[38,39] Lest the reader believe that manufacturers would be severely handicapped by having to redesign their products, it is important to note that manufacturers are clearly conscious of the design process:

> The [product life] cycle is initiated by choices in product design: which materials are going to be used, how they will be joined and which processes are used for manufacturing. Choices made during design have a lasting effect on material and product life cycles. They drive the demand for specific metals and influence the effectiveness of the recycling chain during end-of-life (EOL).[40]

Thus, by redesigning their production process, sources will clearly be better able to reconcile their declining allotment by embedding less of the detrimental characteristics into their products.

All things being equal and in the most ideal of cases, these products will be less complex and/or easier to disassemble and be theoretically reusable by the source that originally manufactured them. Unfortunately, at this stage, without further regulatory or economic inducement to circulate materials at the front end of production, these better-designed products will still likely just end up as waste in landfills, waterways, ditches, and wherever else. Thus, where the ability to disassemble various products does exist, that does not by itself correspond to having established a CE; the line may be curving, but circularity has not yet been achieved. Trading IDPC and IDPC surrogate pollutants to facilitate better product design is just half the battle since it only facilitates resource recovery *readiness*, which is a necessary prerequisite to achieving a CE, but it is not yet sufficient for it to take root. Prodding sources to go from resource recovery readiness to circularity is an acutely difficult problem, particularly when the use of virgin resources is not constrained. Thus, one fundamentally necessary prerequisite to attaining an ideal CE is that it must rely on more Command-and-Control (CaC) and market drivers that both constrain the use of virgin resources and also make material reuse an offer that producers simply cannot refuse (no pun intended). The means to do this is addressed next.

Incentivizing Material Recovery

The discussion to this point has assumed that the sources in the trading scheme will be able to redesign their production process technologies to manufacture products with lower MoDs to sufficiently reconcile their declining allotments for each IDPC and IDPC surrogate pollutant. But what if some sources, regardless of their research and development capabilities, are technologically limited and are unable to significantly redesign their production process(es) sufficiently enough to reduce their MoD pollution generation rate to meet required reductions? What if these technologically limited companies are forced to pay exorbitant prices and taxes in perpetuity for TUs from sources that are able to reduce? In fact, there will be some sources that will be completely unwilling to redesign their products and/or innovate their production process(es). So what can be done for all sources overall to reconcile allotments while at the same time facilitating the use of consumed product materials and hopefully recirculating them as inputs to production rather than as waste to a landfill, ditch, or ocean?

The answers to these questions lie at the very heart of achieving a circular economy.

So let's say a company found itself in the unfortunate situation where its declined allotment at a given time is 160,000 TUs for the complexity characteristic, but it manufactured a product with a total VMoD for complexity generated at the equivalent of 210,000 TUs. The shortfall of 50,000 TUs can be addressed by purchasing TUs in the market, but that can get very expensive due to tighter supplies of TUs and their subsequent taxation upon purchase. Complicating the need to urgently reconcile is when production redesign occurs on a much longer timescale than is sufficient to immediately reconcile the allotment, and as the regional cap on the complexity VMoD continues to tighten over time, the cost per (scarcer) Trading Unit (TU) rises.

It is under this scenario that the recovery of materials may become more cost-effective in an "internalizing the externalities" world. To more readily address the TU shortfall resulting from the need to reconcile the actual manufactured output of IDPC or IDPC surrogates with the declining allotment, companies can utilize and take credit for recovered waste materials[41] at the front end of production. Here, the manufacturer is eligible to receive "internalized externality rebates," which from here on will be called "Equivalent Trading Units" or ETUs.[42] An ETU represents the trading unit equivalent of actual *characteristic* waste pollution that was "off-ramped" before harming the environment.[43] Based on the amount of recovered materials that are actually used in the development of a product, the ETUs for each IDPC and IDPC surrogate, upon proper conversion from recovered material volume to volume of characteristic pollutant avoided, can be calculated to determine the amount of available ETUs for that pollutant during reconciliation.

It is worthwhile to walk through some sample calculations.

We want to see how the use of both redesign and the acquisition of reused materials (and ETUs) would be applied under the adapted strategy for a source generating the complexity surrogate pollutant. We initiate the analysis by first calculating the baseline (base year 0). Let's say that the average production over a two-year span prior to the startup of the trading program is 20,000 ft^3 (see Column B for base year 0). With a current product complexity MoD of 0.8 at the start of the program, the total VMoD generated would be 20,000 x 0.8 or 16,000 ft^3. Thus, the baseline allotment in base year 0 would be 160,000 TUs, signified by μ in the F column for base year 0.

The program requires that the baseline allotment decline 2 percent per two-year period so as to encourage the source to redesign their processes to reduce the MoD of their product and/or acquire the use of recovered materials. As early as year two, their allotment of 156,800 TUs was not sufficient to cover their total generated production of VMoD (equivalent to 168,000 TUs), so they had to purchase 11,200 TUs in the market.

However, in year 4 of the program, the source was able to reduce their product's MoD from 0.8 to 0.7. Upon doing so, even with higher production relative to previous years, we find that they were able to reduce their generated VMoD for complexity to the extent that they had a surplus of 3,100 TUs, which they could sell in the market.

Thereafter, they realize that they can no longer reduce the MoD of the product any further. In fact, in year 6, at 22,500 ft^3 of production, the highest production rate since the start of the program, they see that they will need to find 7,100 TUs in the market. However, rather than paying the cost for these TUs, which have been getting progressively more expensive, they find that the option of acquiring reused materials into their production process will incur less cost.

Of the total 30,000 ft^3 of all input materials that were used to manufacture the 22,500 ft^3 of product in year 6, the source was able to reuse 1,000 ft^3 of material 1 and 500 ft^3 of material 2 as like-for-like replacements of two of the many input materials they use in the manufacture of their product. The question becomes—how does this reuse translate into ETUs?

The best way to calculate creditable ETUs is probably the easiest, namely, by multiplying the amount of complexity generated in year 6, that is, 15,750 ft^3, by the "reuse ratio," which is the ratio of reused materials to the total amount of all input materials[44]; thus the reuse ratio here would be 1,500 ft^3/30,000 ft^3, or 0.05. Thus, the creditable amount of ETUs is 15,750 ft^3 x 0.05 x 10 ETU/ft^3, or 7,875 ETUs.

Table 6.1 Sample TU Reconciliation Tracking

Year	Production (ft^3)	Product Complexity MoD	Sourcewide Complexity VMoD Generated (ft^3)	Generated Complexity to Reconcile (TU)	Allotment in Year A (TU)	Amount to Reconcile (TU)
A	B	C	D = B x C	E = 10 x D	F = μ x (1-.01xA)	G = E-F
Base	20,000[a]	0.8	16,000	---	160,000	---
2	21,000	0.8	16,800	168,000	156,800	+11,200
4	21,500	0.7	15,050	150,500	153,600	-3,100
6	22,500	0.7	15,750	157,500	150,400	+7,100

a. Represents the average production for the previous two years in the base year when A = 0.

So while they needed 7,100 TUs to reconcile their generation of complexity pollution in year 6, upon having acquired and used recovered input materials into their production process, they now have 7,875–7,100 TUs or a surplus of 775 TUs which they can sell in the market.

Note that the more materials that get reused, the higher the reuse ratio. Theoretically, if all input materials in production are those acquired as reused materials (reuse ratio = 1), then that would correspond to the full amount of acquired ETUs that will completely reconcile the generation of characteristic pollution during production; on the other hand, if no reused materials are utilized (reuse ratio = 0), then, as expected, no credit would be given as ETUs.

Where production of an end product consists of an integrated, multi-step process, the specific ETU calculations may not be as straightforward. In general, though, the calculation will follow much like the above. The determination of ETUs will be much easier when the materials recovered are directly usable as a like-for-like input to the process; the use of a different material as a potentially viable substitute in a process is not considered here. The ETU determination calculation in this case will become a more advanced engineering problem, but certainly not an insurmountable one.

So how would the "6 R's"[45] be counted as ETUs where the used product itself or a portion thereof is returned to the manufacturer? In this case, ETUs can be allowed for those portions of the materials returned that are untouched by the manufacturing process and reused in their entirety. Product components that are repaired, replaced, recovered, etc., must be accounted for as additional IDPC or IDPC surrogate pollution as necessary, while nonreused components should be treated as scrap (which counts as on-site generated waste). While innovatively redesigning the manufacturing process is the ideal means to avoid creation of pollution (by lowering product MoD), thereby sitting atop the pollution avoidance hierarchy, one can likewise think of the next step down the hierarchy being the use of those materials with already-embedded energy that requires the next least amount of energy to recover. ETUs, in essence, represent the "currency" of recovered materials.

Rationing and gradually choking off the use of virgin resources, including the use of fossil-based carbon, by taxing their use at the front end of production[46] (a tax on environmental unsustainability) must be required as a disincentive to use them so as to further promote material recovery. Hinton believes that fees rather than taxes would be sufficient to promote the manufacture of environmentally sustainable products.[47] However, much more than simply imposing fees will be required to spur a CE—providing rebates in the form of ETUs will act as that incentive to reconcile source TU shortfalls, thereby facilitating the circularity of recovered materials from solid waste. It is these very ETUs that will create a uniquely robust end market for used materials where the current market for reused materials is woefully underwhelming. It should be stressed that ETUs are never to be provided for the use of virgin materials, so sources that wish to use virgin materials rather than reused materials must pay not just for those virgin materials but also for the TU shortfall, in effect paying twice. In addition, taxes must be dissuasively imposed on the deliberate choice to use virgin resources rather than reused materials, while taxes must never be imposed on ETUs.

Aluminum can manufacturers provide an excellent example of a type of source category that basically follows this method already. They reduce the use of virgin aluminum processed from bauxite by reusing a significant amount of waste cans to offset that need (and also reduce the use of fossil fuels by doing so). Within a CE, aluminum can manufacturers, upon acquiring recovered aluminum from secondary smelters, would easily acquire sufficient quantities of ETUs to reconcile their trading unit shortfall.[48]

What to Expect

To summarize: (1) the setting and corrective tightening of total regional VMoD caps via trading for each subject IDPC and IDPC surrogate pollutant, particularly those for DoD and complexity, (2) the imposition and tightening of product characteristic standards, (3) the use of ETUs as creditable rebates (to facilitate reconciliation of allotments) combined with (4) the dissuasive taxation on the purchase of virgin resources will (5a) facilitate process and product redesign (as a means to reduce product MoD and thus IDPC and IDPC surrogate pollution generated at a source), and (5b) drive the linear economy to transition to a CE. This process will together achieve "CE readiness" at the back end of production and catalyze the actual "kinetic motion" of the CE to the front end of production.[49]

As noted earlier, it may turn out that for some sources deficient allotments can be reconciled much more readily by acquiring ETUs than by redesigning the manufacturing process. In fact, where a product's complexity or its ability to be disassembled is virtually impossible or its means to determine these MoDs is too difficult, the regulatory MoD for them will default to the established characteristic standard, necessitating the acquisition of TUs from other participating sources or ETUs from elsewhere, the latter leading only to circulation, not process and/or product redesign.

Recycling of post-consumption product materials will likely occur on a shorter timescale than would significant changes be made to process redesign, which may occur over a longer timescale. The two avenues to reconcile allotments (product redesign and acquisition of TUs and ETUs) work best in tandem to facilitate circularity. The tighter the reduced cap on the total regional VMoD becomes over time, the more desperate sources will become when they must reconcile their declining allotments with their actual production. This will force them to redesign/innovate further and/or acquire TUs and/or ETUs, the latter requiring them to use recovered post-consumed materials, which may be more accessible and economical to obtain as the CE gains momentum. And where sources cannot innovate or acquire ETUs, they will be forced to acquire both virgin raw materials (with stiffer taxes being imposed) plus pay for their shortfall in TUs—a double whammy.

Thus, *a circular economy begets a circular economy—a product that is easier to disassemble or is less complex is easier to recover later as a resource input to a manufacturing process.*

A few key points on just how to facilitate circularity are useful here:

- Declining caps on total VMoD for the IDPC and IDPC surrogate pollutants and taxing TU purchases provide both carrot and stick. They incentivize redesign of manufacturing processes, material recovery, and the decreased use of virgin resources. Manufacturers that cannot or will not redesign/innovate or recycle will likely pay a hefty price in the TU marketplace to reconcile their allotment shortfall, particularly if they do not acquire ETUs from material recovery.
- An ideal CE requires a "closed" physical system. While certain aspects of the strategy facilitate CE-readiness, starving or choking off virgin resources (while taxing TU purchases) in conjunction with the incentivized use of ETUs is what ultimately facilitates circularity.
- Regulating the difficulty-of-disassembly and complexity characteristics is fundamental to the reduction of actual IDPC surrogate pollution, thereby facilitating material recovery and reducing the use of virgin resources where their use is sufficiently choked off. Virgin resources may still be allowed to address realistic makeup needs due to dissipative losses, but here too, the price to do so should not be cheap since there is so much waste to be recovered and reused.

- There has been wide discussion in the literature about the need to establish the following as part of the CE: reuse, recover, rematerialization (including recycling), refurbishment, remanufacturing, repair, takeback management, *Cradle to Cradle* (i.e., waste-free design), and deposit systems.[50] In the adapted strategy, these aspects of a CE should facilitate both "economic and technological fractionation" of the "R's" and other presumed outcomes (e.g., products that maintain long-term value) within the CE based on which "R" is most cost-effective and practical to implement.[51] Undertaking an "R" will be a direct consequence of the combined rising costs of IDPC and IDPC surrogate TUs in the market, with declining allotments for these pollutants and the use of ETUs to reconcile those allotments. Where manufacturers could not do so themselves, an ecosystem of companies will likely sprout up to repair, refurbish, remanufacture, take back, etc., products so that they are made available to consumers/users[52] to avoid the higher cost of consumer goods. Likewise, product recovery and reprocessing facilities would also sprout up to provide manufacturers with recovered raw materials, which would be used by these manufacturers as both a substitute for virgin materials and toward the acquisition as ETUs.
- Specifically, product takebacks, one aspect of Extended Producer Responsibility or Product Stewardship, would be a special means for manufacturers to acquire ETUs to reconcile shortfalls due to declining allotments. Doing so, however, will entail the significant disassembly of their products and the reuse of materials, thereby encouraging them to later better design their products for disassembly. It should be noted that simply taking products back only to toss the materials away is next to useless because (1) no ETUs will be allowed for such use and (2) such a source will then have to account for the amount of on-site waste pollution generated (including nonreused scrap) requiring them to acquire the appropriate quantity of TUs for these particular pollutants.
- If regulators were ever foolish enough to allow for the significant use of virgin resources in a real-world CE where there is a significant opportunity to recover already-consumed materials instead, then without question, *ETUs must never be granted for their use*. No matter what, taxation on these virgin resources must still be applied to deter their extraction.

It should be clear by now why it is important that only volumetric measures of detrimental characteristics that arise from the manufacture of the product that lead to solid waste pollution should be traded. Where quantifiable, these measures of characteristics represent specific regulatory targets for reduction by the manufacturer. This is why metrics, such as "recycle-ability," must be excluded from regulatory consideration since the term is vague and a function of current recycling capability. In fact, a product may only be recyclable once. To meet ideal *Cradle to Cradle* goals, the product must in theory approach infinite recyclability rather than just being a one-off recycling event. To achieve this requires discrete and definable metrics that can be appropriately regulated.

The Perplexing Problems of Plastics and Toxics

While the developing regulatory strategy addresses, among other outcomes, reductions in the complexity of solid waste and the ability to disassemble many types of products, be they infrastructural, consumable, or disposable, extra measures must be undertaken to address truly ecological hazards. Two such perplexing problems are the production of plastics and embedded toxic materials. While reducing both of them over time via a trading program that facilitates a CE represents progress, will the strategy be enough to sufficiently reduce the harms they incur to ecosystems? Unfortunately, simply recirculating plastics and embedded toxic materials is not enough to reduce harm; reducing their "harm intensity" is also critical to reducing their impacts.

We have already seen harm intensity as it applies to a region, but have not recognized it as such. For example, when a region is nonattainment for an air pollutant, that pollutant's concentration X is greater than the required concentration for which the NAAQS is attained, Y, which can be thought of as the region's performance standard, that is, a measure of health and welfare attainment. The measure of harm intensity of air pollution in a region, X/Y, is a number greater than 1 for which a regional trading program is used as a means to reduce the ratio of X/Y to 1 (or less).[53]

One possible model for the noncompostability harm intensity (NHI) for a plastic *product*, rather than for a *region*, might be defined here similarly as the following ratio: TtD/TtC_{pos}, where TtD is the "Time to Degradation," that is, a measure of the amount of time before which the material degrades but not to compostability; and TtC is the "Time to Compostability," that is, a measure of the amount of time before which the material biodegrades via composting,[54] and TtC_{pos} represents the minimum time to biodegradation via composting to be achieved for the category for which the product belongs, where the subscript "pos" denotes the ideal "product-to-soil" case. For the sake of argument, let's say that the TtC_{pos} for a plastic bag could be set or determined, say, at 3 months while the actual TtD for a bag used today is 50 years, so that the NHI value is 50/0.25 or 200. On the other hand, the actual TtD for plastic used in aircraft components could be 100 years while its TtC_{pos} could be established by regulators as 40 years, with an NHI value of 100/40 or 2.50. The closer the NHI gets to 1 due to innovative product development over time, the better.

The noncompostability of plastics must be discouraged, and many single-use products in particular should be rendered compostable. Since the production of plastics in a region may not be sufficiently discouraged through the simple acquisition of ETUs from recovered plastics, how should the acute NHI of plastic products themselves be regulated? Ideally, excessively noncompostable products must not be allowed to continuously trade this flaw within a trading program. Clearly, it is more appropriate, wherever possible, to set a technologically achievable characteristic standard, with a value of TtC_{cs} that is lower than their current TtD, that is, $TtC_{pos} < TtC_{cs} < TtD$. Ideally, the amount of generated pollution for a product over the characteristic standard would be noncompliant and untradable. However, where that is not possible in the short term, the volumetric harm intensity can be traded downward until attainment, however that is established, is achieved. In this scenario, trading must only occur among other sources that also manufacture high NHI products.[55] However, once a characteristic standard is established, volumetric quantities would only be traded among fellow generators of compliant, compostable plastic, whereas noncompliant generation of NHI would be penalized.

Not all plastics are created equal, so it is critical that materials recovered from toxic-containing plastics only be allowed in the trading program for other such plastics. In addition, the ability to achieve total compostability of some plastic products may be constrained, for example, by federal food safety requirements. But clearly, there is room for major improvement in achieving environmental sustainability with Nature between where we are now and what can realistically be achieved.

In similar fashion to reducing the harm intensity of plastics, toxic harm intensity has to be reduced as well. Material toxicity, an inherently detrimental product characteristic that is relevant to regulating the generation of solid waste, is technically not an aspect of a true circular economy since it is only a characteristic worthy of reduction, rather than circulated for purposes of reducing solid waste. In other words, reducing the harm intensity of toxics is much more critical than simply circulating them and shrinking loops by continually reducing their volume. In much the same way as for plastics, one can require that an achievable characteristic standard be met for the toxic content of a given product. Addressing toxics requires a more holistic approach across all media, so a further discussion is reserved for after the generalized strategy is developed in Chapter 7.

Regulating Supply Chains, Including Imports

Addressing all inputs and outputs encompasses the source as a system. While regulations should not only address basic inputs (e.g., resources, fuels) and standard outputs (e.g., waste pollution, products), they must equally apply to the whole supply chain, which includes all sources and transportation inside and, where possible, outside the country (i.e., shipping and imported products). This proposal clearly is nothing new; what is new, however, involves regulating the generation of environmental pollution in supply chains, including IDPC surrogates.

Regulating the generation of characteristic pollution is actually quite straightforward. When intermediate products possessing a certain VMoD enter a source and where more characteristic pollution is added, then the difference between the VMoD output and the VMoD input is what the source performing the VMoD-additive change to the manufactured product must be held accountable for.

What will be problematic for overseas manufacturers of products are those that are not well-designed for disassembly. Such products should likely be discouraged by importing countries concerned with having to address those products later as waste. As the importing country's environment gets its cut through declining caps on IDPC and IDPC surrogate pollution, the embedded economy within the larger ecosystem will be forced to adapt by establishing a new equilibrium that incorporates these products.

Each source within the supply chain should be required to manufacture products that meet IDPC and IDPC surrogate characteristic standards.[56] As stated previously, this must be required simply because the exporting country should not become a transboundary supplier of landfill-clogging waste products (think "monstrous hybrids," per *Cradle to Cradle*) that cannot be economically recovered for reuse later. The exporting country must also be required to have their manifests (more specifically, digital passports) include for each product its MoD and characteristic standard. Given that certification is already required for the importation of toxic substances per the Toxic Substances Control Act, these additional requirements are not onerous. Imposing these requirements on imports should encourage/coax foreign manufacturers to bend their manufacturing arc toward a CE within their own home countries. In fact, setting international import characteristic standards would help to create an "environmental arms race" to reduce IDPC and IDPC surrogate pollution worldwide.

From an environmental protection standpoint, dispatching those imports with the lowest potential environmental footprint first must be mandated over those imports with higher footprints (to attain sustainability with Nature remember). In addition, if allowances are made out of necessity to import products that exceed characteristic standards, regulators can agree to a lower purchase price and/or, if need be, impose taxes on those imports in proportion to their MoD footprint (i.e., a "landfill clogging tax"). It is critical that the importing country be penalized; simply imposing a tariff on the imported products would only force consumers in the circular economic country to pay for the sins of the noncircular economic country.

Within supply chains, the shipping industry, as one component of transport, must also limit its generation of pollution. While transport by itself is not part of the direct manufacturing process, it does contribute to CO_2 emissions. Thus, the transport sector must be required to participate in the rationing of fossil fuel-based carbon within the broader transport sector as a whole. In this way, cost pinching should make shipping appropriately more energy efficient and, where this is not possible, more expensive. Thus, the pinching of costs will force the market to better reflect shipping costs; this is known as internalizing the externality, a means to achieve sustainability with Nature, which should be welcomed by economists, among others.

Unfortunately, the USEPA does not appear anxious to begin regulating supply chains.[57] In any event, examining inputs and outputs from a full systems standpoint for both supply chains and the manufacturing facilities within them allows future regulators, using the adapted strategy, to address (i) resource inputs that are becoming scarcer (e.g., rare metals), (ii) inputs that are environmentally harmful (e.g., petroleum that can both be refined into fossil fuels or to produce plastics), and (iii) outputs that are environmentally harmful (e.g., air, water, on-site generated waste, and IDPCs/IDPC surrogate pollution).

The Adapted Strategy

We are calling the strategy applied to regulate the generation of IDPCs and IDPC surrogate pollution the adapted strategy because it is an adaptation of the comprehensive strategy for regulating the generation of air pollution. The key components of this strategy are:

- Setting limits on the total regional VMoD for each IDPC and IDPC surrogate pollutant
- Declining caps on these pollutants, whereby trading sorts out who gets what under each cap
- Allowing the use of ETUs through the reuse of waste materials
- Rationing, or choking off the use of virgin resources, including the use of fossil-based carbon, through sufficient taxation
- Requiring that all products meet characteristic standards that must not be exceeded
- The inclusion of supply chains, particularly where VMoD is added per source along the chain and where fossil fuel usage is rationed and
- Any proposed new major source or modification at an existing source of IDPCs and/or IDPC surrogates will require compliance to the latest applicable product characteristic standards and the purchase of trading units.

Up to this point, the discussion has referred to sources that embed IDPCs and IDPC surrogates in major rather than minor quantities. The reason is clear: the bulk of solid waste pollution appears to be due to society's excess consumption of high MoD-embedded IDPC- and IDPC surrogate-laden goods. Nevertheless, minor sources will include small manufacturers of such products. The equivalent notion of Plantwide Applicability Limitation is helpful in this regard, where these can apply to those types of sources where IDPCs or IDPC surrogates are generated in such minor quantities that they are not required to be reduced (although the transfer of innovative technology will eventually reach those sources anyway).

It should be noted that while the above bullet points represent key components of the adapted strategy, the entire strategy must also include the many aspects of the comprehensive strategy covered in Part 2, such as the proper division of labor, the development of Next Gen-based rules and regulations, and the reliance on academic/environmental research centers.

What Role Will Life Cycle Assessment Play?

Life Cycle Assessment (LCA) is the holistic assessment of all impacts for a given product over its cradle-to-grave lifetime, whereby researchers determine how resource-, energy-, and pollutant-intensive certain products are. Engineers have taken sides in this regard in that some support the perspectives offered in *Cradle to Cradle*; others support the perspectives offered in LCA.[58] However, the difference between the two is fairly clear, at least to this author. As noted previously, from a surrogate pollutant standpoint, *Cradle to Cradle* proposes idealized attainment for the particular subset of detrimental characteristics which focus on the nature of products. On the other hand, LCA is a means to holistically examine the entirety of sustainability metrics, including material and energy efficiency. Bjørn and Hauschild summarize it this way:

> LCA generally tells you what is *greener* in today's non-ideal world, while C2C [*Cradle to Cradle*] tells you what is *green* in an ideal future. Often, both things cannot be pursued simultaneously. This is because an ideal future may never be realized if products and systems are optimized according to what is greener in today's non-ideal world, since this optimization of "wrong systems" could serve to lock societies into an unsustainable trajectory.[59]

Although LCA is a means by which to examine the impact(s) of a product, it will be left to policymakers to dictate how critical product characteristic pollutants will be regulated within the broader universe of environmental sustainability for all products. In this context, LCA acts more like a diagnostic tool rather than a policy itself.

LCA and *Cradle to Cradle* coexist in the adapted strategy (and later, the generalized strategy). Squeezing virgin material usage and energy use within the strategy by both regulation (via rationing) and market forces will separate the wheat from the chaff within the two perspectives. Whether one energy-efficient toaster is utilized in the CE over that of a lesser energy-efficient one will, within the implementation of the strategy, be sorted out by the interplay of regulation and market forces. In a theoretical CE, LCA will be utilized to peer forward into the future as to what technologies should be adopted relative to others in a resource- and fuel-constrained world.

In reality, regulators or policymakers will determine the environmental impacts of the production and disposal of products via CaT at ground level. This will require the symbiotic ratcheting down of the caps on the various inputs and outputs (i.e., resources, conventional pollutants, IDPC and IDPC surrogate pollution), and, most importantly, the behavior of consumers/users will play a critical role in driving the kinetic motion of the path-dependent CE. What's missing from LCA and *Cradle to Cradle* to this point is the knowledge of the critically necessary real-world regulatory and economic inducements to reach a CE. So far, the analysis of LCA and *Cradle to Cradle* has only been of a technical nature. It will still take a full team effort by engineers, lawyers, economists, regulators, and consumers/users to solve the environmental problems we all face, even while a cap-and-trade scheme is utilized among manufacturers. In any event, LCA will play its proper diagnostic role supplementing the achievement of *Cradle to Cradle* principles as a long-term goal.

We next address the generalized strategy in Chapter 7. If the adapted strategy results from adapting the comprehensive strategy to the generation of solid waste, then it only stands to reason that the strategy can be generalized to regulate all multi-media pollution.

Notes

1 While the reader is already familiar with nonattainment areas for air pollution, to broaden the reader's thinking further, one can think of nonattainment as noncompliance to or an exceedance above an established standard, usually caused by unchecked upward expansion that exceeds some quantifiable attainment standard. Thus, being frenetically busy can be thought of as being "nonattainment for time management," and, as we'll see later in Chapter 9, runaway urban sprawl can be deemed to be "nonattainment for upward expansion."

2 Unless otherwise specified, in this and the following chapters, resources should be thought of as inputs to industrial production, rather than agricultural production.

3 While the generalized strategy developed in Chapter 7 focuses on the generation of multi-media environmental pollution, legacy pollution, namely pollution that has *already* been generated, will be addressed in Chapter 7 as well.

4 The Ellen MacArthur Foundation, "Towards the Circular Economy" (2013): 7. https://www.ellenmacarthurfoundation.org/publications/towards-the-circular-economy-vol-1-an-economic-and-business-rationale-for-an-accelerated-transition.

5 Kenneth Webster, *The Circular Economy A Wealth of Flows* (Ellen MacArthur Foundation Publishing, 2nd Edition, 2017).

6 Walter R. Stahel, *The Circular Economy: A User's Guide* (Routledge, 2019).

7 Kirchherr, Reike, and Hekkert, "Conceptualizing the Circular Economy."

8 It may very well be possible that a more refined definition would include the minimization of the rate of entropy increase within the economic system, a topic that is briefly explored in Chapter 9.

9 Addressing climate change and social equity as espoused in the CE definition by the Ellen MacArthur Foundation is not expected to directly arise from regulating

the generation of solid waste pollution as developed here. Rather, averting climate change will occur primarily by limiting and reducing the use of fossil fuels and applying first principles to the comprehensive strategy at the global scale (see Parts 2 and 4). Slowing biodiversity loss is a collateral "fringe benefit" of limiting both multi-media environmental pollution and limiting resource use. However, addressing climate change, conversion to renewables, and biodiversity loss are all key components of achieving sustainability with Nature through the use of the mitigation strategy and the application of other techniques developed in Chapter 9, rather than specifically through a CE. Social equity is not addressed as a component of the generalized strategy developed in this book since it is outside the scope of explicitly regulating the generation of environmental pollution. https://ellenmacarthurfoundation.org/topics/circular-economy-introduction/glossary.

10 The more appropriate way to characterize our current "take, make, consume, dispose" linear economy is more accurately: "take, make products more voluminous /complex/difficult-to-disassemble/noncompostable/toxic, consume, dispose."

11 Joseph Fiksel, Tarsha Eason, and Herbert Frederickson, "A Framework for Sustainability Indicators at EPA," EPA/600/R/12/687 (Washington, DC: National Risk Management Research Laboratory, ORD, USEPA, October 2012). See Table 3 (page 22) at https://www.epa.gov/sites/default/files/2014-10/documents/framework-for-sustainability-indicators-at-epa.pdf.

12 World Business Council for Sustainable Development, "Circular Metrics Landscape Analysis," WBCSD and Climate-KIC, May 2018. https://docs.wbcsd.org/2018/06/Circular_Metrics-Landscape_Analysis.pdf.

13 https://www.naem.org/docs/default-source/conference-agendas/conference-metrics-2014-final-agena-naem.pdf?sfvrsn=b5151962_2.

14 The Ellen MacArthur Foundation, "Circularity Indicators: An Approach to Measuring Circularity." https://emf.thirdlight.com/link/yybss1obhtdv-ub419h/@/preview/1?o.

15 WBCSD, "Circular Metrics Landscape Analysis," 15.

16 Michael Saidani, Bernard Yannou, Yan Leroy, et al., "A Taxonomy of Circular Economy Indicators," *Journal of Cleaner Production* 207 (January 2019). https://doi.org/10.1016/j.jclepro.2018.10.014.

17 The reader should be reminded of the task of Dmitri Mendeleev, who pieced together the underlying structure of the periodic table in the nineteenth century. Based on the elements he knew at the time, he formed a periodic table that had missing elements that he predicted should exist and be found later. For example, gallium and germanium were later found to fill two of those spots. The point is that

he deduced what the blueprint of the periodic table should look like before all the elements were even known.

18 It is critical for the reader to note the distinctive use of the term "characteristic" as it is used here, *which applies to the product itself.* This is different than its current application in solid waste regulation, which is (1) as a property of municipal solid waste, such as its density, compressibility, and permeability; and (2) its chemical properties, particularly as it relates to hazardous waste, such as its ignitability, corrosivity, and reactivity.

19 Although these characteristics may not have been uniquely described by the book, they were immediately recognizable.

20 For those readers who might question why these characteristics are precursors to pollution, note that the more recoverable materials are from solid waste, the less likely they will become pollution; for example, aluminum cans are far more recoverable of their constituent materials than mattresses. Note also that these precursors could be more precisely called inherent product irrecoverability characteristics, but the term "IDPC surrogates" will be used instead.

21 A term this author credits to Herman Daly.

22 One article that provides a possible model of determining the difficulty-of-disassembly characteristic is: Paul Vanegas, Jef R. Peeters, Dirk Cattrysse, et al., "Ease of Disassembly of Products to Support Circular Economy Strategies," *Resources, Conservation, and Recycling* 135 (August 2018). The ideal regulatory, rather than tracking, metric would measure the true complexity of the product itself, although the complexity of manufacturing the product may suffice. The following article develops a framework for what may later become a possible measure of complexity: Josue R. Crespo-Varela, Gül E. Okudan Kremer, Conrad S. Tucker, et al., "An Analysis of Complexity Measures for Product Design and Development," *Proceedings of the ASME 2012 International Design Engineering Technical Conferences & Computers and Information in Engineering Conference,* August 2012. https://www.researchgate.net/publication/258022441_An_Analysis_of_Complexity_Measures_in_Product_Design_and_Development.

23 To be clear, the MoD of the IDPCs and IDPC surrogates would simply be numerical values, without assigned units. In the case of the IDPC specific to volume itself, the MoD is 1, since the volumetric MoD will simply be the production volume generated per unit time. In general, the MoD will vary depending on the IDPC or IDPC surrogate, for example, while volume has a MoD of 1, the difficulty-of-disassembly MoD will be a value of 1 or greater, and the complexity MoD will be a number less than or equal to 1.

24 While the generation of IDPC and IDPC surrogate pollution will be measured volumetrically, that is, in units of ft^3 per hour, weight-based measurements could just as easily be used.

25 Note that while a tractor tire and a lawnmower tire may have the same MoD for a given IDPC surrogate, the volumetric MoD for this characteristic surrogate pollutant per product will not be the same due to the large difference in volume between them.

26 Once final consensus is developed on regulating IDPC surrogates, this number may change.

27 C. A. Bakker, R. Wever, Ch. Teoh, et al., "Designing Cradle to Cradle Products; A Reality Check," *International Journal of Sustainable Engineering* 3, no. 1 (March 2010): 2.

28 Marcus Linder, Steven Sarasini, and Patricia von Loon, "A Metric for Quantifying Product-Level Circularity," *Journal of Industrial Ecology* 21, no. 3 (June 2017). https://onlinelibrary.wiley.com/doi/10.1111/jiec.12552.

29 Eléonore Maitre-Ekern, "The Choice of Regulatory Instruments for a Circular Economy," in *Environmental Law and Economics*, Vol. 4, Economic Analysis of Law in European Legal Scholarship, ed. K. Mathis and B. R. Huber (Springer International Publishing AG, 2017).

30 Chris Backes, *Law For a Circular Economy* (Netherlands: Eleven International Publishing, 2017). See also Chris Backes, "Recycling, Law, and the Circular Economy," in *Handbook of Recycling: State-of-the-art for Practitioners, Analysts, and Scientists*, 2nd Edition, ed. Christina Meskers, Ernst Worrell, and Markus A. Reuter (Elsevier, 2024).

31 Backes, *Law For a Circular Economy*, 43.

32 Environmental Law Institute. "The Circular Economy: Regulatory and Commercial Law Implications" (Conference Summary and Materials). https://www.eli.org/sites/default/files/docs/seminars/2_23_16_rfeldmanppt.pdf.

33 It's illuminating to note that trading doesn't just have to be relegated to addressing pollution. Another plausible consideration for the use of trading is applying it to the amount of atmospheric surface area that satellites are allowed to occupy. Astronomers worry that too many satellites could occupy the night sky to such an extent that it interferes with their observations. When the number of satellites causes "nonattainment of skyward observation," then limits could be set on the allowable surface area coverage of satellites, and companies would then be required to trade their excess coverage in order to bring the global coverage back to attainment. We will see in Chapter 9 that reverse cap-and-trade to restore ecosystems is likewise possible.

34 While the author was inspired by *Cradle to Cradle* to apply aspects of the comprehensive strategy to regulate the generation of solid waste pollution at the point of production, Marcotte independently proposed applying an economy-wide, state-participating trading scheme to solid waste at the point of disposal, that is, landfill and incineration, where the goal was to reduce volume. Unfortunately, his approach lacked rigor, particularly with respect to facilitating the kinetics of circularity. https://issuu.com/apwa/docs/201203_reporteronline/s/12177333. It should be noted that Marcotte's paper (Jay Marcotte, "A Paradigm Shift Towards a Cap and Trade-based Solid Waste System" (June 2011)), appears to have been removed from the internet.

35 These tasks are not trivial, but they are temporary and once done, the trading program would likely be no more tedious than what is currently typical for regulating environmental pollution and would also be relatively straightforward to implement.

36 Regulators should directly penalize noncompliance to the characteristic standard rather than allow noncompliance to be reconciled within the trading scheme. This is because the source could meet the characteristic standard but chose not to.

37 For the sake of simplicity, it is assumed that each state must regulate what is generated in its jurisdiction, with either the state or federal government setting the attainment levels. In reality, IDPC and IDPC surrogate nonattainment applies nationwide since this pollution is generated nationally and where consumed domestically, disposed of domestically. Clearly, the idea of having the feds regulating IDPCs and IDPC surrogates is inappropriate.

38 Process redesign is an already familiar concept in air pollution regulation. When a review of Best Available Control Technology is required under Prevention of Significant Deterioration (PSD) for a project at a major stationary source, aside from considering add-on controls, other considerations to minimize emissions are the application of lower-emitting production processes and available methods, systems, and techniques.

39 Some readers may assert that process redesign as laid out here is simply one version of the EU's Extended Producer Responsibility (EPR). This assertion is not quite correct in that EPR in the EU is imposed in a command-and-control fashion, whereas the regulatory strategy here only requires that the total VMoD cap be reduced via a market-based trading program in conjunction with front-end constraints (to be discussed later), which allows for the product's MoD to meet a specified characteristic standard, itself to be reduced over time. Just how the product is flexibly redesigned is a decision left to the manufacturer.

40 T. E. Graedel and Barbara K. Reck, "Recycling in Context," in *Handbook of Recycling: State-of-the-art for Practitioners, Analysts and Scientists*, ed. Ernst Worrell and Markus A. Reuter (Elsevier, 2014).

41 In an ideally functioning CE, a perfectly designed product after consumption would be immediately 100% reusable and/or recoverable. While that is unrealistic at this primitive stage, this is still the goal. In the real world, though, reusable materials can be acquired from various waste streams, such as just-consumed materials or those mined from landfills, oceans, or infrastructure.

42 In this book, the default discussion regarding ETUs applies to *recovered waste materials*, but it can also include the use of "compostability ETUs," that is, ETUs credited for the substitution of compostable materials in the end product (e.g., plastics).

In addition, where products completely biodegrade during composting and where it is also suitable as a fertilizer, the resulting composted materials could be used as an input ETU credit in agricultural production where industrially manufactured fertilizer is rationed and its usage taxed.

43 In similar fashion, we will see in Chapter 9 that sequestering CO_2 via re-/afforestation can also be credited as ETUs (i.e., negative emissions).

44 The calculation should only include materials used as a raw material in production, so water used in an industrial boiler to produce steam is excluded.

45 These are reuse, recover, rematerialization (which includes recycling), refurbishment, remanufacturing, and repair, although more generally, the broader list of R's includes rethink/refuse, reduce, renew, reuse, repair, refurbish, remanufacture, repurpose, recycle, and recover.

46 Generally speaking, trading should only be reserved for collective contributors to reduce regional environmental harm, while taxing, via the purchase of TUs, should only be targeted toward disincentivizing environmentally harmful decisions made by participants.

47 Stephen Hinton, "White Paper: How Flexible Emission Fees Can Drive Sustainable Development," Version 4.02. Swedish Sustainable Economy Foundation, 2013. https://stephenhintondotorg.files.wordpress.com/2013/08/whitepaperfe_v4-02.pdf. His idea simply relies on fees on inputs proposed by Anders Höglund, whereby feedback mechanisms developed throughout the economy would facilitate sustainable development.

48 In other sectors, it may not be so simple. For example, container glass is more recyclable than other types of glass, such as flat glass, which may not be as easy to recover.

49 Regulators could exercise discretion by requiring that an escalating percentage of TUs used during each reconciliation period be ETUs (i.e., 3 percent one year, 6 percent the next, and so on).

50 For one such discussion regarding the "R's" (reuse, remanufacturing, etc.), see Deloitte, "Circular Economy: From Theory to Practice," Infographic, September

8, 2017. https://www2.deloitte.com/content/dam/Deloitte/fi/Documents/risk/Circular%20economy%20FINAL%20web.pdf.

51 Again, a broader list of R's could be expanded, as noted earlier.

52 Per Stahel, once a functional CE becomes the standard, consumers may no longer consume but use products instead.

53 Thinking ahead to its use in a trading program, note that to render harm intensity usable within it, we will subtract 1 from it so that it is simpler to trade (i.e., X/Y-1), and after multiplying by usage volume, trading continues until the total volumetric quantity in a region is targeted to 0.

54 Just because materials such as bioplastics can biodegrade, it cannot necessarily be assumed that this is always a positive outcome if the environment cannot assimilate its degraded residuals. Thus, rather than biodegradability, the term compostability is used here instead since compost's end market product can more likely be used, potentially as fertilizer in some capacity, perhaps with possible tax benefits.

55 We will see something similar to this situation in Chapter 9 with regard to the climate change mitigation strategy, where developed countries that generate noncompliant per capita emissions are responsible for the current harm intensity of global CO_2 emissions.

56 Some policymakers might think that allowing companies to average standards to meet a sourcewide standard is acceptable, but this only creates a complicated, bureaucratic logjam-provoking problem (i.e., bureaucratic pollution) as well as some products that will not be susceptible to material recovery.

57 Heriberto Cabezas, "Using Sustainability Metrics and Indicators to Design Sustainable Supply Chains," Presentation at the University of Pannonia. National Risk Management Research Laboratory, 2010. https://slideplayer.com/slide/10565526/. Here, the USEPA addresses the use of metrics for supply chains but without a proposal to regulate them.

58 Anders Bjørn and Michael Z. Hauschild, "Cradle To Cradle and LCA," in *Life Cycle Assessment: Theory and Practice*, ed. Michael Hauschild, Ralph Rozenbaum, and Stig Irving Olsen (Springer, 2018).

59 Bjørn and Hauschild, "Cradle To Cradle and LCA," 625–6.

7

Generalizing the Adapted Strategy to the Generation of Multi-Media Environmental Pollution

The Full Generalized Strategy

When applying the comprehensive strategy to IDPCs and IDPC surrogate pollution, this new strategy was identified as the "adapted strategy." Because the strategy that addresses the generation of both air pollution (the comprehensive strategy) and solid waste pollution (the adapted strategy) applies many of the same techniques, it stands to reason that the generation of *all* multi-media environmental pollution can be holistically regulated, namely, air, water, on-site waste generation, and IDPC and IDPC surrogate generated pollution. This strategy that unifies the regulation of all environmental media is the "generalized strategy." Key components of this regulatory strategy that fit within a consistent structure for all media are:

- Setting limits on the regional total of each relevant nonattainment area pollutant
- Declining caps for each of those pollutants generated in major quantities in nonattainment areas while taxing Trading Unit (TU) purchases and letting trading sort out reconciliation
- For nonattainment area pollutants, allowing the use of ETUs through the reuse of waste materials, including remediated waste, such as from water pollution or the substitution of compostables
- Choking off the use of resources further through sufficient taxation
- Rationing/choking off and phasing out the use of fossil-based feedstocks and fuels with sufficient taxation
- Requiring that pollution-generating equipment meet performance standards and all products meet characteristic standards and
- Allow PALs for those pollutants emitted in minor quantities.

It should be noted that while the above represents key components of the generalized strategy, the entire strategy must also include many of the administrative aspects of the comprehensive strategy, such as the development of Next Gen rules and the division of labor (i.e., who does what).

Under the generalized strategy, limiting and then tightening the caps on each multi-media environmental pollutant (as applicable) should hopefully coax major generators of nonattainment pollutants of whatever type to redesign and alter some, if not all of their pollution-generating activities and/or production processes, rather than simply relying on reused materials for ETUs. One should note that while the adapted strategy facilitates core components of the circular economy (CE), the integrated, generalized strategy facilitates a broader, more comprehensive redesign that leads to not just the CE but also the overall reduction of pollution, including climate-destabilizing CO_2 emissions, the mitigation strategy for which is developed in Chapter 9. So, while reducing air pollution by the comprehensive strategy directly reduces fossil fuel usage by rationing them and the adapted strategy indirectly reduces fossil fuel usage, the generalized strategy, incorporating multi-media regulation, broadly addresses fossil-based carbon usage by folding in these strategies together.

The generalized strategy can be used to regulate the generation of on-site waste, which includes hazardous waste generated on-site and "sent away," typically regulated under the Resource Conservation and Recovery Act. This typically requires the hazwaste to meet minimal numerical treatment standards. Under the requirements of the generalized strategy, industrial sources that generate hazardous waste should be required to generate their waste to the level that meets pre-determined performance/treatment standards, measured in pounds per unit of product (tightened every five years). Total limits on waste from sources within a state can then be set and forced to decline via trading until attainment (however that is determined for that type of pollution) is reached. As usual, such sources that reduce pollution (via process redesign) more innovatively than other similar generators can be rewarded for that innovation by selling their excess TUs; likewise, sources that do not innovate and who exhibit a TU shortfall must be taxed for acquiring TUs during reconciliation.

Toxic chemicals and products are best addressed holistically through a multi-media approach rather than by addressing each media separately. If toxic chemicals/HAPs cannot be eliminated outright, then the goal is to minimize their use as much as possible, aided by using a trading program to keep them circulating while simultaneously lowering their harm intensity per product and source,[1] thereby minimizing their exposure to the environment. A key line of defense is requiring stringent technologically achievable characteristic standards that minimize toxic content (i.e., via embedded use in product materials).[2] Aggressively declining pollutant caps via trading of the quantity of individual or aggregated toxics must be applied to guarantee reductions, but where toxic content above an achievable characteristic standard is noncompliant and untradeable. Where there are no achievable toxic characteristic standards, trading proceeds until toxic harm intensity is reduced or eliminated. To minimize toxic materials from products escaping into the environment, the ultimate Next Gen strategy of setting higher-than-normal deposits on those toxic material-containing products will encourage their collection and incentivize their reuse via the acquisition of ETUs.

We will see in Chapter 9 that key components of the generalized strategy to regulate industrially generated pollution can be applied even more broadly and generally to basic agricultural production-related processes as well, as one component of a larger strategy to achieve environmental sustainability with Nature.

Where Does Legacy Pollution Fit In?

Regulators already know how to remediate many contaminants in polluted water under the Safe Drinking Water Act to satisfy drinking water quality requirements. Likewise, adoption of the generalized strategy, primarily through a circular economy, will help to address a portion of the legacy air, water, on-site generated, and solid waste pollution that has already been generated. This is accomplished by recirculating whatever waste is recoverable back into the economy.

We will see that the mitigation strategy developed in Chapter 9 will include a means to take credit for recovering legacy CO_2. In addition, where ETUs can be quantified by their material recovery, legacy externalities such as PCBs in sediment and polluted groundwater can be incentivized for remediation and reuse in some capacity, and the heat content of organics in nonchlorinated plastics can be converted to energy, with the resulting CO_2 emissions sequestered where feasible.[3] By extrapolation then, the larger goal of a robust generalized strategy would be to circulate what materials can be circulated, remediate anything that can economically be remediated, and put aside those materials that cannot, until such later time that it is economical to do so. The continual striving for circular inclusion of legacy pollution within the economy is the long-term goal.

Nuances of the Generalized Strategy

Under the generalized strategy, the domain of trading IDPC and IDPC surrogates will likely be the entire state, while the trading domain for nitrogen oxides, as one example, will only be the regional NOx NAAs applied to those sources that emit NOx in major quantities. Although IDPC and IDPC surrogate pollution is truly transboundary in nature, there is still no clearly identifiable "IDPC/IDPC surrogate-shed," which identifies this kind of homogeneously dispersed solid waste pollution throughout the environment. For these reasons, it is appropriate to regulate all relevant IDPC and IDPC surrogate pollutants as if the pollution was generated within the state in which the products were manufactured.

Note that there may be sources that trade more than one pollutant as well: one source may have redesigned its process to reduce their IDPC surrogate footprint while increasing its NOx emissions. It is also possible that, due to process changes, another source in an SO_2 nonattainment area (NAA) that has SO_2 TUs to sell within that area may, on the other hand, have to purchase difficulty-of-disassembly (DoD) pollutant TUs within its state's DoD NAA. Thus, sources within their respective nonattainment areas all have the ability to redesign their process(es), abate and control pollutants, participate in each applicable trading program, and/or stand pat, depending on the pollutant and their particular situation. So while this provides sources flexibility across all media, the environment experiences overall harm reduction in subject NAAs due to the decline in their caps. And where there are increases in attainment area pollutants (of whatever type) over their PAL thresholds, modeling must be conducted to ensure that environmental deterioration does not occur.

> The significance of buying and selling TUs for the various pollution media is that it allows sources to better balance process costs of redesign in proportion to the environmental harm they inflict ("the polluter pays principle"). This significance cannot be overstated. Economists have argued that the costs to businesses associated with trading are not spread equally to all; rather than focusing on just one media, trading where increases and decreases across multiple media are holistically considered allows sources to better exercise flexibility to comply and distribute costs, while environmental harms overall are being reduced.

Further regulatory nuances may apply. For example, if redesigning a process reduces discharges of hydrogen sulfide in a water body, but in so doing it increases SO_2 emissions in an attainment area for SO_2, then the PAL for SO_2

may need to be redetermined and modeling conducted, where doable. There can also be small sources in an IDPC surrogate pollutant NAA that manufacture products that do not meet an IDPC characteristic standard, thereby being a small source that is nevertheless noncompliant.

While ETUs are mostly associated with the recovery of solid waste products as reusable resource inputs, wherever certain contaminants, say from water, are recoverable and reusable as a resource input, then ETUs can be utilized within a trading program for that NAA pollutant.

The whole point of the generalized trading scheme is that it doesn't matter how individual sources reduce pollution (or not); what ultimately matters is that the regional cap on each pollutant is reduced. The environment experiences reductions in pollution while the market simply sorts out who does and does not reduce; environmentalists get what they want (declining caps) while companies get what they want (flexibility). And where pollution is allowed to increase in attainment areas, these increases are designed by regulation to be made progressively more difficult as the amount of that pollutant in the region gets closer to nonattainment levels.

Thus, the generalized strategy demonstrates that the generation of environmental pollution, where measurable, is amenable to holistic, rigorous regulation.

A Note on the Role of the States and the Feds

As noted earlier, it has been assumed that states rather than the feds should regulate IDPCs and IDPC surrogates. Recall that the authors of *Breaking The Logjam* proposed that sources that generate transboundary air pollution (via interstate dispersion) should best be handled by the feds, which begs this question: who should regulate the generation of IDPCs and IDPC surrogates that are typically transboundary by nature (via interstate consumption and disposal)? As in Part 2, setting a limit followed by external trading with an established target, not necessarily federal control, is probably the most critical factor in reducing pollution. In this light, states clearly have the manpower to address the task of regulating IDPCs and IDPC surrogates generated from sources within their regulatory jurisdiction. Likewise, the feds will play a critical factor by overseeing that imports meet minimum characteristic standards.

Where Regulators Must Go from Here

As far as developing a CE is concerned, the European Union (EU) is, in effect, where the United States was decades ago with regard to the early "RACT" stage of air pollution regulation. Regulating air pollution then was often characterized by setting command-and-control-based emission unit standards and developing regulations in a piecemeal, ad hoc fashion. Likewise, with the EU trying to set command-and-control solid waste reduction standards rather than truly establishing a holistic, comprehensive framework for a CE, history is once again repeating itself.

Outsiders to the world of day-to-day regulation might argue that setting up trading programs would be an incredibly burdensome regulatory undertaking, as if regulation is a fate worse than unsustainability itself. Insiders, on the other hand, would recognize that once the regulatory infrastructure for adopting the generalized strategy is set up, the result would be an infrastructure that would be relatively straightforward to navigate. So, policymakers and regulators who wish to adopt a generalized strategy should ensure that the components of the generalized strategy are adopted. As it is now, few are. Clearly, countries around the world have some work to do.

Brief Remarks on the Generalized Strategy

We have seen that Stephen Hinton's idea of taxing resources on the front end is insufficient to develop the framework for a CE. Although taxing resources to discourage their use is certainly one piece of the puzzle and the use of CaT to reduce IDPC and IDPC surrogate pollution is another piece of the larger puzzle, the question begging to be asked is: what exactly is that bigger puzzle and how is it to be clarified?

That bigger puzzle is the regulatory strategy to achieve sustainability with Nature but, for now, the lesser but still large puzzle is regulating the harms resulting from the generation of environmental pollution via the use of the generalized strategy. As for more powerful inducements to change actual practices on a global scale, there are none more powerful. The strategy relies on a smart cocktail of techniques that includes inducements to promote technological innovation, a means to "kinetically incentivize" the reuse of materials and use appropriately applied economic tools. The optimal utilization of the generalized strategy, in conjunction with the confluence of engineering, legal, and economic acumen, will hopefully navigate us out of many of our current environmental crises.

While we may not seem able to actually phase out fossil-based carbon, we must nevertheless do everything in our power to do so, despite the largely political limitations that prevent that. Restricting carbon will be a bitter pill for global citizens to swallow, but there is no other alternative that will flatten and then lower the CO_2 concentration (and plastics) curve. Furthermore, trading of *all* relevant multi-media environmental pollutants, including IDPC surrogates, will give policymakers and regulatory bodies the fighting chance they desperately need to address the environmental impacts that the generation of industrial pollution creates. Companies that subscribe to the outdated principles of Corporate Social Responsibility will be put to the test based on how they accept the holistic regulation of IDPCs and IDPC surrogates and the other multi-media pollutants. Likewise, global citizens will have to decide whether or not they are stewards of the environment who support environmental sustainability programs that facilitate and perpetuate the CE or simply consumers of resources that Nature provides them.

Chapters 6 and 7 have respectively laid out the adapted and generalized strategies. Chapter 8 will discuss their consequences and provide commentary on their use.

Notes

1 A measure of harm intensity would be the ratio of the current measure of toxic harm to a reference measure.

2 In fact, the definition of "National Standards of Performance" under the Clean Water Act, 33 U.S. Code §1316 includes, "where practicable, a standard permitting no discharge of pollutants." Thus, where possible, regulators could expand applicability of this requirement to toxics across all media.

3 Existing (not future) CO_2 emissions generated from the combustion of fossil fuel-based carbon must be sequestered.

8

Commentary on and Implications of the Adapted and Generalized Strategies

An Overview of the Consequences of Trading IDPCs and IDPC Surrogates and Other Pollutants under the Generalized Strategy

This chapter details the implications of applying the generalized strategy to regulate the generation of multi-media environmental pollution, most notably facilitating the transition to a circular economy (CE) in the real world. In addition, applying the methods of the generalized strategy to attain environmental sustainability itself and where future study should progress is proposed.

What then are the implications of regulating the IDPC and IDPC surrogate pollutants?

Attainment of each IDPC/IDPC surrogate pollutant standard nationwide should eventually lead to an economy that will hopefully generate products whose components will be more reusable such that they can conceivably (1) re-enter the economic mainstream; (2) be less toxic; (3) be more biodegradable and compostable (with the targeted focus on plastics); and (4) be more durable (for some critically essential products). Manufacturers will be incentivized to redesign these components for reuse potentially by these same manufacturers and others who will find them cheaper to utilize than buying and processing virgin materials. This is complemented by the requirement that all products' MoDs not exceed established numerical characteristic standards, establishing a floor for minimal recoverability.

The transition over time to something that resembles a CE arises *directly* out of both regulating IDPCs and IDPC surrogates, rationing resources and fossil-based carbon inputs, and creating a robust market for product components. Besides catalyzing a CE, reusing materials that came from disassembled and/or less complex products will create the collateral benefits of reducing the need for energy, and thus the lower need for fossil fuels.

If upon required participation in a trading program, a source cannot reduce its IDPC or IDPC surrogate pollution by process redesign and/or acquisition of ETUs, the source will have to buy trading units for failing to reduce their generation of the subject pollutant. The company may then pass this cost on to consumers who may (1) go without that product, (2) find an adequate replacement, (3) keep, reuse, and refurbish the product that they already have, or (4) purchase it and later toss it into a recycling bin or drop-off center and let the market be incentivized to remediate this pollution for profit, as credited ETUs.

Sources that make no effort to redesign their manufacturing process to reduce their generation of IDPC and IDPC surrogate pollution without acquiring ETUs impose a further requirement upon them. Such sources will need to purchase the necessary TUs when that manufacturer has to reconcile any shortfall of such units above that source's allotment and pay an environmental "unsustainability tax" for having to do so.

Taken together, while unique regulated pollutants apply to each environmental media (e.g., NOx being unique to air pollution while IDPC surrogates are unique to solid waste pollution), the same general methodology is used to regulate the generation of pollution for each. This consistent approach represents a fundamental shift away from the current situation where the generation of environmental pollution is regulated within separate, mutually exclusive silos.

Beyond this basic outline of the implications of applying the generalized strategy, we can now make a number of salient, more detailed points about the guiding principles and consequences of the generalized strategy. We will also provide critical regulatory insights and implications, anticipate likely changes we'll have to make to our current mindsets, and highlight a number of key ecological, economic, and policy considerations.

1 Guiding Principles and Consequences of the Strategy

The following guiding principles are clear:

a. *The Regulatory Coverage Hierarchy*. We saw in Part 2 that there was a hierarchy for regulating the generation of air pollution; the same applies to the generation of environmental pollution in general. The following tiers can be postulated: Top Tier—setting absolute global or regional limits on relevant measurable quantities of resources, fuels and pollutant emissions, discharges, etc., and then declining those quantified caps using a CaT program; Mid-Tier—sourcewide coverage, focusing on the regulation of a source's process equipment or products that generate pollution; and Bottom Tier—minor coverage, with a narrower effect, for example, regulating nuisance odors, conducting required water quality sampling, and imposing tests using approved test methods.

Unfortunately, the application of current regulation in the United States has addressed these tiers in a somewhat ad hoc fashion, without significantly setting absolute regional limits pursuant to the highest tier of the regulatory hierarchy where it could be applied. Be that as it may, US regulators have made headway in addressing air and water pollution via the Clean Air Act and the Clean Water Act, respectively. The two Acts were not optimally designed, so clearly more yet can be done by aiming to be more comprehensive. Regulating the generation of air pollution continues to neglect climate change for the most part (particularly by treating GHG as an attainment area pollutant), and the accumulation of solid waste in the environment offers clear evidence that proper regulation here lags as well.

b. *The Durability Hierarchy.* One can classify a product as belonging to one of three different categories: infrastructure (e.g., buildings), consumables (e.g., a toaster), and disposables (e.g., plastic razors with metal blades). Generally speaking, the longer a product can be kept and maintained in the economy, the better. This is clearly the case with roads and buildings. Consumables will typically last only as long as the product is able to function. Thereafter, upon eking the most out of the R's and/or disassembly, it is critical to circulate the materials within the economy as much as possible. Some disposables, such as hypodermic needles, will by their nature only be used once, but their materials are reusable. True single-use disposables, such as plastic straws, must be phased out using surgically targeted regulation that facilitates the use of compostable plastics or other materials.

c. *The Material Degradation Hierarchy.* While the generalized strategy ideally applies to all materials as if they all potentially possess equal replaceability, the reality is what industrial ecologists already know all too well. There is a hierarchy of degradational disadvantage per material, whereby certain materials like metals will have a much higher capacity for continual circularity relative to paper and concrete, whose usability will degrade more rapidly over time. So while the generalized strategy treats all materials as equally capable of continual recirculation, it cannot directly overcome materials' inherent differences in physical characteristics. Under the generalized strategy, choices, such as redesigning manufacturing processes, are made in response to regulation, but those choices are clearly limited by the unique chemical and physical constraints of the various materials in circulation.

d. *A Means of Measuring Harm*. The generation of a technology-induced[1] environmental pollutant that can be measured means it can be regulated. Determining and quantifying these pollutants is fundamental. As the *Cradle to Cradle* authors noted, we face a design problem. The generalized strategy should go a long way to facilitate process redesign and technology innovation in a timely manner. It should sort out the optimal composition of legal and economic instruments that will achieve the desired outcome of reducing the use of harmful fuels and resources/feedstocks via a CE.

e. *Eco-Effectiveness. Cradle to Cradle* idealizes the "Waste = Food" or zero waste CE[2] paradigm (i.e., where perfect harmony prevails between all generated waste and raw material inputs). Per *Cradle to Cradle*, eco-efficiency (basic meaning—be less unsustainable) must be replaced by eco-effectiveness (i.e., being truly sustainable, in the strictest sense of the word). The generalized strategy attempts to achieve this.

f. *Quantifiable Limits (the Yin)*. Without quantifiable limits, a CE cannot be achieved. *There is no substitute for setting hard limits and tightening those limits to reduce the generation of technology-induced environmental pollution*. The generalized strategy restructures regulation by setting rigorously quantified limits and thereafter adhering to a systematic means of reducing them.

Identifying and applying an enforceable and absolute hard and tightening limit to fossil fuel use, for example, acts as a *guarantee* on reducing post-combustion emissions. In regional terms, the limits on fossil fuel use will affect all sources in the region that combust those fuels—mobile sources, stationary sources, nonroad engines, residential heating, etc. Limiting the amount of fossil fuels as a means to limit emissions is not just a means to flatten the CO_2 concentration curve and curve it back downward, but it also facilitates the internalization of negative externalities.[3]

How anyone, including distinguished academic scholars, can speak of environmental sustainability without discussion of setting and acting to reduce global and regional limits is beyond comprehension. If absolute limits on emissions and other generated discharges of pollution are not set and systematically reduced, how can we ever manage what we could measure but don't, in order to achieve reduction goals? Solely relying on the use of suboptimal baby-step regulatory procedures and the source-by-source imposition of rules for addressing regional air emissions, water discharges, and other pollution will not compensate for reducing total global and regional limits on pollution.

As obvious as it may seem, we cannot simply hope and rely on the sum of best management practices at the individual micro level to solve problems at the global level. The response to a severe crisis and the need for the necessary regulatory capacity has to be in proportion to that severity. Even though many people will deem it unrealistic to expect that global action is required to solve global problems, Nature does not recognize the lack of global cooperation or political boundaries—international treaties will be required. And if global citizens must adopt new behaviors to ensure global sustainability, so be it.

Likewise, if resource usage limits are not set, how would we realistically claim that solid waste pollution can ever be reduced? Yet, we have settled into a flawed mindset that favors reducing pollution at the back end without also accepting that we must limit inputs at the front end.

g. *Trading (the Yang).* The Yang of trading is a critically useful tool, ideally used when multiple generators contribute pollution into an adverse area. Trading, simply a tool like a hammer or chisel, or a device like a trash compactor, is neither worthy of worship or fear. As a tool, we have already seen that trading can be applied to nonattainment areas like an airshed, but it can now apply to the generation of pollution for all environmental media, such as to the regional generation of product and nonproduct waste pollution, including on-site generated hazardous waste and nonreused scrap.
h. *Striking the Right Balance of Limits and Markets.* Applying and declining limits while using trading provides just the right balance in that limits

provide rigor while minimizing bureaucratic pollution, whereas markets sort out who makes the reductions most economically. We have seen that the generalized strategy is characterized by both market incentives and CaC, for example, by using trading and performance standards, respectively, sandwiched between Command-and-Control (CaC)-based regulation both on the upper/macro end (i.e., limits) and at the lower/ micro end (e.g., emissions testing).

It is this balance that provides the flexibility that the European Union (EU)'s Extended Producer Responsibility does not. Rather than using pure CaC-based regulation to demand redesign, the fact that allotments are declining provides that incentive, allowing manufacturers to either redesign their processes and products or acquire reused materials when they can or will not.

i. *Rationing and Phasing Out.* Rationing and phasing out resources and fuels at the front end automatically reduces pollution at the back end.[4] This approach must be adopted in response to how we address climate change and waste plastics pollution—where they are currently treated as two mutually exclusive crises.[5] So when the underlying cause of environmental hazard is the same, that is, fossil-based carbon, it makes no sense to continue bifurcating the approach to regulating CO_2 emissions separately from the approach (or lack thereof) to regulating microplastic pollution.

For skeptics of rationing and phase outs, note that we already possess the historical experience of phasing out CFCs as a guide. When scientists realized that CFCs were destroying the ozone layer, the Montreal Protocol responded with a timed phaseout scheme and Congress responded by imposing a tax on the use of virgin CFCs. In this respect, the article from Pasfield and Paeffgren[6] is instructive by demonstrating how the CFC phaseout program worked, including the issue of the black market for CFCs. Applying a similar program to fossil-based carbon inputs and other resources that must be rationed or otherwise limited (e.g., clean groundwater in overextracted areas) to stymie overexploitation should likewise be feasible.[7]

Time is pressing; we cannot afford to wait to see how well any international-scale CO_2 emissions reduction experiment, such as taxation, pans out while the consumption of microplastics by humans, whales, turtles, fish, and other life within the food chain continues unabated.[8] We cannot agree to limiting the effects of climate change (to ensure the flattening of the CO_2 curve, remember) and promoting a CE without also agreeing to limit the use of fossil-based carbon fuels and feedstocks.[9] It's a package deal.

j. *Resource Constraints*. As total circulated waste (reused and unremediated) increases, the use of virgin resources will ideally drop to zero. Thus, jobs will gradually be lost in the extractive sector while jobs will gradually be gained in the disassembly and recovery/reprocessing sector. To grease the skids even more, reuse of low IDPC-inducing input materials should be subsidized, while use of virgin materials must be taxed (i.e., an environmental "unsustainability tax" intended to dissuade unsustainability-based choices). Obviously, there will be leakage of virgin resources into the economic circulatory system, but the goal remains: remediate as much waste as possible and use less virgin resources. As such, it may be possible to repurpose refineries to process recycled fossil-based carbon materials as feedstocks rather than to refine virgin fossil-based materials.

Unfortunately, it is still possible that there will be stationary waste in the environment that is no longer in demand as a resource in the economy; for example, organized stockpiles of materials that manufacturers or consumers/users no longer need. Let us examine one realistic example: excess synthetic rubber. There may be quantities of such rubber expertly disassembled and ready for reuse, but for which there is no customer need. In fact, there may be stockpiles of low-IDPC surrogate materials that no longer have an economic niche in the short term, which, if nothing else, can be managed better than mixed waste is today. Hopefully, companies will not only be compelled to innovate to reduce the magnitude of their MoD-laden products but will presumably plan ahead for increasing the salvage value of their post-consumption product "waste" as potential credits as ETUs later. This process will be baked into the regulatory scheme, in conjunction with the increased functioning of the materials market that the CE will generate.

Regarding the inefficient use of resources, the following from Webster is insightful:

> The linear industrial economy is best in overcoming situations of scarcity of food, goods, shelter. But in a situation of saturated

> markets, a circular economy is best suited to manage existing stock. In 1980, the market penetration for durable household goods in France was already above 90 percent for all social classes. In Germany, since 1995, the number of cars scrapped each year has been roughly the same as the number of cars newly registered. Continued production in saturated markets constitutes a substitution of, not an addition to, wealth, at the cost of "intensive and often inefficient use of resources."[10]

A question that is rarely asked, and usually only among the industrial ecologists, is the following: are there sufficient amounts of all materials to maintain circularity? The "take, make, dispose"[11] linear economy is sometimes one that is better characterized as "take, make products more voluminous/complex/difficult-to-disassemble/noncompostable/toxic, accumulate (and later dispose)." Accumulating occurs when materials are "sequestered" within the economy as existing infrastructure,[12,13] which are maintained or abandoned (i.e., disposed-in-place) for decades at a time without being brought back into circulation. Is it so necessary to continue to use virgin resources to build new roads and structures when abandoned or underutilized ones exist for material reuse? The case of abandoned infrastructural resources can be just as problematic as the use of single use consumer products that end up in a landfill soon after purchase and consumption.

There is a flipside as well-in a linear economy it is quite rational to reduce the volume of generated waste. However, with the possible exception of plastics and the waste that must still go to landfills, in a CE we paradoxically may not want to reduce waste volume *excessively* for some materials since waste volume is what enables robust circularity. Without adequate waste volume, an already materially streamlined economy would have to "breathe in," that is, make up, more virgin resources. We may even have to rely on cannibalizing materials from existing infrastructural stocks before we resort to breathing virgin resources into the economy.

This begs the following thought-provoking question—what then is the appropriate "steady state" of a CE, where neither excess waste nor excess product accumulates? While this should be a critical project for further study, such a steady-state equilibrium paradigm is proposed in Chapter 9.

k. *Internalizing Externalities.* Some entities may feel an economic sting at the micro level, but setting CaC-based limits on the generation of pollution is clearly necessary at the macrolevel. To alleviate that sting, a market-based trading program, along with other market instruments (e.g., dissuasive taxation of TU purchases), must play a role beneath the larger limit/umbrella. As it turns out, that sting just happens to be the result of internalizing negative environmental externalities by shifting the harm away from the environment (e.g., extinctions, litter in oceans, abandoned buildings) back to the economic perpetrators of that harm.

   It is important to realize that the more external costs are internalized, the fairer the environmental/economic relationship will be. Clearly, internalizing negative externalities will not always be for the faint of heart. We will all have to adjust to the required sacrifice to reduce global pollution. Internalizing externalized costs, while absolutely appropriate in our day and age, will not only be a cost which manufacturers, shippers, and others absorb but also a cost that consumers/users must learn to accept, leading to the concept of "full cost pricing" and "least cost planning" for all of us. Limiting back-end pollution and redesigning front-end processes will cost everybody in the short term, if not longer. It is also very possible that some costs will decrease within the CE, including the cost of energy due to reduced fossil fuel use and increased efficiency.

   Some people will likely wish to go back to "business as usual," that is, a linear economy, but it is important to realize that doing so does not imply that the great reservoir of externalities where waste currently goes "out of sight out of mind" will not have gone away. Any ongoing failure to surrender our current harm-inducing linear economy for the achievement of sustainability with Nature would just be another case of "you can pay me now or . . . pay me later," or "you can run but you can't hide."

l. *Material and Energy Efficiency.* Since a CE arises in part from regulating the generation of IDPCs and IDPC surrogates, achieving a CE is technically independent of, that is, not predicated on, the reduction in the use of fossil fuels. Nevertheless, adopting a CE will indirectly reduce fossil fuel usage because the economy becomes more materially and energy efficient. When we think of energy efficiency, we may simplistically think of an actual piece of technology that was designed to use less energy. However, one can likewise think of energy efficiency at a national scale whereby the throughput of materials within the CE is reusable to the point where much less energy is needed to reprocess them relative to the processing of raw virgin materials and feedstocks. In fact, significant innovations in production will prevent both pollution and an increase in energy usage. Furthermore, ETUs acquired for the manufacture of products meeting characteristic standards are a means to acquire those materials with energy already expended relative to the use of virgin materials (e.g., aluminum can recycling). While industrial ecologists tell us that not all recovered materials save on energy, the strategy will nevertheless help to exploit what advantages do exist. In any event, a fully operational CE will theoretically exhibit *economy-wide* energy efficiency. At the source level as well, aggressively scaling back the use of fossil fuels will also encourage companies themselves to be more energy efficient, including for those companies where cogeneration is feasible. Likewise, individual equipment and the flow of all materials within the entire "economic machine" will ideally exhibit energy-efficient behavior.

The CE is not just efficient in terms of energy economy-wide, but likewise efficient in terms of material use throughout the economy. As we become both more energy and materially efficient, we no longer face a binary choice of either using environmentally harmful quantities of both fuels and resources to maintain our economy or not using them and settling for a pauper economy. Rather, in a CE, less fuel and resources will be used while supporting economic growth by maintaining or improving our quality of life through the transitional development of environmentally *sustainable* sources of materials and, hopefully in time, renewable energy.

Two key points should be noted—(1) as inefficient technologies are discarded in an ideal CE, they will not simply end up in a landfill since they will first get taken back, disassembled, melted down and/or reused in some form; and (2) while we may be inefficient at the micro level (e.g., some products being materially efficient but not optimally energy efficient), when we achieve attainment at the macrolevel by having minimized the generation of pollution, a CE is doing just what it was meant to do.

Lastly, rationing and gradually limiting fossil fuels and virgin resources will limit both an increase in entropy and the rate of its increase. Taking this a step further, by design via application of the generalized strategy, the CE will replace the linear economy's reliance on a higher rate of entropy increase at both the front end (i.e., resource extraction) and the back end (i.e., product manufacture) with a lower rate of entropy increase on both ends due to the lower use of energy.

The astute reader will observe the common thread in this book of minimizing the rate of increase of entropy, whether that occurs via rationing, material recovery, improving work practices, prioritizing the lowest carbon-intensive resource extraction, or simply by minimizing the generation of pollution.

m. *Legacy Pollution.* While the mitigation strategy developed in Chapter 9 will help to address legacy CO_2 emissions, and the generalized strategy can theoretically address legacy pollution, in general though, the strategy cannot do so immediately. And what makes the legacy CO_2 problem a daunting one to solve is that we may begrudgingly have to accept that, as they are being phased down, fossil fuels must still be used (preferably at existing sources) until we find adequate energy substitutes. Making this decision against our better judgment will create yet more legacy CO_2 emissions for future remediation. By doing so, we continue to knowingly add more CO_2 to the atmosphere, and yet we just can't stop ourselves. This is a vicious cycle indeed.
n. *Encourages Shared Use.* "Shared use" of products, such as Uber, should become a later step in the evolutionary process of the CE. Within such a consumptive lifestyle, people will be able to answer the question—what is cherished more, the product itself or the benefit of consuming that product?
o. *Strenuous Scrutiny Still Required.* While the generalized strategy provides increased flexibility, it will still require the necessary tasks of monitoring and verification, such as product testing for determining or verifying MoDs,[14] increased scrutiny of operating/production records, and attaining aggressive reductions. Running such a regulatory program will be no cakewalk. Thankfully, though, there is sufficient regulatory infrastructure capacity existing already in the United States and elsewhere to develop and conduct such a program.

p. *The Continuous Pursuit of Improvement.* While the generalized strategy is, among its regulatory drivers, a catalyst to facilitate the transition to a CE (or, in the worst case, facilitate the *opportunity* for a CE), it fortuitously achieves regulatory clarity and elegance. Declining global and regional caps in conjunction with the tightening of both performance and characteristic standards requires participants to continually strive for optimal process/product redesign as the CE matures. External trading elegantly addresses movement up both the waste/materials management and energy hierarchies by economic incentivizing.

Governments will not have to prescriptively dictate through CaC what companies must do to specifically reduce IDPC and IDPC surrogate pollution at each individual source; the generalized strategy and the market will do it for them. The strategy also highlights this proviso: every source that generates pollution and every person that consumes is obligated to be a citizen-participant in the CE. Limiting the generation of environmental pollution and resource extraction snares us all in the net. Regulation strategically sets boundary conditions (limits) on resources and pollution without the use of brutish command-and-control micromanagement. In contrast to targeted CaC, (1) requiring the rationing of the "scarcity-induced" carbon budget; (2) allowing manufacturers the choice/flexibility to combine process innovation with the ability to reuse materials; and (3) letting consumer/user choices dictate priorities will instead achieve ecological and environmental benefits via simplified but effective "*macro*management."

q. *The Future Cannot Be Predicted.* It is possible that the generalized strategy will not facilitate the transition to a CE, but it should certainly facilitate the process—the rest would be left to engineers, economists, regulators, lawyers, and consumers/users to enable circularity. This assumes that human ingenuity and industrial technology live up to the task of continual innovation and/or that materials are sufficiently recovered throughout the economy to replace the use of virgin resources and the ongoing development of an economic infrastructure for perpetual material reuse. While attainment occurs when solid waste is able to be assimilated and managed, it will not lead to the complete elimination of all pollution (note that the Acid Rain Program *reduced* acid rain; it has yet to eliminate it). Thus, through the use of regulation, we may only be able to reduce but not eliminate IDPC and IDPC surrogate pollution. Hopefully, additional but currently underused (or even unknown market) instruments may further encourage a means to sell waste as later materials and discourage the excessive extraction and use of virgin materials.

At this point, without having firmly developed the category of IDPC surrogates, the means to quantify them, or their allied characteristic standards, adopting the predicates of the CE *in toto* is infeasible at this time.

r. *The Separate Roles of the Generalized Strategy and LCA*. The generalized strategy is a means of regulating the generation of pollution of various media. Life Cycle Assessment (LCA)'s key role will be to provide a means to diagnose which technologies will be best suited to a resource- and fuel-constrained world.

The assumption to this point has been that the generalized strategy and LCA supplement each other, but this may not always be the case. So, while limiting the use of fuels and the resource-constraining generalized strategy will reduce the rate of entropy increase at the overall macro level due to the lower use of energy, what if, at the micro level, LCA indicates that a complex and/or difficult-to-disassemble product (e.g., a lawnmower) is very energy efficient over its lifetime, which more than offsets the higher rate of entropy increase from the manufacture of the product?[15] It is very possible that a product that is materially efficient is more energy *in*efficient than a product that is less materially efficient. How do we sort out the best product for use within the economy in these situations? In an ideal world, the best tradable regulatory metric would be one that factors in both the product's quantifiable material characteristics and its energy use; this is hard to imagine accomplishing at this time.

In any event, while the generalized strategy does not by itself immediately answer these micro-scale questions, the significant result of applying the strategy is that it will eventually achieve attainment for *all* pollution-generating activities at the macroscale. Also, while what we may gain in material efficiency we may lose in energy efficiency, and vice versa, note that by constraining fuels and resources and setting limits on pollution at the global or regional level means the environment has already "gotten its cut up front" for the damage it has incurred (the polluter pays principle) and will receive "installment payments" into the future as caps decline. Market economics, which is embedded within the ecosystem, is relegated to sorting out the "leftovers" of who-gets-what via the market instrument of trading. As limits tighten, the market has lesser quantities of pollution to "allot" among its participants. Pushing the envelope in this way over time will ensure just what niches among highly complex, durable, and material and energy-efficient products survive.

s. *Exposing Genuine and Disingenuous Commitment.* Those companies that are truly committed to the principles of Corporate Social Responsibility (CSR) and who would love nothing better than to participate within an enforceable CE regulatory regime can now "put their money where their mouth is" and exploit those companies with low CSR. No longer will simply relying on piecemeal, socially responsible corporate behavior be sufficient, because participation in the CE will put CSR to the test. Practically speaking, investors and securities regulators who monitor Environmental, Social and Governance (ESG) behavior will now have much better metrics to base their decisions on.

2. Regulatory Insights and Consequences

The following insights can be gleaned from the generalized strategy:

a. *Streamlined Regulation.* If there was ever an Exhibit A that applying a prescriptive, brute force, NSR-like regulation will never work, it is in the regulation of IDPC and IDPC surrogate pollution. The administrative resources needed to regulate these pollutants by using a prescriptive, slow-walking, source-by-source method would be laughably labor-intensive and largely ineffective. As we've seen for regulating air pollution, the SIP process and NSR are just too inefficient and process-oriented, particularly where Food and Drug Administration (FDA)-like regulation is used to avert dangerous health impacts in NAAs (which requires a more CDC-like, targeted approach). Many individual companies will not immediately have the R&D acumen to redesign their processes and products within this kind of prescriptive scheme, nor would they have an incentive to do so. Absent a cap-and-trade program, movement away from the current status quo will only be possible by government dictate, which commonly involves disjointed and inefficient planning.

b. *Developing and Verifying the MoDs for Products.* As necessary, regulators must ensure that the determination of the surrogate characteristics' measures of detriment is as simple as possible. If these MoDs are too difficult and complicated to calculate, then trading would be based on the solid waste pollution equivalent of air pollution stack testing, namely, that calculating MoDs may be the weakest link in the whole chain of regulating the generation of IDPC surrogate pollution.

The core of the regulatory program will be the day-to-day permitting tasks focused primarily on verifying the calculation of the IDPC surrogate MoDs. Assuming that IDPC surrogate MoDs can be accurately determined—fortunately, they are constant rather than varying over time—regulating them should not be problematic.

Besides the development of IDPC and IDPC surrogate MoDs, the difficult aspects of regulating these characteristics and the pollution associated with them include: (1) the multitude and variety of manufactured products; (2) the determination of characteristic standards across the various source categories; (3) calculating and revising such MoDs for the various products at a source upon redesign; and (4) determining other negative environmental metrics that would need to be quantified and regulated.

c. *Three Means for Reconciliation*. Besides simply purchasing TUs from participating sources, the generalized strategy allows sources a combination of two other avenues to meet IDPC and IDPC surrogate volumetric measure of detriment (VMoD) reduction targets. One is to redesign their product to render it more "recycle-compatible," for example, less complex and/or easier to disassemble.[16] The second avenue is to simply acquire the requisite amount of ETUs to maintain the inherent qualities of the product but offsetting its inherently negative effects on the environment by extracting the necessary materials from existing waste supplies and/or accepting takebacks. As we have seen, it is this latter avenue of reconciliation that facilitates true circularity.

In the article by den Hollander and colleagues,[17] it was conceptually demonstrated that companies will want to either redesign for recycling or design their products to maintain product integrity. These two vehicles are none other than what was demonstrated in the development of the adapted strategy in Chapter 6, and also the generalized, multi-media strategy in Chapter 7 and the two alternative avenues cited above. Design for Recycling corresponds to redesigning the manufacturing process so that the product is less detrimental and more recycle-ready, while the Design for Product Integrity alternative allows companies to continue manufacturing a product that may be inherently detrimental to the environment but is durable (i.e., long-lasting). One can expect tension in a future CE whereby designing for recycling respects the need to "smooth the rough edges" of the discontinuity between manufactured products and their material recoverability, while designing for product integrity maintains that discontinuity while preserving product durability. Because recycled materials are degraded relative to the use of virgin materials, it may behoove society to keep certain products in "durability mode" for as long as possible. This does not apply to single-use, undesirably durable products with short consumption lifetimes. On the other hand, the advantage of rendering other products as recycle-compatible exploits the fact that they are less energy-intensive to recover.

The bottom line is that as long as the total IDPC and IDPC surrogate VMoDs are being reduced regionally or even globally, it doesn't matter what choices along the Design for Product Integrity/Design for Recycling spectrum sources use to achieve that end.

d. *Strategies to Address Other Media*. Another problem includes developing a parallel optimal strategy for the generation of both water and on-site waste pollution. Luckily, regulators already have a head start since many of the large sources are already regulated and tracked for the major sources of air, water, and/or on-site generated waste pollution.

However, to address on-site generated waste, such as hazardous waste or nonreused scrap, instead of simply regulating it as off-site pollution as is done currently, regulation must also set on-site generation requirements at the source, such as the development of sufficiently tight lb/unit of product performance/treatment standards for all source categories. For example, if hazardous waste is generated at a source that exceeds a given lb/ton of product performance standard, then the manufacturer must redesign the process and/or treat the waste so as to reduce the generation rate to meet that performance standard.

e. *Rewarding Innovation*. It's useful to compare the environmental benefits of the Acid Rain Program (ARP) relative to the pragmatic use of regulation and technologies to achieve those benefits. The ARP's "lowest of the lowest-hanging fruit" of regulation was successful because options existed within the program, for example, use either add-on controls or switch fuels. It was also easy to measure emissions, albeit with expensive continuous emissions monitoring systems (CEMS). More generally, simply reducing air pollution with add-on technology controls may very well be just the "low-hanging fruit" of pollution control, that is, it is straightforward to simply install controls rather than completely rethink and redesign the entire production process to reduce emissions. On the other hand, reducing other regulated pollution such as IDPC surrogates will be much more difficult because there are no add-on controls; rather this will require changing the actual upstream process itself through technological redesign, perhaps radically and maybe even fundamentally. The innovative thinking behind the creation of the current product has to be replaced with the higher order ingenuity to redesign it. Unfortunately, it may be possible that the radical new upstream technologies that may be necessary may not even exist yet. Even the phaseout of CFCs was possible only because technologies already existed to produce substitutes.

On the other hand, there are responsible companies that have developed reformulations and conducted R&D at their own expense, while other companies have acted irresponsibly by dragging their feet, resisting investment in the search for adequate substitutes. As it is right now, where is the incentive to spend millions on process redesign? What company is willing to take the risk when the downsides outnumber the upsides? With a trading program for IDPC and IDPC surrogate pollution, the socially responsible companies can profitably and socially benefit their bottom line, while the irresponsible companies will suffer both a competitive disadvantage and inconvenient public relations optics to their shareholders and the public.

Aside from sources utilizing ETUs to alternatively reconcile shortfalls, an external trading program is precisely meant to exploit these competitive differences—it rewards those companies that have made reformulations and/or redesigns by allowing them to sell their IDPC and IDPC surrogate pollutant trading units to those sources that were too stubborn and/or recalcitrant to make reductions on their own. To properly add insult to injury, those same companies that must buy TUs will have those purchases taxed as well.

Responsible, early adopting companies can obtain a deferral from the trading program for several years (depending on how much their quantity of IDPC and IDPC surrogate pollution was reduced beforehand), while irresponsible companies that made no reductions at all must participate immediately.

So, for the time being, besides developing simpler calculations for IDPC and IDPC surrogate pollutant MoDs and determining the appropriate characteristic standards, a great deal of technological R&D must be conducted to find substitutes and chemical reformulations to facilitate further solid waste reductions and material circularity.

f. *The Inherent Advantage of R&D*. From a business standpoint, sources that invested in strong R&D capacity will adapt better relative to those that did not. This approach relies on the unforeseen ingenuity arising from R&D versus the "known knowns" of relying on old, conventional production methods and equipment. Since innovation may not occur quickly, the larger sources that are capable of redesigning their products may have to rely on the acquisition of ETUs in the early stages of the trading program.

g. *ETU Acquisitions*. To provide an ETU market for manufacturers, competition between recyclers and recycle bin providers should ensue. Obviously, an Information Clearinghouse should also be developed for buyers and sellers of materials to facilitate and hopefully optimize the circulation of the industrial metabolic process. It's too early to tell at this point what will develop, but the market dynamics that will eventually dovetail with the integrated regulatory strategy should achieve a high level of sophistication once the CE matures.

   As TUs become more and more expensive over time, market phenomena that are idealized today should become realistic in the CE tomorrow. To encourage consumers/users to return materials to a material processor, most every reusable IDPC surrogate-embedded product will ideally have a deposit that is proportional to the expense of acquiring substitutes for virgin resources and the cost of acquiring and holding ETUs.[18] Recall that manufacturers want to avoid paying heavily for the use of virgin resources (due to taxation), so it behooves them to offer an economic incentive to consumers/users to facilitate the return of product materials back to them or to a material reprocessor as a source of ETUs. In fact, one could even envision the development of offtake agreements so that manufacturers can be guaranteed that reused materials will be in plentiful supply in the future. This would obviously grease the skids toward CE facilitation.

h. *Eco-Labeling and Prioritizing*. Virgin resources should only be used when no recycled or remediated materials are available, so where they are to be utilized, regulators must also combine eco-labeling with prioritizing the acquisition of virgin resources from those providers that are the most climate-friendly, cause the least environmental harm, meet specified harm-minimizing performance standards, and operate with the lowest rate of carbon/entropic increase footprint relative to those that are not. Resource providers with good stewardship based on their eco-labels should be the first in line for contracts for purchasing their products.

i. *The Fundamental Flaw of the Premises of Current Circular Economy Theory*. Most studies of the CE to date succumb to a fundamental flaw, namely the premise that a circular economy will be created "from the ground up" within a linear economy. Thus, if we apply CaC to manufacturers while demanding that we all just act circular and give it all we've got, then we can collectively get the global wheels of a CE turning. Exercising our collective will power is a poor substitute for actually overcoming via regulation our choice to pollute. Unfortunately, this thinking is delusional and exhibits the "primitive infancy" that pervades the CE concept within the literature and of policymakers worldwide. To reiterate yet again: solving global problems requires global solutions. This situation is similar to how American regulators decades ago, in response to poor regional air quality, attempted to simply rely on imposing emission standards on individual items of equipment (e.g., boilers having to meet a limitation of 0.1 lb/mmBtu, etc.) at individual sources as the means to reduce the regional generation of air pollution. Attacking the problem from the ground up unit by unit is futile when the total national emissions from the ubiquity of sources are increasing and the air quality in several regions is deteriorating. Likewise, imposing standards on products is not sufficient by itself; the total regional quantity of the pollutant must be regulated as well as incentivizing circulation.

Bocken et al.'s assertion of the evolution of a CE is typical, but her conclusion is prescient:

> Are there circular strategies that do not generate net environmental benefits now, but might do so after they evolve? How do we identify which ostensibly counterproductive strategies fall into this category? Put another way, an analytical foundation is needed to manage a transition to a CE.[19]

As has been developed here in Part 3, the generalized strategy provides just that analytical foundation.

Allwood was also prescient with his following observation:

> Our vision of a future sustainable material economy is therefore not prescribed by the ambition to create a circular economy, but aims to minimize its total environmental impact.[20]

As the most practical tool for doing so, and as developed through the generalized strategy, a CE will get off the ground only by the appropriate application of milestone-based constraints. Prior to the generalized strategy, policymakers worldwide did not know just what leverage they had to regulate the generation of solid waste pollution because the concepts of total VMoD associated with IDPC and IDPC surrogate pollution was not even in existence. Now they are.

At the risk of overstating the obvious at this point, it is inconceivable just how a CE could ever arise without limits on waste pollution and resources. Without setting national limits, the notion of a robust CE taking off is a pipedream, particularly where unsustainable growth is unchecked. Without imposing declining limits and rationing resources, facilitating a CE would be fruitless since there is no incentive for anyone to participate or for companies to motivate themselves to innovate and redesign their processes and manufacture their products for later reuse, remanufacturing, etc. Starting from the ground up relies on conscientious individual behavior and while there are a good number of these individuals and companies, there are still plenty who are not conscientious. Needless to say, without a clearly laid-out strategy, there will be far more discussion of a CE than progress toward developing one.

j. *Avoiding Design Flaws*. It goes without saying that the adoption of the results-oriented aspects of the generalized strategy must avoid the applicable design flaws cited earlier in Chapter 2. As such, one should require and expect that state and federal laws and regulations would be updated to twenty-first-century Next Gen principles and standards. Obsolete methods of regulating will have to be purged and replaced.

k. *Reliance on Academia/Research Centers*. Just like how academia and environmental research centers should assist air pollution regulators (see Chapter 4), the same research must be conducted by sustainability research centers to investigate how to address all the issues associated with IDPC and IDPC surrogates (e.g., determining MoDs, each TtC_{pos}, setting characteristic standards). Clearly, chemical engineers and small business assistance will be in great demand in order to transfer lessons learned (e.g., lesser polluting technologies) from early adopting larger sources to smaller sources.

l. *Adaptation on the Go.* Optimal regulation of IDPCs and IDPC surrogates will be determined over time as a developing chain of regulatory adaptations, progressing with each new link or step, major or minor, at a time, as appropriate. This adaptive, path-dependent method, plus some further market incentives to establish an optimal market between inputs and outputs, should eventually facilitate a fully or nearly fully functioning CE.

m. *Impractical to Plan Everything to the Last Detail.* In a similar fashion, there will clearly be a long transition period to a *Cradle to Cradle* economy, so planning every last detail or nuance is impractical at this time. But while there isn't a detailed roadmap, at least there would be a logical procedure in place that points in the right direction.

n. *Product Takebacks and Complexity.* The market should sort out, or be designed to sort out, the catalyzation of product takebacks. The generalized strategy would facilitate market forces that should promote buybacks/takebacks, rather than the regulations themselves commanding that outcome. In other words, it is not 100% certain whether setting the regulatory trading scheme loose on reducing IDPC surrogate pollution, as well as the other aspects of the strategy, will facilitate ALL the proper market signals that will then support the transition to a CE or whether further regulation, at a later stage, will be required. But the strategy should make significant progress to that end.

On the other hand, if market signals promoted through the generalized strategy do not spur takebacks, the sources that do not redesign or innovate and choose instead to simply pay for the acquisition of TUs may eventually be required (via regulatory nudging) to take back their products for disassembly. For example, if over time these companies have to pay more for TUs and pass the cost on to consumers/users, then the consumer/user may either find other cheaper products elsewhere or repair/refurbish what they have. In this case, the obstinate company may suffer untoward market consequences.

Ideally, so that they take "ownership" of their manufacturing process, manufacturers of "megacomplex" products, such as airplanes and buildings, should in the early stages of the program have to oversee the complete disassembly of their product. To incentivize this, it may probably be best to allow airplane manufacturers to partially reconcile their allotments in part with ETUs via takebacks, depending on the quality of the returned product, perhaps based on the proportion of the amount of energy necessary to bring the product back to high quality. Likewise, building owners will be responsible for the removal and acquisition of building components, thereby encouraging them to construct such buildings as materially optimal as possible to minimize such hassles.[21]

The generalized strategy will more generally create the regulatory guardrails toward the development of Design for Disassembly (DfD). Regulations should be designed to promote DfD and takebacks, and imbue less product complexity, toxicity, etc.[22] Thus, much like designing products at the front end to reduce pollution, regulations must be Next Gen designed for compliance and litigation avoidance at the front end to facilitate those reductions in regional pollution; in particular, they must be well-designed to facilitate and achieve Design for Environment (DfE) goals. Production shouldn't just be designed to dovetail with DfE—the regulations themselves have to be designed that way too.[23]

An airplane is the sum of its many complicated assembled parts, and like many complex products such as a computer or infrastructure (e.g., a building), it is likely that its composite regulated complexity MoD will automatically be defaulted to the maximum value (i.e., no need to run a calculation), thereby necessitating the acquisition of ETUs to reconcile allotments. In addition, unlike a glass bottle, it is far more difficult to discern how to address the recovery of materials from a computer or an airplane and other complex products. It can be anticipated that the less complex products will be subject to simple recovery first. Then, as trading units become more and more expensive, a recycling infrastructure will mature to incorporate the recovery of these more complex products. To minimize costs, it will behoove the computer owner to take it back in for refurbishment or disassembly or for the building owner/operator to first disassemble its components to maximize salvage value. It is very possible that even in the most robust CE, extremely complex products will remain complex and never be disassembled. Nevertheless, an end-of-life vehicle "deproduction" processing facility is being constructed in Poole, located in southern Britain.[24] Airplane disassembly is already common in the Arizona desert.[25]

Among the many goals to achieve is avoiding the production of what the authors of *Cradle to Cradle* call "monstrous hybrids," which are complex, multi-material products that are both very difficult to disassemble and which persist indefinitely in the environment when discarded. In conjunction with the external trading program itself, where regulations and their administration are properly designed both for compliance and litigation avoidance (think Giles's Next Gen),[26] monstrous hybrids would eventually be redesigned for disassembly, any metals recovered for future reuse (as creditable ETUs), and organics replaced by materials that biodegrade via composting, where possible. Regulation must facilitate these measures and reach the goals espoused in *Cradle to Cradle*. Simple-minded, garden-variety recycling is not the goal here. As such, the market will then, as possible outcomes, "encourage by economic coercion" (or "coerce by economic encouragement") the mandatory takeback of waste products or recovered materials (as creditable ETUs), particularly for monstrous hybrids.

o. *Expect Growing Pains*. While adopting the generalized strategy will certainly bring environmental benefits, arriving there cannot be expected to be seamless. As noted earlier, reducing emissions of air pollutants via CaT is the low-hanging fruit of CaT application because controls and fuel switching are feasible (albeit expensive). On the other hand, limiting/rationing fossil fuels in conjunction with a tax on the choice to use virgin fossil-based carbon (to facilitate the use of other energy sources) may be painful both economically and societally. This is because there are no add-on controls for CO_2 emissions at the back end (although fuel substitution can and probably should include remediated waste plastics that are not compostable, and where Carbon Capture and Storage [CCS] is feasible).[27,28] Something similar worked by limiting CFCs except that they were phased out over time and substitutes were available which fit within the CE paradigm. Reducing multi-media environmental pollution via CaT may be equally painful because reformulations and redesigns are unknown beforehand. Thankfully, there is the alternative of obtaining ETUs from the reuse of waste product materials.

p. *Exemptions Not Allowed*. Companies should never be allowed any exemptions that would compromise the achievement of a CE (and thereby sustainability with Nature). For example, companies must not be allowed to get a free pass from participating within a CE by criminalizing the "right-to-repair," which is not compatible with a CE. This also includes those materials reprocessing facilities that would supply manufacturers with resources-as-credited-ETUs. Not allowing exemptions is due to the fact that, if companies claim that they are unable to redesign their products, they are fully capable instead of acquiring ETUs and manufacturing products that must still meet technologically achievable characteristic standards.[29] In this way, manufacturers and consumers alike will be forced to adapt to the new paradigm. Consumers will see that the degradation of the environment is directly tied to their consumptive habits and vice versa. If consumers love their plastics and chemicals, then they must live with the consequences. We will undoubtedly have to adapt to the possible inverse relationship between product quality and generated waste, and vice versa (e.g., the use of inconvenient biodegradable/compostable paper straws as a replacement for plastic straws if a next generation of straws is not available first). This should lead to better decisions by citizens, as opposed to decisions based solely on the traditional needs or choices that consumers commonly make.

Since fossil fuels are to be slowly phased out, there should be no need to shield low-income users from the higher costs associated with the asymmetry of energy access. However, depending on the situation on the ground, policymakers may still need to carve out subsidies for such energy consumers.

In any event, only those citizens who do not cause ecosystem stress are totally exempt from sacrifice within a CE, meaning nobody is.

q. *Regulatory Infrastructure Required*. From a public sector perspective, one thing also appears certain—transitioning to a CE necessitates a regulatory/administrative infrastructure to ensure that it functions properly. A CE is characterized by the need for significant regulatory tracking.
r. *Unilateral Adoption*. While products with embedded detrimental characteristics may not remain in the states in which they were manufactured, states can still adopt this program unilaterally, that is, without having to wait for federal approval.
s. *Success Depends on Design*. It can never be repeated often enough: the success of the CaT program to address multi-media environmental pollution comes down to how well the program is designed, and the

clarity with which lawyers, economists, and regulators structure the program to achieve its end goals. Initial successes, however, will depend on policymakers and regulators not letting industry corrupt the program and/or letting a risk-averse legal and regulatory culture add layers of nonessential bureaucratic and procedural pollution.

To those who might complain that economic costs and social inequities were ignored, let it be said that this was at this point both intentional and justified. It is important to recognize that the generalized strategy is first and foremost a pollution control strategy; the laser-focus is on reducing the generation of environmental pollution rather than getting caught up at this very early stage in peripheral concerns. Had these concerns, commonly found in academic debates—such as cost inequities among sources, which market instruments work best and which don't, and social equity issues—all been treated on par with reducing pollution, the generalized strategy would have suffered from "paralysis by analysis" and would never get off the ground. We have already seen that FDA-like oversight applied to air pollution regulation rendered the pollution-reduction program suboptimal. Similar paralysis would likely immobilize initial adoption of a CE as well. Nevertheless, researchers are certainly welcome to incorporate the above concerns within a strategy to facilitate a CE.

3. Changing Our Current Mindsets

Transitioning from a linear to a circular economy will require a change in our current mindsets:

a. *Requires Readjustment in Thinking*. Unfortunately, there is still too much of a twentieth-century regulatory mindset being applied to twenty-first-century environmental problems. More insidious is the problem of so many people acknowledging the reality of environmental unsustainability as a global problem that happens "out there" somewhere, yet many people reflexively push back aggressively when their own unsustainable behavior is challenged in their own lives (e.g., justifying the loss of biodiversity to construct a subdivision). We must radically reprogram our culture of instant gratification that renders us ill-prepared to address our environmental problems. With the generalized strategy, not only will everyone's consumptive behavior be made more accountable, there will also no longer have to be a false, binary choice between consumption and environmental degradation (e.g., either buy plastic straws or not). As we have seen with the strategy, we will have other options.

The problem of regulating the generation of environmental pollution is made more complicated by requiring a societal team effort. The proper use of CaT to address all relevant pollutants blends the roles of engineering and technology, economics, and environmental law by nudging and modifying requisite behaviors between producers and consumers/users. In fact, adopting a CE requires a course correction, if not redesign, sometimes even fundamentally, of the above disciplines and probably other subdisciplines (e.g., finance, accounting, trade). Scientists and engineers can develop the MoDs associated with the IDPC and IDPC surrogate characteristics, design technological reformulations, and determine what the best available technologies are for various source categories. Likewise, environmental scholars and legal practitioners can begin drafting the "Next Gen"-based rules to facilitate CE-inspired environmental sustainability. As composite materials are light yet strong, so must be rules and regulations. Economists can sort out the interplay of the various aspects of the economy within the CE (e.g., how to restructure the economy for development where resources and fuels are limited, the demand for labor). The above disciplines should also focus on what the regulatory infrastructure should be for addressing the generation of water and on-site waste pollution. Finally, as consumers and citizens, we must all modify our thinking and behavior by adapting to the new paradigm of internalized externalities.

So what is the optimal mix of law, technology, and economics to achieve a CE? While Webster and Stahel have envisioned the CE's future, in the short term, we have a better idea of how IDPC and IDPC surrogate pollution and material resources fit into the environmental protection mosaic. The blend of technology, law, and economics will all evolve, adapt, and self-correct as the CE transitions. While the particulars may call for further study, implementing a generalized strategy will certainly make significant headway. Further detailed study will probably not determine this route *a priori* since the path is dependent on the collective yet unpredictable confluence of process technology, environmental law, economics, and consumer behavior.

b. *Requires Readjustment in Behavior.* The bottom-up, market boycotting of fossil-based carbon by collective citizenship so as to send a message to our leaders and policymakers will not be effective. Collective citizenship has to demand action from the top. When enough pressure is exerted, the generalized strategy (or a near-variant) will be here. In the meantime consensus on how to proceed will have to be reached.

It's the difference between the will to simply lose weight or completely having to change one's lifestyle. Up until recently, the question has incorrectly been framed around how to reduce ubiquitous pollution, but the bigger, more critical question is—can we break our habitual addiction to consume products? An even more salient question is—do we really need to *consume* the product or only obtain the *benefit* of that product?

Climate change is treated as the overriding problem, but it is only a symptom of the much larger problem of consumption. Hence we can't act as if solving the climate crisis alone will bring us back to some nostalgic state of an old normal. Likewise, simply boiling down a CE to recycling alone indicates the primitive infancy of the concept. Let's not forget the role of redesign within the manufacturing process. Rather than relying on the downstream, simple-minded capability to recycle, process redesign forces fundamental upstream changes in thinking. Ideally, the overarching goal is to follow a regulatory hierarchical scheme whereby we must first prevent pollution where possible; then, where that is not possible, innovate redesign upstream in the production process, thereby regulating activities before they later become harmful legacy effects and, where possible, fully incentivizing the use of waste, including legacy pollution, for recovery.

With optimal design of the program and relentless citizen pressure to push the program envelope, the ability to regulate multi-media pollution should spur action, given that there is now a more coherent path forward.[30] As we're already aware, current attempts at achieving environmental sustainability have been relatively static in the absence of direct regulation. However, applying the generalized strategy will facilitate progress toward environmental sustainability in a much more dynamic manner.

c. *Accepting the Rationale for Rationing.* There are many points to be made regarding rationing and the folly of failing to do so:

i. Without question, we must flatten and lower the CO_2 concentration curve to attain climate stability. We noted earlier that limiting and ratcheting down the use of fossil fuel-based carbon directly *guarantees* reductions in CO_2 emissions, while a CE does so only indirectly via economy-wide efficiency improvement. Policymakers could try to rely on a CE to reduce fossil fuel use without rationing them, but that is unlikely to be sufficient. Clearly, adopting a CE is a prerequisite to reducing CO_2 emissions, but to make sufficient reductions, we will have to significantly clamp down on the use of fossil fuels to go beyond flattening the CO_2 concentration curve on to lowering it. Further process innovation is necessary to reduce emissions as well. If rationing fossil fuels turns out even on a small scale to be problematic, that will serve as the flashing yellow light on the dashboard of what could happen at a much larger scale when fossil fuel stocks truly are nearing depletion.

ii. As noted several times, yet bears repeating, rationing fossil fuels is the more genuine tack than taxing carbon use, which is likely to only mildly address the problem. This is because simply taxing (or pricing) carbon at the front end relies on an ideologically driven premise that fossil fuel use is too sacrosanct to strictly limit head-on. This strategy, however, is disingenuous as it only "discourages" the use of fossil fuels in an era of sure calamity if it fails. The use of global CaT limits CO_2 emissions to a specific targeted quantity, which is just one claim that proponents of CO_2 emissions taxation cannot make.

iii. Perhaps the greatest delusion we collectively suffer from is the idea that we don't need to limit inputs if we all just commit to only limiting outputs. But resources and fuels are not inexhaustible. Economists and the rest of us will simply have to adapt to a world with limited resources, with scarcity imposed, as a leading premise at the front end.

As a sign of our societal cognitive dissonance, we psychically comfort ourselves by asserting that we not only want to limit our pollution, fuel and resource inputs but also reverse biodiversity loss; yet, nothing will create societal connip-tion fits more than proposing to *actually set limits*.

- iv. Why are virgin resources critical to consume now when circulating used resources to preserve the environment is more critical?[31] In a finite resource world, profligate use of Nature's credit card cannot ever be a higher virtue than frugality.
- v. We phased out the supply of CFCs. How well did that work out after we committed ourselves to it?
- vi. Realizing that legacy CO_2 and waste plastics *already* in the ambient environment will be difficult enough to remediate as it is, it is only appropriate to significantly phase down fossil-based carbon's current use within the economy as a package deal.[32]
- vii. Looked at from another angle, just how serious does climate change and the horrific problem posed by plastics pollution have to become before we focus on *all* fossil-based carbon inputs if limiting or rationing *all* fossil-based carbon as an *input* is not the wiser approach overall? It must be noted that for those who scoff at the notion of rationing fossil fuels or holding them in reserve, the question that must be asked is how the flattening and lowering of the CO_2 concentration curve is currently progressing.
- viii. Finally, why wait until fossil-based carbon is depleted before we act?

d. *Nevertheless, Fossil Fuels Will Not Vanish Overnight.* In any event, the fossil fuel problem is clearly a very tough nut to crack. While waste generated from production (including IDPC surrogate pollution from the products themselves) and the use of fossil fuels will reduce within a CE, solar and wind are not going to immediately replace them. So, while we must remediate the existing CO_2 in the atmosphere, we must accept that we might have to continue combusting a finite supply of fossil-based carbon into the near future. That said, the mitigation strategy would most importantly require global CO_2 emissions to be reduced to attain climate stability even where it allows fossil fuels to be combusted.

Nevertheless, while there are pro-free market adherents who consider major reductions in fossil fuel use as unrealistic, the need to flatten and lower the CO_2 concentration curve is more critical, since the environment faces force-multiplying stressors from man-made disasters, including the following all-hands-on-deck crises: global climate change, extreme groundwater depletion, forest fires, floating ocean plastics (including microplastics that can be found in all areas of the world), extinctions, low sperm counts (due to certain endocrine-disrupting chemicals), and so on. And as we know, such stressors are accelerating rather than diminishing in harm intensity. These are not textbook abstractions seen only as words on the pages of economics textbooks but rather the global realities we must all face.

e. *Developing a Culture of Disassembly and Reprocessing.* Not only must many products be designed for disassembly, but our infrastructure must also be designed to accommodate it. We must all become accustomed to a culture where this CE infrastructure is fully functional. Discussion of disassembly and reprocessing is usually conducted only in the abstract and typically as it relates to products. As we'll see later, the discussion of the reality of having to apply disassembly at the mega-scale, such as to buildings,[33] has been discussed only relatively recently.

f. *Overcoming The "Right to Pollute" Fallacy.* We must acknowledge again that trading does not give companies the "right to pollute." Instead of framing the debate as the right to pollute,[34] it may be preferable in some cases to frame it as industry not knowing a better means to redesign their processes to be lower polluting within the linear economy model. It is the generalized strategy that will catalyze the means for sources to push the innovation envelope to continually strive to reduce pollution and transition to that CE.

   When one realizes that the economic system is embedded within, nurtured by, but should not be dominant over, the environment, then trading simply sorts out how participants will reconcile the reduction of harm to that "outer" environment.

g. *Responsibility Required by All.* Without appropriate regulation, we have until now only relied on the goodwill of a smattering of socially responsible companies and consumers to reduce pollution. This is clearly not enough for the various sustainability measures to achieve a value of zero for the Additional Earths at Global Development (AEGD), that is, the number of Earths required to maintain a level of development if every global citizen adopted it. As the authors of *Cradle to Cradle* noted, simply being less unsustainable is not sufficient. Not only does our current AEGD represent a global measure of the nonattainment of sustainability with Nature, but it is also a measure of the harm intensity of our impact to the planet. The higher the AEGD, the more harmful and unsustainable the activities are that facilitate that harm and unsustainability. For example, use of a 500 MW coal-fired boiler would contribute to a higher AEGD than a 500 MW wind turbine farm where their materials are recoverable within a circular economy.

At a fundamental level, the generalized strategy will require citizens to adopt more of a scarcity mindset, rather than the abundance mindset that led to the environmental problems we face today. In the short term, many companies, suppliers, and consumers will feel put out. Consumers will expect progress in abating carbon dioxide emissions and other pollution, but how many consumers will actually change their lifestyles rooted in the antiquated mindset of abundance? On its own, the generalized strategy will cover a great deal of ground, but it will achieve only so much if consumers are not incentivized to be responsible citizens.[35]

h. *No Other Alternatives*. It is inevitable that an argument leveled against the generalized strategy will be that it is too radical, so will never happen. While the strategy to address IDPC surrogate pollution may be scoffed at by those who are consumption-focused, no matter how long we dither, this strategy, or some related variant of it, will eventually have to be implemented. We have to push back against relentless environmental degradation, particularly fossil-based carbon, regardless of vested interests and recalcitrant companies and consumers.

   The question isn't whether the strategy is practicable—it's whether there's a better alternative. If producers and consumers aren't willing to adopt any strategy, is leaving a degraded planet to their children's children an acceptable good option? Will leaving the planet be the best alternative? And speaking of leaving the planet, there has actually been discussion about mining planets for resources, as if the problems we face are simply resource problems. The reader is urged to think about the mining of planets for a minute—where exactly are the products manufactured from those resources imported from other planets and consumed here on Earth going to be disposed of? As products of a linear economy, they would doubtless end up in landfills or our waterways.

i. *Feelings of Uncertainty and Grief*. Finally, it is expected that the immediate response to adopting the generalized strategy will either be a feeling of daunting unease or dismissal, which simply demonstrates just how far we have to go. There is an inverse relationship between the extremely complex nature of products that lead to their unrecoverability and the conveniences we take for granted from these products (e.g., cell phones).

To achieve not just a circular economy but also sustainability with Nature requires less complex products that may not be convenient for the consumer/user. Making this transition may not be easy for some to adapt to. Some individuals will undergo the five stages of grief—denial, anger, bargaining, depression, and acceptance—when confronting the loss of the unsustainable quality of life we've come to take for granted. The CE and other outcomes from the generalized strategy will likely be achieved only when a psychological tipping point is reached first.

4. Key Industrial Ecology Considerations

a. *Waste Acquisition Priorities*. Implementing the strategy raises a conservation of mass question—there is only a finite amount of consumed material that can be circulated throughout the economy. Recovering product waste as a new, circulated raw material is not discriminatory. The material can be used from immediately discarded waste or mined from landfills and waterways. To continually circulate all consumed materials would require that the economy be larger, which is itself problematic (think increased energy use). Unfortunately, there will be an amount of waste materials that will remain buried or otherwise out of circulation. The highest priorities for reusing materials are likely to be domestic waste and imported waste that both meet characteristic standards, and then virgin materials. A recoverability hierarchy would likely dictate that the materials that are acquired first will be those that are both easier to recover and inexpensive to transport.

   Infinite circularity will still have significant implications. Ideally this strategy will theoretically allow for infinite re-consumption of reused materials, preferably recovered from remote corners of the polluted Earth, which will still require unacceptable amounts of energy in proportion to the amount of materials used and reused.

b. *Product Niches*. Are washable cloth napkins better for the environment than paper napkins? Are concrete railroad ties better than treated wooden ones? The pollution and resource-constrained market that internalizes negative externalities will clarify the answers to these and similar questions. Just as in Nature, the market will allow the survival of some product niches as others become extinct.

Since they cannot be continuously recycled, what will be the substitute for wood and other critical natural materials? There may not be substitutes, but replenishment may be the next best option. That option will likely be found within the mitigation and ecosystem restoration strategies developed in Chapter 9 and, with any luck, within a more general regulatory agroforestry strategy, whereby sustainability with Nature will determine the proper balance of wood regrowth, use, and replenishment within the economy.

c. *The June 2017 Issue of the Journal of Industrial Ecology*. While environmental law and air pollution regulation already have history between them, one major consequence of the generalized strategy is that it bridges the gap between environmental regulation and industrial ecology, which have been two disciplines that have heretofore existed in virtual isolation from one another.

The June 2017 issue of the *Journal of Industrial Ecology* (JIE) was specially devoted to address the CE. Some of its papers are very relevant to the results that arise from the generalized strategy. A few articles that addressed key issues can find their answers within the strategy. We saw earlier that the generalized strategy nicely addresses the concepts raised by den Hollander and colleagues regarding Design for Recycling and Designing for Product Integrity. Other critical issues from that June 2017 journal will be addressed below:

- *Validity Issues*. In their summary of the June 2017 issue of the JIE, Mulrow and Santos[36] cite what they term the "validity issues" that the journal articles address with regard to what conditions a CE must meet to be deemed valid. Such issues are how to address the rebound effect, ensuring the decoupling of economic quality from virgin resource use, and the requirement for not just the closing of loops, but the slowing, narrowing and shrinking of loops as well.
  - *The Rebound Effect (at the Macro-Scale) Should Now No Longer Be an Issue of Concern*. In their article, Zink and Geyer[37] assert that a flaw of a CE is that there will be a rebound effect whereby materials, characterized by the situation where improvement in material efficiency will be more than offset by an increased use of materials. Much like an increase in an automobile's fuel efficiency "encourages" motorists to drive them more, thereby offsetting improved efficiency,

the rebound effect for materials is likewise due to the desire to consume more products and the lower cost of doing so.

- Zink and Geyer's conclusion is based on the flaw within the premises of the current circular economy paradigm noted above, whereby their conception of a CE is based on a model of open-ended circularity, that is, one *without having to set limits*. Naturally, in a world without the setting of limits, an improvement in efficiency here will only lead to increased consumption elsewhere; within the generalized strategy, where a CE is based on setting macro-scale limits on resources and pollution, the macro-scale rebound effect is eliminated, or at worst minimized. There is no incentive to game the system, voluntarily or otherwise, due to those rigidly set "boundary conditions." However, there may still be localized rebound effects at the micro-scale within a fully functioning and sustaining CE, but not at the macroscale since in such a CE, IDPC and IDPC surrogate pollution will have reached attainment by virtue of having been limited. And regional and localized rebound effects could likewise be eliminated or reduced where respective regional and localized limits are also set.
- Where limits are set and declined to meet attainment of IDPC and IDPC surrogate pollution, the rebound effect goes by another name—a good one this time—flexibility. Analogously, when spending within a constrained budget, buying something cheaper, which allows for the purchase of something else useful within the budget, demonstrates flexibility, which is perfectly acceptable within a closed, properly constrained CE.[38]
- *Decoupling*. Decoupling describes the disconnection between economic growth and the use of virgin resources. If economic growth can proceed without the use of virgin resources, that is ideal decoupling. By specifically limiting pollution and rationing virgin resource materials, the generalized strategy is inherently designed to ensure that economic growth and material use are decoupled within an *ideal* CE. Clearly, there will be some allowance for the use of virgin resources in a real-world CE due to slippage effects, due to, for example, degraded waste materials that are physically unfit for infinite reuse.
- *The Closing, Slowing, and Narrowing of Loops*. Bocken et al. define these concepts in their paper in the JIE special issue:

> The basic premises of the CE appear to be closing and slowing loops. *Closing* loops refer to (postconsumer waste) recycling, *slowing* is about the retention of the product value through maintenance, repair and refurbishment, and remanufacturing, and *narrowing* loops is about efficiency improvements, a notion that already is commonplace in the linear economy.[39]

Mulrow and Santos assert that the shrinking of loops should also be added to the loops list.[40]

The generalized strategy will facilitate the closing, slowing, narrowing and shrinking of these loops through the use of declining limits and the efficient use of market instrument tools. Loop closure occurs via the tightening of virgin material inputs and incentivizing material recovery via ETUs for each subject IDPC and IDPC surrogate pollutant. The slowing of loops occurs most particularly from the tightening of limits on subject IDPC and IDPC surrogate pollutants, thereby incentivizing both the use of existing products and the "R's." The narrowing of loops occurs as a direct outcome of applying the generalized strategy itself, which facilitates the transition to a circular economy. The shrinking of loops occurs when material use within the economy reduces over time. As we have seen, by its very design, the generalized strategy will facilitate this by regulating the generation of waste volume at the back end by applying front-end constraints while at the same time incentivizing material reuse (via ETU creation), thereby facilitating the shrinkage of the volume loop.

- Other Relevant Issues
  - In her article, Goldberg asserts that toxics (e.g., lead and mercury) cannot be neglected in any attempt to achieve a CE.[41] As noted previously, based strictly on the assessment of the adapted strategy to regulate the generation of solid waste, a CE does not ensure the elimination of toxics to the environment, any more than the adapted strategy was meant to address climate change (an air pollution problem rather than a solid waste problem). Nevertheless, the reduction of toxics is accomplished by using (1) declining caps, (2) the imposition by the multi-media-focused generalized strategy to target toxics by setting stringent characteristic standards, (3) the reduction in harm intensity of toxic content (where toxic content

over an achievable characteristic standard is noncompliant and untradeable), (4) trading where appropriate and feasible to facilitate reductions, and (5) incentivized circulation, for example, by the incorporation of ETUs and the imposition of high deposits on toxics-containing materials to encourage circularity.

- *Industrial Symbiosis*. Under the generalized strategy, industrial symbiosis, whereby waste from Company A is used directly as a raw material for Company B, is envisioned by the generalized strategy to be the exception rather than the rule. This is because the acquisition of ETUs will more likely require an infrastructure that allows sources in need of recovered resource materials to obtain them from intermediary reprocessing facilities to provide those necessary resources.
- *Quantity and Quality of Waste Resources*. Cullen[42] reminds us of the limitations and realities of a CE. He makes the point that a CE without limiting growth will not be sufficient:

> We should therefore be wary of proposals to "go circular," which put the economic growth cart before the environmental impact reduction *horse*.[43]

As the generalized strategy has demonstrated, it was designed precisely to put the environmental impact horse before the economic growth cart by first focusing on and limiting environmental impacts. But it is also important to understand the limitations of the CE. A CE can potentially be overtaken by external forces beyond its control, and one such external force is economic growth fueled directly by population growth, which places serious demands on extracted virgin materials. However, where resource use is tightened so strictly to the point where the per capita standard of living is intentionally reduced as the population increases, then that will promote circularity and likely deter population growth. More will be said about this in Chapter 9 with regard to limiting both the global use of fossil fuels and limiting per capita CO_2 emissions so as to mitigate climate change and slow, and hopefully deter, population growth.

Lest we think that achieving a CE solves all problems, Cullen also notes the following reality regarding conserving the quantity of materials circulating within the economy:

> In a perfect CE, the quantity of materials in "closed loops" must be conserved. What goes into the economy must equal what comes out, and there must be no material losses from the closed loop; thus, the quantity of material is always conserved. In practice, materials are leaked from recycling loops or delayed from exiting the economy; this "loss" requires the addition of new material to maintain circularity. Two specific issues make the prevention of material loss challenging.[44]

Those two problems related to conserving the *quantity* of materials are (1) the "sequestration" of existing material stocks (e.g., within the economy's infrastructure), an issue also raised by Fellner et al. in the same June 2017 issue of the JIE,[45] and (2) dissipative material losses, which are basically the loss of recoverable material due to its dispersion throughout the environment.

Cullen likewise notes the difficulty of conserving the *quality* of materials within the economy. "Many common recycling processes degrade and destroy material structure, requiring energy-intensive melting and recasting processes to restore material quality."[46] The issue of material degradation was noted earlier in the discussion of the Material Degradation Hierarchy.

These two problems, that is, quantity and quality of materials, are not the failings of a CE as developed in this book; rather, they are attributed respectively to unchecked economic growth and the limitations imposed by physics.

d. *Allwood.* Julian Allwood's chapter in the *Handbook of Recycling* provides a humbling but clearly necessary reality check to any romanticized notions of delivering a CE. There is much in his chapter worth pondering for all interested readers, such as:

> Approximately half of the world's emissions of CO_2 from industry arise from producing materials for construction, and as we've seen already, most of the resulting built space is unoccupied for most of the time. But on top of this, buildings designed to last for 100 years or more are knocked down and replaced on average every 40 years in the United Kingdom or nearer to every 20 years in China. Not only is the "embodied energy" of construction underused through excess capacity, it is also underexploited and could deliver its intended service over a much longer period.[47,48]

It would be too simplistic to say that developers should just "plan ahead." Allwood's reality check clearly indicates that building developers, owners, and operators must be aware that it behooves them to construct infrastructure for durability, including designing buildings so as to avoid premature deconstruction and demolition where major components are difficult to replace before the building itself (e.g., the Heating, Ventilating, and Air Conditioning system). Clearly, they will likewise be responsible for minimizing the increase in total complexity of their buildings for later material recovery and reuse.

Allwood also raises the issue regarding the efficient generation of scrap:

> The car industry is extremely good at it and confidently scraps about 30 percent of what it purchases, but the real experts at scrap generation are the aerospace industry. Typically the manufacture of an aeroplane involves the conversion of 90–95 percent of all purchased materials into scrap, with the aeroplane left over as a minor by-product. That's efficiency![49]

The production of scrap is an unfortunate artifact of the need to manufacture products economically. Again, Allwood:

> . . . potentially, we could reduce demand for material production and therefore its harmful impacts by one-third by efficient design. Surely that's rational? It's clearly an important strategy, but there is no commercial incentive for this approach at present, because the savings would require a much more tailored approach to producing each component.[50]

The capping of on-site generated waste, including scrappage, trading their TUs, and setting sufficiently tight standards for the generation of waste and scrap will ensure that its generation is reduced over time while production becomes more efficient. In conjunction with this requirement, the scrap sent to a material reprocessor could, via contract or an offtake agreement, be later acquired as material by its generator to provide later credit as ETUs.

As we have seen, stringently tightening the total volumetric amount of regional IDPC surrogates should incentivize upstream redesign of infrastructure by developers, but unlike "simple" products like table lamps and mattresses, buildings and other pieces of infrastructure will clearly present a challenge to the transition to a CE.

While there are other citations that could be taken from Allwood, his chapter provides great food for thought for all readers. He drives home the point that we will need an overhaul in the design of products so as to facilitate material reuse both symbiotically and continually, that is, the same trajectory the generalized strategy promotes as well. He likewise notes the earlier conclusion that a future CE will entail a foundational culture of Design for Recycling and Design for Disassembly.

e. *Energy Used in Proportion to Circularity.* Resources and fossil fuels cannot be treated the same in terms of regulation because resources can theoretically be reused infinitely[51] whereas fossil fuels can only get combusted once. In turn, in the absence of renewable energy, the use of fossil fuels is proportional to the energy needed to make the CE function.

   Suppose attainment is reached for every airshed, watershed, hazardous nonproduct on-site generated waste region, IDPC/IDPC surrogate-"shed," etc.—what amount of energy is required and how efficient does the circular economic system have to be to achieve this ideal situation? Putting resource needs aside, the use of energy within a CE all depends on the size of the economy required to be energized. A large-scale CE obviously needs more energy/fossil fuels than one at a smaller scale. The ultimate question then becomes—what percent of that necessary energy will eventually be from non-fossil fuels?

f. *An Existing Example of Circularity.* It is very likely that fossil fuel extraction and use will significantly decrease as circularity over the long term reduces the need for energy (assuming a stabilized population). The case of recycling aluminum cans is exemplary in this regard: due to the amount of energy already expended and embedded within, it is much less energy-intensive to reprocess aluminum cans in a secondary smelter than to process raw bauxite for full production in a primary smelter. More generally, but not necessarily true in all cases, industry will use less energy to process reused materials than virgin materials.

g. *Theft of Materials.* What if the recovery of materials for profit leads to increased theft or destruction of private property? Hopefully, that will not be a problem, but to prevent this moral hazard, regulators can institute a deterrent for theft of materials by providing value only for materials obtained in bulk quantities.

5. Key Ecological Considerations

a. *Elevating the Role of Ecological Economics.* The fact that ecological and environmental improvement can be facilitated by rigorously regulating the use of quantifiable measures of harm to facilitate sustainability with Nature means that the discipline of ecological economics will now no longer be dismissed as a subordinated subdiscipline of economics, but rather should be elevated closer to the realm of a natural science, justifiably higher in stature than that of a social science. In conjunction with the strategies further developed in Chapter 9 (which includes a strategy for ecosystem restoration), the significance of this assertion cannot be overstated. Mamlyuk would likely agree.[52]

b. *"You Don't Foul Your Own Nest" (YDFYON) School of Economics.* Since the optimal regulation of the generation of environmental pollution and limiting resources is interrelated in a CE, it would be extremely difficult for anyone with a diehard linear economy mindset to argue that they are sincerely pro-environment. *Cradle to Cradle*'s "Waste = Food" circular economy paradigm coincides with Nature, and should be the outcome of a civilized society because it follows the real-world dictate that you don't foul your own nest. It only stands to reason that evolution and natural selection favor those species that follow this basic principle.

Unfortunately, free-market economics, because it advocates minimal regulation, is fully normalized to a linear economy worldview. In a world where the generation of pollution and the use of resources are optimally minimized as a real-world boundary condition to facilitate sustainability with Nature, *it is the unsustainable linear economy that is the special, worst-case of the more general sustainable circular economy without boundary conditions.* Consequent to minimizing the generation of solid waste pollution is the circular economy. One can think of it using this analogy—when looked at from every angle except one, when a circle is viewed from overhead, it is a circle and when looked at from an angle, it has the shape of an ellipse. It is only upon looking at it at ground level that the circle or ellipse looks like a line segment. Figuratively speaking, those with a linear economy mindset have been narrowly looking at the geometric shape at ground level.

Within the School of Economics where fouling one's own nest is still accepted as a foundational postulate, adherents would likely assert that the CE is the general "correction" of the linear economy. Truthfully, however, the CE corrects the flaws overlooked by mainstream economists who have erroneously adopted an infinite abundance, resource spendthrift mindset. We must now wean ourselves away from linear mindsets when the CE is the natural paradigm that engenders finiteness and frugality (by not taking more than is necessary). The CE is not subordinate to the linear economy—just the opposite, since a CE conforms much more to Nature (think *Cradle to Cradle*'s Waste = Food) than does a linear economy. We got to where we are in part because our culture has been indoctrinated with an "out of sight out of mind" mindset, a symptom of "Nature Deficit Disorder" that afflicts many.

Due to the necessary imposition of resource constraints to minimize pollution, it is self-evident that mainstream economics must necessarily be subordinated to ecological economics.

c. *A Major Step Toward Sustainability with Nature.* A well-functioning CE, which ideally internalizes all materials used within the economy, would not by itself adversely affect biodiversity other than by unchecked population growth and a concomitant expansion that destroys ecosystems—issues which must concern us as the CE matures. Let's not forget that limiting pollution and adopting a CE are prerequisite steps but not the final steps toward achieving environmental sustainability with Nature. For example, although the use of timber as a resource in manufacturing will be reduced in a CE, trees will still be felled to clear land and build homes. More will be said about an approach to address this situation in Part 4.

d. *An Algorithm to Mimic Waste = Food.* Conducted properly, the tools of law, economics, and engineering will be utilized to mimic natural processes according to *Cradle to Cradle* principles. One way to think of the mimicking of nature is in the development of robotics. Robots are not made of the same materials as humans, but in combination with algorithms can be designed to mimic certain actions of humans. Likewise, while the generalized strategy is not the same as mimicking Nature, its use as an "algorithm" can attempt to mimic the "Waste = Food" aspect of natural processes.

6. Key Economic Considerations

a. *Ecology Takes Precedence over Economics.* In a CE then, the ultimate goal will be to maximize ecology-preserving development, that is, optimizing development with the minimal use of fossil fuels and virgin resources such that the rate of entropy increase is minimized. This is predicated first and foremost on economic principles appropriately being subordinated to ecological principles since the economy is embedded within the larger ecosystem.

b. *Is Economic Growth Allowed under the Generalized Strategy?* This is a critical question that depends on the definition of economic growth. If it is the type of economic growth that is dependent on and proportional to population growth and the excessive use of virgin resources, much like mimicking a pyramid scheme, then the answer is clearly no. On the other hand, if economic growth is simply the improvement of quality of life in a truly sustainable, steady-state "equilibrium" between a restored Nature itself and the economy embedded within it, then the economy can certainly grow within a CE.[53] As Mulrow and Santos say, "the goal is to grow well-being without growing impact."[54]
c. *Use of Cost-Benefit Analysis Is Suspect.* Wherever harm to Nature or to human health is of concern (e.g., loss of biodiversity to allow for construction of a mining project near freshwater supplies), economists argue that regulating harms to Nature and harms from pollution should consider all costs within a cost-benefit analysis. However, those cost calculations fail to properly factor in the full incalculable costs of all externalities within a noncircular economy. Most acutely, however, the calculations are fundamentally suspect because they are based on a standard of reference from within a nonattainment of sustainability with Nature paradigm. This latter point is of the utmost significance to grasp—the First Fundamental Law of Environmental Regulation does not allow the preservation of the economic exploitation of Nature to take precedence over the preservation and restoration of Nature when sustainability has not yet been attained.[55] When a cost-benefit analysis is predicated on the perpetuation of unsustainability, the analysis is inherently flawed.[56,57]

Unsustainable behavior is justified in the short term "when you're high on your own supply," but when the crash inevitably comes, it's too late to justify it. At the very heart of this problem is that Nature is being subordinated to the economy, a case of the tail wagging the dog. Where environmental sustainability with Nature is attained, the economic system is embedded within and dependent upon Nature which is the supplier of resources to that economic system (not vice versa). Where Nature is the parent and the economy the child, it bears reiterating the metaphor that when oxygen masks drop, Nature must be taken care of first. Thus, when economists determine how much of Nature is expendable within their cost-benefit analyses in our current state of nonattainment of sustainability with Nature, it is absurd to its very core, yet this mindset is pervasive. Thus, anything short of accepting Nature's parental role only justifies and enables the environmentally unsustainable predatory facilitation of resource scarcity and climate instability.

One can think of the nonattainment of sustainability with Nature as being the result of the force multiplication of many environmental problems because collectively they "exponentiate" adverse impacts. As we know, climate change wreaks havoc on more than just the climate alone. So if the climate change genie can be put back into the bottle, then there is a chance that its multiplier effects will diminish also, putting other genies back in their bottles. Thus, crunching cost-benefit analyses can be justified only when the level playing field of attainment is reached for environmental and ecological sustainability.

The bottom line is that, if economic costs continue to be treated as the absolute highest priority in our attempt to reach environmental sustainability, we can kiss attaining a CE and sustainability with Nature goodbye.

d. *The Rule of Law and a Market Economy as Prerequisites.* One key question that arises from the discussion is this—does the minimization of the generation of environmental pollution that leads eventually to a CE dictate that a rules-based and structured market economy be prerequisites? In particular, can a command economy achieve these same results without respect for the rule of law and an underlying market economy? Unless it can be adequately demonstrated otherwise, it would appear the answer to both questions is no. Clearly, further research is necessary.
e. *Externalities Will Only Be Reduced.* In addition to facilitating the transition to a CE, one could conceivably argue that making progress toward full cost pricing by internalizing pollution externalities is a given. It is important not to overlook the fact that negative environmental externalities quietly cost far more now than we think since we pay for them outside the economic mainstream (e.g., via harmful health impacts). Economists have only softly spoken of this issue when addressing environmental concerns. The absence of economists in a fuller discussion of the CE and elsewhere is addressed later in the Conclusion.

f. *Imports as Transboundary Solid Waste Pollution.* While lesser developed countries may use taxation as a last resort rather than CaT, the international trade of consumer products from all countries must ensure that such products meet minimal characteristic standards. This will hopefully facilitate the transition to the trade of recoverable materials since CE-minded nations should only want to trade with other kindred CE-minded nations to avoid becoming repositories of nonrecoverable transboundary solid waste pollution. Accepting products manufactured from only circular economies is not just good for the environment; it is also an economic incentive for noncircular economies to become circular. However, where noncompliant products are imported, taxation and/or a reduced product purchase price should be imposed on the importing country's goods in direct proportion to the material recoverability of those imports.

7. Policy Considerations

Policy Uptake Varies by Country. Unfortunately, the US will probably only adopt the generalized strategy only after the European Union is well on its way. If it's any consolation, the generalized strategy is compatible with the proposed Green New Deal.[58]

Past Use of Suboptimal Market Instruments

In much the same way that we saw in Part 2 how taxing emissions was shown to suboptimally facilitate reductions, taxing IDPC and IDPC surrogates is likewise fraught. While European regulators focus on dissuasive taxation to facilitate improvement of the environment,[59] such taxation—to this point at least—has been unsuccessful in catalyzing even minimal progress toward facilitating a CE. Even if regulators were to tax IDPC surrogates, it is very unlikely that it will decrease their generation anywhere as well as using the incentives of the generalized strategy. Why? Because regulators do not possess a priori knowledge with regard to how IDPC surrogate pollution should be taxed in proportion to the environmental damage those products cause, such as how to tax the production of a battery relative to carpet. In one of the rare exceptions where the economics community in the United States has engaged substantively in a discussion of a CE is the paper by Manderson and Considine, where they assert that industrial ecology can aid in the application of Pigouvian taxes.[60]

Like many economists, Manderson and Considine are fixated on taxation as the only means to address impacts that are inherently detrimental to the environment. Likewise, Peter Sørensen develops a model where environmental waste is taxed, demonstrating "that if it is possible to implement an appropriate mix of Pigouvian taxes and subsidies, there is no need for other policy instruments to promote the circular economy."[61] Besides the use of taxation, the insufficiency of pricing to achieve a CE is the concern of Hans Stegeman, a European economist.[62]

Could simply taxing IDPCs and IDPC surrogates per product and feedstock facilitate the transition to a CE? It's certainly possible in theory that in response to taxation, some manufacturers would be motivated to redesign products to become more "circulation-ready" as these manufacturers innovate their production processes. Taxing the use of virgin resources would likely incentivize some kind of recycling and may even receive a rebate upon doing so. Nevertheless, this would be a very inefficient means to steer the CE ship since it is long on stick and short on carrot, not to mention that necessary environmental outcomes are far from guaranteed.

Both the pro-CaC/anti-trading adherents and the pro-taxation advocates maintain positions that are too far removed from the optimal regulatory center of gravity for addressing the generation of IDPC/IDPC surrogate pollution. By far the best regulatory friend to the environment, setting and declining limits, must be met over established timeframes (the Yin of CaC-based requirements); without declining limits, what is the equivalent environmental friend to taxation? Reaching actual pollution-reduction goals via taxation is faith-based, so while there are certainly likely to be some reductions, there's no guarantee that total quantities will be reduced *sufficiently within an established timeframe.* It seems clear that corrective CaT must be applied regionally, while taxation should have a more surgically and locally targeted niche role as a deterrent, applied to recalcitrant sources for their poor choices. Rather than actually solving the underlying pollution problem, taxation may simply be a source's cost of doing business, with those costs passed on to consumers anyway, without environmental benefit. Thus, the fundamental flaw of taxing pollution is that it has no "Yin."

There are further reasons why taxation is flawed:

- While the whole point of taxation would be to stem the growth of total accumulated VMoDs associated with IDPCs and IDPC surrogates and other types of pollution from *existing* manufacturers, how is the increasing accumulation of pollution from the construction and operation of *new* sources addressed? Again, this is the Yin problem of taxation.

- Also, when would regulators know when to halt or reduce the taxation for certain companies relative to others?
- The philosophical basis for taxation is not conducive to regulating the generation of environmental pollution, which is treated by economists as if it were a behavioral problem, a red flag indicating that the indiscriminate use of taxation across the board is flawed. Simply taxing fossil-based carbon might conceivably be acceptable if the result of its use created a nuisance or discretionary harm *to the user*, but where the combustion of fossil fuels and ubiquitous microplastics creates a global crisis *harming the entire planet*, dissuasive taxation's value is far from optimal.
- Under the generalized strategy, companies that have sufficient R&D capacity would have the ability to redesign their products to reduce IDPCs and IDPC surrogates, while those without this capacity could simply purchase TUs to resolve their shortfall. In contrast, within a taxation scheme, it would be "every source for themself."
- Taxation of pollution sees money go to government coffers, with no guarantee of targeted environmental improvement.
- While taxation of complex products would be used in the country of manufacture, how would imported products from foreign countries be addressed?

If taking half-hearted half-measures that result in environmental calamities takes precedence over full measures that require *guaranteed reductions* to avoid them, then is the abhorrence of regulation really so much more loathsome and unpalatable than those force-multiplied calamities? This is not a rhetorical question; economists' silence would indicate concurrence with the underlying assertion.

On the other hand, the generalized strategy will facilitate the internalization of externalities by the chain reaction of market responses and modified consumer/user behavior that will spur the necessary innovative technological redesigns and material reuse. Moreover, the strategy does this without micromanaging responses and behaviors, providing flexibility for sources to achieve compliance.

Where Do Fossil-Based Feedstocks and Fuels Fit In?

As noted in Part 2 and since, it cannot be stressed enough that rationing/phasing out carbon-based fuels *at the front end* is far more of a guarantee that CO_2 emissions will decrease to a set level, particularly if there is CO_2 emissions trading at the back end as well. This simply reflects the Fundamentals of Pollution Regulation 101: set operating limits on total inputs in order to ensure that output limits are met. To truly address climate change, regulation via rationing and choking off of both fossil fuels and the production of fossil-based petrochemicals can be leveraged to collaterally regulate the generation of both air and plastics pollution. Cutting back on fossil-based carbon provides many environmental co-benefits, e.g., a decrease in microplastics generation and decreased air pollution overall.

To underscore the significance of rationing fossil-based carbon feedstocks, as materials are reused and virgin raw material resource needs are suppressed, the need for fuels, particularly fossil fuels, will likewise decrease on an economy-wide basis. From Stahel:

> The macro-economic impact of such a mature circular industrial economy has been researched pertaining to the Czech Republic, Finland, France, the Netherlands, Poland, Spain and Sweden by Anders Wijkman and Kristian Skånberg. In their 2016 study, they have calculated that a nation-wide shift to a circular industrial economy would reduce greenhouse gas (GHG) emissions by 66 per cent and increase the number of jobs at national level by more than 4 per cent.[63] This reduction of 66 per cent is way above any figures discussed in the political agenda of slowing global warming, such as the COP21 conference in Paris.[64]

Thus, in a CE, fossil fuels won't technically be "replaced"; instead, all things being equal, circularity over the long term will reduce energy demand, and thus fossil fuels. So while fossil fuel use will gradually decrease as the CE transitions and other caps are met, the reduction in the use of fossil-based carbon feedstocks will likewise mitigate ubiquitous plastic pollution. It is the rationing of fossil fuels and trading via the mitigation strategy developed in Chapter 9 that will directly ensure the greatest reductions of CO_2 emissions, while rationing virgin resources, including fossil-based carbon feedstocks, will be what will play a key part in facilitating the transition to a CE.

Chapters 6, 7, and 8 have broken new ground on unifying the regulation of environmental pollution. Chapter 9 further develops a means to apply the concepts learned in Part 3 to, among other outcomes, mitigate global climate change and restore ecosystems. Chapter 10 develops a basic legal framework to facilitate various aspects of sustainability with Nature with profound implications to environmental law, including the necessity of a Global Constitution to preserve and protect Nature.

Notes

1 The qualification of "technology-induced" is included here to preclude the contribution due to natural pollution, such as that generated by volcanoes. Emissions from such sources are measurable but not tradable.

2 While the European Union tends to address the circular economy, the United States focuses on the study of industrial metabolism and ESG metrics.

3 Clearly, we must not succumb to the mindset that the only thing worse than climate change is high gas prices.

4 We saw in Part 2 that rationing is just a special case of CaT, where trading is performed in real time with real currency by all consumers, thereby allowing the environment to get that guarantee up front.

5 If climate change institutes are unconditionally committed to their collective missions to address climate change, these same institutes should actually become "Fossil-Based Carbon Reduction Institutes."

6 Bruce Pasfield and Elise Paeffgen, "How to Enforce a Carbon Tax: Lessons from the Montreal Protocol and the U.S. Experience with the Ozone Depleting Chemicals Tax," *Vermont Journal of Environmental Law* 14, no. 3 (2013).

7 Jonathan Wood, "Building a Groundwater Market from the Bottom Up." Property and Environmental Research Center (PERC), August 16, 2018. A CaT program is being used for redistributing the use of groundwater in California. https://www.perc.org/2018/08/16/building-a-groundwater-market-from-the-bottom-up/.

8 James Garthe, "Burning Plastic for Energy: An Update." Presentation. The reader is encouraged to view slides 33 through 47 at https://www.alfredstate.edu/files/downloads/PVGA11AVI.pdf. The reader is urged to be sufficiently humbled by the sober reality of the waste plastics problem and the sea life that are affected by them. The reader should then ask nonrhetorically whether environmental realities must continue to be subordinated to political and economic dogma.

9 Clearly, that which is causing a life-threatening crisis should be banned outright (e.g., DDT or thalidomide), so it stands to reason that fossil-based carbon should at least be phased out or phased down.

10 Webster, *The Circular Economy A Wealth of Flows*, 92.

11 Unfortunately, when these terms are used together in the literature or elsewhere, rarely is the destruction or loss of biodiversity mentioned.

12 Fridolin Krausmann, Dominik Wiedenhofer, Christian Lauk, et al., "Global Socioeconomic Material Stocks Rise 23-fold over the 20th Century and Require Half of AAnnual Resource Use," *Proceedings of the National Academy of Sciences* 114, no. 8 (February 2017). https://www.pnas.org/doi/10.1073/pnas.1613773114.

13 See Johann Fellner, Jakob Lederer, Christoph Scharff, et al., "Present Potentials and Limitations of a Circular Economy with Respect to Primary Raw Material Demand," *Journal of Industrial Ecology* 21, no. 3 (June 2017).

14 In a similar fashion to approximating emissions by stack tests, determining the complexity and difficulty-of-disassembly (DoD) MoDs may not be exact, but approximations should be good enough for a trading program to function.

15 While this type of product appears to counter the presumption that the impact on the environment is minimized over its operational lifetime, the acquisition of ETUs to manufacture it still ensures that materials will continue to be resupplied, thereby minimizing the generation of solid waste.

16 Two means to reduce steps in the disassembly process are utilizing modular construction methods and keeping the number of connectors in a product to a minimum. Laura Talens Peiró, Fulvio Ardente, and Fabrice Mathieux, "Design for Disassembly Criteria in EU Product Policies for a More Circular Economy," *Journal of Industrial Ecology* 21, no. 3 (June 2017): 733.

17 Marcel C. den Hollander, Conny A. Bakker, and Erik Jan Hultink, "Product Design in a Circular Economy: Development of a Typology of Key Concepts and Terms," *Journal of Industrial Ecology* 21, no. 3 (June 2017).

18 Because no technological solution yet exists for littering, an economic incentive must step in at the point of post-consumption.

19 Nancy M. P. Bocken, Elsa A. Olivetti, Jonathan M. Cullen, et al., "Taking the Circularity to the Next Level: A Special Issue on the Circular Economy," *Journal of Industrial Ecology* 21, no. 3 (June 2017): 480.

20 Julian M. Allwood, "Material Efficiency-Squaring the Circular Economy: Recycling within a Hierarchy of Material Management Strategies," in *Handbook of Recycling: State-of-the-art for Practitioners, Analysts, and Scientists. 2nd Edition,* ed. Christina Meskers, Ernst Worrell, and Markus A. Reuter (Elsevier, 2024), 48.

21 An excellent discussion on the application of CE principles to buildings is David A. Ness and Ke Xing, "Toward a Resource-Efficient Built Environment: A Literature Review and Conceptual Model," *Journal of Industrial Ecology* 21, no. 3 (June 2017).

22 To conceptualize regulation-driven design, imagine disembarking from a plane at any international airport terminal. Once off the plane, the corridors and walking escalators automatically channel the passenger to the immigration counters, then to baggage claim, then to customs, and then out the door to a transport area. Airports have been designed that way.

23 As noted earlier, designing rules, industrial processes, etc., for upfront prevention of harms is a running theme throughout this book.

24 https://www.economist.com/science-and-technology/2023/07/19/scrapyards-adopt-new-high-tech-ways-to-dismantle-cars. July 19, 2023.

25 "Ships of Theseus," *The Economist*, December 21, 2024–Janūary 3, 2025, 30–4.
26 This should also include use of a compliance dashboard administered by regulators that provides full transparency of a source's current and past compliance history to the general public. For example, much like posting grades online for a restaurant's food quality, grades can likewise be posted for a source's environmental track record as well.
27 Carbon sequestration of some sort has to play a role in abating climate change, but it should only be utilized to sequester/remediate existing carbon, not future as-yet unearthed carbon. Reforestating and afforestating will not be enough to remove the enormous amounts of CO_2 emissions already generated by fossil-based carbon either. It thus makes no sense to ask that expensive technology be developed to address the sequestration of *future* carbon emissions when doing so for *existing* CO_2 will be difficult enough as it is.
28 Ideal adherence to circular economic principles will encourage, say, the mining of landfills ("urban mining") for recovering waste plastics for continual reuse as fuel as its final use. Right now, both energy recovery of waste plastics with CCS and product deposits are currently cost-prohibitive, so how do we design our way there? Truly nonrecyclable, nonchlorinated plastic waste can be used as a supplemental fuel in cement kilns. This is not a comforting answer, but if carbon-based fuels are to be combusted, virgin fossil fuels must be displaced, possibly by the plastic that is currently choking landfills and waterways, while sequestering the resulting CO_2.
29 While the production of processed foods would be subject to the generalized strategy for the use of nonagricultural inputs, agriculturally grown food products themselves are not conducive to the strategy at the back end because agricultural goods are a product provided by Nature, so the assumption that the product is "technologically induced" does not apply here. However, while agriculturally grown food products cannot be redesigned, the use of their inputs and the fate of their outputs can still be appropriately regulated. While a strategy to regulate the inputs to agriculturally grown food products is not developed fully in Chapter 9, the strategy proposed there will nevertheless provide a basic initial framework for how future regulators could proceed.
30 Unfortunately, it is to be expected that many citizen-consumers/users who support environmental progress will not sacrifice the loss of some of their conveniences.
31 It behooves nations to adopt a CE for two worthy reasons: first, due to national security concerns, to avoid unnecessary dependency on unstable countries for their rare metals; and second, because receiving a mining permit is a multi-year process.
32 While the focus in this book is mostly on petroleum-based carbon that either gets refined into fuels, plastics, or chemicals, it should be noted that fossil-based carbon also includes natural gas that is a feedstock in the production of nitrogen fertilizer.

33 Lauren Sparandara, Mike Werner, Amanda Kaminsky, et al., "Accelerating the Circular Economy Through Commercial Deconstruction and Reuse." Ellen MacArthur Foundation, 2019. This is a rare paper that discusses the topic well. https://emf.thirdlight.com/link/v6gyhiosoqs7-s9k2oe/@/preview/1?o.

34 Advocates of the so-called right to pollute tend to shame the sinner (i.e., the polluter) rather than the sin (i.e., the act of polluting).

35 This is why economic incentives such as deposits (e.g., bottle returns) should be baked into the CE.

36 John Mulrow and Victoria Santos, "Moving the Circular Economy Beyond Alchemy," *Discard Studies*, November 13, 2017. https://discardstudies.com/2017/11/13/moving-the-circular-economy-beyond-alchemy.

37 Trevor Zink and Roland Geyer, "Circular Economy Rebound," *Journal of Industrial Ecology* 21, no. 3 (June 2017).

38 One can still make unwise purchases while spending within one's budget, so budget consciousness does not necessarily imply cost-consciousness. Likewise, while setting and reducing limits at the global scale will reduce the large-scale generation of environmental pollution, thereby inhibiting the rebound effect, "localized" rebound effects may still occur.

39 Nancy M. P. Bocken, Paavo Ritala, and Pontus Huotari, "The Circular Economy: Exploring the Introduction of the Concept Among S&P 500 Firms," *Journal of Industrial Ecology* 21, no. 3 (June 2017): 487. Here Bocken cites: N. M. P. Bocken, I. de Pauw, C. Bakker, et al., "Product Design and Business Model Strategies for a Circular Economy," *Journal of Industrial and Production Engineering* 33, no. 5 (2016).

40 Mulrow and Santos, "Moving the Circular Economy Beyond Alchemy."

41 Terri Goldberg, "What About Circularity of Hazardous Materials?" *Journal of Industrial Ecology* 21, no. 3 (June 2017).

42 Jonathan M. Cullen, "Circular Economy: Theoretical Benchmark or Perpetual Motion Machine," *Journal of Industrial Ecology* 21, no. 3 (June 2017).

43 Cullen, "Circular Economy," 484.

44 Cullen, "Circular Economy," 484.

45 Fellner, Lederer, Scharff, et al., "Present Potentials and Limitations of a Circular Economy."

46 Cullen, "Circular Economy," 485.

47 Allwood, "Material Efficiency," 53–4.

48 Ness and Xing, "Toward a Resource-Efficient Built Environment."

49 Allwood, "Material Efficiency," 57–8.

50 Allwood, "Material Efficiency," 56.

51 Not all resources are created equal. Aluminum can be recovered far more readily than wood, the fibers of which degrade after reuse.

52 Mamlyuk, "Analyzing the Polluter Pays Principle Through Law and Economics," 76–80.

53 There will be more to say in Chapter 9 about what equilibrium entails.

54 Mulrow and Santos, "Moving the Circular Economy Beyond Alchemy."

55 A rhetorical question for the reader: just how often does cost-benefit analysis indicate that Nature wins out over economic growth?

56 The moral hazard of robbing Peter to pay Paul will always get Paul's endorsement, so if Paul's unsustainable act is scrutinized under a cost-benefit analysis, it should come as no surprise if Paul's team of economic advisors asserts that his robbery/acquisition is unequivocally beneficial.

57 Of course, if cost-benefit analysis is used to determine the best choice among sustainable solutions, then its use is likely justified.

58 Joseph Sarkis, "As I See It: Inclusion of 'Circular Economy' in Green New Deal Could Support Economic Transformation," *Telegram*, May 4, 2019. https://www.telegram.com/news/20190504/as-i-see-it-inclusion-of-circular-economy-in-green-new-deal-could-support-economic-transformation.

59 Withana, Brink, Illes, et al., *Environmental Tax Reform in Europe: Opportunities for the Future* (cited in Chapter 4). As it relates to the circular economy: Peter Birch Sørensen, "The Basic Environmental Economics of the Circular Economy." EPRU Working Paper Series, No. 2017-04, University of Copenhagen, Economic Policy Research Unit (EPRU). https://papers.ssrn.com/sol3/papers.cfm?abstract_id=3064684.

60 Edward J. Manderson and Timothy J. Considine, "An Economic Perspective on Industrial Ecology," *Review of Environmental Economics and Policy* 12, no. 2 (Summer 2018): 306.

61 Sørensen, "The Basic Environmental Economics of the Circular Economy," 3.

62 Hans Stegeman, "True Pricing Is Not Enough to Make an Economy Circular," Trios Investment Management, January 15, 2019. https://www.triodos-im.com/articles/2019/true-pricing-is-not-enough-to-achieve-sustainability. The takeaway of Manderson and Considine, Sørensen, Stegeman, and others is the flawed notion that pollution that causes environmental havoc, for example, climate change, is simply a behavioral modification problem that can simply be addressed by the proper use of dissuasion via taxation and pricing. Rather, pollution is an environmental problem that is best addressed by regulation.

63 Here, Stahel cites Anders Wijkman and Kristian Skånberg, *The Circular Economy and Benefits for Society: Jobs and Climate Clear Winners in an Economy Based on Renewable Energy and ResourceEfficiency* (The Club of Rome, 2015). https://www.clubofrome.org/wp-content/uploads/2020/03/The-Circular-Economy-and-Benefits-for-Society.pdf.

64 Stahel, *The Circular Economy: A User's Guide*, 19.

Part 4

Pursuing a Grand Unified Theory of Environmental Law and Regulation

9

Expanding the Use of the Strategies

Thinking Beyond the Circular Economy and the Generalized Strategy

This book has so far developed an optimal, generalized strategy to minimize via regulation the *generation* of multi-media environmental pollution (principally by industrial sources), thereby facilitating the transition to a circular economy (CE) and plugging some of the gaping holes in the linear economy dyke by correcting market failures that negatively impact our ecology, environment, and health.

Let's now look beyond where the generalized strategy will take us and see whether we can push the envelope even further. First, if the industrial sources that significantly contribute to a number of ecological calamities can be regulated through the generalized strategy, are there other problem areas where we could extrapolate the use of the strategy's methods to address these other calamities? Along these lines, mitigating climate change is amenable to the application of the comprehensive/generalized strategy, and if the same strategy can be used to reduce harms to Nature, it only seems logical that aspects of the strategy can be used in reverse to *restore* Nature, the general framework of which will later be developed. Reaching a "sustainable equilibrium" between a restored Nature and humanity is next examined. Lastly, generalizing regulation further to measures of complexity and the rate of entropy increase is explored.

Can the Regulatory Strategies Be Applied Elsewhere?

Regulating pollutant harms to Nature is one thing, but what if we try to see whether there are higher order problems that can be addressed?

If one conducts an internet search for "Top Ten Environmental Problems," a number of sites on the web provide a list of their various selected top ten (or more) problems. Here is a compilation of several of those common problems:

Acid Rain	Ocean Acidification
Air Pollution	Overfishing
Climate Change	Overpopulation
Deforestation	Ozone Layer Depletion
Endangered Species	Soil Degradation
Loss of Biodiversity	Solid Waste Pollution
Melting Polar Ice Caps	Urban Sprawl
Natural Resource Depletion	Water Pollution

To expand on the discussion, the following will also be added: excess use of inputs (e.g., water, energy, fertilizers, and pesticides) within agriculture; and pre- and post-consumption food waste.

So what current regulatory strategies, if any, can be applied to these problems? We first note that strategies for regulating acid rain and industrial air pollution have already been discussed in Parts 1 and 2 and the generation of on-site and solid waste pollution can be addressed by the generalized strategy developed in Part 3; ozone depletion has been addressed by the Montreal Protocol; but what about the other problems above? Despite their daunting nature, can we somehow categorize them, identify commonalities, and see if certain regulatory strategies can render them more manageable and amenable to regulation in some fashion?

The above global problems have been practically categorized and rearranged below, as seems appropriate. The point is to see how their regulation could be better approached if their underlying causes are classified.

A. *Technology-Induced Combustion/Rate of Entropy Increase*[1]

Climate Change (includes melting polar ice caps and ocean acidification)

B. *Technology-Induced Production/Rate of Entropy, Disorder and Complexity Increase*

Industrially Generated Air, Water, and Solid Waste Pollution (including combined animal feeding operations)
Ozone Layer Depletion

C. *Large Scale Human-Driven Ecological and Environmental Stressors*

Pre- and Post-Consumption Food Waste
Area Source Generated Air Pollution (e.g., stubble burning) and Water Pollution (e.g., farm runoff)
Overpopulation

D. *Large Scale Industrial and Human-Driven Resource and Biodiversity Loss*

i. Production-Based Activities:
Agriculture/Food-Based Resource Depletion (includes Soil Degradation, Excess Use of Water, Energy, Fertilizers, and Pesticides; Meat Production and Overfishing)
Natural Resource Depletion (includes Deforestation)

ii. Destruction-Based Consequences:
Urban Sprawl (i.e., "expansion pollution," including Land Clearance)
Runoff from Land Clearance
Loss of Biodiversity, Endangered Species

First, the category "Technology-Induced Combustion/Rate of Entropy Increase" refers to post-production outcomes where the use of technology increases the rate of entropy increase (i.e., accelerates entropy), such as through the combustion of fossil fuels. We have already seen that setting total limits on air pollution, using the comprehensive and generalized strategy's resource/fuel limiting/rationing scheme, and in some cases a back-end air pollutant trading program can address the decrease in technology-induced pollution from combustion. In particular, to specifically mitigate climate change, a rigorous method will be developed in the next section that combines the comprehensive strategy with a reuse equivalent of the circular economy whereby credit for reforestating and restoring ecosystems is counted toward the reduction in CO_2 emissions.

Second, the category "Technology-Induced Production/Rate of Entropy, Disorder and Complexity Increase" refers to those post-production environmental harms where technology induces a large rate in the increase of entropy, disorder, and complexity that are very difficult to "uncomplicate." This includes, but is not limited to, the creation of complex products/solid waste that are inherently difficult to recover. We have seen that setting total limits on the generation of multi-media waste pollution, using the generalized strategy's resource/fuel limiting/rationing scheme, a back-end pollutant trading program, and the mandatory imposition and periodic decline of performance or characteristic standards can address the decrease of this type of technology-inducing pollution. As noted earlier, ozone layer depletion under the Montreal Protocol was addressed by the timed phaseout of ozone-depleting substances with taxation imposed by Congress.

The third category, "Large Scale Human-Driven Ecological and Environmental Stressors," comprises those hazards that pose unique difficulties to manage; caused, as they are, by large numbers of individuals acting on their own volition. Unfortunately, there are no simple answers here since regulation, up to this point, is not practically applicable to area source pollution generated by individuals; one would hope that global citizens' conscientious behavior would be positively modified due to the escalating need to remediate the planet. It would appear at first glance that overpopulation is the toughest nut to crack because it is an ecological force multiplier of so many other environmental calamities. However, the problem of overpopulation is likely that of a linear economy mindset because in a strictly fuel- and resource-capped world, overpopulation becomes a drag on the standard of living. Thus, overpopulation can and should be addressed indirectly by strategically limiting the resources that feed it, forcing society's desired standard of living to adjust population. Achieving ecosystem equilibrium with humanity, which includes reducing the "harm intensity" of resource use, will likely be a prerequisite to how regulating this specific category is best accomplished. In addition, creation of a circular economy "bubble" within the larger ecosystem that the CE is embedded within will not by itself directly address the big ticket items that also contribute significantly to climate change, such as lack of family planning and meat-based diets. Only when ecosystem equilibrium[2] is sought and attained with humans will it be likely that we can focus on stabilizing population growth through social measures. It should be noted that simply providing rights to Nature, while necessary, will not be sufficient to accomplish these goals.

Once the generalized, multi-media strategy and a CE are in place, it will become clearer as to what combination of strict Command-and-Control (CaC) measures, market instruments, and/or appropriately applied subsidies in the future will facilitate the critical changes that will be required to address this category's problems. Hopefully, with appropriate regulation, the adoption of a CE should motivate more individuals to act as responsible stewards of the environment so as to mitigate these problems.

The fourth and final category, "Large Scale Industrial and Human-Driven Resource and Biodiversity Loss," includes those (1) ubiquitous "production-based activities" that lead to depletion and (2) "destruction-based consequences" that result in the loss of ecosystems. Applying rationing or CaT on the use of resources in conjunction with the use of reverse CaT when applied to ecosystem restoration (to be described later) can both be employed to respectively reduce excessive resource depletion in the production of agricultural goods and recover ecosystems.

Besides deforestation, which can be better addressed by the climate change mitigation strategy and reverse cap-and-trade, production-based agricultural activities can best be addressed by using (1) rationed resource inputs, (2) the imposition of resource usage performance standards that cannot be exceeded, and (3) trading and declining total input usage to replenish resources (e.g., water) while using reverse cap-and-trade to restore water and other resources.

It should be noted that the following discussion will only scratch the surface of the framework for how to address resource use in agricultural production, so filling in the details will be left for further study.

While rationing can be thought of as the resource analogy of CaT for reducing pollution,[3] the resource inputs for the production of agricultural consumables, including feed later used as a resource input for livestock production, can likewise be required to meet basic nature-based resource usage standards at the input side. This would be accomplished by imposing usage standards for the use of water, fertilizer, and energy applied per acre. As usual, for the purposes of addressing "nonattainment of natural input usage," trading would let the market sort out which profit-seeking companies innovate sufficiently to reduce excess resource usage impacts and those that do not.

For example, if Nature requires X gallons of water to produce Y bushels of an agricultural commodity per acre while a company uses 1.5X for that same commodity, then trading of water usage TUs can be applied to all major agricultural consumers of that water supply to reach "Nature-based" attainment for food production. Assuming that the source meets a usage standard, it would have a baseline of (1.5X/X - 1) x Z, where Z here is the acreage of resource application at the source. The observant reader will note that the ratio of 1.5X/X is a measure of harm intensity, in this case, the harm associated with the overuse of water.

The primary goal of the corrective trading program is to replenish surface and groundwater that would promote the achievement of sustainability with Nature. The secondary goal is to preserve only enough of the resource such that usage is sustainable for short-term future use but without replenishment.

It is not sufficient to simply trade usage downward to achieve sustainability where the harm intensity due to overuse is too high. Thus, as one should expect, users of resources must also meet usage performance standards. Water usage standards might be based on the amount of acre-feet of water used per bushel of product; if that amount is exceeded, the amount of total water used over that usage standard throughout the entire acreage is noncompliant and, if regulatorily realistic, untradeable. Where permits cannot realistically be issued to individual farms to regulate measures of resource overuse, then promoting green agriculture can be incentivized instead. Prioritization may be another alternative, for example, farmers that are willing to maintain accurate records demonstrating that their footprint relative to that of a "natural baseline" for their product is minimal could, say, be taxed at a lower rate.[4]

Likewise, resource inputs for food production could include the imposition of eco-labeling (e.g., X gallons of water were used per 100 tons of almonds harvested). In any event, by reducing extraction at the national level, rationing and prioritizing would represent the route to the minimization of the rate of entropy increase.

In like fashion to the dictates of the generalized strategy, usage of resources exceeding a given usage performance standard footprint must be penalized and not be allowed to trade usage allotments above this standard. Unfortunately, reducing these activities at the international level by these methods would be difficult at the present time, but supply chain recordkeeping should be used to ensure that suppliers meet those measures. Sanctions should also be applied to those resource input suppliers that deliberately avoid these requirements.

Expansion pollution via population growth, land clearance, and urban sprawl is included in this category. Land clearance and urban sprawl can both be subject to trading programs (to encourage building up rather than out) since they can each be feasibly treated as quantifiable "nonattainment area growth pollutants" and thus limitable.[5] As a result, runoff would be reduced as urban sprawl is reduced, and likewise, farmland, ecosystems, and biodiversity preserved, and losses recovered.

Using the Comprehensive Strategy to Mitigate Global Climate Change

Under both the comprehensive and the broader generalized multi-media strategy (but oddly, not the current Clean Air Act), CO_2 is treated as a global climate-altering, that is, climate stability "nonattainment area" pollutant. The atmosphere must be remediated of excess CO_2, but to do so is still technologically and economically out of reach. Relying solely on reforestation and afforestation to remediate existing fossil fuel-generated legacy carbon in the atmosphere is futile since there's just too much of it there already.[6] If reforestation and afforestation are simply used to offset the CO_2 absorptive capacity from forests already felled,[7] what means will be used to remove the existing legacy CO_2 generated from the combustion of fossil fuels? Thawing of permafrost as the century proceeds will only generate even more methane, which has a higher global warming potential than CO_2. It obviously makes no sense to continuously generate unlimited amounts of fossil fuel-based CO_2 emissions when we don't even know how to remediate the legacy fossil fuel-based CO_2 that has already been generated.

The holistic generalized strategy only deals with optimally reducing the generation of multi-media pollution and facilitating the transition from the current linear economy into a dynamic CE instead. In contrast, addressing the removal of static, noneconomic legacy pollution would require the development of extremely expensive remediation technologies that may or may not yet even exist.[8,9]

At the annual Conference of Parties (COP) sessions that focus on addressing climate change, nations across the world have argued over how greenhouse gas emissions should be reduced, who should do what, and to what degree. A modified comprehensive strategy is timely to settle this matter. But won't mitigating global climate change be far more complicated?—politically, sure, but mechanically, not as much. As we've seen, the comprehensive strategy has generally been applicable to regional air pollution, particularly for nonattainment areas. Here, capping the global use of fossil fuel-based carbon is the first critical step in the process, assuming the appropriate treaties and ground rules are agreed to. Thereafter, declining the global limit using a cap-and-trade program between requisite participating countries, applying an underlying per capita performance standard, and providing rigorously recognized credit for CO_2 sequestration essentially rounds out the strategy.

In the development of the mitigation strategy that follows, for the sake of simplicity and because limiting fossil fuels is an assumed prerequisite, we will only focus on regulating CO_2. This is done in part because not all GHGs are carbon-based (e.g., sulfur hexafluoride) and tracking such noncarbon-based GHGs is likewise not as straightforward as tracking CO_2 by itself. In any case, it is the process that matters most here, so regulating GHGs can be adapted from the process developed here for regulating global emissions of CO_2.

Development of the CO_2 Mitigation Strategy

Starting from first principles, the CO_2 mitigation strategy will be developed through a rigorous step-by-step procedure, using the comprehensive strategy as a guide. If the strategy is simply provided without any motivation, that is, without showing the reasoning as it proceeds, the reader will miss out on significant conclusions and decisions along the way that arise out of it and will likely question the conclusion. Upon doing so, we will see that the final outcome of the step-by-step process will result in a trading program centered around those countries that exceed a globally agreed-upon "per capita performance standard," while those countries that emit below it will not be required to participate. In addition, whether countries participate or not in the trading program, some countries may be eligible to supply CO_2 ETUs within the scheme to take credit for having facilitated negative emissions.

To first motivate the ongoing discussion, and before the actual methodology of the modified comprehensive strategy is developed in more detail, as stated previously, countries must agree that fossil-based carbon must be limited. With that as a prerequisite, we must next conduct a preliminary investigation to determine the total metric tonnage of CO_2 emissions generated in the year that corresponded to the CO_2 concentration of 350 ppm (i.e., attainment of climate stability, which represents the "CO_2 performance standard" for the planet). This will be the reference global baseline we must achieve to "re-attain" climate stability. This value is 22.08 metric Gigatons (mGigatons).[10] Likewise, we conduct a little more research to uncover the per capita CO_2 emissions during that baseline attainment year when the CO_2 concentration was 350 ppm; that per person value was 4.3 metric tons (mtons).

In the spirit of the comprehensive strategy, we will next treat each individual country as an emission unit that emits CO_2. For practical purposes, the mitigation strategy will for our purposes only apply to non-minor emitters. Several countries that emit virtually negligible amounts of CO_2 emissions, where the total of their combined emissions is less than 10 percent of the total annual global emissions, will automatically be exempt from the program unless they later become non-minor emitters or they are noncompliant because they emit CO_2 above the per capita performance standard, or PCPS, a globally agreed-to value that applies equally to each "emission unit"/country. These countries are exempted because they are not the root cause of the climate change problem and, due to their status as small emitters, may not possess the necessary governance capacity anyway to even participate in the program.

Next, all countries must collectively determine via negotiation what the initial PCPS will be, in units of CO_2 generated per capita, that applies equally to all countries. In effect, by agreeing to this starter PCPS, countries are accepting a proxy for what is in effect the "compliant level of global development," an entitlement that applies to the average individual around the world regardless of their country's current level of development. In other words, this is done so that the program does not favor one country over another. The initial determination of this global PCPS will likely be the most controversial aspect of developing and applying the mitigation strategy since some developed countries will have per capita emissions higher than this value and will be "noncompliant," reflecting their past and ongoing damage to climate stability. Once it is agreed to, the comprehensive strategy is easily modified with an additional wrinkle related to taking credit for negative emissions, as will be discussed later.

We know that we have to get from our current global CO_2 concentration down to that of the year of climate stability at attainment (i.e., 350 ppm). So what are the ground rules for reaching attainment? At this stage, based on our approach, the simplistic answer lies in requiring countries to be ideally and instantaneously "compliant" to the PCPS while ongoing global attainment milestones are being achieved. (As we'll see later, this requirement will have to be altered but we don't know that just yet.) Since we are considering each country as a stand-alone emission unit, just as in the comprehensive strategy whereby an emission unit must meet a performance standard, each such country must meet the agreed-upon PCPS to be compliant; emissions over that standard are "internationally noncompliant." We are already well aware that regional nonattainment areas for a pollutant (e.g., SO_2) can be comprised entirely of emission units (e.g., boilers) that are each individually compliant to these standards but where the combined emissions generated from all such units in the area nevertheless render the air quality in that geographical area to be in nonattainment to that pollutant's national Ambient Air Quality Standard. The same can apply to CO_2 emissions at the national level where a country complying with the PCPS can still render global climate stability to be in nonattainment.[11] As it turns out, this scenario will not apply here; it will be the *PCPS-noncompliant* countries that play the major role here.

So knowing what attainment goal must again be reached in the future and the compliant level of development that countries are allowed to achieve, we next look at how to get there from where we are today.

So now it's the current year, which is several years beyond the baseline year; emissions are now much greater and the global population has likewise increased significantly. We will follow along with how this strategy plays out for four different participating (nonexempt) countries in the program. Figures 9.1a and 9.1b show the corresponding emissions and population profiles for today's current situation.[12]

Unsurprisingly, the current year's total global CO_2 emissions of 39.0 mGigatons are much higher than the 22.08 mGigatons of the baseline year. Note from the current year's emissions data that 7.8 billion is roughly the current year's global population, and the global CO_2 emissions per capita are roughly 39/7.8 or 5.0 mtons. Note that this rate represents the current year's per capita generation of emissions during nonattainment of climate stability; clearly, this includes a number of countries that exceed this PCPS. While we have to reduce the 39.0 mGigatons downward until attainment is reached, what trading scheme for CO_2 emissions will be required when some countries are internationally noncompliant to the global PCPS? We will sort this out momentarily.

Let's say that countries collectively agree to an allowable initial PCPS equal to the current per capita emissions of 5.0 mtons in the first year of the trading program. Using per country CO_2 emissions and population data, we can develop Figure 9.1c, where the hashed areas indicate those emissions that are in excess of

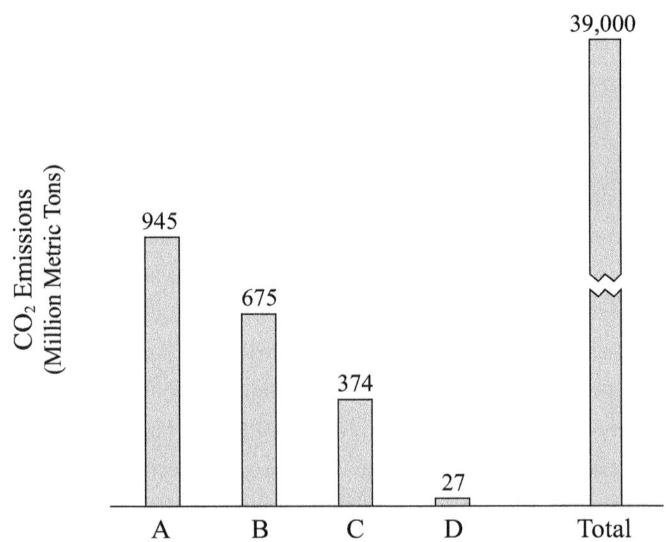

Figure 9.1a Current year CO_2 emissions for countries A, B, C and D, and global total

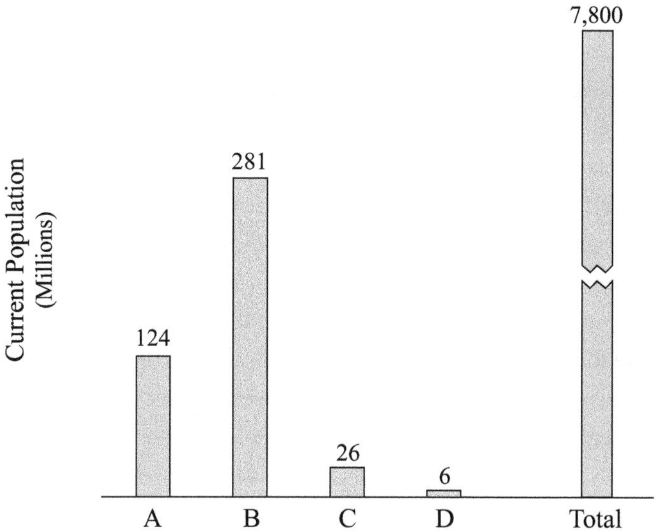

Figure 9.1b Current year population for countries A, B, C and D, and global total

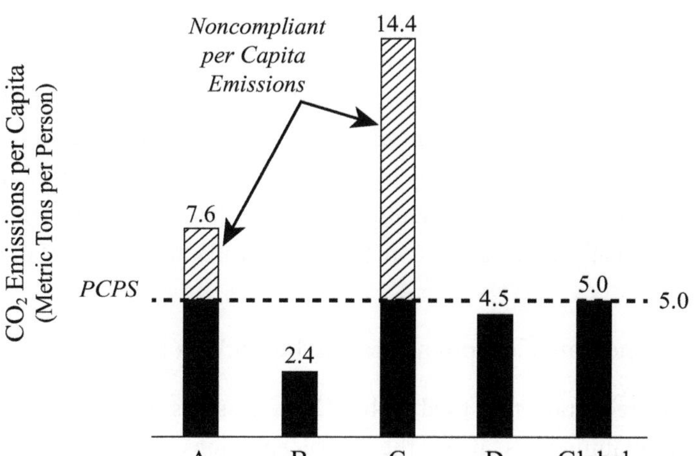

Figure 9.1c Current year CO_2 emissions per capita for countries A, B, C and D, and globally

the initial PCPS of 5.0 mtons per capita. Note, as an example, that the per capita emissions for Country A are 945 million metric tons/124 million persons, or 7.6 mtons per capita. The darkened areas where emissions are below the PCPS represent compliant emissions.

The four countries are all major emitters. Countries A and C generate emissions over the PCPS. Based on current year emissions, we see in Figure 9.1c that Country A generated emissions over the allowable initial PCPS of (7.6–5.0) x 124 million, or 322.4 million mtons/year noncompliantly. Under this methodology, developed countries such as A and C are unsustainable CO_2 emitters, or arguably "unsustainably developed," for their current rate of per capita CO_2 emissions. In theory, there should be no way under the mitigation strategy that countries should be allowed to generate CO_2 emissions that exceed the PCPS. As far as the ideal mitigation strategy is concerned, only current emissions that are at or below the PCPS should be tradable while those that are over this value are both noncompliant and untradable. Thus, much like a noncompliant boiler that generates emissions over the applicable performance standard, those noncompliant emissions must be reduced unilaterally and the country penalized. Unfortunately, unsustainably developed countries are not items of equipment that can easily be replaced with a compliant unit, so it is not practical to demand that such countries comply immediately upon initiating the trading program. At the same time, however, where any country exceeds the international PCPS-compliance standard, they must be required to compensate those affected most by climate change, justifiably throughout all the past years since the baseline year that their emissions have been noncompliant.[13]

The crux of the program is how to resolve the dilemma of ongoing PCPS noncompliance and the timely need to become compliant. We will motivate the resolution of this dilemma by treating emissions that are noncompliant to the PCPS as separate from the emissions that are compliant. We will see that following this path will lead to a conclusion that will alter our initial premises.

What If Immediate Compliance to the PCPS Was Required?

The percent reduction that total global CO_2 emissions have to be reduced by to achieve attainment is, using the global emissions data from Figure 9.1a, [(39.0–22.08)/39.0] x 100, or 43.4 percent. Again, according to our current approach, a portion of those global CO_2 emissions is noncompliant, nontradable, and addressed by the imposition of harsh penalties. The total limit of CO_2 emissions allowed to be traded within the program would thus be much lower than 39 mGigatons, the rest comprising those emissions that must be reduced unilaterally by the violators of the noncompliant PCPS.

Upon crunching the numbers, it turns out that the total noncompliant emissions for the top thirty or so nonexempt countries, i.e., the total emissions that are over the PCPS of 5.0 mtons from these countries, are roughly 14 mGigatons, which is only 3 mGigatons short of the roughly 17 mGigatons[14] of total noncompliant emissions. If we were to simply reduce the allowed PCPS to 4.0 mtons, we would add about five more PCPS-noncompliant countries as participants in the trading program, and by doing so the total noncompliant emissions for the thirty-five or so nonexempt countries would reach that 17 mGigaton quantity of noncompliant emissions. In short, one can see that nonattainment to climate stability is primarily due to just thirty-five or so countries. While this may not be surprising to some, it is nevertheless a significant result.

What this tells us is that once noncompliant emissions from these participating sources within the trading program are reduced to the PCPS and assuming there is little to no growth in emissions from the other countries that together emit less than 30 percent of global CO_2 emissions, then the whole point of having a broadly inclusive trading program in the first place is rendered moot. This requires a fundamental pivot in the approach. If emissions from the PCPS-noncompliant countries alone were reduced to below the PCPS, total CO_2 emissions would be below the total emissions generated during the baseline year. This situation is in contrast to the comprehensive strategy where sources are presumed to be compliant but whose collective generation of an air pollutant in an area renders that area nonattainment. With the mitigation strategy, the seriousness of nonattainment for climate stability is an order of magnitude worse because the sources/countries are noncompliant to the PCPS.

Demanding immediate compliance from the PCPS-noncompliant sources would be practically unrealistic; as the next best option, trading the emissions from only these PCPS-noncompliant emitters downward is necessary. Such a global trading program should therefore be focused on the PCPS-noncompliant countries that together exceed at least 70 percent of total global CO_2 emissions. So while the original motivation was to require trading when emissions were below 5.0 mtons while emissions over that could be treated as noncompliant with penalties applied, that idea has to be scrapped, overridden, and replaced by the new requirement that both (1) the total emissions from thirty-five or so PCPS-noncompliant countries must be reduced to a PCPS-compliance level of 4.0 mtons and (2) attainment of a CO_2 concentration of 350 ppm is achieved. This result should not be surprising, particularly to members of the United Nations Framework Convention on Climate Change (UNFCCC). However, what brings comfort is that this determination arose out of the rigorous application of first principles to the comprehensive strategy.

It should be noted that among the fifty or so countries that are the largest contributors to CO_2 emissions, there are just a few that emit below the PCPS of 4.0 mtons. From a rational perspective, in no way should PCPS-compliant countries be allowed or required to participate in the trading program with the noncompliant countries since this allows compliant countries to be "farm teams" to those noncompliant countries, defeating the whole purpose of the program.[15] Noncompliant countries must fight among themselves to the point of exhaustion to each reduce their noncompliant emissions. Thus, it is this author's contention that these compliant countries should not participate in the trading scheme with the "noncompliants." However, since they are still major contributors, what should be done about them? The more general question is—as emissions decrease from the trading program and more and more countries become compliant while nonparticipants increase their emissions, how should compliant countries that increase emissions be addressed? We will look into this issue next.

The tradable global emissions could be reduced by a set per-year percentage for a specified number of years, or if nonparticipating countries are increasing their emissions too quickly while the trading program is operating, then a more aggressive percentage reduction must be applied. This percent reduction will have to be intentionally aggressive for two reasons: (1) nonparticipants will likely be increasing their CO_2 emissions, so there should be a net global reduction overall as the program proceeds; and (2) this aggressive rate will encourage the facilitation of negative emissions and the subsequent acquisition of CO_2 ETUs (discussed in the next section).

To achieve the required reductions, not only must participating countries' allotments be reduced by possibly variable per-year percentages, but the allowable global PCPS must also be ratcheted downward over time, perhaps aggressively. If PCPS-noncompliant countries' emissions decrease and compliant countries' emissions increase, while the attainment goal itself has yet to be achieved, this situation suggests a possible second stage within the trading program. Here, regulators must continue to ratchet down the PCPS such that at least thirty to forty countries that together generate at least 70 plus percent of the total PCPS-noncompliant emissions are always included within the program. If nothing else, this will prevent gaming of the system by noncompliant countries by sending manufacturing to nonparticipating countries to avoid operation in these noncompliant countries. Trading is conducted until compliance to the baseline concentration of 350 ppm is achieved and, even where that is achieved, every participating country must still meet the applicable PCPS at the time that attainment is achieved; and should any nonparticipants increase emissions over that PCPS in the meantime, they too would be required to participate as well.

Clearly, as the first stage proceeds, those conducting the trading scheme would determine whether any second stage is even necessary and how that new scheme should be tailored.

To assist participants in seeking an easier means of achieving compliance within the trading program, the essential wrinkle of folding in the crediting of negative emissions by the use of CO_2 ETUs is discussed next.

The Added Wrinkle with regard to Negative Emissions

If the globalized trading of CO_2 emissions to reduce the global cap downward was all that was involved in the program, it would be relatively straightforward, for example, just replace fossil fuels with renewables to reduce CO_2 emissions. However, the problem is a little more complicated because, while some countries possess natural CO_2 sinks, such as rainforests, there is very little incentive to maintain those forests or even expand them as CO_2 sinks.

To address this critical issue, a resourceful wrinkle encourages all countries, particularly developing countries, to preserve their rainforests (and other ecosystems) by treating CO_2 sequestration by these forests and other sinks as negative emissions.[16] Rather than subtracting CO_2 emissions from a country's generated emissions, be it the same country sequestering the CO_2 or that of another, it is more practical to treat negative emissions as ETUs within a trading scheme to better facilitate their transfer through a global ETU clearinghouse and/or auction. Incorporation of ETUs would be no different than that of the adapted and generalized strategies for achieving a circular economy for material reuse.[17,18,19] Here, these emissions represent the *recovery (or long-term off-ramping) via sequestration of actual* CO_2 from the atmosphere since the commencement of the program. Let's say that over a period of time since the mitigation strategy was implemented, a South American country expanded their rainforest by 100,000 hectares, which is the equivalent of X mGigatons of sequestered or "negative" CO_2 emissions. If they are a participant in the program, after verification by their certified sustainability accountant and later by the clearinghouse, they can add these ETUs to their allotment for that year and if they are above the Trading Unit (TU) equivalent of their generated emissions, they can sell the TUs in excess of their total allotment to those countries that wish to purchase them. And if they are not a participant, they can auction these ETUs through the clearinghouse. Contributing such ETUs commits these countries to ongoing tracking and verification thereafter, to ensure that the contributing country's total CO_2 emissions do not decrease in the future (e.g., due to wildfires), in which case they may later have to *purchase* TUs. Thus, while long-term planning is required by participating countries to be future buyers or sellers in the trading program, long-term planning is also required by nonparticipating contributors of ETUs.

Ideally, the mitigation strategy should be expanded to apply to all countries, participants and nonparticipants alike, where the acquisition of ETUs can apply to the full restoration of ecosystems rather than just forests. Within the restoration strategy that will be addressed further later in this chapter, minimal ecologically achievable quotas are required. In fact, when global CO_2 concentrations continue to be over 350 ppm, one key requirement that must be adhered to without exception is that there must be a severe penalty to be paid for the intentional, unsustainable harvest of timber (i.e., removal of a natural "CO_2 control device") where there is a greater than de minimis increase in CO_2 emissions. This is the near-cousin of countries that must be penalized for having generated noncompliant emissions of CO_2. It should be expected that when the supply of TUs gets tighter, countries will be more incentivized to make a profit by re-/afforestating, when they are able to provide future ETUs to participants that need them rather than by selling the timber and having to meet the additional obligation of buying TUs and being taxed upon doing so.

Again, in an ideal mitigation strategy, each country would inventory their soils, forests and other natural CO_2 sequestration sinks, where quantifiably possible, so that nonparticipants and participants alike that restore ecosystems and rainforests can facilitate the creation of ETUs for use by participants in the trading program via the global ETU clearinghouse and/or by auction. It may not be absolutely necessary to inventory every existing sink at the initiation of the trading scheme since only quantifying the incremental growth or loss of sequestered CO_2 is all that is necessary thereafter. To reiterate, the loss of forests requires the purchase and taxation of TUs while growth allows ETUs to be sold/auctioned.

Thus, for major emitters to reconcile allotments, many countries now have a much stronger economic incentive to reforestate and afforestate,[20] because it allows them to be compensated by those higher-emitting countries and to use those funds to develop their own economies. This is particularly significant as allotments decline and the acquisition of ETUs from countries that reforestate and afforestate become more expensive as the program continues.

So What About Nonparticipants?

There are two types of nonparticipating countries that collectively emit less than 30 percent of global CO_2 emissions: (1) those low-emitting countries that generate emissions noncompliantly over the PCPS and (2) those countries that emit below that standard. With regard to the first group, regulators can exercise one of two options: (a) participating in the trading program with the other "noncompliants" and accepting the responsibilities associated with it, or (b) continually paying a noncompliance penalty until emissions become compliant. Compliant nonparticipants are regulatorily off the hook, until, of course, they emit over the applicable PCPS.

A Key Loose End

Lastly, to address noncompliant emissions over the PCPS for the years from the baseline year to the start of the trading program, PCPS-noncompliant countries must put funds into an escrow account for possible compensation to countries damaged by climate change. However, certain countries affected by climate change should not be immediately compensated, specifically those that have been bad actors themselves with regard to environmental harm. In this case, compensation could be used instead to directly improve governing capacity and/or be put into an escrow account until governance improves.

A number of points regarding the mitigation strategy can be noted and further reiterated:

1. Countries are responsible for the CO_2 emissions generated from the sources within them, so if they wish to be world leaders in mitigation, they will have to improve their capacity to regulate those sources' emissions. Nations that want to be sellers rather than buyers of global TUs will have to regulate the generation of CO_2 from the states and provinces within them, and those states and provinces will have to regulate CO_2 from the sources within them, and so on. Likewise, irresponsible participating countries will have to acquire TUs and pay a further "unsustainability tax" for excess emissions over their current allotment. In fact, countries that house multinational corporations can require that those corporations' CO_2 emissions be accounted for and reimburse that country for their contribution to that country's generated emissions.

The mitigation strategy not only adds teeth to regulating CO_2/GHG beyond what the United Nations Framework Convention on Climate Change (UNFCCC) and the Paris Agreement established previously, but it also provides compliance options. Two major goals that the UNFCCC has struggled to achieve have been determining common but differentiated responsibilities among developed and developing nations for CO_2 emissions and an equitable means of addressing climate change while attaining full participation of all affected parties. The mitigation strategy provides this framework. In addition, rather than each country being mandated under the Paris Agreement to meet rigid, nationally determined contributions (NDC) via command-and-control, the mitigation strategy provides flexibility for countries to do so as long as they all collectively emit under a globally declining cap and are accountable for their CO_2/GHG-generating behavior. In addition, the UNFCCC's program of Reducing Emissions from Deforestation and Forest Degradation is rigorously enhanced by the determination and use of ETUs via re-/afforestation and/or direct air capture as a means to provide credit for negative emissions.

It should be noted that regulating GHG would add more "CO_2 equivalents" that would need to be regulated. Not all GHG are carbon-based; while methane is, other GHGs such as nitrous oxide (N_2O) and sulfur hexaflouride (SF_6) are not. In addition to limiting fossil fuel usage, the process to regulate GHGs would follow a similar fashion to the CO_2 mitigation strategy, but doing so would require more countries to participate and more involved tracking.

2. At the heart of the mitigation strategy is the fact that climate change is not an economic problem that is solved by the dissuasive tools of economics, such as taxation; nonattainment of climate stability is a CO_2/GHG-generation problem solved first and foremost by corrective, limit-based CaT measures to sort out how those declining limits are to be met. Taxation is then used to dissuade the purchase of TUs by penalizing the choice not to reduce the generation of CO_2.
3. As the reader may have concluded by now, the mitigation strategy will allow for the situation where, while global attainment is in the process of being reached, all countries can achieve their own choice of a "happy medium" whereby they can decide their own level of development and/or

ecosystem restoration depending on how they wish to pay for it, or have other countries pay them.

4. Based on the country-by-country example above, reduction-wise, Countries A and C have the worst of it because of the harm intensity of their emissions, that is, they are unsustainably developed (noncompliant to the PCPS) but have the most capacity to adapt to the need to reduce. Not only do they have to compensate countries harmed by climate change due to their likely decades-long noncompliant emissions, they will also have to continue achieving large reductions. It is presumed that with their development, their access to and possession of capital will allow them to achieve these reductions.
5. Next Gen principles must be developed and incorporated into the regulatory structure to build in compliance to the international mitigation strategy. This is especially critical since per country tracking and verification of emissions will be a weak link of the strategy, particularly for certain low-capacity and/or unwilling or corrupted countries. These possible realities are not deficiencies of the mitigation strategy; they exist already, independent of any such strategy. Thus, a key component of Next Gen will be the incorporation of "certified sustainability accountants," who must be higher in stature than certified public accountants since sustainability is a much higher order goal (recall the first FLoER). Their role is to verify pollutant quantification used in the trading program. It should be expected that there will still be pariah states that refuse to participate, so participating countries have to ensure such states are punished by applying global pressure on them to address those countries' contributions to the problem. There will need to be a global tracking and verification team that independently monitors countries' emissions to ensure that they are calculated properly and to ensure that fraud does not taint the program's integrity.
6. The mitigation strategy, just like the other pollution control strategies developed in this book, does not attempt to adjust, nor is it a miracle cure for, the world's underlying unresolved North-South developmental equity issues, nor should it. This is because it is first and foremost a CO_2 reduction strategy, not a means to promote economic development. As far as the strategy is concerned, underdeveloped, PCPS-noncompliant countries can still be significant CO_2 emitters, so these emissions have to be reduced. It is inappropriate to carve out softer treatment for these

countries because "fungibly speaking," pollution is pollution regardless of the country that emits it. Lesser developed countries, and clearly all countries in general, have options, e.g., reforestate/afforestate, develop a circular economy, negotiate with other countries for acquiring TUs and/or ETUs, swap out inefficient technologies with much more efficient ones, improve governance, etc. With any luck, the mitigation strategy will spur an aggressive race toward reforestation/afforestation, use of direct air capture, energy efficiency, etc.

Some countries have high capacity and good governance but are unsustainably developed relative to their population due to the overreliance on fossil fuels. On the other hand, other countries' emissions are low relative to their population but suffer from low capacity and sometimes poor governance. The former countries will have to sacrifice capital to maintain their standard of living while the latter countries will have to improve their governance if they wish to develop while keeping their emissions relatively low.

7. Clear-cutting forests as practiced today would be killing the goose that lays the golden egg within the mitigation strategy. ETUs from reforestation (and restoring ecosystems in general) have value although it may take many years for them to be of significance (because of the timescale to reach forest/ecosystem maturity). In the meantime, countries can purchase them as future investments, that is, a layaway plan whereby developed countries could contract with lesser developed countries to assist them with development today while acquiring reforestation/afforestation and ecosystem ETUs for later years. In absolutely no way, however, should ETUs ever be provided earlier than when the CO_2 emissions have been sequestered.

   As it stands now, when a major project is undertaken that increases CO_2 emissions, many global leaders believe that the acquisition of carbon offsets from reforestation justifies offsetting the emissions generated from the project. Since the planet is already in nonattainment for climate stability, it is not only absurd to accept a feckless 1:1 offset ratio when a much higher ratio is demanded, but also where the reductions are at a far-off international location with lax regulatory oversight and insufficiently rigorous measurement and verification capability, then enforceability is highly questionable. Under the rigorous mitigation strategy, which speaks well to the proper means to incorporate CO_2

removal and sequestration within a CaT system, emitters of CO_2 must bite the bullet and reduce their noncompliant emissions with other noncompliant CO_2 generating participants. Likewise, reforestation and afforestation can provide offsets only when there is rigorous accounting conducted by certified sustainability accountants and the ETUs are processed through the ETU clearinghouse.

8. While fossil fuels have to be rationed/phased down, the use of all fuels combusted has to be tracked regardless since waste plastics and/or biomass could be used as substitutes. Since global CO_2 emissions are correlated to global CO_2 concentrations, their emissions have to be tracked, particularly since they include biomass-generated CO_2 emissions. It is only at the global level that tracking and regulating global emissions is sensible, and why national trading by only a few countries acting unilaterally is suboptimal.
9. While the mitigation strategy excludes shipping and aviation, these sectors must have their supply of fossil fuel limited separately or included within the allotment of the country of ownership.
10. The mitigation and generalized strategies do not directly regulate population growth since they both focus on regulating pollution as an output and fuel and resource inputs. Given specifically set limits on fuels, resources, pollution, and the allowable PCPS, individual countries that encourage population growth do so at the risk of potentially accepting a lower standard of living. Under the mitigation strategy, it is first compliance to the PCPS and secondarily the overall amount of a country's generated CO_2 emissions (in conjunction with meeting its corresponding declining TU allotment and other required collateral declines in sustainability measures) that matters above all else.

As critical as lowering the CO_2 concentration is, and the necessity to reduce CO_2 emissions to do so, it is difficult to imagine how to accomplish these ends without also reducing population as ongoing development continues to push the envelope. Since a country's CO_2 emissions are the product of its per capita emissions and its population, to keep its emissions PCPS-compliant requires keeping either its per capita emissions low or its population low, or both. Thus, there is a trade-off for many developed and some developing countries between achieving and maintaining both a compliant PCPS and a large population to avoid noncompliance and contributing to the calamities resulting from climate change; long story short, trying to have per capita emissions and population as high as possible only invites further calamities.

11. It should be possible in theory to develop a global solid waste mitigation strategy for the use of virgin materials to achieve a global CE. While we do not possess a baseline year's total volumetric measure of detriment (VMoD) for the various IDPC and IDPC surrogate pollutants, countries could still conceivably trade current amounts downward once agreed-upon global per capita performance standards for these pollutants are established.
12. Upon taking a bird's-eye view perspective, one can observe that environmental regulation provides a means to regulate a source's pollution outputs (e.g., air pollution, IDPC surrogates), while regulating total regional quantities of these pollutants can facilitate a circular economy and that global regulation can facilitate the mitigation of climate change. No one source facilitates a circular economy; a CE comes about only by regionally and globally regulating the generation of solid waste from multiple sources. Likewise, neither one source in one country nor one country itself can mitigate climate change by itself; combating climate change is only facilitated by acting globally.

    While international consensus will hash out the specific details of the mitigation strategy, most of the discussion above should form its core.

Restoring Nature and the Tools to Do So

It is one thing to reduce humanity's harm to Nature, as this book has shown, but it is another thing to regenerate Nature to some degree of restoration. Unfortunately, the current approach to restoring Nature has followed a similar one addressing air pollution in the very early years and the current approach to establishing a CE in the European Union (EU), namely, using a small-scale, bottom-up application of ad hoc methods to rehabilitate ecosystems. In contrast, this section will instead provide a conceptual framework for how to do so by applying some of the techniques learned so far but "in reverse."

Throughout this book, we set limits on a "bad" and declined it using the economic tools of corrective cap-and-trade and dissuasive taxation on individual TU purchases. Who is to say we can't apply reverse "cap-and-trade" instead on a "good" to restore Nature by increasing certain ecological measures above a given baseline?[21]

Restoring ecosystems is not an exact science, but at this stage, it appears amenable to a reverse CaT system where the state and/or landowners would be subject to requirements to restore or otherwise upgrade Nature's ecosystems (which includes reviving endangered species). We focus on the work of Gann et al.,[22] who provided a detailed description of how to use ecological tools to move ecosystems through "The Restorative Continuum." The steps are as follows: (1) Reducing societal impacts; (2) Improving ecosystem management; (3) Repairing ecosystem function; (4) Initiating native recovery; (5) Partially recovering native ecosystems; and (6) Fully recovering native ecosystems.

Gann uses a Five-Star System and Ecological Recovery Wheel to measure the restoration of ecosystems at the site level.[23] In theory, and likely in practice, the Five-Star System can be used to evaluate local ecosystems within counties of a state and the total number of "stars" summed over those regions. With that total set as a baseline for that state's counties and individual baselines set for each location, regulators could require that the initial total be increased over the baseline by an established regulatory percentage every ten years without allowing for any decreases within any region. As usual, each participant must meet a performance standard, which can be thought of as a minimum ecologically achievable restoration quota. Localities that do not meet prescribed ecosystem growth milestones must pay to reconcile their deficient TU allotments (measured as ecosystem growth points), all facilitated by the use of a reverse CaT program where TU purchases (due to insufficient restoration) are taxed. Counties are incentivized to increase over their allotment so that they may be paid by those that do not. The process continues until a prescribed equilibrium state between Nature and humans (with its embedded economy) is attained. So, while reducing harms to Nature by the generalized strategy internalizes externalities, restoring Nature attempts to de-externalize those harms.

Formulating a Steady-State Equilibrium Theory for Sustainability with Nature

As we know, an enemy of sustainability is the assumption of infinite abundance, which leads to slash-and-burn, destructive, unchecked growth, all so as to maintain the existing oxymoronic "unsustainable status quo." On top of that, we have normalized the notion of growth, destruction, externalities, and other unsustainable practices in our culture yet have the cognitively dissonant audacity to say that we need to achieve sustainability, much like an addict with life-threatening health issues who admits that he must overcome his addiction but is wholly dismissive of the very thought of attending rehab because it would severely impact his lifestyle.

The United Nations defines sustainable development as "development that meets the needs of the present without compromising the ability of future generations to meet their own needs,"[24] an anthropocentric interest which says nothing of the destruction of ecosystems (think loss of endangered species, old-growth forests, and groundwater). Where there is a need to achieve a CE and sustainability on a large scale, there is no economic justification for continued expansion that relies on the destruction of wetlands, habitat and biodiversity loss, etc. If expansion and destruction can ever be deemed to be sustainable by pro-free market advocates, it is incumbent upon them to prove it.[25]

While one goal is to restore ecosystems, the greater goal is to find the sustainable, "steady-state equilibrium point" between the attainment of the restored natural environment (that sustainably supplies the economy with the proper amount of nourishing resources) and the CE that is embedded within it. Where the number of additional Earths needed to sustain life on the planet is zero, a sustainable economy is embedded within a sustainable ecosystem, where the economy is constrained on a leash from wreaking havoc on the greater ecosystem it must be in equilibrium with.

When the program to minimize the generation of pollution from both industrial and agricultural sources occurs such that it is below a given national standard (analogous to the National Ambient Air Quality Standards [NAAQS] to protect both human health and Nature itself), then that standard has been attained. The equivalent concept applies as well with regard to attainment of ecosystem restoration, applied regionally, nationally, and globally. One can think of it this way: achieving attainment for both environmental harms (e.g., pollutants, resource overuse) and the restoration of Nature, as well as for all environmental stressors (e.g., urban sprawl, soil degradation), is to full environmental sustainability with Nature and achieving an Additional Earths at Global Development [AEGD] of zero as achieving attainment for all multi-media pollutants is to a fully functioning CE. To achieve these goals, regulators must make unflinching use of rationing, the setting of limits, the gradual decline of limits for harms, the mandated increases over ecosystem baselines, trading and taxation where necessary, performance/characteristic standards, etc.

While a Holy Grail of any Grand Unified Theory will be described further in Chapter 10, a natural fringe benefit of such a strategy that achieves a CE at the optimal point of steady-state equilibrium with a restored Nature is that not only will the loss of biodiversity significantly decrease, but it will have been restored to some capacity.[26] Thus, the unnecessary destruction of ecosystems must not be allowed; rather, a steady-state equilibrium must be established between the "circular economy under the bubble" and the restored ecosystem within which it is embedded.

Drawing the Lines between Sustainability with Nature, Physics, and a CE

As was noted in the previous chapter, Cullen, among others, raised issues about the quantity of waste that was able to be recovered and reused as well as the quality of that recoverable waste. It is important to note that many of the criticisms directed at a CE are obstacles it is not designed to overcome (e.g., dissipative losses). While relevant to the ability of materials to circulate, these issues are actually outside the regulatory scope of a CE, typical of recent literature that attempts to "pile on" more responsibility onto the achievement of a CE when those responsibilities lie elsewhere. The counterargument here is simply that physics happens—material degradation within a CE will be no different than the corrosion of water treatment equipment or the deteriorating performance of air pollution control equipment over time, so material degradation within a CE is to be expected and does not represent a flaw of a CE, just a flaw of misplaced attribution. Note that, with appropriately applied constraints, a CE is just the regulation of the generation of solid waste pollution by another name, and with it comes physical limitations.

On the other hand, while quality issues which render a CE as nonideal (e.g., dissipative losses) are attributed to physics and thermodynamics, the issue regarding the increasing quantity of waste also misses the target due to what may be called "nonlinear unsustainability." This is the force multiplier of ubiquitous unsustainable behavior that ultimately results from population growth, explicitly manifested by, citing two examples, the economy's hunger for resources and urban sprawl.[27] Thus, it is important to avoid the pitfall of perceiving a CE as being flawed when it is coerced into functioning within an unsustainably growing population and economy that relies on urban sprawl, the extraction of virgin resources, and other stressors. Allowing economic growth due directly to an increase in population by feeding virgin resources into a CE undermines the viability of that CE. A CE may be a key step in solving the overall problem of regulating the generation of environmental pollution, but it is nonetheless just one necessary, but not a sufficient, condition for achieving sustainability with Nature. Clearly, to achieve a CE, the sustainable steady-state equilibrium point between Nature and humanity will be reached by also regulating other critical drivers such as urban sprawl and (indirectly) population growth, which should also stabilize the quantity of material throughput in the economy.

Such a system must allow only enough virgin resources to address the immediate amount necessary to supplement the maximum possible quantity of recovered materials. Clearly, in a truly sustainable world, extracting virgin resources for the sake of expanding growth itself cannot be allowed. A stable CE, on the other hand, requires an adequate material surplus in a state of steady-state equilibrium, acquiring only enough virgin resources to replenish losses and maintain the economy without expanding beyond that sustainable steady-state equilibrium. The notion that we need to use virgin materials because maintaining existing infrastructural stocks has a higher priority and must remain outside the CE is not a sufficient reason to continue using more such materials. This is because the expanded use of materials that later comprise our existing infrastructure is a consequence of nonattainment of sustainability with Nature. Energizing a CE with excess virgin resources while perpetuating a state of unsustainability is not only a violation of the first FLoER but a fool's errand.

In the middle of this entire discussion about seeking a steady-state equilibrium CE, it is absolutely critical not to lose sight of the fact that, at the risk of overstatement, achieving sustainability with Nature requires restoring ecosystems. Hence, an ideal steady-state equilibrium point must be found between the actual CE and the restored ecological environment in which that CE is embedded. That same embedded CE must likewise determine the proper equilibrium point between existing stocks of materials and the use of virgin resources, all while Nature is being restored contemporaneously.

In this regard, the concepts of degrowth and a spiral economy are noteworthy.[28] While Mulrow and Santos expounded on the topic of shrinking and slowing material throughputs,[29] Assadourian and Mulrow[30] speak of seeking "degrowth" by way of a "spiral economy" rather than simply via a CE. This concept simply reflects the need to reach attainment for sustainability with Nature and not just circularity. So while economists may recoil in horror at the very concept of "degrowth," it is incumbent upon them to take the study of economics to a more advanced level whereby economic growth is allowed while sustainability with Nature and an AEGD of zero is achieved.

Postulating the Strategy to Regulate the Rate of Complexity Increase

The term "complexity" describes the complex assemblage of resources (altered or otherwise) that constitutes a product. So when the complexity of a product is reduced, the resulting rate of entropy increase is also reduced since less energy, particularly where fossil fuels are combusted, was required to facilitate that reduction.

Ecological economist Herman Daly made this very profound statement:

> The Second Law [of Thermodynamics], that the entropy (or disorder) of the universe is always increasing, imposes a qualitative degradation of the environment – by extracting low-entropy resources and returning high-entropy wastes. The Second Law of Thermodynamics thus imposes an additional conflict between expansion of the economy and preservation of the environment, namely *that the order and structure of the economy is paid for by imposing disorder in the sustaining ecosphere.*[31] (Emphasis added)

With this in mind, when a complex product such as a cellphone is manufactured, not only was energy use increased relative to that for a less complex cellphone, and likely due to an increase in fossil fuel use as well, that same device becomes a major hindrance to recovery of materials for later reuse due to its high complexity. If we take a step back and observe how we regulate the generation of environmental pollution, including that for IDPCs and IDPC surrogates in a future generalized strategy, we observe this: what is being regulated (the aforesaid cellphone's characteristics) is the generation of increased complexity (paid for by an increase in entropy, remember). The generalized strategy in effect seeks to limit the total complexity within a region and forces its reduction via a corrective trading program. Just to be clear, the actual entropy as defined by physicists is not itself regulated, but a proxy (e.g., in the form of VMoD) that acts in its place, where we only need to leverage reductions measured as differences in this proxy rather than its absolute value.

The less complex manufactured products become, the more reusable their constituent materials are, with less energy/fuel required in the recovery/manufacturing process. Where then does economic growth fit into the picture? No matter what, since economics is subordinate to the larger ecosystem within which it is embedded, the minimization of disorder and material complexity increase is paramount. Thus, the expansion of the global economy is allowable where the increase in the total global "rate of disorder/entropy increase" is minimized while attaining an AEGD of zero.

The Next Steps

The strategies developed in this book point to a possible means of circumscribing environmental law into a systematic and far better-defined framework of application. This framework in turn points to the pursuit of a Holy Grail of a Grand Unified Theory of Environmental Law and Regulation as well as the development of a Global Constitution for Nature that would subordinate national constitutions as far as protecting and preserving Nature is concerned. These discussions and more are subjects covered in Chapter 10.

Notes

1 It is critical to note that this is *not* the increase in entropy. Entropy is always increasing, but it is the *rate* of that entropy increase that can be regulated.

2 It should be noted that the notion of an equilibrium state of Nature is disputed by ecologists because Nature is characterized as a complex adaptive system that changes over time. For purposes of this book and for the sake of simplicity, steady-state equilibrium is assumed to be between Nature and humanity (although humanity is part of Nature) and not that for Nature as a stand-alone entity by itself.

3 It does so by setting a limit and letting the market sort out who gets what, where everyone participates in real time and the trading units are actual dollars.

4 While regulation appears to work best with a relatively small number of participants, incentivizing a large number of participants, e.g., by using deposits to encourage material recovery from consumers, is a better alternative to regulation.

5 A variant has already been tried in Germany: Ralph Henger and Kilian Bizer, "Tradable Planning Permits for Land-Use Control in Germany," *Land Use Policy* 27, no. 3 (2010).

6 Natural remediation (e.g., planting trees), preferably via an economic instrument, is likely to be far more efficient than adopting a more expensive technological solution first.

7 Unless a complete mitigation strategy is adopted and implemented that restores Nature, including a means to incentivize reforestation, we may only be able to decelerate deforestation.

8 In this regard, the work of the Global CO_2 Initiative at the University of Michigan is noteworthy. https://www.globalco2initiative.org/.

9 In the meantime, if it is at all possible, the focus of most environmental violation penalties should ideally be put toward addressing the remediation of legacy pollution, such as CO_2 sequestration, since this is absolutely critical to our and Nature's survival.

10 While some readers may quibble about the numerical values used in the subsequent analysis, the key takeaway here is the methodology and the conclusions drawn.

11 For the same reason as asserted within the adapted strategy, it was strongly advised not to default the characteristic standard to the worst-case value, so we cannot let the initial PCPS be set to the worst-case value. High-emitting countries should have to meet some stringent standard of achieving an agreed-upon PCPS.

12 To guide the discussion, sample country emissions and population data were respectively taken from the European Commission's Emissions Database for Global Atmospheric Research (EDGAR) Joint Research Center (JRC) Report for 2024, found at https://jrc.ec.europa.eu/report_2024?vis=co2tot#emissions_table and https://jrc.ec.europa.eu/report_2024?vis=co2pop#emissions_table. Actual country names and per country numbers are irrelevant to this analysis.

13 An article that provides an approach on how responsibility can be assigned to those countries that have contributed past legacy emissions of CO_2 that have already contributed to climate change is: Jason Hickel, "Quantifying National Responsibility for Climate Breakdown: An Equality-Based Attribution Approach for Carbon Dioxide Emissions in Excess of the Planetary Boundary," *Lancet Planet Health* 4 (September 2020). https://www.thelancet.com/action/showPdf?pii=S2542-5196%2820%29960. As an alternative, the PCPS approach can certainly be used to march back each per-year level of noncompliance to determine the total amount of noncompliant emissions that exceeded the PCPS since the base year.

14 This result is arrived at as the difference between the currently generated CO_2 emissions (39 mGigatons) minus the CO_2 emissions during the attainment year (22.08 mGigatons); or 39.0–22.08 ~ 17 mGigatons.

15 Some readers may object that as long as CO_2 emissions are to be reduced planetwide anyway (since the planet is just one large CO_2 nonattainment area), then there should be no harm if PCPS-noncompliant developed countries acquire TUs from lesser developed compliant countries. The mitigation strategy as developed here is predicated upon and maintains the integrity of applying both the imposition of performance standards at the source/country level and emissions trading at the global level. Integrity adherence aside, furthering the glaring asymmetry between higher-emitting developed countries and lower-emitting developing countries, reflecting a moral hazard outside the scope of the mitigation strategy, is an inequity that seems difficult to rationalize. It allows well-developed higher emitters to effectively "pay off" the lesser developed lower emitters to maintain the asymmetric status quo.

16 This wrinkle adds rigor to the United Nations Framework Convention on Climate Change's program of Reducing Emissions from Deforestation and Forest Degradation.

17 It would be incorrect to assert that ETUs for the recovery of CO_2 participate in the "circular economy." This is because forests are a fundamental aspect of Nature's "circular natural process," not of the human-created economy.

18 In no way should ETUs for CO_2 be viewed as TUs for "pollutants not yet emitted," but as *actual recovery* or *permanent sequestration* such that it no longer participates in climate instability (e.g., CO_2 captured and sequestered back into biomass or converted into mineral form). This requirement forestalls the absurd situation where ETUs are provided simply for keeping fossil fuels in the ground, which would corrupt the integrity of the program.

19 It bears reminding the reader that the incorporation of a CE, as noted in Part 3, will by its nature also reduce the use of fossil fuels and energy in general.

20 Where measuring emissions reductions is quantifiable, other alternatives are possible, such as other biomass CO_2 extraction (e.g., Bioenergy Carbon Capture and Storage [CCS]), or installing technologies such as direct air capture that directly extracts atmospheric CO_2, which may be economical sometime in the future.

21 An interesting application of reverse cap-and-trade is the following: Jordan Farenhem, "Reverse Cap-and-Trade for Refugees: A Proposal to Ameliorate the Refugee Crisis in the European Union through a System of Quotas and Markets," *The Yale Review of International Studies*. https://yris.yira.org/wp-content/uploads/2020/03/yris-acheson-issue-2019-draft-2-1.pdf.

22 George D. Gann, Tein McDonald, Bethanie Walder, et al., "International Principles and Standards for the Practice of Ecological Restoration," Second edition. *Restoration Ecology* 27, no. S1 (2019).

23 Gann, et al., "International Principles and Standards for the Practice of Ecological Restoration," S17–S19.

24 UN Brundtland Commission, *Report of the World Commission on Environment and Development: Our Common Future*, 1987, 41. https://sustainabledevelopment.un.org/content/documents/5987our-common-future.pdf.

25 For example, how can the deforestation of old-growth forests or the loss of ancient groundwater be offset from a sustainability point of view? This is not a rhetorical question.

26 This notion fits in well with Mamlyuk's biosphere quality model, cited in the Introduction.

27 We clearly have to get beyond the mindset that the only thing worse than urban sprawl and habitat loss is high housing prices. Given the need to restore ecosystems to achieve an AEGD of zero, we will more often have to address the issue of facilitating "ecosystem sprawl." Our homework assignment is taking the growth versus loss problem far more seriously than we do now and determining how to address it.

28 Erik Assadourian and John Mulrow, "'Til Sustainability' Do You Part: Arranging a Marriage Between Degrowth and the Circular Economy," *Resilience*, October 3,

2018. https://www.resilience.org/stories/2018-10-03/til-sustainability-do-you-part-arranging-a-marriage-between-degrowth-and-the-circular-economy.

29 Mulrow and Santos, "Moving the Circular Economy Beyond Alchemy."

30 Assadourian and Mulrow, "'Til Sustainability' Do You Part: Arranging a Marriage Between Degrowth and the Circular Economy."

31 Herman Daly, "Economics for a Full World," Great Transition Initiative, June 2015. www.greattransition.org/publication/economics-for-a-full-world.

10

The Implications for Environmental Law

Formulating a Blueprint for Environmental Law

This chapter postulates the existence of a global blueprint of environmental law. We will first propose the existence of the Holy Grail of a Grand Unified Theory of Environmental Law and Regulation. Within that paradigm, we will also observe the regulatory interplay that applies to harms, resource use and Nature arising out of the methods developed in this book. In fact, a Global Constitution for Nature can be posited that takes primacy over human-based constitutions.

Can a New Framework Be Postulated for Environmental Law?

We see that there are two regimes where regulation can be applied: one where human harms to Nature must be reduced (e.g., abating acid rain, reducing excess water use) and the other where Nature's ecosystems are restored. As both are being achieved, patching the two goals together is clearly compatible. For example, there is an obvious collateral benefit of restoring ecosystems by the sequestration of legacy CO_2 from the atmosphere (e.g., via reforestation), so there will fortunately be a "two for the price of one" opportunity where abating pollution also restores Nature. Hopefully, there will be more such opportunities.

The more difficult problem we face is how to address the interfacial problem whereby ecosystems are destroyed without violating the first FLoER, such as when a forest is cleared locally to extract metals used in solar power generation to further the goals of sustainability with Nature on a larger scale. This conflict is a red flag that we have obviously grown beyond our carrying capacity by having to confront this very dilemma. Since this situation is a violation of the first FLoER, the correct solution is to avoid this situation in the first place, noting that it occurs when we put our needs first and those of Nature a distant second.

One can think of reactively resorting to using greenfields over brownfields as the macrolevel equivalent of using extracted virgin raw materials over that of reusing existing materials. Thus, before we commit to destroying ecosystems, considered by many as having no value, we must ideally 'max out' opportunities elsewhere, such as utilizing energy efficiency and accessing renewable energy (e.g., by using existing space via rooftop solar panels) before reflexively deciding to expand outwards unsustainably. In no way, however, should Nature be destroyed merely for the sole purpose of furthering economic interests.

The problem is clearly ripe for further study, not first by economists, legal scholars, engineers, or policymakers, but by environmental scientists and ecologists.[1]

The extraction of resources and the harms incurred to ecosystems are the near-cousins of the harms incurred by pollution. Thus, one can further observe the interplay of two semi-discrete impact components that interact between humans and Nature, namely, pollutant harms and the role of resource overuse. Pollutant harms inflicted onto Nature, such as air, water, and on-site generated hazardous waste pollution, are just one component of the impact in that they are the direct outcome of human activities or production by sources, the latter of which has primarily been the focus of this book.

With regard to the other related impact component, resource overuse, resources can either be (1) those resources used for industrially manufactured products, where we have seen that durable materials within consumed products can be returned to the economy via a circular economy; and (2) resources such as water or soils that are overused and degraded in the generation of agriculturally produced goods.

Unlike their industrial material siblings, materials that flow through the agricultural economy, such as water and fertilizers, are best regulated by setting usage performance standards and trading the compliant usage downward until either complete replenishment of the resource is achieved (strongly preferred) or, at the very least, regional usage of the resource simply sustains future usage (least preferred).

Nature itself participates in its own natural cycles, such as forests absorbing CO_2 from the atmosphere. By its very "nature," Nature sets its own natural performance standards.

How to Regulate the Interplay between Harms, Resource Use, and Nature

Having now developed the strategies in this book, we can sift out how to regulate the interplay between harms, resource use, and Nature.

With regard to the first impact component, pollutant harms, we know to use the generalized strategy to regulate them directly from pollution generators, particularly by using cap-and-trade (where appropriate) to reduce regional and product harm intensity and the use of technologically achievable performance (and characteristic) standards at all times.

With regard to the second component, industrial resource use, we note that while the extraction of resources must meet their own achievable performance standards, the use of resources in manufactured products that are later consumed must also use CaT in conjunction with characteristic standards and setting limits on, and taxing the acquisition of, virgin resource use to facilitate the transition to a circular economy. Regional reduction of product harm intensity is targeted in large part to reduce the harm of toxics and nonbiodegradable products.

Next, we note that resources used in agriculturally produced goods must likewise require the use of regional trading and usage performance standards to reduce resource usage. As always, usage above an achievable performance standard is not just noncompliant but penalized. This strategy facilitates the overall reduction of excess resource use.

Reducing pollutant harms and resource use is "easy" due to the one-dimensional focus on one discrete harm at a time, namely, by simply limiting a pollutant and reducing it. Restoring natural ecosystems at the macroscale is also one-dimensional since reverse CaT only requires regional macro-scale measures of ecosystem health to be increased. Where possible, the opposite of harm intensity, namely the *restoration intensity*, a measure of *too little* of a good within ecosystems, such as endangered species, must be increased to facilitate their growth. As noted earlier, restoring Nature also includes the sequestration of CO_2 by forests via the interaction with the human-based economy. In every case of pursuing restoration, the performance standard for each participating area is a minimum ecologically achievable restoration quota.

On the other hand, restoring natural ecosystems and degraded soil nutrients at the micro-scale will likely be much more difficult due to the multidimensional nature of measuring improvement, for example, soil health being measured by the various nutrients, pH, carbon content, and moisture to name just a few variables. It is possible that the strategy to agro-ecologically restore soils, etc., may be similar to the Nature restoration strategy developed in Chapter 9, where reverse CaT is utilized. Just what the measures of replenishment will be will require further study.

The ultimate macro-measure of achieving sustainability with Nature is reaching an Additional Earths at Global Development [AEGD] of zero, that is, no additional Earths being necessary if global citizens were to live at the level of the most developed countries. Even where developed countries stabilize their own unsustainable behavior while lesser developed countries ramp up theirs is still not necessarily a globally sustainable path to an AEGD of zero. More must be done to avoid just being less unsustainable; true sustainability must be the goal.

While it is encouraging to observe certain sustainability micro-measures of resource use and harms each being below a given per capita performance standard in many countries, this is not always the case for each country. We saw that within the mitigation strategy certain countries were above the PCPS for CO_2 emissions, but in the case of water usage, as just one example, some countries that may be well below the PCPS for CO_2 may very well be above the applicable standard for groundwater usage. This necessitates that all countries be responsible for correcting their own contributions to unsustainability, whether it is CO_2 emissions, groundwater usage, biodiversity loss, etc.

As far as ecosystem restoration is concerned, a minimal globally achievable ecosystem PCPS (quota) must also be met if not exceeded. With regard to the problem of the water-energy-food-ecosystem (WEFE) nexus[2]—the combined product resulting from the force-multiplied impacts by humans on water, energy, food, and ecosystems—it is likewise insufficient to simply manage or stabilize unsustainability. Rather than resorting to tactical adaptation, tackling the multifaceted WEFE problem requires strategic mitigation by unwinding its multiple impacting components by setting usage standards on their individual resource inputs as a means to more broadly achieve sustainability.

In any case, accelerating development now while worrying about achieving sustainability "later" is a lost cause, if for no other reason that there is no exit criterion to determine when to finally reverse course. In its place, we have to plan for a world where sustainability and our quality of life take primacy over the short-term gratification of economic growth based on the unsustainable destruction of ecosystems and the gluttonous use of fossil fuels, raw materials, water, forests, etc.

A Rationale for Respecting the Rights of Nature

Up to this point, we have looked at Nature as if it were a passive partner with respect to the role of humans on this planet. To preserve the planet, law must conform to the protection of Nature as if it were a more active planetary participant. We will develop a basic foundation to do so in this section.

From a real-world perspective, when an individual person is being abused, simply stopping the abuse does not rectify the problem. The damage incurred has to be healed and the abused individual allowed to recover, with all of this predicated on the fundamental notion that the abused has underlying fundamental rights, including the right to be made whole (e.g., payment for damages incurred). It should be clear, however, that being made whole does not imply that simply compensating the abused resolves and excuses the underlying abuse.

By all rights, the same must apply to Nature. Since one cannot financially compensate Nature, restoring it to a state where humanity lives in harmony with it (self-evident since humans are a part of Nature) is the final endpoint. Thus, we can see at one end of the regulatory spectrum that humans have the duty to reduce and eliminate their harms on Nature and the reciprocal duty to restore it back to a state of equilibrium, all predicated on Nature's fundamental right to exist. The last step in filling out the foundational model of environmental regulation is ensuring that, as a backstop to the above, Nature is provided with those fundamental rights.

Table 10.1 is the author's attempt to lay out the possible applicable twenty-first-century matrix of environmental law and regulation for protecting and restoring Nature, acknowledging its rights, as well as the harms imposed on Nature by the generation of environmental pollution and the harms already imposed on it by legacy pollution.

Each category requires a strategic legal instrument, such as regulation or tortious lawsuit. This author is unaware whether this type of legal and regulatory map has ever been developed before, so legal scholars are encouraged to weigh in with their thoughts.

Postulating the Holy Grail of a Grand Unified Theory of Environmental Law and Regulation

Due to the fragmentation of environmental law, Fisher et al. expressed doubt of the existence of a grand theory of international environmental law,[3] but we shall see that the siloed regulation of environmental media can be configured into a holistic regulatory framework, as we have already seen with the generalized strategy for the generation of multi-media pollution.

Table 10.1 Legal Regimes Applicable to Nature

Legal Regime	Category	Scale	Examples
Protecting & Restoring Nature (e.g., via Reverse CaT)	Inherent Foundational Rights	Macro	The Planet
		Mid	Forests
		Micro	Flora/Fauna
	Eco-Restoration	All Scales	Reforestation
			Endangered Species Reintroduction
Regulating Possible & Present Harms to Nature	Prevention[a]	Macro	Keeping Fossil Fuels Sequestered
		Mid	Refinery Malfunction Prevention Plan
		Micro	Landfill Liner
	Generation	Macro	Set & Decline CO_2 Global Limits
		Mid	Unit Performance Standards
		Micro	Stack Testing
Addressing Past Harms to Nature	Legacy/Torts[b]	Macro	Criminal Deforestation
		Mid	Superfund Sites
		Micro	Past Use of Lead Paint in Homes

a. Not addressed via legal means until only after the hazard occurs.
b. Where legacy pollution creates harm that leads to a tort action, this would not technically be classified as environmental law.

There are actually three prongs to the regulation of pollution—(1) harm prevention (e.g., accidental releases, discharges, and spills) which requires carefully siting sources to prevent, minimize if not eliminate the likelihood of harms with a healthy dose of intensive occupational workplace inspections, (2) minimizing the generation of pollution, as much of this book has already discussed, and (3) remediating legacy pollution. The Holy Grail of a Grand Unified Theory of Environmental Law and Regulation[4] would be the perfect alignment of environmental pollution abatement and remediation with ecological/biodiversity preservation that facilitates the complete ecological stewardship of the environment and its expansion, in conjunction with markets that incorporate consumer behavior, all playing a major role. The Grand Unified Theory would include an embedded economic system whereby the flows of *all* materials are circular, including the generation of CO_2 emissions being removed while Nature's biodiversity is not only preserved but allowed to rewild and prosper again. It is not enough to simply slow the loss of biodiversity; we have to reverse course and facilitate biodiversity *regrowth* so as to achieve an AEGD of zero thereby avoiding having to move to other planets.

While we can set limits on air, water, and on-site generated pollution to address immediately generated harms, we can also set limits on resource extraction and IDPC and IDPC surrogate production and pollution, as well as set national and hopefully international limits on harmful "economic fuel," specifically on the unsustainable use of fossil fuel-based energy, thereby limiting CO_2 emissions. In fact, we may be able to set limits on other regulatory measures of harm, both known and as yet unknown, which implies that we must have the fortitude to address, for example, a city's "nonattainment of upward expansion" by setting limits and externally trade and reduce the cap on that city's area in order to limit and reverse localized habitat intrusion and biodiversity loss.[5]

So where else can limits be used to further the pursuits of attaining sustainability from the grip of nonattainment, and with that in mind, what will be the optimal interplay between regulations and markets?

Developing the Grand Unified Theory is much like creating a "regulatory periodic table," similar to Dmitri Mendeleev's periodic table—the framework is there but more 'elements' need to be found. This is accomplished through the complete and proper integrated balance between economics, law, engineering, the environment, ecology, etc., such as by the incorporation of negative emissions and economic incentivizing to not only reverse biodiversity loss but *revive* biodiversity (e.g., by using reverse CaT based on Gann et al.). Are there missing or underutilized tools which may aid in the development of the Grand Unified Theory? Are there other measures of detriment that engineers or ecologists could develop that can be leveraged via regulation? Are there other fundamental sustainability regulatory measures that are necessary to fill in the Grand Unified Theory's "periodic table"?

Thus, enterprising, ecology-respecting economists, industrial ecologists, and engineers now have a homework assignment—find the set of all tools that will complete the Holy Grail of a Grand Unified Theory. In the meantime, we might be able to develop a broad framework to restore Nature back to health by creatively using the tools we already have at our disposal.

Nature's Global Constitution

As a consequence of reacting to effects rather than regulating causes, practitioners of environmental law have until now been trying for decades to keep up with finding and applying legal methods to address global and regional pollution, resource depletion, ecosystem loss, etc., but our capacity to address these problems have been overwhelmed. Environmental law's response, particularly in the United States, has been to focus on torts and Nature's rights to passively address the gaps in environmental law where suboptimal regulation has heretofore failed to.

Unfortunately, and as noted in Chapter 5, current regulation of air pollution in the United States and elsewhere has often had a pathological focus on the problems at the more localized level (e.g., the factory belching out pollution just upwind), where source compliance rather than regional pollution reduction is the main concern. The best approach would focus on tackling all the necessary tiers of the regulatory hierarchy, that is, at the global, national, and regional levels downward, through a systematic, top-down approach.

When sustainability must be the greater goal, we must break from this myopia and instead adopt a global "Top-Down Hierarchy" of regulation and if that means a few more (efficiently) moving parts than what we have currently, including attaining the global capacity to facilitate this type of "global federalism" via treaties, then so be it. This book, through the broader use of environmental regulation, has circumscribed the necessary tools at the global level to holistically reduce environmental pollution and using many of these same tools to restore Nature. With global regulation so circumscribed, we only need the capacity and political will to achieve these goals.

Speaking of the United States in particular, where it relies on statutes to address human harms onto, and the preservation of, Nature, such statutes are subordinated to the rights engendered by the US Constitution due to its anthropocentric focus, notwithstanding assertions that the US Constitution does address environmental rights to some capacity.[6] To avoid this flaw, we must protect and preserve Nature and the planet so that they coexist sustainably in equilibrium with humanity. Rather than simply establishing a less-than-optimal Bill of Rights for Nature, a more comprehensive Global Constitution/Treaty representing Nature's foundational rights *and* "interests," as if it did not have to grovel with humanity for them, must be developed. Failing to do so would only allow the continual and likely spiral of unsustainability, which begs the question—what is the point of promoting the rights of humanity in an unsustainable world where those very same rights are de facto jeopardized in a calamitous future?

To avoid this scenario, the US Constitution and those of other countries as well must be subordinated to Nature's "Global Constitution" to reflect that humans are a member of Nature but not legally superior to it. The statutes that would represent the operational strategies and policies developed in this book would form the foundation for Nature's Global Constitution. In such a world, the protection and preservation of Nature, human rights, and an embedded economic system must not each be separately siloed, but instead, they should all work symbiotically together in an equilibrium-seeking, steady but evolving state where the AEGD is zero in perpetuity.

A Point That Must Not Be Overlooked

We cannot put a price on fundamental aspects of Nature (e.g., determining the price of insects to birds), so using anthropocentric measures of value to price only what is valuable to humans but not to Nature itself must be remedied, and quickly. Likewise, our current 'primitive' legal system constructed around what is only a means to mediate disputes, maintain order or seek justice for humans and their institutions is also problematic for preserving and sustaining Nature forever. However, the strategies developed in this book indicate that we can at least put a price on preventing humanity's harms imposed on Nature. While not being an immediate cure for these ills, the regulatory architecture of these strategies lend themselves to advancing the reversal of humanity's harmful impacts.

Notes

1 It should be noted that the loss of biodiversity and habitat by clearing an acre of land to construct a house is obviously not a zero-sum game for Nature because as far as the effect on Nature is concerned, the house is more than just an isolated house. A great deal of infrastructural support is baked into "interacting" with it, such as roads, sewer lines, natural gas service lines, etc., and the associated traffic and pollution all acting as harm force multipliers inflicted onto Nature.

2 European Commission, "Water-Energy-Food-Ecosystem Nexus." https://international-partnerships.ec.europa.eu/policies/climate-environment-and-energy/water-energy-food-ecosystem-nexus_en#:~:text=The%20Water%2DEnergy%2DFood%2D,land%20%E2%80%93%20that%20underpin%20that%20security.

3 Elizabeth Fisher, Bettina Lange, Eloise Scotford, et al., "Maturity and Methodology: Starting a Debate about Environmental Law Scholarship," *Journal of Environmental Law* 21, no. 2 (2009): 241.

4 While past authors speak of the "Next Generation" of environmental regulation, one can think of the Holy Grail of a Grand Unified Theory as the "Last Generation," that is, one that is both protective and restorative of Nature (not just for the welfare of humans) and allows humanity to live in "balance" with Nature (as accepted by ecologists).

5 This would encourage growth up rather than out. The reader who considers the idea of using trading to alleviate urban sprawl to be draconian must again be reminded that we are currently in a *severe* state of nonattainment of sustainability with Nature by many different metrics, where reaching an AEGD of zero is critical. Without an exit criterion from our current trajectory, the goal must obviously be to reverse course and achieve sustainability with Nature for the generations that follow.

6 Robin Kundis Craig, "Constitutional Environmental Law, or, the Constitutional Consequences of Insisting that the Environment is Everybody's Business," University of Utah School of Law Research Paper No. 302, *Environmental Law* 49 (2019). https://dc.law.utah.edu/cgi/viewcontent.cgi?article=1262&context=scholarship.

Conclusion

Looking Back and Looking Forward

Looking Back: So Where Have the Economists, Legal Scholars, and Environmental Organizations Been?

This book has shown that, among its accomplishments, attaining a circular economy and achieving some semblance of sustainability with Nature can be facilitated by milestone-based regulation. Besides minor quibbles that the reader may have, this author would assert that at its core, the book's strategies are likely to be the only way to achieve these outcomes. And based on how far our regulatory capabilities can potentially reach in the foreseeable future relative to where it is currently, the strategies show just how primitive environmental regulation has been up to this point. Who knew that a circular economy could be facilitated by holistically regulating detrimental characteristics inherent to products that later become solid waste? Who knew there was a rigorous method to mitigate climate change? Who knew that a trading program could be utilized to restore Nature? Who knew that we can formulate a framework to remediate the planet that fits the outline of a Grand Unified Theory of Environmental Law and Regulation? Who foresaw that based on this framework, we can now contemplate the existence of a Global Constitution that represents the Rights of Nature, without them being subordinated to those of humanity?

This book has exposed major gaps in scholarship, particularly in economics and environmental law. It should be noted that an engineer with an academic background in applied mathematics and a career in environmental regulation added a layer of rigor in conjunction with redesigned environmental regulation to create a far more rational framework to systematically address many of our major global environmental problems. To be abundantly clear, this is not the author expressing arrogance; rather, this is a warning about our current state of scholarship, where few should escape blame. Scholars in economics and environmental law, among others, had ample capability and opportunity to discover these strategies, yet failed to do so in part due to their insular cultures and narrowly focused scope of scholarship.

The Insular Economics Community

Nicholas Stern and Andrew Oswald, both professors of economics themselves, decry the dearth of attention paid to climate change by economists by asserting that "Economists have been too silent on the greatest problem of our age," noting that "the Quarterly Journal of Economics, currently the most-cited journal in our discipline, has published zero articles."[1] The fact that these statements come from economists is as much striking as it is praiseworthy.

So where do mainstream economists stand with regard to the study of the circular economy (CE)? The reader might assume that the literature, unlike that for climate change, is replete with copious amounts of articles written on the subject because "economy" appears in the term, so clearly economists must be studying the subject, right? Oddly enough, this is not the case.[2] The economics community is far more insular than most other academic fields, and it clearly shows with regard to the subject of the CE.[3]

While the CE is a subject of interest in the European Union (EU),[4] although with relatively scant coverage within the economics community itself, it barely registers in the United States.[5] Even the topics of industrial ecology or industrial metabolism are rarely given serious attention except among industrial and environmental engineers.[6] Fullerton et al.[7] conducted a 2021 search of all economics journals and found seventy-one published mentions of the term "circular economy," of which five were published prior to 2016. Of the seventy-one papers, sixty-eight were not from authors in North America; Fullerton indicates that for the most part, economists have never heard of the term. So while the CE has been studied by industrial ecologists, Fullerton encourages economists to conduct research in the various economic aspects of a CE, implicitly indicating that economists have a lot of catching up to do.

Had economists read *Cradle to Cradle* with an eye toward finding the "Waste = Food" solution, they may have discovered the existence of product pollutants (e.g., IDPC surrogates) that they could quantify, the total volumetric limits of which could be declined via one of their favorite market instruments, namely, trading. Yet, economists appear squeamish to even speak of the concept of limits, as if it would challenge their antiquated twentieth-century orthodoxy in this new era. In effect, their silence regarding setting limits to mitigate climate change and facilitate a CE reflects concurrence that they do not yet see any need to repair harms and restore ecosystems; rather, they appear content with the existing status quo.

While economists have weighed in on the water-energy-food nexus problem, this author has little faith that US economists will catalyze further study on the adoption of the generalized strategy to address environmental pollution. By fighting against a true scarcity-based mindset, economists apparently have an engrained bias toward an abundance- and consumption-based linear economy. *Cradle to Cradle* is a book as much about resources and their reuse as it is about pollution, so where some mainstream economists may have read the book, perhaps the words "scarcity" and "limit" are what inhibit them from thinking outside their insular, siloed box to entertain new, fundamentally profound ideas. Apparently economics, again, *the study of the allocation of scarce resources*, is not a subject where economists have seriously postulated the *actual scarcity of resources*. In fact, in times of resource scarcity, many economists have resorted to the faith-based and risk-seeking beliefs that resources can simply be substituted or that technologies will be discovered in the future to address the problems caused by resource scarcity.[8,9,10]

The failure of mainstream economists to appreciate the real-world scarcity of resources and faith in material substitutability is an indication that they have little grounding in the physical characteristics of materials and their limitations. And worse, they have abstracted Nature itself within their academic discipline, a symptom of Nature Deficit Disorder. If one does not see, experience, or acknowledge the impacts of climate change, massive ocean gyres of plastics, or even a tortoise with a plastic straw stuck in its nostril, then the more one would expect that simplistic, dissuasive economic instruments, such as taxation, are the ideal instrument.[11] It is not surprising, then, that achieving sustainability with Nature is not on economists' radar. Apologists and doubters should ask themselves whether mainstream economists factor in the concept of Additional Earths at Global Development in any form in their research, or whether they consider sustainability with Nature to even be a critical goal. When one subscribes to the real-world-based "You Don't Foul Your Own Nest" (YDFYON) School of Economics, a CE is the paradigm that follows Nature more closely. On the other hand, economists, who tend to view ecosystems as an expendable entitlement and waste as valueless, fail to appreciate or factor in real-world ecological "boundary conditions" with Nature within their research, a symptom of their not adhering to the YDFYON School. So while mainstream economists often preach austerity to the have-nots (think of measures proposed by the International Monetary Fund on third-world nations), by their silence, they accept the unsustainable extraction of Nature (natural capital in their eyes) unflinchingly, which smacks of hypocrisy when an austere approach is necessary. The true test of economics is not to immediately default to the convenient and expendable exploitation of Nature and its ecosystems but to truly working within the "pure" economic system embedded within and minimally dependent on Nature.

The study of the CE should already be an economic subdiscipline generating argument, perspective, and solutions, yet based on how little the subject arises in the economics literature, one can only conclude that it is treated as a quaint topic, where such publications are not likely to ensure tenure.

As environmental agencies adopt the generalized strategy to minimize pollution and set the CE and climate change mitigation strategies in motion, economists can no longer ignore the concept where setting limits on pollution gains primacy. It would be difficult for a social science that prides itself on rigor to be dismissive of the rigor that promotes sustainability with Nature. There should be nothing controversial about adopting a CE and mitigating climate change unless we actually don't want to minimize the generation of environmental pollution and restore ecosystems.

It has been stated multiple times that the engineering, legal and economic disciplines, regulators, and the public will all play a part, and that no one discipline "solves" the problem of controlling and eliminating pollution.[12] While environmental scholars wish to find the right blend of laws and regulations to facilitate reform of the CAA, this author has not seen much from the mainstream economics community regarding how they would optimally regulate the generation of environmental pollution (putting a dissuasion-based price on greenhouse gases does not qualify).

As a consequence of their insularity, economists are rarely experts in natural or physical science, particularly ecology or thermodynamics; in fact, they are likely unaware of the very critical role that the Second Law of Thermodynamics plays in the economic system (recall Herman Daly's quote from Chapter 9). Yet the fact that they assert that scientists and engineers will somehow find future solutions to today's calamities is another red flag that mainstream economists are out of their element when it comes to addressing ecological problems.[13] It would seem that economists' only solution is the same old canards regarding taxing and pricing, with a little CO_2 emissions trading thrown in for good measure.

If we truly want to stay on one planet, the mainstream economics community must pivot quickly to catch up with other scholarly disciplines with regard to the seriousness of the mission at hand. Their key role will be to research how to transition from our current growth economy to a sharing economy where the benefit of a consumer good replaces ownership instead. This will help alleviate our global environmental calamities by properly addressing twenty-first-century ecological realities. If, on the other hand, they cannot muster the will to contribute to the solution, the least they can do is avoid being part of the problem.

The Community of Environmental Legal Scholars

Much of what has been leveled at the economics community can also be laid at the feet of the current generation of environmental legal scholars. There was discussion of legal reform in years past, but what has come of it since? More practically, where in the US legal community has there been any discussion of how to reform environmental laws to achieve a circular economy and address sustainability with nature?

In conducting the research for this book, the author read a large number of articles, many of which, of course, were written by environmental legal scholars. Besides a few scholars who have an excellent grasp of environmental law, it is not uncommon for many environmental legal scholars to use their writing in law review journals to assert that someone (else) ought to do something rather than doing the heavy lifting themselves; the reader does not have to take this author's word for it:

> While some law review articles are largely descriptive, a normative claim is an element of most legal scholarship. Often that normative claim takes the form of an argument that legal decision-makers—legislators, agency officials, or, particularly often, judges—ought to do something differently.[14,15]

Does not legal scholarship imply active "upstream" problem-solving ability, much like an offensive coordinator developing strategies in football? Or has the law degree entitled many scholars to simply articulate a problem in detail or only provide passive "downstream" color commentary to the play on the field?

Physicists Ralph Alpher and Robert Herman predicted *here on Earth* (!) the existence of a 5 degree Kelvin background temperature in deep space, and several years later scientists measured it to be 2.7 degrees Kelvin—not too far off. Atmospheric chemists, F. Sherwood Rowland and Mario Molina, predicted that CFCs harm the ozone layer, which was later discovered to be true. In contrast, the fact that virtually all environmental legal scholars have not even theorized how to rigorously achieve a circular economy as an outcome of regulating the generation of solid waste indicates not only that such environmental legal scholars have been asleep at the switch but also that the field is still in a relatively primitive state of development.

Within mathematics scholarship, one sees research in both abstract and applied mathematics scholarship, the latter of which is conducted to solve real-world problems in engineering and science. There is mutual respect among mathematicians for both abstract and applied mathematics, both inside and outside the university. There is certainly a role for abstract mathematics, but without the applied version, a good chunk of engineering research would be handicapped. In contrast, it seems that most everyone within environmental legal scholarship wants to be a nonrigorous, pondering theorist and/or commentator/pundit; to add insult to injury, there appears to be a condescending culture where rigorous research in or the teaching of "applied environmental law" is discouraged as a means to actually *solve* real-world environmental problems at the macrolevel.[16] As a consequence, there is little interest in exchanging knowledge and lessons learned with practitioners in the trenches. If this gap had been filled decades ago in law schools throughout the country, the regulatory means to facilitate a circular economy and broaden the concept of sustainability with Nature would likely have been uncovered and encouraged long before now.

If the role of environmental legal scholars is not to solve problems, what exactly *is* their role within the university where conducting top-notch, problem-solving research is the norm at the other colleges and departments at the university (think physics or biology)?[17] And if environmental legal scholars feel that they are not equipped to solve problems but where their op-ed/punditry-like review articles implore someone else to do so instead, who *exactly* do they expect *will* solve these problems?[18,19,20] One need speculate no further as to why environmental regulatory reform has proceeded at a glacial pace over the decades—legal scholars have been expecting someone else to do it. And if the expectation is for politicians to solve them, that is a recipe for disappointment, if not outright disaster.

Legal scholars cannot have it both ways—they cannot call themselves scholars, equivalent to those in, say, the chemistry department, but then claim that they are entitled to only provide normative color commentary to the world of law.

Brent Newton, formerly with the United States Sentencing Commission at American University, would understand this author's incredulity. Newton's two papers on the flaws of legal scholarship[21] speak very well to this author's experience reading a multitude of journal articles written by environmental legal scholars. There are many flaws that could be cited here, but of those that Newton addresses, what drives the point home well is the fact that Supreme Court Justice John Roberts[22] and former Appellate Court Judge Richard Posner both consider legal review articles to be of little use to them as members of the bench.[23] In addition, while interdisciplinary research is strongly advocated, it is usually done where crossing disciplines is undertaken in the social sciences. While this is in some cases useful, this approach has been favored far more than crossing into the natural or physical sciences, where breakthroughs such as those inspired by *Cradle to Cradle* could have been discovered much earlier. Lastly, with rigorously peer-reviewed journal articles in science and engineering as the standard of reference, the fact that there is a lack of equivalent rigorous peer review of many law review articles should give the reader great pause as to the quality of those articles.

The author, who came from an academic background in engineering, physics, and mathematics, finds it perplexing and frightening that many law journals have such lower standards for legal scholarship. The reader does not have to take this author's word for it; the skeptical reader is strongly urged to read through Newton's articles or Adam Liptak's piece in the *New York Times*.[24] They are an eye-opener, and they explain much of what this author has encountered as part of his background research.

In contrast to academic legal scholars, it is worthwhile noting that critical innovations to environmental regulation have in fact been proposed by practitioners like Cynthia Giles, who has spent much of her career with the USEPA. She and her USEPA colleagues proposed Next Gen principles whereby compliance is built into the rules. In addition, this author has been a career air pollution regulator/practitioner with a state agency. The point is that practitioners clearly observe problems and craft solutions in much finer detail than academics that tend to be far removed from the action. Giles has arguably given a homework assignment to legal scholars and others to develop Next Gen regulatory solutions that will have real-world application, yet this author is doubtful that those same scholars will undertake the challenge.[25]

While legal experience practiced "in the trenches" can focus on a wider array of problems, when legal scholarship in the academic literature is put under the microscope, one observes an almost pathological obsession to continue tinkering at the margins of environmental legal theory by beating to death the minutia of certain general topics, such as the use of cap-and-trade versus market instruments, the track record of the Acid Rain Program, or the pros and cons of using cost-benefit analysis.[26] These topics usually apply to situations that are narrowly encountered in air pollution regulation that are also not all that relevant to and/or do not address multifaceted real-world realities at the macrolevel where these realities are manifested.[27] Metaphorically speaking, one can think of legal scholars examining individual jigsaw puzzle pieces under a microscope when the far more critical problem is that of macroscopically determining how those pieces must be put together to complete the larger puzzle.

In general, assembling multiple micro-scale pieces together to actually apply environmental regulation to solve macro-scale problems in the face of worldwide calamity is not common. Mamlyuk's paper comes immediately to mind, but to their credit also, Schoenbrod et al. and Robert Nordhaus were scholars who at least attempted to assemble a few of those pieces to reform the CAA, while Maitre-Ekern was a rare legal scholar who attempted to tackle the circular economy problem.

The "fiduciary" obligation of environmental law should be its unwavering focus on achieving sustainability with Nature; anything less is malfeasance. The technical solutions developed in this book will very likely scare off the insular legal community, yet it is the very technical aspects of the generalized strategy that will make all the difference in making significant progress in addressing our global, regional, and local environmental problems. There is clearly creative talent in the legal community[28] but what problems have they been tackling that justify their lack of attention to true reform and solving the problem of achieving sustainability with Nature? Without question, the legal community, just like the economics community, must also get with the twenty-first-century program, and quickly.

The Environmental Community Including Anti-Trading Dogmatists

An entrenched culture is not unique to economists and the legal community. Let's not forget about many members of the environmental community who, much to their credit, have been on the front lines of the climate crisis but not so much as it pertains to the subject of the CE, a cause one would think would be a top priority for them. Other than their cynicism that manufacturers are greenwashing when they claim to be in favor of a CE, it is surprising to find little progressive discussion from American environmental NGOs regarding how to achieve a CE. Simply proposing the banning of single-use plastics is woefully inadequate.

Some close-minded environmentalists and environmental NGOs have also been strong opponents of trading (because it supposedly gives polluters the so-called "right to pollute"),[29,30] helping to easily lose more than a decade of potential progress for failing to, even theoretically, posit how trading could be applied to *Cradle to Cradle* principles. If they had been more open-minded, this may have led to a strategy to facilitate the transition to a CE much, much sooner.

As this author was reading *Cradle to Cradle*, soon after having just developed the comprehensive strategy, it was apparent that the concept of IDPC/IDPC surrogates could be developed, quantified, and thus rendered tradable. This created a huge opening for exploring the transfer of external trading to more general use by regulating the technology-induced generation of multi-media environmental pollution, including its utility as a means to transition to a CE.

Environmental lawyers employed by environmental NGOs seem to suffer from the same afflictions as their colleagues in academia, namely, lacking the know-how to, and/or being fearful of, applying technical concepts and tools to creatively and rigorously improve regulation. That deficiency, coupled in some cases with close-minded anti-trading mindsets, rendered the NGO community impotent to even propose plausible reform of environmental regulation. NGOs' skittishness to compromise their loyalty to existing Old Green Laws to accept new approaches shows just how mired they are, a great point made by Ruhl and Salzman as it pertains to the Green New Deal.[31]

One could argue that those with access to the proper legal skills and economic tools, and most at the forefront to solve environmental problems, that is, environmental legal professionals and economists, respectively, suffer from apathy and antipathy to do so. On the other hand, those with the strongest passion to solve those problems, that is, the environmental NGOs, either do not possess the proper skills and tools or they lack the interest to do so. Here's the odd irony—as an environmental engineer with a strong applied mathematics and regulatory practitioner background, this author promoted regulation (within the domain of environmental law) and the use of cap-and-trade (within the domain of economics), the latter of which is distrusted if not disliked by some in the environmental community. The point is that, unlike academics, this author was unencumbered by insular mindsets or fears to use advanced tools that allowed for the development of strategies to address major global environmental problems.

And Then There Is Everyone Else . . .

The economics, legal, and environmental NGO communities are not the only ones to have been stuck in twentieth-century linear mindsets. Only a fraction of corporations claim to be socially responsible, and a subset of those probably are, implying that many companies recoil at the very thought of regulating their manufactured products for the benefit of Nature, the environment, and society at large. It goes without saying that policymakers have also been absent, other than by proposing half-hearted, half-measure solutions to environmental problems. And only a fraction of consumers seem to care.

It is no wonder we've fallen behind, chasing after approaches to major environmental problems that continually outpace us, particularly in the US—people in various disciplines and professions have been locked into antiquated mindsets and are unable to think outside their respective boxes. These failures reflect a decades-long dark era in environmental legal reform.

Looking Forward

While this book presents a model for moving environmental regulation in a significantly different direction to achieve sustainability with Nature, there is still much more homework to do. Getting the generalized strategy up and running will require the following:

- So that trading programs can function with more accurate data, improved methods must be found to better measure air pollution emissions from various emission units.
- Environmental engineers and legal scholars must determine the appropriate strategies for the generation of water pollution, on-site generated waste, and scrap pollution.
- Determining the performance standards for on-site generated waste and other pollution that have not yet been determined.

- Developing the applicable, Next Gen-friendly regulations for the various media (e.g., air, water, on-site).
- Developing, measuring, and simplifying IDPC/IDPC surrogate pollutant MoDs and those of other necessary "quantifiables."
- Developing the characteristic standards for the wide variety of products, including those for plastic and other nonbiodegradable products.
- Very critically, the process redesigns and technological innovations to facilitate product changes must be determined. This task will proceed in perpetuity.
- Next Gen principles must be furthered:
  - The work of Giles and her colleagues must undertake the "science of compliance," for example, by examining when rules achieve the greatest level of compliance; the legal theorists in academia should put their efforts to work on this and not rely on practitioners to do the work.
  - Giles notes that with regard to a trading program, "The entire program has to be structured to be self-executing; leaving out just one element that results in significant need for continuous government intervention has the potential to derail program effectiveness."[32] The strategies developed in this book will not facilitate compliance by themselves, so Giles's advice must be respected and followed.

    A key question to answer is whether it is better to use the strategies developed in this book if they are not yet Next Gen-friendly but we work to upgrade them, or is it better to have a less optimal strategy that is far more Next Gen-friendly? It is this author's opinion that the former has to be the primary goal.
- Economists have plenty of research to conduct with regard to the economic mechanics of a circular economy. Fullerton's paper is a great place to find research ideas.
- How to prevent pollution such as accidental and nonpoint source pollution via design is a homework assignment targeted at environmental engineers.

The significance of Next Generation Compliance cannot be stressed enough. The first step is getting the goal and its underlying regulatory process to achieve it correct, and only then applying Next Gen glue to that package to build in compliance. If Next Gen is unworkable for a rule, then it likely means that the rule is fundamentally flawed to begin with and/or the underlying methodology is not yet firm enough (e.g., it relies too much on trust without verification).

Next Gen is only compatible with sound policy and cannot patch shoddy policy; instead, such policy must be reformed. As stated previously, a key component is the incorporation of "certified sustainability accountants," whose role is to verify pollutant quantification that is used in trading programs. These are not environmental consultants but instead highly credentialed professionals who are randomly assigned to review the calculations of the trading program participants. Rather than putting the burden of determining compliance on the backs of the regulators, the goal is to put the onus onto the polluters (i.e., the polluter pays).

Beyond the generalized strategy itself, there are additional homework assignments to hand out:

- We must strategize how we transition from where we are to where we must go. In the same vein as Ruhl and Salzman, we have to determine how we transition away from our current Green Laws to applying the generalized strategy, restoring ecosystems and achieving sustainability with Nature.
- While this book focuses more on addressing global problems that require global and regional measures, there are still work practice-related problems created at the local level by individual actors who will remain unaffected by enforceable regulation. These problems include overfishing, the burning of residual crops, farmland erosion, and forest clear-cutting. While the methods developed in this book will help to indirectly mitigate these problems, there will always be individual rogue actors who are unfazed by regulation. There are other regulatory gaps that must be filled in, including the patching of regulations that are designed to reduce the harms to Nature and those that attempt to restore Nature. Establishing the underlying "Rights of Nature" and compensation for inflicted harms will play a significant role by creating a solid backstop to environmental regulation.
- The details of a global mitigation strategy for the use of virgin materials to facilitate a global CE should also be developed, including the applicable PCPSs for them.
- For a regulatory strategy to achieve agricultural sustainability (that only just scratches the surface of regulation), the resource usage performance standards for the various inputs must be determined.
- Expanding on the early work of Monteduro,[33] the agricultural sustainability problem based on agroecological principles has to be developed, probably

much like Gann et al.'s ecosystem restoration scheme, with the likely use of reverse cap-and-trade.

- Research needs to be conducted with major input by ecologists to determine how to patch the interface between harm reduction and ecological restoration, particularly those tough cases where ecosystems are locally harmed with the intent to achieve regional and global sustainability; how to minimize these situations is a key assignment.
- The complete set of all tools that will lead to the achievement of the Holy Grail of a Grand Unified Theory must be found.
- Legal scholars should also address the issues raised by Farber regarding rule enforcement "slippage," that is, the tendency for rule enforcement to be unenthusiastically applied, neglected, ignored, etc.[34]
- One suggestion is for law departments to develop courses on Next Generation Compliance 101, including how to write crisp rules and regulations that conform to Next Gen principles. Since the mere existence of regulatory strategies is no guarantee of future compliance, legal scholars must also take Giles's lead and develop "legal enforceability manuals" that rigorously demonstrate how to build compliance into the rules and the corresponding enforceable boilerplate conditions that permits should incorporate. If achieving sustainability is as important as we claim it is, rather than associating their all-too-common interdisciplinary studies with economics, legal scholars should instead develop the legal expertise in eco-studies and ecological restoration. They can start with the work of Gann et al. (see Chapter 9) and that of Cliquet and Decleer.[35]
- It is not enough to only focus on externally regulating the generation of externalities that harm the environment. Sustainability with Nature includes regulating structural issues that undermine it. Thus, sustainability includes (1) building in Next Gen-like compliance, including setting and enforcing corporate performance standards and specifying corporate purpose directly within the corporate charter itself,[36] (2) properly delineating the applicable (and nonapplicable) rights of corporations to constrain corporate excess, and (3) designing corporate law as necessary to balance the interests of stakeholders.
- Beyond what has already been developed in this book, to avoid the sluggish regulatory process and lawsuits due to excess discretion, scholars and practitioners of all types must determine which aspects of regulation need the least built-in discretion to achieve its environmental goals.

- Since regulated entities resent anything resembling "regulation by enforcement," attorneys should develop "certainty guidelines" for regulated entities, such as categories of violations and penalties based on deviations, excursions, minor violations, etc. In the spirit of Schakenbach, Vollaro, and Forte, enforcement attorneys should specify the relationship between violations and penalties, in some cases spelling out the penalty within the rule itself (much like the Acid Rain Program).
- Developing an international global environmental legacy treaty, much like Flournoy's National Environmental Legacy Act, is critical.[37]
- One last major assignment is changing the inertially entrenched, insular economics and legal culture within academia (and within society itself) to facilitate the cultivation of fresh new ideas. Innovation and reform have stagnated within environmental economic and legal scholarship, due in part to cultures that resist innovative and nonconformist ideas from scholars outside and within their respective scholarly ecosystems. It would not be an exaggeration to assert that such scholars must focus their professional attention on the mission of achieving sustainability with Nature rather than writing abstract journal articles that few people read for the purpose of achieving tenure. Although likely to be wishful thinking, economics and environmental legal scholars must be required to have sufficient coursework in ecology and environmental science to understand their role within the larger ecosystem. To conform to scholarship in the hard sciences and mathematics today, law schools must complement abstract legal research in environmental law with applied research so as to fill the major void that exists between the current plethora of color commentary and the rare development of usable legal strategies applied to real-world environmental problems. Again, while a great number of legal review articles had been written so that legal scholars could achieve tenure, the development of a *regulatory* strategy to achieve a circular economy and much more was discovered by an engineer.

This is an incomplete listing of the necessary homework assignments, but the results will provide significant benefits. Accomplishing these tasks will not be easy, but they are necessary. That said, it is certainly possible that the methodologies developed in this book may be too clunky, but even more efficient ways to achieve the same ends may be discovered by subsequent researchers.[38]

If an economist touts a car's stellar fuel efficiency while onlookers raise alarms about the car careening toward a cliff, which factor takes priority? Thus, whenever anyone proposes a project that will incur environmental or ecological damage, the immediate question one must ask is, will it promote an Additional Earths at Global Development [AEGD] goal of zero? What externalities are created that will not be "priced in"?

Changing Behavior and Overcoming Hurdles

Will advanced economies change their habits and adopt the generalized strategy? Maybe, but there will be hurdles.

It should be expected that there will be plenty of environmental calamity skeptics who will refuse to be socially conscious and responsible. The "abundance mindset" diehards who are only comfortable with incremental change will scoff at capping and phasing down the generation of waste, not to mention the need to restore Nature, seeing it as an infringement on economic growth at literally all costs. Such skeptics inflicted by Nature Deficit Disorder should only voice their skepticism after viewing the various visual depictions of the existing and ongoing calamities found in videos and photos scattered across the internet, if not view them in person.

There are also likely to be environmental advocates who may avidly support the concept of sustainability with Nature but who subconsciously like their conveniences more and exhibit cognitive dissonance when they ask if there is a better, less inconvenient way. One need only observe here in the United States just how little regard there is with achieving a circular economy.

Just like we saw earlier in Chapter 4 with nonattainment areas and mandatory external trading, if we say that CO_2 emissions and IDPC/IDPC surrogates create truly *major* problems for our environment, *then we must treat them like it.* Commerce that relies on a "take, make, consume, dispose"-based paradigm must adapt to a new commercial paradigm with a material reuse component, and all the aspects of the paradigm shift that come with it.

Likewise, we—consumers, companies, decision makers, etc.—can't simply think selfishly about how inconvenienced we would be in the here and now by a new regulatory paradigm without taking steps to resolve the environmental issues we currently face and their long-term impacts for the generations that follow.

Notes

1 Nicholas Stern and Andrew Oswald, "Why are Economists Letting Down the World on Climate Change?" September 19, 2017. https://cepr.org/voxeu/columns/why-are-economists-letting-down-the-world-climate-change.

2 It cannot be comforting for economists to learn that McDonough (co-author of *Cradle to Cradle*) and Stahel (author of *The Circular Economy: A User's Guide*) were two architects who theorized the nature of a CE before they did.

3 Marion Fourcade, Ettienne Ollion, and Yann Algan, "The Superiority of Economists," *Journal of Economic Perspectives* 29, no. 1 (2015). This article speaks quite well to this insularity.

4 Beyond David Pearce, R. Kerry Turner, Ken Webster, and Kate Raworth, there just aren't that many scholars in the field of economics who are known prominently for their study of the CE. Even the suggestions made by those in the EU tend to focus on post-production economic tools (e.g., taxing and pricing) rather than point-of-production regulation.

5 One exception, discussed earlier in Chapter 6, was the paper by Manderson and Considine, where on page 318, they advocate for economists to play a greater role in the field of industrial ecology.

6 One exception is the following paper that contrasts industrial ecology, ecological economics, and circular economy: Aurélien Bruel, Jakub Kronenberg, Nadège Troussier, et al., "Linking Industrial Ecology and Ecological Economics," *Journal of Industrial Ecology* 23, no. 1 (2018).

7 Don Fullerton, Callie W. Babbitt, Melissa M. Bilec, et al., "Introducing the Circular Economy to Economists," *Annual Review of Resource Economics* 14 (2022).

8 Allwood, "Material Efficiency," 74–5. Allwood provides excellent counterarguments to these economists' assertions. Besides Allwood's counterarguments, another obvious one is the fact that while groundwater can theoretically be replaced by distant surface water sources, albeit at enormous cost, it cannot realistically be substituted for. Note that finding alternate sources may only be a temporary solution since population and economic growth will simply render the resource becoming scarce anyway.

9 Given that economists assert that resources can simply be substituted, it would seem that they believe that the goal is sustainability with something other than Nature (e.g., physical or monetary capital). This notion is cringeworthy on many levels since it fails to respect, among other considerations, the Second Law of Thermodynamics (e.g., the increased heating due to climate change); the economists' answer to which is simple dissuasive taxation and the overreliance on future technological development. Economists have no answer to how to remediate

legacy pollution such as groundwater polluted by persistent chemical contaminants. Lastly, many mainstream economists disrespect the inherent value of biodiversity and ecosystems; to them, these are simply commodities whose only purpose is for the exploitation by humankind. See Heather Klemick and R. David Simpson, "Market Economy and Biodiversity," in *Encyclopedia of Biodiversity, Volume 5, (2nd Edition)*, ed. Simon A. Levin (Academic Press, 2013).

It is difficult to imagine the dystopian world where economists view raw materials nonchalantly being substituted when virgin materials are depleted, unremediable legacy pollution is simply taxed, and where biodiversity is treated as nothing more than a resource input.

10 Just to be clear, this author does not lump Herman Daly, an ecological economist, in with mainstream economists.

11 While dissuasive methods can be useful during periods of attainment to *prevent* deterioration, once a state of nonattainment is reached, corrective measures are called for instead. These latter measures will reduce the ongoing impact on Nature, but may not by themselves remediate physical harms already inflicted on it; more intensive ecosystem restoration techniques would likely be required.

12 In Chapter 1, the article "How Economics Solved Acid Rain" (https://www.edf.org/approach/markets/acid-rain) was shown to be flawed because (1) it was the setting and declining of caps, a regulatory prescription (clearly not economics), that "solved" the acid rain problem, where trading was only a tool that facilitated the necessary reductions; and (2) the task of abating pollution *is a team effort* whereby the engineering, legal, and economic disciplines, as well as regulators, all played a part.

13 Needless to say, economists expecting and relying on the physical science disciplines to solve global problems exacerbated by the social science of economics smacks of professional malfeasance. This includes the assumption that we will have the ability to emigrate timely to another planet after ours becomes unlivable. Economics cannot be foundational if it must rely on outside solutions; ecological economics, since it would be far more tethered to respecting Nature's preservation, is clearly more foundational.

14 Dave Owen and Caroline Noblet, "Interdisciplinary Research and Environmental Law," *Ecology Law Quarterly* 41, no. 4 (2015): 44. https://repository.uchastings.edu/cgi/viewcontent.cgi?article=2230&context=faculty_scholarship.

15 Unfortunately, as much as Giles espouses the need to adopt critical Next Gen concepts, she is long on providing wise suggestions for improvement and what doesn't work; she is short on the actual substance of how Next Gen rules should specifically be written.

16 Exhibit A in this regard is the paucity of any quality papers that moved the needle over the last several years regarding environmental regulatory reform or how

to write better regulations and facilitate better enforcement based on Next Gen principles.

17 This is not meant to be a rhetorical question.

18 To support the assertion, see: Daniel C. Esty, "Red Lights to Green Lights: From 20th Century Environmental Regulation to 21st Century Sustainability," *Environmental Law* 47, no. 1 (2017). Esty's otherwise insightful paper paints with broad strokes what needs to be done to reform environmental regulation to reach sustainability, but much like other environmental legal scholars, he fails to provide any rigorous how-to specifics, presumably leaving the solution to others.

19 As a reality check, scholars in mathematics, engineering, and the hard sciences who provide sideline pontifications and pass the buck to other scholars to do the heavy lifting of problem-solving would not get tenure.

20 This is also not a rhetorical question.

21 Brent E. Newton, "Preaching What They Practice: Why Law Faculties' Preoccupation with Impractical Scholarship and Devaluation of Practical Competencies Obstruct Reform in the Legal Academy," *South Carolina Law Review* 62, no. 1 (2010); and Brent E. Newton, "Law Review Scholarship in the Eyes of the Twenty-First Century Supreme Court Justices: An Empirical Analysis," *Drexel Law Review* 4 (2012).

22 Newton, "Law Review Scholarship," 399. Newton cites Bravin, among other authors, to provide support for his discussion: Jess Bravin, "Chief Justice Roberts on Obama, Justice Stevens, Law Reviews, More," *Wall Street Journal Law Blog*, April 7, 2010. http://blogs.wsj.com/law/2010/04/07/chief-justice-roberts-on-obama-justice-stevens-law-reviews-more. The reader is strongly urged to see the other citations in Footnote 1 of Newton's Law Review Scholarship article.

23 That said, cynics may be justified to assert that some Supreme Court justices choose to use their position to set policy, so that they see no need to read the relevant works of legal scholars.

24 Adam Liptak, "The Lackluster Reviews That Lawyers Love To Hate," October 21, 2013. https://www.nytimes.com/2013/10/22/us/law-scholarships-lackluster-reviews.html.

25 The following is not a rhetorical question—do environmental legal scholars have something more important to do than solve critical environmental legal problems posed by legal practitioners in the trenches?

26 On the other hand, except for the work of Driesen and Sinden, squeamishness to even discuss the necessary imposition of limits as a prerequisite to reducing harms or achieving sustainability is conspicuous by its absence within the legal literature despite the oft-cited success of the Acid Rain Program.

27 An obvious example is again the use of the misguided notion of taxing CO_2 emissions as a means to attain climate stability. As population grows, so do

emissions; thus, taxing emissions only discourages them rather than actually reducing the global total to levels that *guarantee* achievement of attainment. Yet, after Mamlyuk published his paper in 2010 (cited in the Introduction and later in Chapter 4), this zombie idea continues to crop up.

It is this author's opinion that Mamlyuk's article is grossly underappreciated. In his paper, he postulated the need for holistic regulation that presciently factored in ecosystems, a rarity within environmental legal scholarship. While he was not rigorous, his "head-in-the-game" insights far outpaced the vast majority of legal and economic scholars at that time. Unfortunately, little work has been conducted since 2010 to further the biosphere quality model, scholars having apparently ignored his work.

28 One legal scholar that this author feels belongs on the Mount Rushmore of environmental legal scholars is Dan Tarlock. The following articles provide outstanding insights: "Is There a There There in Environmental Law?" *Florida State University Journal of Land Use and Environmental Law* 19, no. 2 (2018); "Is a Substantive, Non-Positive United States Environmental Law Possible?" *Michigan Journal of Environmental & Administrative Law* 1 (2012); and "Why There Should Be No Restatement of Environmental Law," *Brooklyn Law Review* 79, no. 2 (2014). Readers may find it of interest that Mount Rushmore was named after Charles Rushmore, a New York lawyer.

29 Excluded are the Environmental Defense Fund and the Nature Conservancy since they are pro-trading.

30 As a reminder to the reader, the National Research Council (NRC) highlighted the major reductions in pollution through the use of trading programs.

31 J. B. Ruhl and James Salzman, "What Happens When the Green New Deal Meets the Old Green Laws?" *Vermont Law Review* 44, no. 4 (Summer 2020).

32 Giles, *Next Generation Compliance*, 17.

33 Massimo Monteduro, "Environmental Law and Agroecology. Transdisciplinary Approach to Public Ecosystem Services as a New Challenge for Environmental Legal Doctrine," *European Energy and Environmental Law Review* (2013).

34 Daniel A. Farber, "Taking Slippage Seriously: Noncompliance and Creative Compliance in Environmental Law," *Harvard Environmental Law Review* 23 (1999).

35 An Cliquet and Kris Decleer, "Linking Restoration Science and Law," in *Ecological Restoration Law*, ed. Afshin Akhtar-Khavari and Benjamin J. Richardson (Routledge, 2019).

36 While this endeavor would break new ground and raise concerns among corporations, embedding compliance into the corporate charter would be little different than embedding source-specific requirements within a pollution permit, a charter effectively being an "operating permit" for the corporation itself.

37 Alyson C. Flournoy, Ryan Feinberg, Margaret Clune Giblin, et al., "The Future of Environmental Protection: The Case for a National Environmental Legacy Act," Center for Progressive Reform White Paper #1002 (2010).

38 The author is reminded of Edward O. Thorp's book, *Beat The Dealer* (Vintage, 1966), which showed readers how to count cards when playing Blackjack. The numbers in Thorp's tables were difficult to memorize, which made the task of counting cards difficult also. Subsequent authors devised better methods to count cards, likely motivated by Thorp being the first mover.

Bibliography

Allwood, Julian M. "Material Efficiency: Squaring the Circular Economy: Recycling within a Hierarchy of Material Management Strategies." In *Handbook of Recycling: State-of-the-art for Practitioners, Analysts, and Scientists, 2nd Edition*, edited by Christina Meskers, Ernst Worrell, and Markus A. Reuter. Elsevier, 2024.

Assadourian, Erik, and John Mulrow. "'Til Sustainability Do You Part: Arranging a Marriage Between Degrowth and the Circular Economy." *Resilience.* October 3, 2018. https://www.resilience.org/stories/2018-10-03/til-sustainability-do-you-part-arranging-a-marriage-between-degrowth-and-the-circular-economy.

Assessment of the Effectiveness of European Air Quality Policies and Measures. Case Study 2: Comparison of the EU & US AQ Standards & Planning Requirements. https://ec.europa.eu/environment/archives/cafe/activities/pdf/case_study2.pdf.

Backes, Chris. *Law For a Circular Economy.* Eleven International Publishing, 2017.

Backes, Chris. "Recycling, Law, and the Circular Economy." In *Handbook of Recycling: State-of-the-art for Practitioners, Analysts, and Scientists, 2nd Edition,* edited by Christina Meskers, Ernst Worrell, and Markus A. Reuter. Elsevier, 2024.

Bakker, C. A., R. Wever, Ch. Teoh, and S. De Clerq. "Designing Cradle to Cradle Products: A Reality Check." *International Journal of Sustainable Engineering* 3, no. 1 (March 2010).

Bjørn, Anders, and Michael Z. Hauschild. "Cradle To Cradle and LCA." In *Life Cycle Assessment: Theory and Practice*, edited by Michael Hauschild, Ralph Rozenbaum, and Stig Irving Olsen. Springer, 2018.

Bocken, Nancy M. P., Elsa A. Olivetti, Jonathan M. Cullen, José Potting, and Reid Lifset. "Taking the Circularity to the Next Level: A Special Issue on the Circular Economy." *Journal of Industrial Ecology* 21, no. 3 (June 2017).

Bocken, Nancy M. P., Paavo Ritala, and Pontus Huotari. "The Circular Economy: Exploring the Introduction of the Concept Among S&P 500 Firms." *Journal of Industrial Ecology* 21, no. 3 (June 2017).

Bratspies, Rebecca. "Sustainability: Can Law Meet the Challenge?" *Suffolk Transnational Law Review* 34, no. 2 (2011).

Bruel, Aurélien, Jakob Kronenberg, Nadège Troussier, and Bertrand Guillaume. "Linking Industrial Ecology and Ecological Economics." *Journal of Industrial Ecology* 23, no. 1 (2018).

Cabezas, Heriberto. "Using Sustainability Metrics and Indicators to Design Sustainable Supply Chains." Presentation at the University of Pannonia. National Risk Management Research Laboratory, 2010. https://slideplayer.com/slide/10565526.

Case, David. "The Lost Generation: Environmental Regulatory Reform in the Era of Congressional Abdication." *Duke Environmental Law & Policy Forum* 25, no. 1 (Fall 2014).

Cliquet, An, and Kris Decleer. "Linking Restoration Science and Law." In *Ecological Restoration Law*, edited by Afshin Akhtar-Khavari and Benjamin J. Richardson. Routledge, 2019.

Coglianese, Cary. "Evaluating Regulatory Performance." *University of Pennsylvania Journal of Law & Public Affairs* 8, no. 1 (2023). https://scholarship.law.upenn.edu/jlpa/vol8/iss1/8.

Congressional Research Service. *The Regional Greenhouse Gas Initiative: Background, Impacts, and Selected Issues.* Congressional Research Service, 2019. https://fas.org/sgp/crs/misc/R41836.pdf.

Copeland, Claudia. *Clean Air Permitting: Implementation and Issues.* Congressional Research Service, 2016. https://fas.org/sgp/crs/misc/RL33632.pdf.

Craig, Robin Kundis. "Constitutional Environmental Law, or, the Constitutional Consequences of Insisting that the Environment is Everybody's Business." University of Utah School of Law Research Paper No. 302. *Environmental Law* 49 (2019). https://dc.law.utah.edu/cgi/viewcontent.cgi?article=1262&context=scholarship.

Crespo-Varela, Josue R., Gül E. Okudan Kremer, Conrad S. Tucker, and Lourdes A. Medina. "An Analysis of Complexity Measures for Product Design and Development." *Proceedings of the ASME 2012 International Design Engineering Technical Conferences & Computers and Information in Engineering Conference*, August 2012. https://www.researchgate.net/publication/258022441_An_Analysis_of_Complexity_Measures_in_Product_Design_and_Development.

Cullen, Jonathan M. "Circular Economy: Theoretical Benchmark or Perpetual Motion Machine." *Journal of Industrial Ecology* 21, no. 3 (June 2017).

Daly, Herman. "Economics for a Full World." Great Transition Initiative, June 2015. www.greattransition.org/publication/economics-for-a-full-world.

Davenport, C. "After Nobel in Economics, William Nordhaus Talks about Who's Getting His Pollution-Tax Ideas Right." *New York Times*, October 13, 2018. https://www.nytimes.com/2018/10/13/climate/nordhaus-carbon-tax-interview.html.

Davies, Terry, Robert Hersh, Aracely Alicea, and Ruth Greenspan Bell. *Reforming Permitting.* Resources for the Future [RFF], 2001.

Deloitte. "Circular Economy: From Theory to Practice." Infographic, September 8, 2017. https://www2.deloitte.com/content/dam/Deloitte/fi/Documents/risk/Circular%20economy%20FINAL%20web.pdf.

den Hollander, Marcel C., Conny A. Bakker, and Erik Jan Hultink. "Product Design in a Circular Economy: Development of a Typology of Key Concepts and Terms." *Journal of Industrial Ecology* 21, no. 3 (June 2017).

Driesen, David M., and Amy Sinden. "The Missing Instrument: Dirty Input Limits." *Harvard Environmental Law Review* 33, no. 1 (2009). https://harvardelr.com/wp-content/uploads/sites/12/2019/07/33.1-Driesen-and-Sinden.pdf.

The Ellen MacArthur Foundation. "Circularity Indicators: An Approach to Measuring Circularity." 2015. https://emf.thirdlight.com/link/yybss1obhtdv-ub419h/@/preview/1?o.

The Ellen MacArthur Foundation. "Towards the Circular Economy." 2013. https://www.ellenmacarthurfoundation.org/publications/towards-the-circular-economy-vol-1-an-economic-and-business-rationale-for-an-accelerated-transition.

Elliott, E. Donald. "Environmental Markets and Beyond: Three Modest Proposals for the Future of Environmental Law." *Capital University Law Review* 29 (2001). https://openyls.law.yale.edu/bitstream/handle/20.500.13051/1512/Enviro_markets.pdf?sequence=2&isAllowed=y.

Environmental Defense Fund. "How Economics Solved Acid Rain." September 2018. https://www.edf.org/approach/markets/acid-rain.

Environmental Law Institute. *Barriers to Environmental Technology Innovation and Use.* ELI, 1998.

Environmental Law Institute. "The Circular Economy: Regulatory and Commercial Law Implications" (Conference Summary and Materials). https://www.eli.org/sites/default/files/docs/seminars/2_23_16_rfeldmanppt.pdf.

Esty, Daniel. "Next Generation Environmental Law: A Response to Richard Stewart." *Capital University Law Review* 29 (2001–2002).

Esty, Daniel. "Red Lights to Green Lights: From 20th Century Environmental Regulation to 21st Century Sustainability." *Environmental Law* 47, no. 1 (Winter 2017).

European Commission. "Water-Energy-Food-Ecosystem Nexus." https://international-partnerships.ec.europa.eu/policies/climate-environment-and-energy/water-energy-food-ecosystem-nexus_en#:~:text=The%20Water%2DEnergy%2DFood%2D,land%20%E2%80%93%20that%20underpin%20that%20security.

European Environment Agency. *Environmental Taxation and EU Environmental Policies.* EEA Report No. 17/2016. Publications Office of the European Union, 2016.

Farber, Daniel A. "Taking Slippage Seriously: Noncompliance and Creative Compliance in Environmental Law." *Harvard Environmental Law Review* 23 (1999).

Fellner, Johann, Jakob Lederer, Christoph Scharff, and David Laner. "Present Potentials and Limitations of a Circular Economy with Respect to Primary Raw Material Demand." *Journal of Industrial Ecology* 21, no. 3 (June 2017).

Fiksel, Joseph, Tarsha Eason, and Herbert Frederickson. "A Framework for Sustainability Indicators at EPA." EPA/600/R/12/687. National Risk Management Research Laboratory, ORD, USEPA, October 2012. https://www.epa.gov/sites/default/files/2014-10/documents/framework-for-sustainability-indicators-at-epa.pdf.

Fiorino, Daniel. *The New Environmental Regulation.* The MIT Press, 2006.

Fischman, Robert L. "Letting Go of Stability: Resilience and Environmental Law." *Indiana Law Journal* 94, no. 2 (2019).

Fisher, Elizabeth, Bettina Lange, Eloise Scotford, and Cinnamon Carlarne. "Maturity and Methodology: Starting a Debate about Environmental Law Scholarship." *Journal of Environmental Law* 21, no. 2 (2009).

Flournoy, Alyson C., Ryan Feinberg, Margaret Clune Giblin, Heather Halter, and Christina Storz. "The Future of Environmental Protection: The Case for a National Environmental Legacy Act." Center for Progressive Reform White Paper #1002 (2010).

Fourcade, Marion, Ettienne Ollion, and Yann Algan. "The Superiority of Economists." *Journal of Economic Perspectives* 29, no. 1 (2015).

Fowlie, Meredith, Stephen P. Holland, and Erin T. Mansur. "What Do Emissions Markets Deliver and to Whom? Evidence from Southern California's NOx Trading Program." *American Economic Review* 102, no. 2 (2012). https://faculty.tuck.dartmouth.edu/images/uploads/faculty/erin-mansur/mansur_emissions_markets.pdf.

Freeman, Jody, and Daniel A. Farber. "Modular Environmental Regulation." In "Thirty-Fourth Annual Administrative Law Issue: Incrementalism and the Administrative State." *Duke Law Journal* 54, no. 4 (February 2005). https://scholarship.law.duke.edu/dlj/vol54/iss4/1/.

Fullerton, Don, Callie W. Babbitt, Melissa M. Bilec, Shan He, Condy Isenhour, Vikas Khanna, Eunsang Lee, and Thomas L. Theis. "Introducing the Circular Economy to Economists." *Annual Review of Resource Economics* 14 (2022).

Gann, George D., Tein McDonald, Bethanie Walder, James Aronson, Cara R. Nelson, et al. "International Principles and Standards for the Practice of Ecological Restoration." Second edition. *Restoration Ecology* 27, no. S1 (2019).

Garthe, James. "Burning Plastic for Energy: An Update." Presentation. https://www.alfredstate.edu/files/downloads/PVGA11AVI.pdf.

Giles, Cynthia. *Next Generation Compliance: Environmental Regulation for the Modern Era*. Oxford University Press, 2022.

Goldberg, Terri. "What About Circularity of Hazardous Materials?" *Journal of Industrial Ecology* 21, no. 3 (June 2017).

Graedel, T. E., and Barbara K. Reck. "Recycling in Context." In *Handbook of Recycling: State-of-the-art for Practitioners, Analysts, and Scientists,* edited by Ernst Worrell and Markus A. Reuter. Elsevier, 2014.

Gray, Wayne, and Jay Shimshack. "The Effectiveness of Environmental Monitoring and Enforcement: A Review of the Empirical Evidence." *Review of Environmental Economics and Policy, Association of Environmental and Resource Economists* 5, no. 1 (Winter 2011). https://www.journals.uchicago.edu/doi/full/10.1093/reep/req017.

Henger, Ralph, and Kilian Bizer. "Tradable Planning Permits for Land-Use Control in Germany." *Land Use Policy* 27, no. 3 (2010).

Hickel, Jason. "Quantifying National Responsibility for Climate Breakdown: An Equality-Based Attribution Approach for Carbon Dioxide Emissions in Excess of

the Planetary Boundary." *Lancet Planet Health* 4 (September 2020). https://www.thelancet.com/action/showPdf?pii=S2542-5196%2820%2930196-0.
Hindin, David A. "Next Generation Compliance: Research Questions." Slideshow presented at Session 4: Enhancing Compliance by Leveraging Forces Beyond Inspections and Enforcement of the Research on Effective Government: Inspection and Compliance Workshop, June 2015. https://mcep.umd.edu/sites/mcep.umd.edu/files/David%20Hindin%20Next%20Gen%20Research%20Questions%202015.pdf.
Hindin, David A., and Jon D. Silberman. "Designing More Effective Rules and Permits." *George Washington Journal of Energy & Environmental Law* (Spring 2016).
Hinton, Stephen. "White Paper: How Flexible Emission Fees Can Drive Sustainable Development." Version 4.02. Swedish Sustainable Economy Foundation, 2013. https://stephenhintondotorg.files.wordpress.com/2013/08/whitepaperfe_v4-02.pdf.
Hirschhorn. Joel S. "Why the Pollution Prevention Revolution Failed-And Why It Ultimately Will Succeed." *Pollution Prevention Review*, Winter 2000.
https://ellenmacarthurfoundation.org/topics/circular-economy-introduction/glossary
https://issuu.com/apwa/docs/201203_reporteronline/s/12177333
https://jrc.ec.europa.eu/report_2024?vis=co2pop#emissions_table.
https://jrc.ec.europa.eu/report_2024?vis=co2tot#emissions_table.
https://knowledge4policy.ec.europa.eu/glossary-item/do-no-significant-harm_en.
https://sustainabledevelopment.un.org/content/documents/5987our-common-future.pdf.
https://www.economist.com/science-and-technology/2023/07/19/scrapyards-adopt-new-high-tech-ways-to-dismantle-cars. July 19, 2023.
https://www.eia.gov/totalenergy/data/monthly/.
https://www.epa.gov/acidrain/acid-rain-program.
https://www.epa.gov/clean-air-act-overview/progress-cleaning-air-and-improving-peoples-health.
https://www.epa.gov/nsr/prevention-significant-deterioration-basic-information.
https://www.footprintnetwork.org/our-work/earth-overshoot-day/.
https://www.globalco2initiative.org/.
https://www.naem.org/docs/default-source/conference-agendas/conference-metrics-2014-final-agena-naem.pdf?sfvrsn=b5151962_2.
https://yris.yira.org/wp-content/uploads/2020/03/yris-acheson-issue-2019-draft-2-1.pdf.
Huntington, Lawrence, Philip Sharp, E. Donald Elliott, and David T. Buente Jr. "How Did We Get into the Logjam, and How Do We Get Out of It?: Summary of Panel I Discussion at the Breaking The Logjam Conference Held at the NYU School of Law, March 28–29, 2008." *New York University Environmental Law Journal* 17, no. 1 (2008). https://nyuelj.org/wp-content/uploads/2013/03/HOW-DID-WE-GET-INTO-THE-LOGJAM.pdf.
Kavitha, B. V., Chirag Bhimani, and A. Sudhakar. "Issues and Challenges for Emission Trading Scheme for Particulate Matter in India." *Journal of Environmental Research and Development* 9, no. 3 (January–March 2015).

Kernighan, Brian W., and P. J. Plauger. *The Elements of Programming Style*, 2nd Edition. McGraw-Hill, 1978.

Kirchherr Julian, Denise Reike, and Marko Hekkert. "Conceptualizing the Circular Economy: An Analysis of 114 Definitions." *Resource, Conservation and Recycling* 127 (2017). https://doi.org/10.1016/j.resconrec.2017.09.005.

Klemick, Heather, and R. David Simpson. "Market Economy and Biodiversity." In *Encyclopedia of Biodiversity, Volume 5, (Second Edition)*, edited by Simon A. Levin. Academic Press, 2013.

Kotzé, Louis J. "Reflections on the Future of Environmental Law Scholarship and Methodology in the Anthropocene." In *Perspectives on Environmental Law Scholarship*, edited by Ole W. Pedersen. Cambridge University Press, 2018.

Krausmann, Fridolin, Dominik Wiedenhofer, Christian Lauk, Willi Haas, Hiroki Tanikawa, Tomer Fishman, Alessio Miatto, Heinz Schandl, and Helmut Haberl. "Global Socioeconomic Material Stocks Rise 23-fold over the 20th Century and Require Half of Annual Resource Use." *Proceedings of the National Academy of Sciences* 114, no. 8 (February 2017). https://www.pnas.org/doi/10.1073/pnas.1613773114.

Kruger, Joseph. *Companies and Regulators in Emissions Trading Programs*. Resources For the Future. DP 05-03, February 2005.

Krupp, Fred, and Ernest J. Moniz. "Cutting Climate Pollution Isn't Enough—We also Need Carbon Removal." September 23, 2019. https://thehill.com/opinion/energy-environment/462609-cutting-climate-pollution-isnt-enough-we-also-need-carbon-removal/.

Kuklinska, Karolina, Lidia Wolska, and Jacek Namiesnik. "Air Quality Policy in the U.S. and the EU—A Review." *Atmospheric Pollution Research* 6 (2015).

Linder, Marcus, Steven Sarasini, and Patricia von Loon. "A Metric for Quantifying Product-Level Circularity." *Journal of Industrial Ecology* 21, no. 3 (June 2017). https://onlinelibrary.wiley.com/doi/10.1111/jiec.12552.

Liptak, Adam. "The Lackluster Reviews That Lawyers Love To Hate." *New York Times*, October 21, 2013. https://www.nytimes.com/2013/10/22/us/law-scholarships-lackluster-reviews.html.

Maitre-Ekern, Eléonore. "The Choice of Regulatory Instruments for a Circular Economy." In *Environmental Law and Economics*, Vol. 4 of Economic Analysis of Law in European Legal Scholarship, edited by K. Mathis and B. R. Huber. Springer International Publishing AG, 2017.

Mamlyuk, Boris N. "Analyzing the Polluter Pays Principle Through Law and Economics." *Southeastern Environmental Law Journal* 18, no. 1 (2010). https://ssrn.com/abstract=1679245.

Manderson, Edward J., and Timothy J. Considine. "An Economic Perspective on Industrial Ecology." *Review of Environmental Economics and Policy* 12, no. 2 (Summer 2018).

McDonough, William, and Michael Braungart. *Cradle to Cradle: Remaking the Way We Make Things*. North Point Press, 2002.

Monteduro, Massimo. "Environmental Law and Agroecology. Transdisciplinary Approach to Public Ecosystem Services as a New Challenge for Environmental Legal Doctrine." *European Energy and Environmental Law Review* (2013).

Mulrow, John, and Victoria Santos. "Moving the Circular Economy Beyond Alchemy." *Discard Studies*, November 13, 2017. https://discardstudies.com/2017/11/13/moving-the-circular-economy-beyond-alchemy.

National Academy of Public Administrators. *A Breath of Fresh Air: Reviving the New Source Review Program*. Report by a Panel of the National Academy of Public Administration. NAPA, 2003. https://napawash.org/academy-studies/a-breath-of-fresh-air-reviving-the-new-source-review-program.

National Research Council. *Air Quality Management in the United States*. National Academies Press, 2004.

Ness, David A., and Ke Xing. "Toward a Resource-Efficient Built Environment: A Literature Review and Conceptual Model." *Journal of Industrial Ecology* 21, no. 3 (June 2017).

Newton, Brent E. "Law Review Scholarship in the Eyes of the Twenty-First Century Supreme Court Justices: An Empirical Analysis." *Drexel Law Review* 4 (2012).

Newton, Brent E. "Preaching What They Practice: Why Law Faculties' Preoccupation with Impractical Scholarship and Devaluation of Practical Competencies Obstruct Reform in the Legal Academy." *South Carolina Law Review* 62, no. 1 (2010).

Nordhaus, Robert. "Modernizing the Clean Air Act: Is There Life After 40?" *Energy Law Journal* 33, no. 2 (2012).

Office of Air and Radiation. *Clearing the Air: The Facts About Capping and Trading Emissions*. EPA-430F-02-009. U.S. Environmental Protection Agency, 2002. https://www.epa.gov/sites/default/files/2016-03/documents/clearingtheair.pdf.

Office of Air and Radiation. *Tools of the Trade: A Guide to Designing and Operating a Cap and Trade Program for Pollution Control*. EPA-430-B-03-002. U.S. Environmental Protection Agency, 2003. https://www.epa.gov/sites/default/files/2016-03/documents/tools.pdf.

Oren, Craig N. "Is the Clean Air Act at a Crossroads?" *Environmental Law Review* 40, no. 4 (Fall 2010).

Owen, Dave, and Caroline Noblet. "Interdisciplinary Research and Environmental Law." *Ecology Law Quarterly* 41, no. 4 (2015). https://repository.uchastings.edu/cgi/viewcontent.cgi?article=2230&context=faculty_scholarship.

Pasfield, Bruce, and Elise Paeffgen. "How to Enforce a Carbon Tax: Lessons from the Montreal Protocol and the U.S. Experience with the Ozone Depleting Chemicals Tax." *Vermont Journal of Environmental Law* 14 (2012–2013).

Peiró, Laura Talens, Fulvio Ardente, and Fabrice Mathieux. "Design for Disassembly Criteria in EU Product Policies for a More Circular Economy." *Journal of Industrial Ecology* 21, no. 3 (June 2017).

Potts, Brian. “Trading Grandfathered Air—A New, Simpler Approach.” *Harvard Environmental Law Review* (2006). https://harvardelr.com/wp-content/uploads/sites/12/2019/07/31.1-Potts.pdf.

Ruhl, J. B., and James Salzman. “What Happens When the Green New Deal Meets the Old Green Laws?” *Vermont Law Review* 44, no. 4 (Summer 2020).

Saidani, Michael, Bernard Yannou, Yann Leroy, Francois Cluzel, and Alissa Kendall. “A Taxonomy of Circular Economy Indicators.” *Journal of Cleaner Production* 207 (January 2019). https://doi.org/10.1016/j.jclepro.2018.10.014.

Salzman, James, and J. B. Ruhl. “‘No Net Loss’: Instrument Choice in Wetlands Protection.” In *Moving To Markets in Environmental Regulation, Lessons From Twenty Years of Experience*, edited by Jody Freeman and Charles D. Kolstad. Oxford University Press, 2006.

Sarkis, Joseph. “As I See It: Inclusion of ‘Circular Economy’ in Green New Deal Could Support Economic Transformation.” *Telegram*, May 4, 2019. https://www.telegram.com/news/20190504/as-i-see-it-inclusion-of-circular-economy-in-green-new-deal-could-support-economic-transformation.

Schakenbach, John, Robert Vollaro, and Reynaldo Forte. “Fundamentals of Successful Monitoring, Reporting, and Verification under a Cap-and-Trade Program.” *Journal of the Air & Waste Management Association* 56 (November 2006).

Schmalensee, Richard, and Robert N. Stavins. “Lessons Learned from Three Decades of Experience with Cap and Trade.” *Review of Environmental Economics and Policy* 11, no. 1 (Winter 2017).

Schoenbrod, David, Joel Schwartz, and Ross Sandler. “Air Pollution: Building on the Successes Breaking the Logjam: Environmental Reform for the New Congress and Administration: Panel III—Climate Change, US Domestic Regulation, and the Future of the Car.” *New York University Environmental Law Journal* 17, no. 1 (2008–2009).

Schoenbrod, David, Richard B. Stewart, and Katrina M. Wyman. *Breaking the Logjam: Environmental Protection That Will Work.* Yale University Press, 2010.

Schreifels, Jeremy. “Emissions Trading in Santiago, Chile: A Review of the Emission Offset Program of Supreme Decree No. 4.” (2012). https://papers.ssrn.com/sol3/papers.cfm?abstract_id=1910156.

“Ships of Theseus.” *The Economist*, December 21, 2024–January 3, 2025.

Sørensen, Peter Birch. “The Basic Environmental Economics of the Circular Economy.” EPRU Working Paper Series No. 2017-04, Economic Policy Research Unit (EPRU), University of Denmark, Department of Economics, 2017. https://papers.ssrn.com/sol3/papers.cfm?abstract_id=3064684.

Sparandara, Lauren, Mike Werner, Amanda Kaminsky, Libby Finch, and Kelly Douglas. *Accelerating the Circular Economy Through Commercial Deconstruction and Reuse.* Ellen MacArthur Foundation, 2019. https://emf.thirdlight.com/link/v6gyhiosoqs7-s9k2oe/@/preview/1?o.

Stahel, Walter R. *The Circular Economy: A User's Guide*. Routledge, 2019.

Stegeman, Hans. "True Pricing Is Not Enough to Make an Economy Circular." Trios Investment Management, January 15, 2019. https://www.triodos-im.com/articles/2019/true-pricing-is-not-enough-to-achieve-sustainability.

Stern, Nicholas, and Andrew Oswald. "Why are Economists Letting Down the World on Climate Change?" September 19, 2017. https://cepr.org/voxeu/columns/why-are-economists-letting-down-the-world-climate-change.

Stewart, Richard. "A New Generation of Environmental Regulation." *Capital University Law Review* 29, no. 1 (2001).

Tarlock, Dan. "Is a Substantive, Non-Positive United States Environmental Law Possible?" *Michigan Journal of Environmental & Administrative Law* 1 (2012). https://repository.law.umich.edu/mjeal/vol1/iss1/5.

Tarlock, Dan. "Is There a There There in Environmental Law?" *Florida State University Journal of Land Use and Environmental Law* 19, no. 2 (2018). https://ir.law.fsu.edu/cgi/viewcontent.cgi?article=1281&context=jluel.

Tarlock, Dan. "Why There Should Be No Restatement of Environmental Law." *Brooklyn Law Review* 79, no. 2 (2014). https://brooklynworks.brooklaw.edu/cgi/viewcontent.cgi?article=1034&context=blr.

Telle, Kjetil. "Monitoring and Enforcement of Environmental Regulations: Lessons from a Natural Field Experiment in Norway." *Journal of Public Economics* 99 (March 2013).

Thorp, Edward O. *Beat The Dealer*. Vintage, 1966.

UN Brundtland Commission. *Report of the World Commission on Environment and Development: Our Common Future*. 1987. https://sustainabledevelopment.un.org/content/documents/5987our-common-future.pdf.

U.S. General Accounting Office. *"Air Pollution: EPA Should Improve Oversight of Emissions Reporting by Large Facilities." Report to the Ranking Minority Member, Committee on Government Reform, House of Representatives*. General Accounting Office, 2001.

U.S. General Accounting Office. *Drinking Water: EPA Could Use Available Data to Better Identify Neighborhoods at Risk of Lead Exposure. Report to Congressional Requesters* GAO-21-78. General Accounting Office, 2020. https://www.gao.gov/assets/gao-21-78.pdf.

Vanegas, Paul, Jef R. Peeters, Dirk Cattrysse, Paolo Tecchio, Fulvio Ardente, Fabrice Mathieux, Wim Dewulf, and Joost R. Duflou. "Ease of Disassembly of Products to Support Circular Economy Strategies." *Resources, Conservation, and Recycling* 135 (August 2018).

Webster, Kenneth. *The Circular Economy: A Wealth of Flows*. Ellen MacArthur Foundation Publishing, 2nd Edition., 2017.

Williams, J. H., B. Haley, F. Kahrl, J. Moore, A. D. Jones, M. S. Torn, and H. McJeon. *Pathways to deep decarbonization in the United States*. The U.S. report of the Deep

Decarbonization Pathways Project of the Sustainable Development Solutions Network and the Institute for Sustainable Development and International Relations, 2014. https://biotech.law.lsu.edu/blog/US-Deep-Decarbonization-Report.pdf.

Withana, Sirini, Patrick ten Brink, Andrea Illes, Silvia Nanni, and Emma Watkins. *Environmental Tax Reform in Europe: Opportunities for the Future: Final Report.* A Report by the Institute for European Environmental Policy. Institute for European Environmental Policy, 2014.

Wood, Jonathan. "Building a Groundwater Market from the Bottom Up." Property and Environmental Research Center (PERC). Posted August 16, 2018. https://www.perc.org/2018/08/16/building-a-groundwater-market-from-the-bottom-up.

World Business Council for Sustainable Development (WBCSD). Circular Metrics—Landscape Analysis. WBCSD and Climate-KIC, May 2018. https://docs.wbcsd.org/2018/06/Circular_Metrics-Landscape_analysis.pdf.

Wyeth, George. "'Standard' and 'Alternative' Environmental Protection: The Changing Role of Environmental Agencies." *William & Mary Environmental Law and Policy Review* 31, no. 1 (October 2006).

The Yale Review of International Studies. "Reverse Cap-and-Trade for Refugees: A Proposal to Ameliorate the Refugee Crisis in the European Union through a System of Quotas and Markets." https://yris.yira.org/essays/3299.

Zink, Trevor, and Roland Geyer. "Circular Economy Rebound." *Journal of Industrial Ecology* 21, no. 3 (June 2017).

Index

Note: Page numbers in *italics* indicate figures and tables, while 'n' denotes note numbers

AA. *See* attainment areas
academia 110–13, 135 n.40, 146, 176–7, 258–9, 339–42, 348
Acid Rain Program (ARP) 25, 26, 30, 40 n.4, 41–2 n.11, 64, 65, 69, 97–8, 152, 157, 164, 169–70, 175, 254, 352 n.26
adapted strategy
  development 198–9
  vs. generalized strategy 232–3
  key components 221
  LCA in 221–3
  transition to CE and 196
  use of term 220–1
Additional Earths at Global Development (AEGD) 1, 4, 10, 268–9, 316, 328, 330, 334 n.5, 337
adverse areas 91, 104–7
AEGD. *See* Additional Earths at Global Development
afforestation 288 n.27, 299, 308, 312
agriculturally grown food products 288 n.29, 297–8, 327
air pollution. *See also* US Clean Air Act
  comprehensive strategy 25
  core mission of addressing problem of 28
  HAP 31, 42 n.13
  interstate 72–4
  reducing generation of 4–5
  regulating generation of 23, 332
  regulation hierarchy 93, *94*, 144–5
air quality management (AQM). *See also* US Clean Air Act
  assumptions of knowledge about 10–11
  CaC *vs.* market instruments debate 27–9
  complexity of as a design flaw 45–6
  design flaws 40
  essential concepts of 26–7
  "Fundamental God Particle" of 29, 87, 183 n.8, 202
  logjam 64–5
  for Nature's sake 146
  public inclusion 58–9
  reforming 57
  regulations 5, 10
  regulatory modification 42 n.15
  successful program qualities 51
  US systems 12–13, 23–4
  use of source-wide emissions 30
Allwood, Julian M. 258, 275–7, 350 n.8
ambient air-quality standards 10
ambient monitors 38
AQM. *See* air quality management
ARP. *See* Acid Rain Program
Assadourian, Erik 318
attainment areas (AA) 34, 35, 99–100, 104–7, 106, 183 n.13
attainment of sustainability with Nature
  achieving 1–2, 4, 16–17 n.2
  biosphere quality model 1
  defining 17 n.3
  FLoER 4
  minimizing pollution 4–5
  nonattainment 195, 281
  source thresholds for pollutants emitted in major amounts *101*
attorneys 57–8, 62 n.23, 113, 115, 120–1, 343, 348
austerity 162, 338

Backes, Chris 207
BACT. *See* Best Available Control Technology
Best Available Control Technology (BACT) 26, 34–6, 43 n.22, 45, 102–4, 111–12, 135 n.44, 185 n.35
bioplastics 229 n.54

biosphere quality model 1, 186 n.41
Bocken, Nancy M. P. 257, 272
Bratspies, Rebecca 3
Breaking the Logjam (BTL) 72–5, 169–74, 235
Breaking the Logjam Symposium 63, 65, 72–5
Brenner, Rob 62 n.26, 133 n.29
BTL. See Breaking the Logjam
bureaucratic pollution 5, 6, 25, 32, 39, 54–7, 87, 118–19

CAA. *See* Clean Air Act
CaC. *See* Command-and-Control
Campbell, Colin 102, 133 n.28, 133 n.31, 181
capacity-based emissions growth 91–2, 104
cap-and-trade (CaT)
  in comprehensive strategy 122–4
  as a corrective process 6–7, 60 n.8, 90–1
  effectiveness of 25, 69
  as facilitating integrity 156–7
  in generalized strategy 5
  interstate air pollution regulation 73–4
  as a market instrument 28–9
  NRC support for 69–70
  NSR preferred to 49
  opposition to 131 n.6
  rationing 95–6
  reverse 18 n.17, 297, 322 n.21, 327
carbon capture and sequestration (CCS) 135 n.45
Carbon Capture and Storage (CCS) 112
carbon dioxide (CO_2)
  climate effects of 40 n.2
  external trading 125
  fossil-fuel based 93, 95–6, 132 n.18, 155, 160–3, 166, 237, 244, 284–5, 331
  as a global climate-altering pollutant 298–9
  impracticality of controlling 163–8
  legacy 233, 249, 267, 299, 320 n.9, 325
  misapplication of labor 321 nn.11–17, 322 nn.18–20
  mitigation strategy 9, 300–14, *302–3*
  negative emissions 307–8
  rationale for not using economic instruments to reduce 165–6
  remediation of 9, 267–8
  sequestration 237 n.3, 288 n.27, 307, 320 n.9, 325, 327
  taxation as a component of regulating 166–7, 244, 352 n.27
Case, David 65–7
CaT. *See* cap-and-trade
CE. *See* circular economy
CEMS. *See* continuous emissions monitoring system
Centers for Disease Control (CDC) 50
certified sustainability accountants 311
CFCs. *See* chlorofluorocarbons
chlorofluorocarbons (CFCs) 25, 244, 340
circular economy (CE)
  adoption of 18 n.20, 288 n.31
  approach to achieving theoretical/ideal 197–9
  attaining 1, 17 n.5
  characteristics of 203–4
  criticisms of 317–18
  economics community and 336–9
  Ellen MacArthur Foundation description 196, 223–4 n.9
  environmental legal scholars community and 339–42
  facilitating circularity 215–17
  fundamental flaw of premises of current 257–8
  JIE issue devoted to 271–5
  material recovery in 209–14
  metrics 199–200
  proper pollutants to regulate in 200–4
  readiness 214–17
  regulatory foundation for 23
  transition to 2, 4–5, 15, 90, 263–70
  use of term 13, 193, 197
  zero waste paradigm 242, 278
circularity metrics 203–4
Clean Air Interstate Rule 51
Clean Water Act 237 n.2, 241
climate change institutes 286 n.5

climate change mitigation 5, 9, 15, 164, 166–7, 294–5, 298–9
climate stability NAA 91
closing loops 273–275
Coglianese, Cary 46, 115, 182
command-and-control (CaC)
  vs. market instruments 27–9, 68, 152–3, 175–7
  performance standards 182 n.2
  prescriptive regulation under 131 n.6
  role of 29–30
  suitability of in current regulatory system 64
  trading and 175–6
complexity, product 259–60, 318–19
compostability, use of term 229 n.54
comprehensive strategy. *See also* adapted strategy; generalized strategy
  adoption of 177–8
  CAA downsides addressed by 25
  CO_2 mitigation strategy developed from 298–314, *302–3*, 321 nn.11–17, 322 nn.18–20
  critical aspects 141–6
  design flaws 114–22
  division of labor 93, 110–11, 138 n.70
  economics 153–4
  encouraging adoption of 179–81
  external trading role 97
  framework for 92–130
  key changes resulting from adopting 128–9
  key points 191–3
  legal aspects 151–3
  mitigating global climate change with 299
  need for 87–91
  permitting under 126–7, 150–1
  putting to the test 179
  regulatory elements of *109*
  remarks on 129–30
  sample scenarios 107–10
  streamlining existing NSR 147–9
  terms of usage 91–2
  trading scheme 122–4, 155–60
  underlying assumptions for understanding 10–13
  underlying basis 140–1
Conference of Parties (COP) 299
Considine, Timothy J. 282–3, 350 n.5
construction 48, 104–10, 127, 143, 149, 275–7
Construction and Modification Permitting and Emission Determination Unit (CMPED Unit) 127
consumption 265, 288 n.30
continuous emissions monitoring system (CEMS) 29, 30, 38, 65, 70, 99, 127, 184 n.16, 186 n.47
Corporate Social Responsibility (CSR) 237, 252, 344
cost–benefit analysis 280–1, 290 n.57
Cradle to Cradle (McDonough and Braungart) 8, 159–60, 185 n.31, 201, 202, 216, 222–3, 227 n.34, 242, 259, 261, 268, 278, 336–7, 341, 343
Cross State Air Pollution Rule (CSAPR) 26, 96, 169–70
CSAPR. *See* Cross State Air Pollution Rule
Cullen, Jonathan M. 274–5, 317

Daly, Herman 225 n.21, 319, 351 n.10
debottlenecking 37
decarbonization 166
decoupling 272
deforestation 320 n.7
degrowth 318
demand-based emissions growth 91, 92, 104
Den Hollander, Marcel C. 253, 271
design flaws
  CAA 45–6, 59–60
  complicated rules and requirements 114–18
  comprehensive strategy 114–22
  minimal inclusion of the public 121–2, 137 n.60
  misapplication of labor 119–21
  multiple bureaucratic procedures 118–19
  sluggish emission reduction process 114
Design for Disassembly (DfD) 260, 277
design for product integrity 253, 271
design for recycling 253–4, 271, 277
development, maximizing per capita 2

difficulty-of-disassembly (DoD) 201, 214, 234, 287 n.14, 287 n.16
disassembly
design for 260
developing a culture of 268
difficulty of 201, 214, 234, 287 n.14, 287 n.16
division of labor
entropy in comprehensive strategy 93, 110–13
in generalized strategy 235, 258–9
making regulating rewarding 154–5
misapplication of labor 57–8, 119–21
optimality 192
role of academia and environmental research centers 111–13, 135 n.40, 258–9
role of feds and states 110–11, 135 n.43, 138 n.70, 227 n.37, 235
role of regulatory engineering and legal staff 113, 126–7
DoD. *See* difficulty-of-disassembly
"do no significant harm" policy 18 n.15
Driesen, David M. 132 n.18, 352 n.26
durability hierarchy 241

Earth Overshoot Day 16 n.1
eco-efficiency 242
eco-labeling 256–7, 298
ecological adaptation 3
ecological economics 277–8
economics
austerity 162, 338
climate change not to be solved by 166–7
cost considerations 11–12, 19 n.22
ecological 277–8
economists and the CE 336–9
generalized strategy considerations 279–82
problem with using anthropocentric measures 186 n.42
"You don't foul your own nest" school of 278–9, 337–8
ecosystem restoration 10, 14, 18 n.17, 23, 314–16, 327
ecosystem sprawl 322 n.27
efficiency
eco-, 242
energy 247–8
material 247–8, 276
EJ. *See* environmental justice areas
Ellen MacArthur Foundation 196, 200, 223 n.9
Elliott, E. Donald 28, 68, 89–90, 97, 178
emission determination factors (EDF) 150
emissions
actual 31, 42 n.12
auto 25
CAA reduction process 46–51
capacity-based growth 91–2
CEMS 29, 30, 38, 99, 184 n.16, 186 n.47
demand-based growth 91, 92
fugitive 32
grandfathered 47–8, 76, 97, 133 n.21
major sources 31, 38, 42 n.13, 43 nn.21–22, 104–7
minor sources 31–2, 38
monitoring and measuring 28, 30, 38, 141–3, 149–50, 184 n.18, 187 n.51
negative 307–8
potential 31, 42 n.12
quantifiable limits 25, 242–3
reductions in 24
regulation hierarchy 93, *94*, 144–5
role of limits and SIP process 32–3
setting and declining limits 88–9
source-specific 31–2
source-wide 29, 30, 41 nn.7–8
stack testing 29, 38, 41 nn.9–10, 65, 127–8, 182 n.3
standards 10
stationary source 32
synthetic minor 31–2, 38, 42 n.14
tax 90
trading 7, 25, 27–30, 41–2 n.11, 65, 80 n.7
trading programs 68–9, 89–91
unit performance standards 103
VOC 33
EMS. *See* Environmental Management System
energy efficiency (EE) 162–3, 247–8
Energy Information Administration 185 n.33

engineers 57–8, 113, 115, 126–7, 142, 145–6, 154–5, 335
entropy 223 n.8, 294–5, 318–19, 320 n.1
Environmental, Social and Governance (ESG) metrics 200
Environmental Defense Fund 41 n.11, 353 n.29
environmental justice (EJ) areas 14, 51, 91, 131 n.10, 157–9, 185 n.29
environmental law. *See also* Grand Unified Theory of Environmental Law and Regulation
  backwardness of 183 n.12
  blueprint for 325–6
  FLoER 4, 98–9, 280, 311, 325
  legalistic nature of 59, 62 n.29
  limits of existing 12, 19 n.23
  rights of Nature and 328–9, *330*
  sustainability as an area of study 3
  sustainability with Nature as underlying purpose of 4, 18 n.14
Environmental Law Institute (ELI) 65, 103, 207
environmental legal scholars 2, 3, 6, 17 n.6, 339–42, 352 n.25
Environmental Management System (EMS) 66, 80 n.12
environmental NGOs 342–4
environmental protection God Particle 146, 184 n.17
environmental research centers 110–13, 135 n.40, 258–9
Environmental Technology Verification (EVT) Program 136 n.36
environmentalists 342–4
equilibrium 1–3, 10, 15, 16 n.2, 315–16, 320 n.2
Equivalent Trading Units (ETUs) 198, 210–14, 228 n.42, 235, 256, 307–8
Esty, Daniel 59, 178, 181, 352 n.18
ETUs. *See* Equivalent Trading Units
EU. *See* European Union
European Union (EU)
  CaC solid waste reduction standards 236
  CE as subject of interest in 336
  "do no significant harm" policy 18 n.15
  Ecodesign Directive 207
  emission limits 42 n.17
  emissions tax 90
  Extended Producer Responsibility 196, 227 n.39, 244
  focus on post-production economic tools 350 n.4
  zero waste CE paradigm 286 n.2
exemptions 261–2
existing source performance standard (ESPS) program 76
expansion pollution 298
Extended Producer Responsibility (EPR) 196, 216, 227 n.39
external trading 89, 91, 96–9, 125, 143–4, 183 n.10

Farber, Daniel A. 68, 347
Federal Emergency Management Agency (FEMA) 50
Federally Enforceable State Operating Permit (FESOP) 31
FESOP. *See* Federally Enforceable State Operating Permit
Fiorino, Daniel 65, 66
Fischman, Robert L. 3
Five-Star System 315
FLoER. *See* Fundamental Laws of Environmental Regulation
Food and Drug Administration (FDA) 50
Forte, Reynaldo 120, 348
fossil fuels, rationing
  CO_2 emissions from 95–6, 125, 160–3, 267–8, 284–5, 331
  critics of 163
  limits on 132 n.15, 140–1, 184 n.21
  rationale for 266–7
  reasons for 161–3
  in regulatory hierarchy 93, 95–6
  solid waste pollution and 185 n.34
  tracking 313
Freeman, Jody 68
fuel switching 163–4
fugitive emissions 32
Fullerton, Don 336
"Fundamental God Particle" of air quality management (AQM) 29
Fundamental Laws of Environmental Regulation (FLoER) 4, 98–9, 280, 311, 325

Gann, George G. 315, 347
GAO Report 113, 138 n.76, 142, 182
generalized strategy
applicability of to multiple pollution media 199
ecological considerations 277–9
economic considerations 279–82
guiding principles 240–52
industrial ecology considerations 270–7
key components 231
LCA in 251–2
legacy pollution in 233
looking forward 344–9
policy considerations 282
regulatory insights 252–63
remarks on 236–7
role of feds and states 235
trading scheme 234–5
Geyer, Roland 271–2
Giles, Cynthia 52, 56, 76–9, 115, 116, 151, 175, 187 n.51, 341, 345, 351 n.15
Global Constitution for Nature 16, 331–3
Global Footprint Network 16 n.1
Grand Unified Theory of Environmental Law and Regulation 15–16, 185 n.32, 195, 316, 320, 329–31, 334 n.4
Gray, Wayne 67, 78, 142, 182
Green New Deal 343
greenhouse gases (GHG) 31, 40 n.2, 42 n.13, 42–3 n.20, 91, 93, 107, 125, 132 n.13, 166–7, 184 n.21, 299, 310
guidance documents 45, 60 n.2, 62 n.27

habitat loss 333 n.1
Handbook of Recycling 275
HAP. *See* hazardous air pollutants
harm intensity 217–19, 229 n.53, 237 n.1
hazardous air pollutants (HAP) 31, 42 n.13, 125, 137 nn.65–66, 184 n.22, 232–3
Hindin, David 77–8
hotspots 157–9
"How Economics Solved Acid Rain" (Environmental Defense Fund) 41 n.11
human–driven environmental problems 295–8

IDPC pollutant surrogates 8–9, 201–9, 225 n.20, 239–40. *See also* adapted strategy; generalized strategy
IDPC. *See* inherently detrimental product characteristics
imports 9, 219–20, 282
increment consumption 105–6, 135 n.38
industrial ecology 350 n.5
industrial pollution 5
industrial resources 327
industrial symbiosis 274
inherently detrimental product characteristics (IDPC) 5, 6, 8–9, 159–60, 201–9, 219–20, 239–40. *See also* adapted strategy; generalized strategy
inspections 38, 141–3
Inspector General of Bureaucracy 119, 146
internal trading 89, 91, 99–100
internalized externality 115–16, 136 n.54, 247
International Monetary Fund 162, 338
interstate pollution 72–4, 96–8, 132 n.17, 135 n.40

Journal of Industrial Ecology (JIE) 271–5

Kirchherr, Julian 13, 197
Kotzé, Louis 3

LAER. *See* Lowest Achievable Emission Rate
LAER Retrofit Contingency Plan 98–9
landfill mining 270, 288 n.28
lawyers 57–8, 62 n.23, 113, 115, 120–1, 343, 348
LCA. *See* Life Cycle Assessment
legacy pollution 9, 15, 223 n.3, 233, 249
Life Cycle Assessment (LCA) 221–3, 251–2
linear economy 119 n.22, 195, 196, 214, 224 n.10, 246, 257, 273, 278–9, 286 n.11
Liptak, Adam 341
logjam 40, 43 n.26, 59–60, 64–5, 82 n.40
loop closure 272–3
Lowest Achievable Emission Rate (LAER) 26, 35–6, 102–4, 111–13, 133 n.31

MACT. *See* Maximum Achievable Control Technology standards
Maitre-Ekern, Eléonore 207, 342
Mamlyuk, Boris N. 1, 182, 186 n.41, 342, 352–3 n.27
Manderson, Edward J. 282–3, 350 n.5
Marcotte, Jay 227 n.34
market instruments. *See also* cap-and-trade; taxation
  vs. CaC 27–9, 68, 152–3, 175–7
  past use of suboptimal 282–4
Material Circularity Indicator (MCI) 200
material degradation hierarchy 241–2
material efficiency 247–8, 276
material recovery 209–14, 228 n.41, 277
Maximum Achievable Control Technology (MACT) standards 113, 118
McCutchen, Gary 133 n.31
McDonough, William 350 n.2
measures of detriment (MoD) 198–9, 207–8, 219, 249, 252–3, 287 n.14
Mendeleev, Dmitri 224 n.17, 331
metrics 199–200
microplastics 166, 244
mobile source emissions 167–8
MoD. *See* measures of detriment
modifications 32, 42 n.15
monstrous hybrids 219, 261
Montreal Protocol 244
Mulrow, John 271, 273, 318
multi-media pollution
  generalized strategy for generation of multi-media pollution 231–7
  generalized strategy for regulating generation of 7–9
  reducing generation of 14
  regulating generation of 159–60
NAA. *See* nonattainment areas
NAAQS. *See* National Ambient Air Quality Standards
narrowing loops 273–4
National Ambient Air Quality Standards (NAAQS) 23, 25, 28, 30, 33–5, 95, 132 n.16, 204–5
National Emission Standards for Hazardous Air Pollutants (NESHAP) 51
National Environmental Legacy Act 348
National Research Council (NRC) 54, 69–72, 167–9, 353 n.30
national security 18 n.20
National Transportation Safety Board (NTSB) 50
nature
  as a complex adaptive system 16 n.2
  equilibrium between humanity and 2, 10, 15, 296
  equilibrium state 1, 16 n.2, 315–16, 320 n.2
  Global Constitution for 16, 331–3
  harm-reduction strategies 2–3, 17 n.7
  performance standards 326
  resources of not infinite 10
  restoring 2, 10, 314–15
  rights of 328–9, *330*, 346
  sustainability with 1–2, 16–17 n.2, 17 n.3
Nature Deficit Disorder 279, 337, 349
NESHAP. *See* National Emission Standards for Hazardous Air Pollutants
netting 36–7
New Source Performance Standard (NSPS) 27, 42 n.16, 51, 102–4, 133 nn.29–30
New Source Review (NSR)
  bureaucratic pollution 48–51, 134 n.35
  complexity of 45–6
  complications of 36–7
  construction at major sources 25, 33–7, 83 n.51
  preferred to CaT 49
  reforms 67
  streamlining existing 147–9, 183 n.15
New Unit Performance Standards (NUPS) 111–12, 133 n.27, 158, 172–3, 206
Newton, Brent 341
Next Generation Compliance (Giles) 76–8
Next Gen principles 52, 58, 64–5, 76–8, 116, 119, 151–2, 175–7, 311, 341, 345–7, 351 n.15
nitrogen oxides (NOx) 26, 31, 36–7, 40, 97, 155, 164, 234
nonattainment areas (NAA)

emissions growth allowed in 183 n.14
extreme ozone 35
hotspots 157–9
LAER in 34
NSR rules and 36–7, 133 n.31
PALs 100, 106–7
RACT rules and 33
role of external trading to address emissions in 96–9
source pollutants 43 nn.23–24
source thresholds for pollutants emitted in major amounts *101*
use of term 223 n.1
noncompostability harm intensity (NHI) 217–19
Nordhaus, Robert 45, 47, 63, 65, 75–6, 87, 139, 174–5, 179, 342
Nordhaus, William 165
NOx. *See* nitrogen oxides
NSPS. *See* New Source Performance Standard
NSR. *See* New Source Review
NUPS. *See* New Unit Performance Standards

optimality 11, 14, 18 n.21, 92
Oswald, Andrew 336
overpopulation 296, 313–14

P2. *See* pollution prevention
PALs. *See* Plantwide Applicability Limitation
Paris Agreement 9, 310
particulate matter (PM) emissions 125, 155, 164
PCPS. *See* per capita performance standard
per capita performance standard (PCPS) 300–16, 328
performance standards 10, 74–5, 135 nn.41–42, 145, 172–3, 182 n.2
permitting
in AQM 27
complications 36–7
comprehensive strategy and 126–7, 150–1
EDF 150
FESOP 31–2
incentive clauses 138 n.71
issuance procedures 55–7, 61–2 nn.21–23
new construction and modifications 48, 104–7, 143, 149
in NSR programs 35–6
Title V 26, 31, 42 n.14, 53–4, 62 n.26, 116–17, 120, 151, 171
phase outs 244–5
Plantwide Applicability Limitation (PALs) 91, 99–100, 106, 131 n.11, 133 n.24, 148–9
plastics, harm intensity of 217–19, 286 n.8
PM. *See* particulate matter emissions
pollutants
externally traded 96–9, 125, 137 n.65, 137 n.68, 143–4, 183 n.10
performance standards 74–5
PTE 106
regulating harms 327
regulation of in CE 200–4
setting and declining limits 87–8
sources emitting 91, 95
trading programs 89–91
pollution. *See also* air pollution; solid waste pollution
abatement 351 n.12
addressing 290 n.62
as a design problem 8
expansion 298
harms to Nature 326
interstate 72–4, 96–8, 132 n.17, 135 n.40
legacy 9, 15, 223 n.3, 233–4, 249
limits on 1, 17 n.5
major sources 91, 95
minor sources 91, 95
multi-media 7–9, 14, 159–60, 231–7
reducing generation of 4–5, 13
regulation hierarchy 93, *94*, 144–5
regulation of 330–1
remediation of 9
taxation 182 n.1
technology-induced 11, 242, 286 n.1, 293–6
waste 254
pollution prevention (P2) 67, 162–3
population growth 313–14
Posner, Richard 341

potential to emit (PTE) 92, 106
pre-solid waste 15
Prevention of Significant Deterioration (PSD) 34–5, 45, 92, 100–1, 106–7
process redesign 208–9, 227 nn.38–39
product characteristic standards 203–6, 227 n.36, 262, 282
Product Stewardship 216
product takebacks 216, 259–60
product-based pollution 15
project summaries 26, 53
Project XL 66, 138 n.74
PSD. *See* Prevention of Significant Deterioration
PTE. *See* Potential to Emit
public
  inclusion of in AQM process 58–9
  minimal inclusion of 121–2, 137 n.60
  role of 39

R&D 252, 256, 284
RACT. *See* Reasonably Available Control Technology
rationing 93, 244–5, 286 n.4, 297, 320 n.3. *See also* fossil fuels, rationing
Reasonably Available Control Technology (RACT) 26, 27, 33, 47, 97, 182 n.4
rebound effect 271–2, 289 n.38
recycling 4, 13, 166, 196, 200, 201, 203–4, 215, 216, 228 n.48, 253, 275, 277
reforestation 9, 288 n.27, 299, 308, 312, 320 n.7
Regional Greenhouse Gas Initiative (RGGI) 163–4
regulated NSR pollutant 34, 42 n.20
regulations. *See also* Grand Unified Theory of Environmental Law and Regulation
  alternative regulatory models 66–7
  applicability of strategies to global problems 293–8
  bureaucratic pollution and 54–7
  compliance with 288 n.26
  complicated rules and processing requirements 51–4, 114–18, 136 n.50
  comprehensive strategy elements 109
  effectiveness God Particle 87–8
  EPA study 46
  FLoER 4, 98–9, 280, 311, 325
  on generation of pollution 5
  global 93–6
  hierarchy of 93, *94*, 144–5, 240–1, 332
  holistic application of 2–3
  IDPC/IDPC pollution surrogates 8–9, 206–9
  large scope 155–6
  making regulating rewarding 154–5
  Next Gen principles 52, 58, 64–5, 76–8, 116, 151–2, 175–7, 351 n.16
  optimal 5, 93–5
  overburden on 13, 19 n.7
  at point of production 8–9
  policy logjam 40, 43 n.26, 59–60, 64–5, 72–5, 82 n.40
  of pollution 330–1
  reforming 26, 41 n.5
  regional 94–9
  role of CaC 29–30
  source allotments 95
  supply chains 219–20
  unit level 95
regulatory food chain (RFC) 114, 116, 119
remediation 9, 261, 267–8, 288 n.28, 299, 320 n.6, 350 n.9, 351 n.11
resilience 3
Resource Conservation and Recovery Act 232
resources
  constraints on 245–6
  extraction of 325–6, 331
  industrial 327
  inefficient use of 245–6
  infinite use of 277
  limits on use 1, 17 n.5, 195
  overuse of 326
  rationing and phasing out 244–5
  scarcity 337
  transformation of 202
  use of term 223 n.2
  virgin 215–16, 245, 256–7, 267, 272, 317–18
restoration intensity 327
reuse ratio 211, 213
"right to pollute" fallacy 90, 191, 268, 289 n.34, 343

rights, Nature's 328–9, *330*, 346
Ruhl, J. B. 343, 346
rule development 38, 39, 116–18

Salzman, James 343, 346
Sandler, Ross 72
Santos, Victoria 271, 273, 318
scarcity mindset 269
Schakenbach, John 120–1, 348
Schmalensee, Richard 68–9, 122
Schoenbrod, David 25, 72–5, 87, 96, 97, 139, 143, 169–74, 179, 186 n.47, 342
Schwartz, Joel 72
scrap generation 276
sequestration 9, 237 n.3, 275, 288 n.27, 307, 320 n.9, 325, 327
shared use 249
Shimshack, Jay 67, 78, 142, 182
Silberman, David 77–8
Sinden, Amy 132 n.18, 352 n.26
SIP. *See* State Implementation Plan
slowing loops 272–3
SO_2. *See* sulfur dioxide
social inequities 11, 14
solid waste pollution
- IDPC/IDPC pollution surrogates 201–3, 225–6 nn.23–24, 226 nn.25–26, 239–40
- mitigation strategy 314
- noncompostability harm intensity 217–19
- regulating generation of 23, 27, 195–6

source allotments 132 n.17
source(s)
- allotments 95, 126, 136 n.37, 138 n.69
- category 105, 134 n.35
- construction of new 104–10
- density 101–2
- location 100–2
- major 31, 38, 42 n.13, 43 nn.21–22, 91, 95, 104–7
- minor 31–2, 38, 91, 95
- mobile 167–8
- stationary 32, 87–8, 122–4
- thresholds *101*, 105–7, 134 n.34

stack testing 29, 38, 41 nn.9–10, 65, 127–8, 182 n.3
Stahel, Walter 196, 229 n.52, 264, 285
State Implementation Plan (SIP) 10, 25, 32–3, 42 n.19, 71–2
Statement of Basis (SoB) 26, 53, 117, 136 n.56
stationary source regulation 87–8, 122–4
Stavins, Robert N. 68–9, 122
Stern, Nicholas 336
Stewart, Richard 5, 64, 72, 129, 178, 181
sulfur dioxide (SO_2) 40, 48–9, 97, 101, 115, 122, 125, 134 n.34, 155
supply chains 9, 219–20
sustainability, use of term 193
sustainability with Nature
- AEGD of zero 1, 4, 10, 161, 316, 319, 322 n.27, 328, 330, 334 n.5
- attainment of 1–2, 4, 16–17 n.2, 17 n.3
- CE and 279
- critical natural resource replenishment 271
- as a legal area of study 3
- nonattainment of 11–14, 334 n.5
- regulation of structural issues 347
- steady-state equilibrium theory 315–16
- as underlying purpose of environmental law 4, 18 n.14
- use of term 193

sustainable development 17 n.3, 316

"take, make, dispose" linear economy 224 n.10, 246, 286 n.11, 349
Tarlock, Dan 353 n.28
taxation 27, 29, 90, 153, 165–7, 182 n.1, 186 n.40, 213, 236, 245, 282–4, 352 n.27
technology-induced pollution 242, 286 n.1, 293–8
theft of materials 277
time to compostability (TtC) 217–18
time to degradation (TtD) 217–18
Title V permits 26, 31, 42 n.14, 53–4, 62 n.26, 116–17, 120, 151, 171
toxic harm intensity 217–19, 232–3, 273
Toxic Substances Control Act 219
toxics, reduction in 273–4
trading programs. *See also* cap-and-trade
- Acid Rain Program 25

application of trading scheme 155–60
balance of limits and markets 243–4
CaC and 175–6
in comprehensive strategy 122–4
external 89, 91, 96–9, 125, 143–4, 183 n.10
in generalized strategy 234–5
internal 89, 91, 99–100
as a market instrument 7, 27–30, 41–2 n.11
multi-media pollution regulation 80 n.7
opposition to 342–4
in regulatory reform 65
skeptics of 89
success of 68–9
support of 89–91
transition to CE and 90
uses for 226 n.33

trading units (TU) 91, 104–5, 107, 131 n.9, 159, *212*, 234, 256. *See also* Equivalent Trading Units

Tragedy of the Commons 17 n.7

transparency 146, 184 n.17

TU. *See* trading units

United Nations Framework Convention on Climate Change (UNFCCC) 310

universality of strategies 12–13, 19 n.24

urban mining 288 n.28

US Clean Air Act (CAA)
Acid Rain Program 175
amendments (1999) 64
BTL reform ideas 72–5, 169–74
bureaucratic pollution 54–7
Case's reform ideas 65–7
complicated rules and processing requirements 51–4
design flaws 45–6, 59–60, 179–80, 241
downsides of 25, 87–8
emission reduction process 46–51
Freeman and Farber's reform ideas 68
grandfathering in 47–8, 76
Gray and Shimshack's reform ideas 67
misapplication of labor 57–8
NAAQS 132 n.16
Next Gen principles 76–8, 175–7
Nordhaus' reform ideas 75–6, 174–5
NRC reform ideas 69–72, 168–9
NSR program 25, 33–7, 43 nn.21–22, 45–6, 48–51
past success of 24–5
prescriptive regulation under 23
public inclusion 58–9
reform skeptics 178
reforming 6–7, 27, 39–40, 63–79
regulators' perspective needed for reform 78–9
Schmalensee and Stavins' reform ideas 68–9
SIP process 25, 33, 42 n.19
Stewart's reform ideas 64
Title V permits 26, 31, 42 n.14, 53–4, 62 n.26, 116–17, 120, 151, 171

US Congress 66, 73, 171–2, 180, 244

US Constitution 332

US Environmental Protection Agency (USEPA)
Acid Rain Program 25, 26, 30, 40 n.4, 41–2 n.11, 64, 97–8, 169–70
Air Pollution Control Department 127
The Clearinghouse 103, 134 n.32
Cross State Air Pollution Rule 25, 96, 169–70
division of labor and 110–11
Environmental Technology Verification Program 136 n.36
Next Gen principles 52, 341
Office of Enforcement and Compliance Assurance 76
"Progress Cleaning the Air and Improving People's Health" 24
SIP approvals 33
study of air pollution regulations 46
supporting documents 53

USEPA. *See* US Environmental Protection Agency

vehicle miles traveled (VMT) 164, 167–8

virgin resources 215–16, 245, 256–7, 267, 272, 317–18

VMoD. *See* volumetric measure of detriment

VOC. *See* volatile organic compounds

volatile organic compounds (VOCs) 33, 156, 164, 167
Vollaro, Robert 120, 348
volumetric measure of detriment (VMoD) 203, 207–8, 219, 254
voluntary programs 156

waste acquisition 270
water–energy–food–ecosystem (WEFE) nexus 328, 337
Webster, Ken 196, 245–6, 264
World Business Council for Sustainable Development 199
Wyman, Katrina M. 72

"*You don't foul your own nest*" (YDFYON) 278–9, 337–8

Zink, Trevor 271–2

About the Author

Robert Smet, PhD, PE, has spent the bulk of his career "in the trenches" as an environmental protection engineer in a state regulatory agency capacity for over three decades, developing construction permits for several types of new and existing major stationary sources of air pollution. The author received a PhD in Theoretical and Applied Mechanics from the University of Illinois at Urbana-Champaign.

www.ingramcontent.com/pod-product-compliance
Ingram Content Group UK Ltd.
Pitfield, Milton Keynes, MK11 3LW, UK
UKHW020222290926
15470UKWH00001B/322

9 781666 947755